HISTORICAL DICTIONARIES
OF WAR, REVOLUTION, AND CIVIL UNREST
Edited by Jon Woronoff

1. *Afghan Wars, Revolutions, and Insurgencies*, by Ludwig W. Adamec. 1996.
2. *The United States–Mexican War*, by Edward H. Moseley and Paul C. Clark, Jr. 1997.
3. *World War I*, by Ian V. Hogg. 1998.
4. *The United States Navy*, by James M. Morris and Patricia M. Kearns. 1998.
5. *The United States Marine Corps*, by Harry A. Gailey. 1998.
6. *The Wars of the French Revolution*, by Steven T. Ross. 1998.
7. *The American Revolution*, by Terry M. Mays. 1999.
8. *The Spanish-American War*, by Brad K. Berner. 1998.
9. *The Persian Gulf War*, by Clayton R. Newell. 1998.
10. *The Holocaust*, by Jack R. Fischel. 1999.
11. *The United States Air Force and Its Antecedents*, by Michael Robert Terry. 1999.
12. *Civil Wars in Africa*, by Guy Arnold. 1999.
13. *World War II: The War Against Japan*, by Anne Sharp Wells. 1999.
14. *British and Irish Civil Wars*, by Martyn Bennett. 2000.
15. *The Cold War*, by Joseph Smith and Simon Davis. 2000.
16. *Ancient Greek Warfare*, by Iain Spence. 2002.
17. *The Vietnam War*, by Edwin E. Moïse. 2001.
18. *The Civil War*, by Terry L. Jones. 2002.
19. *The Crimean War*, by Guy Arnold. 2002.
20. *The United States Army, a Historical Dictionary*, by Clayton R. Newell. 2002.
21. *Terrorism, Second Edition*, by Sean K. Anderson and Stephen Sloan. 2002.
22. *Chinese Civil War*, by Edwin Pak-wah Leung. 2002
23. *The Korean War: A Historical Dictionary*, by Paul M. Edwards. 2002.

The United States Army, a Historical Dictionary

Clayton R. Newell

Historical Dictionaries of War, Revolution, and Civil Unrest, No. 20

The Scarecrow Press, Inc.
Lanham, Maryland, and Oxford
2002

SCARECROW PRESS, INC.

Published in the United States of America
by Scarecrow Press, Inc.
A Member of the Rowman & Littlefield Publishing Group
4720 Boston Way
Lanham, Maryland 20706
www.scarecrowpress.com

PO Box 317
Oxford
OX2 9RU, UK

British Library Cataloguing in Publication Information Available

Library of Congress Cataloging-in-Publication Data

Newell, Clayton R., 1942-
  United States Army, a historical dictionary / Clayton R. Newell.
    p. cm. — (Historical dictionaries of war, revolution, and civil unrest ;
  no. 20)
  Includes bibliographical references.
  ISBN 0-8108-4311-0 (cloth : alk. paper)
    1. United States. Army—History—Dictionaries. 2. United States.
Army—Biography—Dictionaries. I. Title. II. Series.
  UA25 .N48 2002
  355'.00973'03—dc21   2002002507

Contents

Illustrations

All photographs courtesy of the U.S. Army Military History Institute

Editor's Foreword

From rather inauspicious beginnings, the U.S. Army has become one of the largest and most powerful military forces in the world, even after reductions following the end of the Cold War. It is also more professional than ever and continues to operate smoothly after desegregation and the expansion of the role of women. In short, there is no other army, coalition of armies, or rogue regime that can stand up to it. While the U.S. Army could rest on its laurels, however, it dare not if it is to remain an effective military force. Thus it has assumed new, broader functions within international organizations, such as the United Nations and the North Atlantic Treaty Organization (NATO). Yet, as so often in the past, the direction it should take in the future remains uncertain.

This *United States Army, a Historical Dictionary* provides a wealth of information about the U.S. Army's past and present, through dictionary entries covering campaign streamers, top military and civilian leaders, notable foes, various component bodies, and logistics and weaponry. The wars it has fought are described at length and additional information is given for each campaign. The appendixes contain several important military documents and lists of top personnel, campaigns, casualties, and insignia. The substantial bibliography provides a tremendous amount of additional resource material, organized into specific and quite usable sections.

This book was written by Clayton R. Newell, who spent nearly three decades of active duty in the U.S. Army. He was educated in outstanding army schools and taught at the U.S. Army War College. He has written extensively on the U.S. Army, including a number of campaign histories for World War II that he prepared for the U.S. Army Center of Military History as chief of historical services. He has published books on the American Civil War and operational warfare, as well as the *Historical Dictionary of the Persian Gulf War*.

This latest addition to Scarecrow Press's Historical Dictionaries of War, Revolution, and Civil Unrest is bound to interest readers who have either served in the U.S. armed forces or want to know more about the world's premier army.

Jon Woronoff
Series Editor

Preface

An army is shaped by its leaders and remembered by its accomplishments. For more than two centuries, the U.S. Army has been serving the nation in peace and war. The foundation for this historical dictionary rests on two themes: the people who have led the army and the campaigns it has fought on battlefields around the world.

Millions of soldiers have served in the U.S. Army during its more than 227 years of service to the nation, while many of its leaders, both uniformed and civilian, have become national figures. Knowing them and their part in the army's history is an important part of understanding the army's role in the nation's affairs. The army's leaders have included the civilian heads of the army, that is, the secretaries of war until 1947 and the secretaries of the army after that; all of the senior military officers, including the commanding generals until 1903 and the chiefs of staff since then; and the sergeants major of the army, those who have served as the senior enlisted soldier in the army since 1966. The secretaries, senior officers, and senior enlisted soldiers are listed in chronological order in appendixes and each has an entry in the dictionary. While not all of these individuals made significant contributions, in the interest of completeness all have an entry, however brief. Many other people who did make significant contributions to the army, a few members of the army whose deeds brought them notoriety, and some of the army's prominent battlefield opponents also have entries.

The army flag carries 174 campaign streamers. Each of those streamers represents the deeds of countless soldiers in myriad battles in the United States and abroad. Although some may be more significant in the history of the army and the United States than others, every campaign involved American soldiers going in harm's way, so each has an entry in the dictionary. Appendix 6 contains a list of the campaigns arranged chronologically by war. In the dictionary, each of the campaigns is designated according to the name of the campaign streamer that commemorates it.

In addition to the people and the campaigns, the dictionary covers a variety of terms and events that have some significance to the army's history. In order to provide appropriate cross references, terms shown in bold in the introduction and in the dictionary indicate an entry. The entries and the appendixes provide basic information on the significant people and events in the army's history and the bibliography provides a guide to more comprehensive sources.

With the army's long history of faithful service to the American nation, this dictionary cannot hope to cover the U.S. Army's past in any detail. This dictionary's purpose is to offer a brief introduction to the people and events that have made the army one of the most important institutions in America and the foremost proponent of land power in the world.

Abbreviations and Acronyms

AAA	anti-aircraft artillery
ABDACOM	American-British-Dutch-Australian Command
ARNG	Army National Guard
CAS3	Combined Arms and Services Staff School
CBI	China-Burma-India
CCC	Civilian Conservation Corps
CCF	Chinese Communist Forces
CCS	Combined Chiefs of Staff
CSM	Command Sergeant Major
DMZ	demilitarized zone
ETO	European theater of operations
FM	field manual
HE	high explosive
JCS	Joint Chiefs of Staff
MLRS	Multiple Launched Rocket System
NATO	North Atlantic Treaty Organization
NCO	noncommissioned officer
NVA	North Vietnamese Army
POW	prisoner of war
RA	regular army
RC	reserve components
ROAD	Reorganization Objective Army Division
ROTC	Reserve Officers' Training Corps
SHAPE	Supreme Headquarters Allied Powers Europe
USA	United States Army
USAR	United States Army Reserve
USMA	United States Military Academy
UN	United Nations
VC	Viet Cong
WAAC	Women's Army Auxiliary Corps
WAC	Women's Army Corps

Chronology

1775 April: Lexington campaign. **May:** Ticonderoga campaign. **June:** The Continental Congress passes a resolution to adopt the Continental Army. The date of the resolution, 14 June, is considered to be the birth of the U.S. Army. The next day, the Continental Congress passes a resolution appointing George Washington as commander in chief of the Continental Army. The Adjutant General, Engineer, Finance, and Quartermaster Corps are established. The Boston campaign begins with the Battle of Bunker Hill; the campaign ends in March 1777. **July:** The Army Medical Department and the Chaplain and Judge Advocate General Corps are established. **August:** The Quebec campaign begins; it ends in July 1776.

1776 June: Charleston campaign. **August:** Long Island campaign. **December:** The cavalry branch and the army inspector general are established. Trenton campaign.

1777 January: Princeton campaign. **July:** The Saratoga campaign begins; it ends in October. **September:** Brandywine campaign. **October:** Germantown campaign. **December:** The Continental Army establishes its winter camp at Valley Forge in Pennsylvania.

1778 February: Baron Friedrich Wilhelm von Steuben arrives at Valley Forge. **June:** Monmouth campaign. **December:** First part of the Savannah campaign.

1779 September: The Savannah campaign continues; it ends in October.

1780 March: Charleston campaign begins; it ends in May.

1781 January: Cowpens campaign. **March:** Guilford Court House campaign. **September:** The Yorktown campaign begins; it ends on 19 October. **October:** British general Charles Cornwallis surrenders to General George Washington at Yorktown, effectively ending the Revolutionary War.

1782 August: George Washington establishes the badge of military merit.

1783 September: The Treaty of Paris ends the Revolutionary War. **December:** Henry Knox becomes commanding general of the army, replacing George Washington.

1790 October: The Miami campaign begins when an American force of 1,500 is decisively defeated in Ohio; it ends in August 1795.

1798 July: George Washington becomes commanding general of the army for the second time.

1803 March: The U.S. Military Academy established at West Point, New York. **August:** Captains Meriwether Lewis and William Clark begin the exploration of land west of the Mississippi River. They return in September 1806, after a journey of 8,000 miles to the Pacific Ocean and back.

1811 September: Tippecanoe campaign against the Indians begins; it ends in November.

1812 May: The Ordnance Corps is established. **June:** Congress declares war against Britain, beginning the War of 1812. The Canada campaign of the War of 1812 begins; it ends in February 1815.

1813 July: The First Creek Indian War begins; it ends in August 1814.

1814 July: Chippewa and Lundy's Lane campaigns. **August:** Bladensburg campaign. **September:** Fort McHenry campaign. The New Orleans campaign begins; it ends in January 1815. Neither side knew a peace had been signed in December. **December:** The Treaty of Ghent ends the War of 1812.

1817 November: The First Seminole Indian War begins; it ends in 1818.

1824 May: The Artillery School of Practice is established at Fort Monroe, Virginia.

1832 April: The Black Hawk Indian War begins; it ends in September. **August:** The Battle of Bad Axe, in which an estimated 300 Indians are killed, effectively ends the Black Hawk War.

1835 December: The Second Seminole Indian War begins; it ends in August 1842.

1836 February: The Second Creek Indian War begins; it ends in July 1837.

1845 March: Congress annexes the Republic of Texas, but Mexico has never recognized Texas independence, thus Mexico considers annexation an act of aggression. Mexico breaks diplomatic relations with the United States.

1846 March: Congress declares war against Mexico, beginning the Mexican War. **May:** Palo Alto and Resaca de la Palma campaigns. **September:** Monterey campaign.

1847 February: Buena Vista campaign. **March:** Vera Cruz campaign. **April:** Cerro Gordo campaign. **August:** Contreras and Churubusco campaigns. **September:** Molino del Rey and Chapultepec campaigns.

1848 February: The Treaty of Guadalupe Hidalgo ends the Mexican War.

1855 December: The Third Seminole Indian War begins; it ends in May 1858.

1860 June: Signal Corps established.

1861 April: The bombardment of Fort Sumter opens the Civil War. **July:** Bull Run campaign.

1862 February: Forts Henry and Donelson campaign. The Mississippi River campaign begins; it ends in July. **March:** The Peninsula campaign begins; it ends in August 1863. **April:** Shiloh campaign. **May:** The Valley campaign begins; it ends in June. **August:** Antietam campaign. The Manassas campaign begins; it ends in September. **November:** The Fredericksburg campaign begins; it ends in December. **December:** The Murfreesborough campaign begins; it ends on 4 January 1863.

1863 March: The Vicksburg campaign begins; it ends in July. **April:** The Chancellorsville campaign begins; it ends in May. **June:** The Gettysburg campaign begins; it ends in July. **August:** The Chickamauga campaign begins; it ends in September. **November:** Chattanooga campaign.

1864 May: Wilderness campaign. The Atlanta campaign begins; it ends in September. Spotsylvania campaign. The Cold Harbor campaign begins; it ends in June. **June:** The Petersburg campaign begins; it ends in April 1865. **August:** The Shenandoah campaign begins; it ends in November. **November:** Franklin campaign. **December:** Nashville campaign.

1865 April: Appomattox campaign. Robert E. Lee surrenders to Ulysses S. Grant. **May:** Remaining Confederate forces surrender.

1867 Comanches campaign begins. It ends in 1875.

1870 February: The Signal Corps creates the first Weather Service.

1872 Modoc Indian wars begin; they end in 1873.

1873 First Apache Indian War.

1876 Little Big Horn Indian war campaign begins; it ends in 1877.

1877 Nez Perce Indian War.

1878 Bannock Indian War. The Cheyenne Indian War begins; it ends in 1879.

1879 Ute Indian War begins; it ends in 1880.

1881 The School of Application for Infantry and Cavalry is established at Fort Leavenworth, Kansas.

1885 The Second Apache Indian War begins; it ends in 1886.

1890 The Pine Ridge Indian War begins; it ends in 1891.

1898 April: Spain breaks off diplomatic relations with the United States on 21 April and the United States subsequently declares war retroactively to that date, beginning the Spanish–American War. **June:** The Santiago campaign begins; it ends in July. **July:** The Puerto Rico and Manila campaigns begin; they both end in August. **December:** The Treaty of Paris ends the Spanish–American War.

1899 February: The Philippine Insurrection begins. The Manila campaign begins; it ends in March. Iloilo campaign. **March:** The Malolos campaign begins; it ends in August. **April:** Laguna de Bay campaign. The First San Isidro campaign begins; it ends in May. **June:** Zapote River campaign. **October:** The First Cavite campaign. The Second San Isidro campaign begins; it ends in November. **November:** Tarlac and San Fabian campaigns.

1900 July: The China Relief Expedition begins with the Tientsin (Tianjin) campaign. **August:** The Yang-tsun and Peking (Beijing) campaigns end the China Relief Expedition.

1901 The Army Nurse Corps and Army War College are established.

1902 July: The Mindanao campaign of the Philippine Insurrection begins; it ends in December 1904.

1903 January: Congress revises the 1792 Militia Act. **February:** Army general staff established. **August:** Samuel B. M. Young becomes the first chief of staff of the army when Nelson A. Miles retires as the last commanding general of the army.

1905 May: First Jolo campaign of the Philippine Insurrection.

1906 March: Second Jolo campaign of the Philippine Insurrection. **August:** Third Jolo campaign of the Philippine Insurrection.

1912 August: The Army Reserve Corps is established and the Quartermaster, Subsistence, and Pay Departments are consolidated to become the Quartermaster Corps.

1913 June: Fourth Jolo campaign in the Philippine Insurrection.

1916 March: The Mexican Expedition begins; it ends in February 1917. **June:** The National Defense Act authorizes a five-year expansion of the regular army to 220,000, establishes a National Guard of 440,000, and establishes an Officers Training Corps in colleges.

1917 February: The United States breaks diplomatic relations with Germany. **April:** Congress declares war on Germany, making the United States a participant in World War I. **June:** John J. Pershing, commander of the American Expeditionary Forces, arrives in Paris. **October:** Mindanao campaign in the Philippine Insurrection. **November:** The Cambrai campaign begins; it ends in December.

1918 March: The Somme Defensive campaign begins; it ends in April. **April:** Lys campaign. **May:** The Aisne campaign begins; it ends in June. **June:** Montdidier–Noyon campaign. The Chemical Corps is established. **July:** Aisne–Marne campaign. The Champagne-Marne campaign begins; it ends in August. **August:** The Somme Offensive, Oise–Aisne, and Ypres–Lys campaigns begin; they end in November. **September:** The St. Mihiel and Meuse–Argonne campaigns begin; they end in November. **October:** The Vittoria Veneto campaign begins; it ends in November. **November:** World War I ends at 1100 on 11 November.

1923 World War I occupation of Germany ends.

1926 The Army Air Corps is established.

1928 The Army Staff College at Fort Leavenworth becomes the Command and General Staff College.

1933 The Civilian Conservation Corps is created.

1940 The War Department creates the Armored Force.

1941 September: The Military Police Corps is established. **December:** The Japanese Imperial Navy attacks Pearl Harbor. Congress declares war on Japan. Germany and Italy declare war on the United States; Congress adopts a resolution recognizing a state of war with both countries. The United States enters World War II. The Philippine Islands and Burma 1942 campaigns begin; they end in May 1942. The Central Pacific campaign begins; it ends in December 1943. The Antisubmarine campaign begins; it ends in December 1945.

1942 January: The East Indies campaign begins; it ends in July. **April:** The India–Burma campaign begins; it ends in January 1945. The Air Offensive campaign against Japan begins; it ends in September 1945. **May:** The Women's Army Auxiliary Corps is established. **June:** The Aleutian Islands campaign begins; it ends in August 1943. The Egypt–Libya campaign begins; it ends in February 1943. **July:** The China Defensive campaign begins; it ends in May 1945. The Air Offensive campaign against Europe begins; it ends in June 1945. The Papua campaign begins; it ends in January 1943. The Transportation Corps is established, assuming part of the mission of the Quartermaster Corps. **August:** The Guadalcanal campaign begins; it ends in February 1943. **November:** Algeria–French Morocco campaign. The Tunisia campaign begins; it ends in May 1943.

1943 January: The New Guinea campaign begins; it ends in December 1944. **February:** The Northern Solomons campaign begins; it ends in November 1944. **July:** The Sicily campaign begins; it ends in August. **August:** The Naples-Foggia air campaign begins; it ends in January 1944. **September:** Italy signs an armistice with the Allies, but Germany continues the war in Italy. The Naples-Foggia ground campaign begins; it ends in January 1944. The Women's Army Auxiliary Corps becomes the Women's Army Corps. **December:** The Bismarck Archipelago campaign begins; it ends in November 1944.

1944 January: The Anzio campaign begins; it ends in May. The Rome–Arno campaign begins; it ends in September. The Eastern Mandates campaign begins; it ends in June. **June:** The Normandy campaign begins; it ends in July. The Western Pacific campaign begins; it ends in September 1945. **July:** The Northern France campaign begins; it ends in September. **August:** The Southern France campaign begins; it ends in September. **September:** The Northern Apennines campaign begins; it ends in April 1945. The Rhineland campaign begins; it ends in March 1945. **October:** The Leyte campaign begins; it ends in July 1945. **December:** The Luzon campaign begins; it ends in July 1945. The Ardennes–Alsace campaign begins; it ends in January 1945.

1945 January: The Central Burma campaign begins; it ends in July. **February:** The Southern Philippines campaign begins; it ends in July. **March:** The Central Europe campaign begins; it ends in May. The Ryukyus campaign begins; it ends in July. **April:** The Po Valley campaign begins; it ends in May. **May:** The China Offensive campaign begins; it ends in September. Germany surrenders unconditionally to the Allies, ending World War II in Europe. **August:** The Japanese agree to a cease-fire. **September:** Japan signs a formal surrender on the American battleship Missouri, ending World War II.

1947 July: President Harry Truman signs the National Security Act, which unifies all branches of the armed forces under a secretary of defense. Under the act, the air force becomes a separate branch of service from the army and the secretary of war becomes the secretary of the army. Kenneth C. Royall becomes the last secretary of war. **September:** Royall becomes the first secretary of the army, in accordance with the National Security Act of 1947.

1948 May: The Key West Agreement establishes roles and missions for the armed forces.

1950 June: North Korean forces invade South Korea. The UN Defensive campaign begins in Korea; it ends in September. **July:** The North Korean People's Army attacks and destroys Task Force Smith in Korea. **September:** The UN Offensive campaign begins; it ends in November. **November:** The Communist China Forces Intervention campaign begins; it ends in January 1951.

1951 January: The First UN Counteroffensive campaign begins; it ends in April. **April:** The Communist China Forces Spring Offensive campaign begins; it ends in July. **July:** The UN Summer–Fall Offensive begins; it ends in November. **November:** The Second Korean Winter campaign begins; it ends in April 1952.

1952 May: The Korea, Summer–Fall, campaign begins; it ends in November. **December:** The Third Korean Winter campaign begins; it ends in April 1953.

1953 May: The Korea, Summer, campaign begins; it ends in July. **July:** An armistice goes into effect in the Korean War, establishing a cease-fire line along the boundary between North and South Korea.

1955 August: The Civil Affairs branch is established.

1962 March: The Advisory campaign begins in Vietnam; it ends in March 1965.

1964 The Tonkin Gulf incident results in the U.S. Congress passing the Tonkin Gulf Resolution, which committed major American forces to Vietnam.

1965 March: The Defense campaign begins in Vietnam; it ends in December. **April:** The Dominican Republic campaign begins; it ends in September. **December:** The Counteroffensive campaign begins in Vietnam; it ends in June 1966.

1966 July: The Counteroffensive, Phase II, campaign begins in Vietnam; it ends in May 1967. William O. Woolridge becomes the first sergeant major of the army.

1967 June: The Counteroffensive, Phase III, campaign begins in Vietnam; it ends in January 1968.

1968 January: The Tet Counteroffensive campaign begins in Vietnam; it ends in April. **April:** The Counteroffensive, Phase IV, campaign begins; it ends in June. **July:** The Counteroffensive, Phase V, campaign begins; it ends in November. William C. Westmoreland, former U.S. commander in Vietnam, becomes chief of staff of the army. **November:** The Counteroffensive, Phase VI, campaign begins; it ends in February 1969.

1969 February: The Tet 69 Counteroffensive campaign begins; it ends in June. **June:** The Summer–Fall 1969 campaign begins; it ends in October. **November:** The Winter–Spring 1970 campaign begins; it ends in April 1970.

1970 May: The Sanctuary Counteroffensive campaign begins; it ends on 30 June. **July:** The Counteroffensive, Phase VII, campaign begins; it ends in June 1971.

1971 July: The Consolidation I campaign begins in Vietnam; it ends in November. **December:** The Consolidation II campaign begins; it ends on 29 March 1972.

1972 March: The Cease-Fire campaign begins; it ends in January 1973. **October:** Creighton W. Abrams Jr., former U.S. commander in Vietnam, becomes chief of staff of the army.

1973 January: The U.S. Army Sergeants Major Academy opens at Fort Bliss, Texas. **March:** The last U.S. Army units depart Vietnam.

1981 January: John O. Marsh becomes secretary of the army. He remains in office until August 1998, making him the longest-serving secretary of the army.

1983 April: Aviation branch established. **October:** Grenada campaign begins; it ends in November.

1987 August: Special Forces branch established.

1989 December: The Panama campaign begins; it ends in January 1990.

1990 August: Iraq invades Kuwait. The Defense of Saudi Arabia campaign begins; it ends in January 1991.

1991 January: The Liberation and Defense of Kuwait campaign begins; it ends in April. **April:** The Cease-Fire campaign begins in southwest Asia; it ends in November 1995.

1995 December: U.S. Army forces move into Bosnia-Herzegovina to enforce the Dayton Peace Accords.

1999 April: U.S. Army forces move into Kosovo to enforce the peace.

2001 September: The war on terrorism begins. **October:** The United States initiates military action against Afghanistan.

Introduction

The U.S. Army dates its creation from 14 June 1775, when the Continental Congress passed a resolution creating the **Continental Army**. Since then, the army has been shaped by more than two centuries of peace and war. In the process, it has grown from a collection of part-time militia forces held in contempt by the regular armies of Europe to become the world's most dominant land force.

Since its founding, the army has participated in 10 major wars: the **Revolutionary War**, the **War of 1812**, the **Mexican War**, the **Civil War**, the **Spanish–American War**, **World War I**, **World War II**, the **Korean War**, the **Vietnam War**, and the **Persian Gulf War**. It also conducted a lengthy series of so-called **Indian wars** against Native Americans during the nineteenth century. Its twentieth-century operations include campaigns during the **Philippine Insurrection** and the **China Relief Expedition**, as well as campaigns in **Mexico**, the **Dominican Republic**, **Grenada**, and **Panama**.

COLONIAL FOUNDATIONS

The foundations of the U.S. Army were laid well before the creation of the Continental Army in 1775. During America's colonial period, agriculture required considerable manpower, so the solution to providing for defense was a part-time militia called to arms as needed. All males of military age were required to serve when called, provide their own weapons, and attend periodic musters. For prolonged expeditions or patrols along the expanding frontier, communities called for volunteers or they drafted young men into service. These expeditions were frequently planned and conducted by European officers, so the officers in the colonial militias gained practical military experience. The militia tradition of friends and neighbors banding together in battle made American officers sensitive to unnecessarily wasting lives. It has become characteristic of American military operations to use firepower to preserve American lives. Today, **Army National Guard** forces are the modern descendants of the colonial militia.

The American militia developed during a period of rapid and constant change in military affairs. The necessity for constantly adapting to change differed from the European military experience of lengthy periods of stability. In the eighteenth century, American colonists learned to conduct land operations against an opponent who did not adhere to the rules of European warfare. American Indians used stealth and surprise; their battles were a melee of individual combat with no disciplined formations or easily identifiable uniforms to distinguish friend from foe, and individual initiative counted more than rigid discipline. Individual initiative remains a highly regarded attribute in the army.

BIRTH OF AN ARMY

The militia system had its weaknesses, but on the whole served the colonists well until the Revolutionary War, when the requirement for a well-trained, disciplined force that could face the British regulars resulted in the creation of the Continental Army. The end of the Revolutionary War saw the beginning of the American tradition of drastically reducing its defense establishment as soon as any overt threats to the nation disappeared. To protect the young nation from future threats, **George Washington**, the first **commanding general of the army**, proposed establishing a small regular force, enrolling males between the ages of 18 and 50 for emergency service, and organizing young men into volunteer units under national control that were ready to serve on call. But a society characterized by localism and distrust of power remained highly distrustful of a permanent military establishment. With an ocean separating the United States from potential European enemies and no large land forces in either Mexico or Canada, Americans had no great concern for protection against a surprise invasion. The Congress, therefore, reduced the Continental Army to 80 men, barely enough to garrison the post at West Point, New York. With only a small regular army, there was no incentive to develop a professional officer corps, thus studying the art and science of war was left to European armies. That changed in 1802, when President Thomas Jefferson established the **U.S. Military Academy** at West Point as a school for training officers and engineers who could assist with national development. In 1803, two army officers, **Meriwether Lewis** and **William Clark**, made a significant contribution to the nation when they led four sergeants, 23 privates, and a number of Indian interpreters to explore the continent west to the Pacific. At about the same time, Lieutenant **Zebulon Pike** led another army expedition to explore the headwaters of the Arkansas River. These expeditions began an army tradition of exploration that continued through the nineteenth century.

GROWING PAINS

In 1812, the United States was again at war with Great Britain. While the army's initial operations were largely unsatisfactory, it learned from its mistakes and eventually prevailed over the British. When the War of 1812 finally ended in 1815, the army was once again quickly reduced in size. The nation faced almost no external threat and, with the model of the self-made military hero **Andrew Jackson** as president by the 1830s, professional soldiers were not held in high regard. But as one of few established national institutions in a growing United States, the army made a significant contribution to national development. Soldiers, with their organization, discipline, and training for survival in a hostile environment, could effectively display the government's authority while exploring the nation's extensive territory. In the tradition of Lewis and Clark, army officers led expeditions westward, making maps and gathering data that helped open frontier regions to settlers.

Until 1835, the U.S. Military Academy was the country's only school producing qualified engineers, and its graduates played a vital role in the nation's growth. Army engineers surveyed roads, canals, and railroads and frequently went on to supervise the construction. They were also instrumental in river and harbor improvements. In Washington, D.C., army engineers built aqueducts, bridges, and public edifices, including the Capitol dome, the Washington Monument, and the Smithsonian Institution's main edifice. Toward the middle of the nineteenth century, as the United States expanded westward, the nation became involved in a boundary dispute with Mexico. The army, drastically reduced in size after the War of 1812, had to be hastily enlarged in 1846 with militia and **U.S. Volunteers** when the United States declared war on Mexico. While there was friction between the regulars and the militia, the army led by **Winfield Scott** as a whole performed well during the war, which proved to be a testing ground for many of the army officers who would lead both Union and Confederate forces in the Civil War.

AN ARMY DIVIDED

For both the army and the nation, the Civil War was the defining event of the nineteenth century. The **regular army**, numbering only about 16,000 soldiers when the war started at Fort **Sumter**, South Carolina, in April 1861, was clearly insufficient for the task of restoring the Union. The initial rush to the colors following President **Abraham Lincoln**'s call for volunteers reflected the American tradition of citizens ready and willing to take up arms when the nation was in danger. Within months, the Union Army numbered almost 500,000 men. Regular army officers, U.S. Military Academy graduates returning from civilian life, and self-educated citizen-officers transformed the multitude of raw recruits into an effective fighting force. The **War Department** and its supply bureaus fed, clothed, equipped, and armed the Union forces for the war.

The army's role in reunifying the nation did not end with **Robert E. Lee**'s surrender to **Ulysses S. Grant** at **Appomattox** in April 1865. To restore Southern allegiance to the United States, the army established military governments in occupied areas and military governors expedited the South's physical recovery from the war. Through the Freedmen's Bureau, the army provided 21 million rations, operated more than 50 hospitals, arranged labor for wages in former plantation areas, and established schools for freedmen or former slaves. The army's thankless but essential role in Reconstruction ended with the withdrawal of the last federal troops from the South in 1877.

The Civil War was a preview of wars to come, in which civilians would bear as much of the suffering of war as the front-line troops. War had widened its influence; no longer would armies fight battles in relative isolation from the population at large. Ironically, while American officers had learned and attempted to apply their interpretation of European military theory in the Civil War, European officers observing and analyzing the Civil War did not immediately recognize that defensive **tactics** had far outstripped the capabilities of an offensive **strategy**. They would learn that hard lesson for themselves in 1914.

In the period immediately after the Civil War, the army endured the traditional drastic reduction in its force structure. As the nation tried to put the war behind it, a renewed sense of duty emerged within the army. From 1790 until 1891, the army conducted a lengthy series of campaigns against Native Americans as the new country expanded west to the Pacific Ocean. With the pacification of the western frontier late in the nineteenth century, the army's small officer corps turned inward to focus on professional development for a war that few civilians believed would ever come. The army began educating its officers in tactics and other aspects of the art of war. Taking its cue from the development of military staffs in Europe, which assisted commanders in controlling the growing complexities of war, the U.S. Army established schools for engineers, the **signal corps**, and the hospital corps, as well as combined schools for **infantry**, **cavalry**, and **artillery**. The most influential army school to appear in the latter half of the nineteenth century was at Fort Leavenworth, Kansas. Known by a variety of names throughout its history, this school remains in existence as the **Command and General Staff College**. For more than a century, the college has prepared army officers for staff duty in peace and war.

During the 1870s and 1880s, the army had little visibility, although soldiers finished mapping the vast continent and made other contributions to the nation's internal development. Surveys conducted from 1867 through 1879 completed the work of Lewis and Clark, while explorations at Yosemite, Yellowstone, and elsewhere led to the establishment of a system of national parks. Army expeditions explored the territory of Alaska and the northwest coast of Greenland. The Army **Corps of Engineers** became involved in flood control, particularly on the Mississippi River, where it built the levee system. The corps also continued work on improving harbors, constructing lighthouses, and developing navigation on the Great Lakes. The Signal Corps put in thousands of miles of underwater cables and telegraph lines, most of which were available for civilian use. But as the nineteenth century drew to an end, the army again found itself being used as an instrument of American expansion.

The explosion of the American battleship *Maine* in Havana harbor in 1898 prompted the United States to become involved in Cuba's war of liberation from Spain. The army's performance in the Spanish–American War left much to be desired. When the inept planning became public knowledge, the outcry caused significant changes in both the army and the U.S. Navy. The bungled operations during the war and the occupation of distant lands prompted a reform of army organization, education, and promotion policies. In 1901, the **secretary of war**, **Elihu Root**, established the **Army War College** and replaced the commanding general of the army and the War Department bureaus with a **chief of staff of the army** and a **general staff** to conduct long-range war planning. Shortly thereafter, the **Militia Act** of 1903 laid the foundation for improved cooperation between the regular army and the Army National Guard.

The army's role in the tropical areas that came under U.S. jurisdiction after the Spanish–American War led to significant medical accomplishment. In 1899, an army medical officer discovered that hookworms were responsible for Puerto Rican anemia; a year later, the **Army Medical Department** created a commission headed by **Walter Reed** to determine the source of yellow fever. After years of difficult research, including the use of volunteers who contracted the disease, the commission traced its transmission to the *Aedes aegypti* mosquito, and the army moved to eliminate the insect in its breeding grounds. The army's eradication of yellow fever opened the door for a new challenge in the tropics.

With America's acquisition of the Philippine Islands in 1898 as a result of the Spanish–American War, and with the accompanying expansion of U.S. interests in the Far East and elsewhere around the globe, came a desire for a canal across the Central American isthmus that would shorten sailing time and reduce the danger ships encountered sailing around the southern tip of South America between the Atlantic and Pacific Oceans. After President **Theodore Roosevelt** acquired what is now the canal zone from Panama, the War Department assumed responsibility for building the canal in 1907, and army engineer **George W. Goethals** was named to head the project. It was a massive undertaking. After **William C. Gorgas**, an army doctor building on the work done by Walter Reed, had the threat of malaria and yellow fever under control, construction workers moved more than 267 million cubic feet of earth and constructed a series of locks so ships could negotiate the 85-foot elevation change over the course of the canal. After years of work, the first ocean-going vessel traversed the Panama Canal in August 1914.

The Panama Canal was not the army's only challenge in the opening years of the twentieth century. In 1900, soldiers participated in the China Relief Expedition, which relieved the legations under siege by Boxer rebels in Beijing. Closer to home, when Mexican rebels led by **Pancho Villa** killed 15 American soldiers and civilians in a raid on Columbus, New Mexico, in March 1916, President Woodrow Wilson sent **John J. Pershing** on a punitive expedition into Mexico to find them. When the Mexican government threatened war, Wilson called up 112,000 National Guardsmen and sent most of the regular army to the border. In the end, the United States was distracted by the war in Europe and Wilson withdrew the punitive expedition.

ENTERING THE WORLD'S STAGE

The United States attempted to continue its traditional isolation as the European continent became embroiled in war in 1914, but global interests eventually forced America into the conflict. The army faced a daunting challenge when President

Woodrow Wilson made the United States a participant in World War I. Although the army sent forces to Cuba during the Spanish–American War and had been fighting guerrillas in the Philippines for some time, Europe's Western Front demanded vastly greater numbers of men than either of the former operations entailed. The army was much better prepared for war than it had been in 1898 and it quickly made good the U.S. commitment. Under Pershing's leadership, the American Expeditionary Force arrived in July 1917, raising Allied morale, and army soldiers were soon making a significant contribution to the fighting alongside the French and British armies on the Western Front. By November 1918, the army had seven corps and more than 40 divisions in France, enough to ensure the Allied defeat of Germany. At 1100 hours on 11 November, the guns fell silent as a truce ending the war went into effect.

Despite some desire to return to a policy of isolationism, the United States remained involved in international politics after World War I. The army endured the traditional reduction in force, but American troops occupied the German Rhineland alongside other Allied contingents, working to restore normal economic life in their zone of responsibility. At home, the Corps of Engineers' role in flood control on the nation's rivers expanded as it experimented with ways to divert excess water into cutoffs and holding reservoirs. Dams constructed by army engineers in the Missouri Valley helped prevent floods and supplied hydroelectric power and recreation on reservoir lakes.

The army was involved in a number of activities during America's Great Depression in the 1930s. In 1932 soldiers led by the chief of staff of the army, **Douglas MacArthur**, evicted World War I veterans from Washington, D.C., where they had gathered in the **Bonus March** to ask Congress for immediate payment of a promised bonus for their military service. A year later, the army played a key role in the **Civilian Conservation Corps**, part of President Franklin D. Roosevelt's program to provide work for the unemployed through public improvements. The War Department built camps for the program and provided food, fuel, vehicles, medical care, and supervision. More than 20 percent of the army's officers were involved with getting the program started. The experience of supervising large numbers of young men paid dividends when the army began mobilizing America's manpower for World War II.

As America sought to emerge from the Great Depression, it faced new challenges overseas. Nazi Germany was supreme on the continent of Europe, while imperial Japan dominated the Asian mainland. With only 230,000 soldiers and a force structure that still included horse cavalry, the army seemed ill prepared to face the armies of either power. But since World War I, the army had been making mobilization plans and preparing for a major expansion. In 1940, Congress authorized the president to federalize the National Guard and passed the Selective Service Act of 1940, thus instituting the nation's first peacetime draft. Under the leadership of Chief of Staff **George C. Marshall**, the army increased its strength to more than 1.6 million soldiers by the end of 1941. When the war ended in 1945, more than 8 million men and women wore the army uniform.

World War II was not one war; it was a complicated series of concurrent, related wars, as the army faced a variety of opponents in several different theaters. The United States and its allies, primarily Great Britain, were all fighting the military forces of Germany and Japan, but the theaters of operations were so large that no one country was able to take the lead everywhere. The United States entered the war after Japan's surprise attack on Pearl Harbor. After initial setbacks in its first battles in North Africa and the Pacific, the army was soon on the long road to success. It made significant contributions in the Mediterranean and European theaters; provided forces in the Middle East, China, Burma, and India; and conducted major operations in the Pacific. **Dwight D. Eisenhower** led the Allies to victory over Germany in the European theater of operations in May 1945, while Douglas MacArthur, commanding Allied forces in the Southwest Pacific Area accepted the Japanese surrender in September of the same year.

When the fighting stopped in Germany and Japan, the army's occupation governments restored order and economic prosperity, eliminated prewar fascist and militaristic parties and cultures, and nurtured democratic forms of government through innovative political reform. In Germany, occupation authorities revived comprehensive health insurance for 80 percent of the population; in Japan the army instituted a massive program to prevent and treat communicable diseases and raise the standards for medical personnel. The accomplishments of the occupation governments started both countries along the road to becoming strong allies of the United States.

At the end of World War II, the United States had one of the most formidable armies in the world. Its soldiers had mastered military operations in a wide variety of climates in a wide variety of geographical locations around the globe. Army commanders and their staffs planned and conducted joint and combined operations quickly and effectively. The army's only real potential challenger appeared to be the Soviet Union. The Soviets, however, with sparse access to the sea, were geographically limited to continental operations, while the United States, with two broad coasts, could project its massive military power virtually anywhere in the world. America also had the atomic bomb, and in 1945 it was widely believed that the American nuclear monopoly would last a long time.

Within two years of the end of World War II, the United States began a long-term global power struggle against the Soviet Union and international communism that became known as the **Cold War**. With the demands of the Cold War and the higher prestige the military had earned with its performance in World War II, Americans accepted the necessity of a larger peacetime army. Along with a bigger army came major changes in the U.S. government's defense establishment. In 1947 the **Department of the Army** replaced the War Department and became part of the new Department of Defense. At the same time, the air force became a separate service. Although drastically reduced in size, as was usual after a major war, the army remained large enough to provide a deterrent to Communist expansion and to support American foreign policy on a greater scale than ever before. The army continued to have global responsibilities. In Greece and the newly independent Philippines, it administered aid programs and supplied training expertise to governments fighting Communist insurgents. In Western Europe, it helped launch the North Atlantic Treaty Organization (NATO), a large, multinational force intended to deter Soviet attack. However, the army's next challenge was not in Europe, but the Far East.

ADJUSTING TO A BIPOLAR WORLD

In June 1950, North Korea surprised the world when its forces crossed the 38th parallel and attacked the Republic of Korea. The United States and the United Nations (UN) reacted quickly. Within two days of the North Korean invasion, President **Harry S. Truman** authorized American air and naval forces to aid South Korea. The UN established a unified command and asked member nations to contribute forces. Douglas MacArthur, commanding the U.S. occupation forces in Japan, was given command of the UN forces.

The army forces that remained in existence after World War II were focused on occupation duties in Europe and Japan, as the army generally gave little serious thought to another war. Consequently, the four army divisions immediately available to MacArthur in Japan were all understrength, equipped with weapons and equipment left over from World War II, and had only enough ammunition for 45 days of fighting. Training had been largely neglected because of occupation duties. None of the divisions were ready for combat, so the army's initial response was a hasty, piecemeal commitment of forces that tried desperately to stem the North Korean invasion before it overwhelmed the peninsula. **Task Force Smith**, an ill-equipped, hastily organized unit that tried in vain to stop the fast-moving invasion forces, exemplified the army's lack of readiness for war. Although Task Force Smith was quickly swept aside, MacArthur managed to establish a defensive perimeter around Pusan and then organize the **UN Offensive** campaign in the fall of 1950, which forced the North Koreans to abandon their invasion. But MacArthur's push north brought the Chinese Communist Forces into the war. After three years of back-and-forth fighting on the Korean peninsula, the two sides signed a cease-fire agreement. The truce preserved South Korea's independence and strengthened the United States' stand against communism, but it was not seen as a clear victory by many Americans.

After the Korean War, the army prepared to support the U.S. policy of containing communism and meet the threat of wars of national liberation by developing its **Special Forces**, an elite counterinsurgency cadre designed to train indigenous paramilitary forces for unconventional warfare. That capability was soon put to good use in Southeast Asia. In the early 1950s, the United States began helping France to suppress a revolt by the Communist-dominated Viet Minh in French Indochina. When the French withdrew from French Indochina following the Geneva Accords of 1954, army personnel provided assistance to the new South Vietnamese government. President John F. Kennedy increased the aid in the early 1960s, as Vietnam became a test case of American ability to resist Communist wars of national liberation. The

containment policy led the army to a major commitment of forces in the rice pad-
dies and jungle-covered mountains of Southeast Asia. By 1965, there were 184,000
American troops committed to the Vietnam War. Vietnam was not the only place the
army had troops in 1965. That year, an army division deployed to the Dominican
Republic, where it intervened to stop marxist revolutionaries from seizing control
of that country. The American commitment to the war in Vietnam eventually
reached 550,000 troops before resolve faded at home and the troops started returning to the United States. Although North and South Vietnam signed peace accords
in 1973, the North Vietnamese overran the south and forced the last Americans into
a frantic exodus from the country in 1975.

With all of its soldiers out of Vietnam, the army tried to put the experience behind it
as force structure, troop morale, and the budget all dropped rapidly. In the decade after
Vietnam, the army struggled to understand what had happened to it in the jungles of
Southeast Asia. To cleanse itself of Vietnam, the army returned to what it had done in
World War II, which in many minds, both military and civilian, was the last war America had clearly won. By the 1980s, after considerable internal debate and hard work,
the army had largely rid itself of its Vietnam ghosts and developed a doctrine and an
organization to counter the Soviet threat in Europe, where the focus was on **tanks** maneuvering across rolling plains, rather than **infantry** creeping through tangled jungles.

The army also began to work more closely with the other services to improve the
U.S. capability to conduct joint operations in which air, land, and sea forces could
work together toward a common objective. In 1983, the invasion of Grenada
showed that, while there had been some progress on the joint front, the army and
the other services still had much work ahead of them. Prodded by Congress, the services continued to develop joint doctrine, and in late December 1989 army **rangers**
led a successful joint invasion of **Panama** that removed Manuel Noriega's drug-
trafficking rogue regime from power.

A NEW WORLD ORDER

As the twentieth century drew to a close, the army's primary concern was Europe,
where the Soviet Union and the Warsaw Pact continued to pose a threat to NATO.
But in November 1989 the Soviet symbol of defiance of Western Europe, the Berlin
Wall, crumbled. As the year ended, the rise of prodemocracy movements in Eastern
European countries marked the end of the Cold War and brought significant changes
to the world's political landscape. In keeping with tradition, the end of the Cold War
also brought plans for a dramatic reduction in the army's force structure, but world
events would soon see army forces deployed more frequently than at any time in its
history. In Europe, the Soviet Union dissolved, Warsaw Pact members withdrew
from that alliance, and the ethnically diverse country of Yugoslavia began to unravel. Outside Europe, Iraq invaded and occupied Kuwait in August 1990, prompting the UN, led by the United States, to initiate a military buildup in Saudi Arabia
to prevent further Iraqi action.

The Persian Gulf War ended any illusions of a peaceful post–Cold War world, as the army quickly deployed its light forces to Saudi Arabia to deter an invasion of that oil-rich country and buy time for the UN coalition to position a strong military force along the Saudi-Kuwaiti border. By January 1991, the army had seven divisions and two armored cavalry regiments, along with their support forces, in Saudi Arabia. After prolonged negotiations failed to dislodge **Saddam Hussein**'s army from Kuwait and an overwhelming bombing offensive softened the enemy defenses, General **H. Norman Schwarzkopf** and his Saudi counterpart, Lieutenant General Khalid ibn Sultan, sent the UN coalition ground forces across the border in late February 1991. Within 100 hours, the coalition destroyed almost 4,000 Iraqi tanks, captured an estimated 60,000 Iraqis, and ruined 36 Iraqi divisions, at the cost of only 148 American dead.

The war brought only a temporary stop to the army's reduction in size. Ironically, however, as the army got smaller, its challenges increased. In 1995, in response to the rapidly deteriorating situation that resulted from the breakup of Yugoslavia, NATO conducted an operation to occupy Bosnia-Herzegovina, where three ethnic groups had been fighting among themselves to control the newly created Balkan country. Designed to enforce the uneasy peace that had been negotiated at Dayton, Ohio, under the auspices of the United States, and led by U.S. Army **armored** forces to give credence to the operation, NATO for the first time deployed its forces outside Central Europe. But what was originally planned as a one-year contingency operation that would provide the warring factions in the area time to settle their differences soon turned into a semipermanent U.S. presence in the Balkans with no time limit. In 1999 the army deployed additional forces to the Balkans as part of another NATO force designed to maintain calm in Kosovo, which was then an integral part of Serbia.

The United States suffered a severe shock on 11 September 2001, when New York City and Washington, D.C., were attacked by international terrorists using commercial airliners. The suicide attacks left more than 3,000 people dead and the nation stunned. President George W. Bush declared a **war on terrorism** and promised the world that the United States would find those responsible for the attack and punish them, as well as any country that harbored terrorists. In early October, the United States initiated military action against Afghanistan, a country long suspected of being a haven for terrorists. The army deployed elements of its **special operations forces** into the region to support what was expected to be a long and difficult struggle.

LOOKING AHEAD

With conflict and chaos reigning in many parts of the world, the army is now smaller, but much busier, than in recent history. In Korea, its forces stand ready to defend an armed border against a powerful enemy dedicated to the reunification of the peninsula under Communist rule. Despite the destruction of much of Saddam

Hussein's military capability in the Persian Gulf War, the threat of further military action in the region remains. The war on terrorism promises to be a lengthy conflict and the army's special operations forces will no doubt remain heavily involved. The army continues to support American foreign policy with peacekeeping missions in such diverse locations as Haiti, Bosnia, Kosovo, and East Timor and with its work with foreign and domestic agencies to curb terrorism. It also cooperates with the Drug Enforcement Agency, the U.S. Customs Service, and foreign agencies to halt the flow of illicit drugs into the United States. From California and Florida to Kurdistan and Somalia, the army has provided vital aid to victims of floods, earthquakes, hurricanes, war, famine, oil spills, forest fires, and other natural and manmade disasters.

The army is not resting on its past accomplishments. Today, it works to transform itself into a force capable of dominating tomorrow's battlefields as completely as it has those of the past. The army has virtually always been successful when given time to conduct deliberate planning and a methodical buildup of force to overwhelm an opponent with firepower and maneuver. The stunning success in the Persian Gulf War is an excellent recent example. But the army has also frequently stumbled in its first encounter with a new foe, and it has glaring examples of failure when a situation demands a quick reaction. The watchword of "no more Task Force Smiths" refers to the catastrophic opening engagement of the Korean War and is testament that the army is very much aware of the importance of maintaining its forces in a constant state of high readiness.

The United States has the finest army in the world. It has always faithfully served the nation no matter the challenges it has faced. Having successfully adapted to change for more than two centuries, the army will continue its long tradition of service to America and remain on point for the nation, confidently leading it into the twenty-first century.

The Dictionary

— A —

ABRAMS, CREIGHTON WILLIAMS, JR. (1914–1974). Chief of staff of the army from 1972 to 1974. Born in Massachusetts, Abrams graduated from the **U.S. Military Academy** in 1936. During **World War II**, he was a battalion commander in the 37th Armored Regiment and from his tank, named "Thunderbolt," led the **armored** column that relieved U.S. Army forces at Bastogne during the **Ardennes–Alsace** campaign. He graduated from the **Command and General Staff College** in 1949 and from the **Army War College** in 1953. From 1967 until 1972 he commanded the U.S. Military Assistance Command, Vietnam, before becoming the chief of staff of the army in 1972. While he was chief of staff, Abrams led the army in the final stages of the **Vietnam War** and supervised the force reductions and organizational restructuring that immediately followed the war. He died while in office, on 4 September 1974, in Washington, D.C. *See also* Appendix 3, Commanding Generals and Chiefs of Staff of the Army; RESERVE COMPONENTS.

ADJUTANT GENERAL. The post of adjutant general was established 16 June 1775. **Horatio Gates**, a retired British army major was appointed to the post on 17 June with the rank of brigadier general. His primary duty was to serve as key adviser and principal assistant to **George Washington**; he also organized the state militias into what became the **Continental Army**. Early in the nineteenth century the Adjutant General's Department became the central bureau of the **War Department** and adjutants general became the only officers invested with the authority to speak and sign official correspondence "for the commander." After the **Civil War**, the adjutant general corps compiled the records of the war for both the North and the South. *The War of the Rebellion: A Compilation of the Official Records of the Union and Confederate Armies*, or the *Official Records* as the work is popularly known, is an invaluable contribution to American military history. By the beginning of the twentieth century the position had acquired a great deal of influence. After the **Spanish–American War** Major General Fred C. Ainsworth, the adjutant general, opposed the efforts of **Elihu Root, secretary of war**, to establish a **general staff** for the army. The Adjutant General's Department was established on 3 March 1813 and was redesignated the Adjutant General's Corps in 1950. *See also* BRANCHES OF THE ARMY.

ADVISORY (15 March 1962 to 7 March 1965). Vietnam War campaign streamer. During this campaign, direct U.S. involvement in Vietnam increased steadily. The United States hoped that a strong Vietnamese government would result in improved internal security and national defense. By the end of 1962, the United States commitment was 11,000, which included 29 U.S. Army **Special Forces** detachments. These elements operated under the commander, U.S. Military Assistance Command, Vietnam, a position established on 8 February 1962. The object of American military assistance was to counter the threat to the government of the Republic of Vietnam posed by the insurgency of an estimated 30,000 regular communist Viet Cong and civilian sympathizers among the population. Despite what appeared to be considerable successes in consolidating the population in a series of defended strategic hamlets, and in establishing local defense forces, the U.S. equipped Army of the Republic of Vietnam repeatedly demonstrated an unwillingness to close with the enemy. A corrupt government and bitterly contending Vietnamese political factions further hampered a coherent prosecution of the war in cooperation with American advisers.

AFRICAN AMERICANS. Americans of African descent have participated in all of America's wars, but they sometimes have faced as much hostility from fellow Americans as from the enemy. During the **Revolutionary War** some 5,000 African Americans, the majority from New England, served with the American forces, often in integrated units. Some served as artillerymen and musicians, the majority as infantrymen or as unarmed pioneers or engineers who repaired roads and bridges. African Americans could not serve in the **regular army** and under the provisions of the **Militia Act** of 1792 they were not allowed to serve in state militias. They did serve in the **War of 1812**, most notably at the battle of **New Orleans**, where LaCoste and Daquin's Battalions of Free Negroes fought with **Andrew Jackson**'s forces. In 1862, during the **Civil War**, Congress passed the Second Confiscation Act, which authorized recruiting African Americans. After the Emancipation Proclamation the **War Department** established a Bureau of Colored Troops, a volunteer organization without ties to specific states, and by the end of the war 100,000 African Americans were enrolled as U.S. Colored Troops. In addition to the 149 combat regiments, thousands more black soldiers served unofficially as laborers, teamsters, and cooks. After the war, in 1866, Congress authorized the creation of permanent all-black regiments, which in 1869 were designated the 9th and 10th Cavalry and the 24th and 25th Infantry.

Some 3,300 African American regular army soldiers and approximately 10,000 volunteers served in the **Spanish–American War**. During **World War I** 40,000 African American officers and men performed a number of vital jobs, such as construction work, most notably in 16 specially formed pioneer-infantry regiments. African Americans also served as combat troops in the all-black 92d and 93d Infantry Divisions. The 92d was in the **Meuse–Argonne** campaign and the 93d served with distinction among the French forces. In **World War II** more than 700,000 African American soldiers served in the army, with more than 500,000 going overseas. Most were in supply and construction units, but the 92d Infantry Division from World War I was reactivated as a black unit and served in Italy. During the **Ardennes–Alsace** campaign in 1944 some 4,500 African American soldiers volunteered for duty as infantrymen to shore up the Allied defenses against an unexpected German counterattack. The volunteers were organized into provisional platoons and companies and fought with distinction at the Battle of the Bulge.

In 1948 President **Harry S. Truman** signed an executive order directing the armed forces of the United States to provide equal opportunity for all servicemen and eliminate segregation of troops by race. By June 1950 the navy and air force no longer had segregated units, but it took the army another four years to comply. The catalyst was the **Korean War**, which required the army to double its size in five months. In April 1950, African Americans accounted for about 10 percent of the army's total **enlisted** strength, while in December 1952 they accounted for 13.2 percent, as the number of African Americans enlisting in the army increased dramatically for the first time. Black reenlistment increased from 8.5 to 12.9 percent of the total reenlistment during the same period. These increases had a tremendous impact, as black units throughout the army reported having larger numbers than they were authorized to, particularly in the combat arms, and by June 1951 they were being assigned to the combat branches in approximately the same percentage (41 percent) as white soldiers. In 14 May 1951 **Matthew Ridgway**, commanding the U.S. Eighth Army in Korea, forced the issue of integration by formally requesting authority to abolish segregation in his command.

During the **Vietnam War** African Americans made up 11 percent of the American population, but they constituted 12.6 percent of the soldiers serving in the war from 1965 to 1969. Most were in the infantry, where they suffered a disproportionate fatality rate in combat. Frustration with the slow rate of racial progress in the army increased tension between blacks and whites and led to the creation of interracial councils and racial sensitivity training throughout the army. The **All-Volunteer Force**, introduced in 1973, increased the percentage of African Americans in the army. Since the 1970s the army has made a serious effort at racial integration and African Americans now serve at all levels. In 1977 **Clifford Alexander** became the first black secretary of the army and in 1989 **Colin Powell** was named chairman of the Joint Chiefs of Staff. *See also* DAVIS, BENJAMIN OLIVER, JR.; DAVIS, BENJAMIN OLIVER, SR.; FLIPPER, HENRY OSSIAN.

AILES, STEPHEN (1912–). Secretary of the army from 1964 to 1965. Born in West Virginia, Ailes graduated from Princeton University in 1933 and received a law degree from West Virginia University in 1936. He was the under secretary of the army from 1961 until 1964, when he was appointed secretary of the army. While he was secretary, the army provided disaster assistance after earthquakes in Yugoslavia and Alaska, made an agreement with the Federal Republic of Germany to jointly develop a main battle tank, provided troops to end a Civil War in the **Dominican Republic**, and dispatched its first combat units to Vietnam. After leaving office, Ailes was director of the Panama Canal Company and president of American Railroads. *See also* Appendix 4, Secretaries of War and Secretaries of the Army.

AIRBORNE. Shortly after **World War I**, **William Mitchell** proposed the concept of parachuting troops from aircraft into combat. In a demonstration at Kelly Field at San Antonio, Texas, six soldiers parachuted from a Martin Bomber, safely landed, and in less than three minutes after exiting the aircraft, had their weapons assembled and were ready for action. U.S. observers dismissed the concept, but the Soviets and Germans in attendance were impressed with the demonstration. In the Soviet Union, static-line parachuting was introduced as a national sport and people were encouraged to join the Russian Airborne Corps. German planners developed an effective military parachute organization and used it to spearhead assaults at the start of **World War II**.

Spurred by the Germans' use of airborne troops, U.S. military branches began an all-out effort to develop this new form of warfare. In April 1940, the **War Department** approved plans for the formation of a test platoon of airborne infantry to form, equip, and train under the direction and control of the army's Infantry Board. In July 1940, First Lieutenant William T. Ryder from the 29th Infantry Regiment was designated to lead the test platoon and 48 **enlisted** men were selected from a pool of 200 volunteers. Shortly thereafter, the platoon moved to the Safe Parachute Company at Hightstown, New Jersey, for training on the parachute drop towers used during the New York World's Fair, where the troops trained for a week on the 250-foot free towers. The training was effective and proved to the soldiers that their parachutes would function safely. The army purchased two of the towers and erected them at Fort Benning, Georgia. Two more were added later, and three of these four towers remain in use for training paratroopers at Fort Benning.

Less than 45 days after its organization, the platoon made its first jump from a Douglas B-18. Before the drop, the test platoon held a lottery to determine who would follow Ryder out of the airplane and Private William N. (Red) King thus became the first enlisted soldier to make an official jump as a paratrooper in the U.S. Army. On 29 August, the platoon made the first platoon mass jump held in the United States. The first airborne combat unit to be organized was the 501st Parachute Battalion, and the original test platoon members formed the battalion cadre. The traditional paratrooper cry "Geronimo!" was originated in the 501st by Private Aubrey Eberhart to prove to a friend that he had full control of his faculties when he jumped. Airborne experimentation of another type was initiated on 10 October 1941 with the activation of the army's first glider infantry battalion.

The army formed six divisions of parachute and glider regiments during World War II. They saw their first combat in North Africa in 1942, followed by a larger airborne assault during the **Sicily** campaign in 1943. The 82d and 101st Airborne Divisions jumped into **Normandy** ahead of the Allied invasion of France in 1944 and, despite some units being dropped in the wrong place, captured key bridges and road intersections during the campaign. At Bastogne, during the **Ardennes–Alsace** campaign, the 101st denied the Germans control of a critical road junction while completely surrounded. During the **Korean War, helicopters** began to replace the paratroopers and in the **Vietnam War** there was only one brigade-sized airborne assault. Today, the army has only one airborne division, although **Rangers** and **Special Forces** soldiers are all qualified paratroopers.

AIR DEFENSE ARTILLERY. Branch of the army. It became a separate branch in 1968, when the former **artillery** branch was separated into **field artillery** and air defense artillery. The branch originated from the Coast Artillery Corps, which was created after the **Revolutionary War** to defend American coasts against naval attack and bombardment. The coast artillery was abolished in 1950, after aircraft and high-velocity guns made concrete coastal fortifications vulnerable and obsolete. At the time, it had been performing in the air defense role since **World War I**, when the **War Department** created an antiaircraft artillery (AAA) corps to protect ground forces from aerial bombardment. Coast artillery units were detailed as AAA units because they had experience firing at moving targets; they were available because the threat of the German fleet to the East Coast had been neutralized by an Allied blockade. In **World War II** AAA units were the first army units to engage the Japanese at Pearl Harbor and, in the **Korean War**, AAA units at Suwon airbase were again the first army units to engage the enemy, this time the invading North Korean forces. During the **Vietnam War**, the United States enjoyed virtual air supremacy, but air defense units used their rapid firing weapons to good advantage against ground targets to protect fire bases and other fixed installations.

In the **Persian Gulf War**, the army's Patriot air defense system gained a worldwide reputation as it defended the coalition forces against repeated attacks from Iraqi Scud missiles. Designed to protect ground forces against enemy planes and tactical ballistic missiles, the system includes remotely operated four-canister launch stations, a radar unit, and an engagement control center. The Patriot system usually deploys in batteries of five to eight launchers. Each of the missiles carries a high-explosive warhead and has a velocity of Mach 3.7 and a range of 160 kilometers. Twenty-one Patriot batteries with 132 launchers were deployed to Saudi Arabia to provide air defense for coalition forces, while seven batteries were deployed in Israel to counter the Iraqi Scud threat there. During the war 158 missiles were fired at Iraqi Scuds over Israel and Saudi Arabia. *See also* BRANCHES OF THE ARMY.

AIR OFFENSIVE, EUROPE (4 July 1942 to 5 June 1944). World War II campaign streamer. The U.S. Army Air Forces, in close coordination with the British Royal Air Force, conducted strategic bombing of Germany from mid-1942 through May 1945. The offensive was a major factor in the war, but it was the subject of continuous political and military debate. Although the buildup of air forces in Britain was supposed to be the first priority for the Army, the **Algeria–French Morocco** campaign in North Africa diverted aircraft from the offensive. The initial results of the bombing were not as productive as the predictions by air power advocates. The wartime training did not produce crews that could match prewar accuracy, short-range fighters could not accompany the bombers all the way to targets in Germany, and the weather frequently prevented accurate bombing. However, the campaign caused Germany to divert considerable resources from the battlefield. Two million German troops manned air defenses, the German aircraft and ball-bearing industries had to be dispersed, and high-velocity artillery and communications equipment were devoted to combating the air offensive. By 1944, radar allowed planes to hit targets through the cloud cover and longer-range escort aircraft equipped with drop tanks engaged German fighters that attacked the bombers.

The first American air raid in the campaign was on 4 July 1942, when six light bombers from the U.S. Eighth Air Force bombed Dutch airfields, although U.S. heavy bombers flying from Egypt had hit the oil refinery in Ploesti, Romania, in June to open the **Egypt–Libya** campaign in North Africa. Throughout the campaign, the raids grew in size, as more aircraft became available. On 27 January 1943, 55 aircraft conducted the first American attack on Germany, hitting the naval base at Wilhelmshaven. In May 1943 the Combined Chiefs of Staff had given high priority to a bombing offensive to be waged by the British Royal Air Force and the U.S. Army Air Forces, and by late summer of that year Allied bombers were conducting round-the-clock bombardment of German industry and communications. As more aircraft became available to the Allied air forces, the campaign increased in intensity. An air raid by 200 planes was considered large in June 1943, but a year later the average strike consisted of 1,000 heavy bombers. In general, British planes bombed by night, while American planes bombed by day.

As the Allies prepared for the invasion of the continent in 1944, the bombing effort focused on oil production, and as the landing date approached, French railways were hit repeatedly. By 6 June 1944, when the Allied landings took place at **Normandy**, the air offensive had virtually eliminated any threat from the German air force. After the successful invasion, the German oil industry remained the primary target for Allied bombing, which forced a brief halt in production in late 1944. During the winter of 1944–1945, when weather inhibited the pinpoint bombing needed to hit oil refineries, the U.S. Eighth Air Forces concentrated on the German transportation system, and by the end of February 1945, the railroads were in ruin, crippling Germany's war economy.

AIR OFFENSIVE, JAPAN (17 April 1942 to 2 September 1945). World War II campaign streamer. American bombing operations against Japan began on 18 April 1942, when a flight of 16 bombers led by Lieutenant Colonel James Doolittle took off from U.S. Navy aircraft carriers and flew 650 miles to raid Tokyo and other Japanese cities. The famous raid caused little material damage, but it was a great boost to American morale and embarrassed the Japanese military. A plan to fly further raids against the Japanese home islands from bases in China had to be delayed when Japanese forces closed the Burma Road during the **Burma 1942** campaign. The aircraft and crews that had been preparing to fly out of China were then diverted to participate in the **Egypt–Libya** campaign, in which they supported the British in North Africa and the Mediterranean. Although American bombers would not challenge the home islands of Japan for another two years, the air offensive supported Allied operations across the Pacific. By June 1944, American air forces were flying raids from China to bomb Japan using the B-29 Superfortresses. In November 1944, the army initiated flight operations from airfields in the Mariana Islands.

Plagued with difficulties, the raids failed to achieve significant results with high-altitude, precision bombing operations during the day, so General Curtis LeMay shifted to low-level, incendiary raids flown at night. On 9 March 1945, 334 bombers set fire to 16 square miles of Tokyo, destroyed 22 key targets, and killed between 80,000 and 90,000 civilians, making this the deadliest air raid of the war. Eventually more than eight million Japanese fled from the cities to avoid the fire raids. With the end of the war in Europe, additional American air forces were deployed to the Pacific. Although in anticipation of an invasion of Japan, there was an attempt to change the bombing strategy from incendiary bombing to concentration on transportation facilities, the momentum was too much to overcome and the fire raids continued. The raids burned some 180 square miles in 67 Japanese cities, killed at least 300,000 people, and wounded another 400,000.

American scientists working on the Manhattan Project produced two types of atomic bomb by mid-1945 and the first atomic detonation was at Alamogordo, New Mexico, on 16 July. After debating if a demonstration of the new weapon would suffice to end the war, a panel of scientists determined saving American lives was the primary consideration and recommended using the bomb against a city. Concerned that conventional bombing would not defeat Japan, on 30 July 1945, U.S. president **Harry S. Truman** approved using an atomic bomb prior to launching an invasion of the home islands. The primary target was Hiroshima, a industrial city of 250,000. On 6 August, at 8:15 in the morning, an atomic bomb killed 60,000 people and destroyed 81 percent of the structures in the city. Another 60,000 fatalities resulted from injuries or radiation poisoning. When the Japanese government did not immediately concede, three days later the U.S. dropped a second atomic bomb, on Nagasaki, killing another 35,000 people, followed by 40,000 additional deaths from radiation and injuries. While awaiting a response from the Japanese government, Truman ordered the resumption of conventional bombing on 15 August and more than 1,000 bombers attacked Japan. Japan surrendered unconditionally that night and signed the agreement on 2 September, ending the war and the bombing campaign.

AISNE (27 May to 5 June 1918). World War I campaign streamer. On 27 May 1918, the Germans attacked thinly held but formidable terrain along the Aisne

River in France. French and British defenders, taken by surprise, were rapidly overrun on a 40-mile front. German progress on the first day was so rapid (advances up to 13 miles were made at some points) that the diversionary attack became the main effort. Most of the Aisne bridges were captured intact and by 31 May the Germans had reached the outskirts of Chateau-Thierry on the Marne, less than 40 miles from Paris. The Germans tried to exploit and expand the salient, but by 4 June they had been stopped everywhere. Some 27,500 American troops helped stop the German advance. During the first four days of June, the U.S. 3d Division foiled German attempts to secure a bridgehead across the Marne River at Chateau-Thierry. West of the town, the U.S. Army's 2d Division, which included a U.S. Marine brigade, defended the road to Paris and on 6 June successfully counterattacked in Belleau Wood.

AISNE–MARNE (18 July to 6 August 1918). World War I campaign streamer. Several days before the Germans launched the **Champagne-Marne** drive, the French made plans for a general converging offensive against the Marne salient. Spearheading the attack were the five divisions of the French XX Corps, two of which were from the American Expeditionary Force. On 18 July the two American divisions and a French Moroccan division launched the main blow near Soissons. Surprised German troops initially gave ground, but resistance stiffened after an Allied penetration of some three miles. Before the two U.S. Army divisions were relieved, they had advanced almost seven miles, made Soissons untenable for the enemy, and captured 6,500 prisoners at a cost of over 10,000 American casualties.

Other French armies also made important gains and the Germans began a general retreat from the Marne salient. The French Sixth Army advanced steadily from the southwest, reaching the Vesle River on 3 August. By 28 July this army included four American divisions, two of which were controlled by the U.S. I Corps headquarters. On 4 August a second American corps headquarters entered combat and by 5 August the entire Sixth Army front was held by the two American corps. On 6 August the Aisne–Marne offensive was over. Eight U.S. Army divisions had spearheaded much of the advance, demonstrating offensive capabilities that helped inspire new confidence in the war-weary Allied armies. About 270,000 Americans took part in the battle.

The excellent showing made by American troops gave General **John J. Pershing**, commander of the U.S. forces in France, an opportunity to press for his goal of forming an independent American army. Preliminary steps in the organization of the U.S. First Army started in early July 1918 and on 10 August the First Army activated its headquarters near Chateau-Thierry, with Pershing as the commander. The new organization had two sectors of responsibility, a temporary combat sector in the Chateau-Thierry region, where the U.S. I and III Corps were conducting operations, and a quiet sector farther east that would become the First Army's theater of operations once the American divisions could be moved there. However, stabilization of the Vesle River front in early August led Pershing to al-ter his plans. Instead of organizing the First Army in the Chateau-Thierry region and moving it eastward for the planned **St. Mihiel** offensive, he concentrated the First Army units in the vicinity of the St. Mihiel salient.

ALEUTIAN ISLANDS (3 June 1942 to 24 August 1943). World War II campaign streamer. The Japanese became interested in the Aleutian Islands shortly after the Doolittle raid on Tokyo in April 1942 made them aware of the vulnerability of the home islands from an attack from the northern Pacific. Although their subsequent seizure of Attu, Kiska, and Agattu Islands in June 1942 was strategically unimportant, it did provide the Japanese a potential base for raiding Alaska and limiting American air and sea operations in the northern Pacific. When the Japanese occupied the islands, the United States did not have enough ships, planes, or troops available to recapture them, but in August 1942 the United States established airfields on the islands of Adak and Amchitka, from which bombers could attack Kiska and Attu.

In the spring of 1943, the United States began to assemble an invasion force to recapture Kiska and Attu. The operation was under the overall command of Vice Admiral Thomas E. Kinkaid, commander of the North Pacific theater, while Major General Albert E. Brown commanded the army forces making the landing. Although Kiska, with the only operational airfield and a better harbor, was the more important of the two islands, landings were made on Attu first with the idea of cutting the supply line to Kiska. On 11 May 1943, army forces supported by air and naval units landed on Attu. The Japanese desperately defended their positions, but they were destroyed almost to a man, and the fighting ended by 30 May. Americans found 2,351 dead Japanese on the island and estimated that several hundred more were buried in the hills during the fighting. The U.S. force of more that 15,000 suffered 549 killed and 1,148 wounded.

Taking heed of the Japanese determination on Attu, a more powerful Allied amphibious force, including a U.S. infantry division and elements of the Royal Canadian Army commanded by Major General Charles H. Corlett and a naval escort commanded by Admiral Kinkaid, assaulted the island of Kiska on 15 August 1943, expecting to find about 10,000 defenders. To the surprise of the Allies, however, the island had been secretly evacuated by the Japanese under cover of heavy summer fog that had prevented aerial observation or interception. Although the massive invasion of an unoccupied island was somewhat embarrassing, the preparations for fighting in severe weather conditions and mountainous terrain proved to be useful lessons in the Allied campaigns in Italy. However, the Japanese withdrawal from Kiska without a fight gave American commanders something of a false picture of what they could expect in future island invasions in the Pacific. The fierce fighting at Attu, not the unopposed landing at Kiska, proved to be the pattern of future battles. *See also* AIR OFFENSIVE, JAPAN,

ALEXANDER, CLIFFORD LEOPOLD, JR. (1933–). Secretary of the army from 1977 to 1981. Born in New York City, Alexander graduated from Harvard University in 1955 and from Yale University Law School in 1958. He served briefly in the New York **Army National Guard**. While secretary he concentrated on making the all-volunteer army, emphasized professionalism, and focused on awarding contracts to minority contractors. After leaving office he formed a consulting firm, served on the boards of directors of several national corporations, and became a member of the Board of Governors of the New York Stock Exchange. *See also* Appendix 4, Secretaries of War and Secretaries of the Army.

ALGER, RUSSELL ALEXANDER (1836–1907). Secretary of war from 1897 to 1899. Born in Ohio, Alger studied law, was admitted to the bar, and began a practice in Cleveland. He enlisted as a private soldier at the beginning of the **Civil War** and ended the war with a brevet promotion to major general of volunteers. While secretary of war he recommended adding a second assistant secretary of war and establishing a constabulary force for Cuba, Puerto Rico, and the Philippines. He was criticized for inadequate preparations and inefficient operations of the department during the **Spanish–American War** and resigned at the request of President William McKinley. He became a U.S. senator from Ohio in 1902 and died in Washington, D.C., on 24 January 1907. *See also* Appendix 4, Secretaries of War and Secretaries of the Army.

ALGERIA–FRENCH MOROCCO (8–11 November 1943). World War II campaign streamer. The United States wanted to launch an invasion of the European continent as early as possible after entering World War II, but when it became evident by mid-1942 that it would not be possible to do so that year, American planners agreed to a British proposal to invade North Africa. The primary objective of the invasion was to relieve pressure on the Russians fighting massive German forces on the Eastern Front. Secondary objectives were to gain French Morocco, Algeria, and **Tunisia** as a base for enlisting the French colonial empire in the war, to assist the British in destroying Axis forces threatening Egypt and Suez, to open the Mediterranean to Allied shipping, to shorten the route to the Far East, and to prepare for future operations in Europe. The British and American Combined Chiefs of Staff approved the plan and named **Dwight D. Eisenhower** commander in chief of the Allied Expeditionary Force that was to invade North Africa. Allied Force Headquarters, North Africa, was established in London on 11 August 1942 to plan the operation.

In North Africa, the Germans and their Italian allies controlled a narrow strip along the Mediterranean coast between Tunisia and Egypt with an army numbering some 100,000 men under Field Marshal **Erwin Rommel**. French forces in North Africa also numbered about 100,000 men, plus considerable naval strength, but since the loyalties of the French forces had become split following their defeat in 1940, it was not clear how they would react to the Allied landings. The need for secrecy to achieve strategic surprise hampered Allied attempts to enlist French support before the landings. The Allied plan for invading North Africa involved concentric attacks. The British Eighth Army under Lieutenant General Bernard L. Montgomery was to attack from the west out of Egypt, while a combined Anglo-American force under Eisenhower was to invade French

North Africa and hit the enemy's rear. The British Eighth Army was to come under Eisenhower's command when the two forces converged on Tunisia.

There were three simultaneous landings in North Africa: one outside the Strait of Gibraltar near Casablanca, Morocco, and two inside the strait in Algeria, near Oran and Algiers. Once these landings were accomplished, additional troops were to land near the eastern border of Algeria and move rapidly into Tunisia, presumably before the Germans could block the move. The British Eighth Army opened an offensive at El Alamein on 23 October 1942 and on 8 November the U.S. Navy landed U.S. Army forces near Casablanca, while the British Royal Navy put American and British troops ashore near Oran and Algiers. The invasion force included more than 400 ships, 1,000 planes, and some 107,000 men. The U.S. I **Armored** Corps of three divisions under Major General **George S. Patton Jr.** landed at Casablanca after sailing directly from ports in the United States, the only time during the war when a force of more than division size was combat-loaded in U.S. ports for landing directly on a hostile beach. The forces landing near Oran and Algiers included the U.S. II Corps, commanded by Major General Lloyd W. Fredendall, with elements of three divisions. The campaign also included an **airborne** battalion of paratroopers making the first U.S. combat jump of the war. The Allies achieved strategic surprise, but the operation was delayed by the French forces, who challenged most of the landings, although by 11 November negotiations had succeeded both in ending French resistance and winning their cooperation.

ALL-VOLUNTEER FORCE. Prior to 1940, America relied on volunteers to man its army, but meeting the manning levels required by **World War II** and the subsequent **Cold War** forced the nation to begin conscription. In 1973 the secretary of defense announced the end of conscription and the beginning of the All-Volunteer Force, in which the army and other armed forces would once again rely on volunteers to maintain their strength. The concept enjoyed early success as a troubled economy made military service an attractive option, but the late 1970s saw a reduction in funding for recruiting. That, combined with a pay rate that was not keeping up with the economy led to problems in manning the force as the army fell 17,000 soldiers short of its recruiting goal in 1979. The situation improved in the 1980s with pay raises and educational incentives. In 1983 the Department of Defense dropped the term "All-Volunteer Force."

ANTIETAM (3–17 September 1862). Civil War campaign streamer. Known also as Sharpsburg. On 4 September 1862, shortly after their success at **Manassas**, Confederate forces under the command of General **Robert E. Lee** began moving north, with the hope of gaining diplomatic recognition from Britain and France by inflicting a major defeat on Union forces in their own territory. On 4 September Lee's Army of Northern Virginia, with some 5,500 men, began crossing the Potomac River north of Washington, D.C. When the army reached Frederick, Maryland, Lee detached General **Thomas J. Jackson**'s column to guard against interference from the Union garrison at Harper's Ferry, while the rest of the army moved across the Blue Ridge Mountains to Hagerstown. In Washington, U.S. president **Abraham Lincoln** ordered General **George B. McClellan** to use the Army of the Potomac to find and destroy Lee's forces. McClellan moved north with 90,000 men and arrived on 12 September at Frederick, where in an amazing stroke of good luck, he obtained a copy of Lee's orders wrapped around a package of cigars lost by a Confederate officer. Learning from the order that Lee's army was divided, McClellan had an opportunity to defeat Lee piecemeal. But McClellan did not move fast enough. The garrison at Harper's Ferry surrendered to Jackson on 15 September and Lee was able to concentrate most of his army near the town of Sharpsburg on Antietam Creek.

Although McClellan outnumbered the Confederates, he assumed that he had the inferior forces. On 17 September, after deliberate preparations to attack the Confederate lines on the left and right at the same time, McClellan's forces began their assault. But the Federal attacks were not well coordinated, giving Lee the opportunity to shift his forces along the line to stop each Union threat as it materialized. Late in the afternoon, Major General **Ambrose Burnside**, after spending most of the day forcing his troops across a small stone bridge, finally presented a threat to Lee's rear and line of retreat back across the Potomac River. But a forced march from Harper's Ferry by Major General A. P. Hill with a division of Confederate troops arrived in time to stop the Union move. It was the bloodiest single day in the Civil War and American military history. Of 75,316 Federals engaged, 2,108 were killed, 9,549 were wounded, and 753 were missing; of 51,844 Confederates engaged, 2,700 were killed, 9,024 were wounded, and about 2,000 were missing. The next day Lee moved his army back across the Potomac, escaping further damage. McClellan did not pursue the Confederates. He remained on the battlefield and declared himself the victor. In spite of McClellan's claims of victory, Lincoln relieved the general of command in November.

ANTISUBMARINE (7 December 1941 to 2 September 1945). World War II campaign streamer. To protect shipping from enemy submarines, Army Air Forces planes flew antisubmarine patrols along the coastlines of the Atlantic and Pacific Oceans and the Gulf of Mexico. Perhaps the most important of these operations were flown from bases in Newfoundland and along the East Coast of the United States. By the fall of 1942 these patrols, working in coordination with naval operations, had stopped the German U-boat packs that had been taking a heavy toll of shipping in the western Atlantic. In late 1943 the U.S. Navy assumed the antisubmarine responsibilities that had been assigned to the army when the United States entered the war in December 1941.

ANZIO (22 January to 24 May 1944). World War II campaign streamer. In December 1943 the U.S. and British forces in Italy were reinforced by a French corps equipped with American arms. With this added strength at his disposal, General **Mark Clark** used the U.S. VI Corps, which included both British and American troops, in an attempt to envelop the western flank of the German line, while he simultaneously tried to break through the Gustav Line, which had halted the Allied advance during the **Naples-Foggia** campaign. To get behind the German defensive line, the VI Corps made an amphibious landing at Anzio, about 35 miles south of Rome, on 22 January 1944 with the mission of linking up with Allied forces fighting north through Italy. After a successful surprise landing, the corps halted to establish port and depot facilities before moving inland. The delay gave the Germans time to move troops to the beachhead and mount an attack that pushed the corps back to the water's edge. The counterattack reached a peak of intensity on 17 February and threatened to wipe out the beachhead. But the VI Corps' defense of the perimeter, supported by artillery, tanks, planes, and naval gunfire, brought the attacks to a halt on 4 March. Fighting continued until the two Allied forces made contact on 25 May.

Although not as successful as hoped, the campaign eventually opened the way for the Allies to enter Rome on 4 June. While the Anzio campaign failed to turn the German defenses in the south or create an immediate Allied breach of the Gustav Line, the presence of a significant Allied force behind the German main line of resistance and very close to Rome represented a constant threat. The 135,000 German troops that surrounded the beachhead could not be moved elsewhere and caused a steady drain on German reserves. The end of the campaign came on 24 May, when soldiers from the Allied forces broke through the Gustav line and linked up with troops from the Anzio beachhead. During the four months of the campaign the Allies suffered more than 29,200 combat casualties, two thirds of which came between the initial landings and the end of the German counteroffensive on 4 March.

APACHES (1873, 1885–1886). Indian wars campaign streamer. Brigadier General **George Crook**, who assumed command of the Department of Arizona in 1871, began training his troops to conduct rapid pursuits and enlisted Apache scouts. He took to the field during the winter of 1872–1873 to move the Indians onto reservations, hitting them in hideouts they had considered safe refuges. The largest battle of the campaign came on 28 December 1872, when army troops attacked a band of Indians at Skull Cave, killing some 75 Yavapais. The winter campaigning demoralized the Indians and by April 1873 the Apaches had stopped fighting and the Yavapais surrendered at Camp Verde. In the years that followed, the Indian Bureau's policy of frequent removal created new dissatisfaction among the Apaches. Led by Chato, Victorio, **Geronimo**, and other chiefs, dissident bands left the reservations and raided settlements along both sides of the international border, escaping into Mexico or the United States as circumstances dictated. In 1882, the two nations agreed to reasonable pursuit of Indian raiders by the troops of each country across the boundary. Victorio was killed by Mexican troops in 1880, but Chato and Geronimo remained at large until May 1883, when they surrendered to Crook in Mexico.

In 1885 Geronimo and about 150 Chiricahua Apaches left their White Mountain reservation in Arizona and began terrorizing the border region. Army cavalry and Apache scouts took up pursuit of the Chiricahua renegades. When Captain

Emmet Crawford and 80 Apache scouts attacked Geronimo's main band some 200 miles south of the border in January 1886 the Indians escaped into the mountains. Crawford was killed by Mexican irregulars shortly thereafter, but his second in command, First Lieutenant M. P. Maus, was able to negotiate Geronimo's surrender to General Crook in late March 1886. Within a few days Geronimo and part of his band escaped. Captain Henry W. Lawton's column of cavalry, infantry, and Apache scouts surprised Geronimo in Mexico on 20 July. Although the Apaches eluded capture, by the end of August they indicated a willingness to surrender. On 4 September 1886, First Lieutenant Charles B. Gatewood negotiated Geronimo's formal surrender to Brigadier General **Nelson Miles**, who had replaced Crook in April. Geronimo and his band were moved to Florida and finally to the Fort Sill military reservation.

APPOMATTOX (3–9 April 1865). Civil War campaign streamer. The beginning of 1865 found Confederate resistance practically at an end at Petersburg and Richmond, where General **Robert E. Lee**'s Army of Northern Virginia grimly held its position. In late March, General **Ulysses S. Grant** began a major effort to destroy this last island of Confederate resistance. Union troops under Grant in the Richmond area numbered 101,000 infantry, 14,700 cavalry, and 9,000 artillery, while Lee had 46,000 infantry, 6,000 cavalry, and 5,000 artillery. Except for a holding force at Richmond, most of Lee's troops were manning the long line of fortifications that extended north and south of Petersburg.

On 29 March, Grant began an encircling movement with part of his force around Lee's right (south) flank at Petersburg, while his main body of troops moved to strike directly at that flank. The movement was halted by Confederate forces under Generals George E. Pickett and Richard S. Ewell in battles around White Oak Road on 31 March and at Five Forks on 1 April. But the next day Grant mounted an assault on Lee's right that broke the Confederate line. As the Confederates withdrew toward Petersburg, Lee pulled General **James Longstreet**'s corps away from Richmond to help hold the line.

Forced to abandon the fortifications, Lee struck out with his army on 3 April and hastened west along the Appomattox River, hoping to break loose and eventually join forces with General **Joseph E. Johnston** to the south. But Grant pursued relentlessly, and a four-day running fight ensued during which Lee's army began to disintegrate. Finally a Union cavalry force under General **Phillip Sheridan** raced ahead of the Confederates, occupied a position at Appomattox Court House, blocked Lee's line of retreat, and ended the fight. On 9 April 1865 Lee met Grant in Appomattox and surrendered. Confederate losses in killed and wounded from 29 March through 7 April were estimated to be more than 6,000. Lee surrendered with 26,765, but many others, individually or by unit, escaped capture or deserted. Federal losses during the same period were 1,316 killed, 7,750 wounded, and 1,714 missing. On 26 April 1865 Johnston surrendered to General **William T. Sherman** near Raleigh, Virginia, and by the end of May the remaining Confederate forces had given up the struggle and the Civil War was finally over.

ARDENNES–ALSACE (16 December 1944 to 25 January 1945). World War II campaign streamer. Known also as the Battle of the Bulge. In December 1944 Adolf Hitler directed an ambitious counteroffensive with the object of regaining the initiative in the west and compelling the Allies to settle for a negotiated peace. Hitler's generals were opposed to the plan, but the Führer's will prevailed and the counteroffensive was launched on 16 December by some 30 German divisions against Allied lines in the Ardennes region, where defenses had been thinned to provide troops for the American offensive during the **Rhineland** campaign. Hitler's intent was to drive through Antwerp and cut off and annihilate the British 21st Army Group and the U.S. First and Ninth Armies north of the Ardennes. The Germans hoped that a successful offensive would lead to a negotiated settlement of the war in the east. The offensive achieved complete surprise, as two Panzer (armored) armies, supported by nearly 1,000 aircraft and as many as 250,000 troops, attacked the U.S. First Army of five divisions, most of which were new or resting. Taking advantage of fog and snow, German tanks and infantry moved swiftly into the American lines using English-speaking soldiers in American uniform to further confuse the surprised defenders. Because the German attack created a huge bulge in the Allied lines, the campaign is frequently referred to as the Battle of the Bulge.

Aided by stormy weather that grounded Allied planes and restricted observation, the Germans initially made rapid gains, but firm resistance by a number of isolated American units provided time for the U.S. First and Ninth Armies to shift against the northern flank of the penetration and for the British to send reserves to secure the line to the Meuse. On 19 December, **Dwight D. Eisenhower**, supreme commander of Allied forces in Europe, ordered **George S. Patton** to move his U.S. Third Army north and cut off the German attack. Eisenhower also sent the 101st and 82d **Airborne** Divisions into battle by truck. As German troops poured through the porous defenses, the troops of the 101st Airborne Division moved to and held the town of Bastogne, a vital road junction. Referring to themselves as the "Battered Bastards of Bastogne," they held the town until Lieutenant Colonel **Creighton Abrams** led Patton's forces into Bastogne on 26 December. Denied vital roads and hampered by air attack when the weather cleared, the German offensive had run out of steam on 24 December. The U.S. First and Third Armies began to counterattack on 3 January from either side of the bulge. Hampered by cold and deep snow, they did not join forces for 13 days, allowing most of the German troops to escape.

Americans suffered some 75,000 casualties in the campaign, but the Germans lost an estimated 81,000 to 103,000 and their strength had been irredeemably impaired. By the end of January 1945, when the campaign ended, American units had retaken all ground they had lost and the defeat of Germany was clearly only a matter of time. The aborted offensive also spent the last German reserves of veteran troops and finally opened the way to the Allied invasion of Germany during the **Central Europe** campaign.

ARMED FORCES EXPEDITIONS. *See* DOMINICAN REPUBLIC; GRENADA; PANAMA.

ARMED FORCES RESERVE ACT (1952). Prompted by weaknesses in the army's reserve forces and inequities for veterans revealed by the partial mobilization for the **Korean War**, Congress sought to improve the army's reserve organization and protect the Korean veterans from future service. The act established three categories of reserve forces: ready, standby, and retired. The ready reserve included the entire **Army National Guard** and was authorized a strength of 1.5 million soldiers. The act also allowed individual reserve and National Guard soldiers to volunteer for active duty, which allowed the army to use them in routine peacetime operations and contingencies without their being mobilized. *See also* RESERVE COMPONENTS; UNITED STATES ARMY RESERVE.

ARMOR. Branch of the army. The branch is equipped with **tanks**, but it traces its origin to the **cavalry**. The Tank Service was formed on 5 March 1918 and American **armored** units equipped with French-supplied tanks first saw combat in **World War I**. After their inauspicious debut in 1918, tank forces virtually disappeared from the army when the National Defense Act of 1920 disbanded the fledgling Tank Corps. In spite of the efforts of officers such as **George S. Patton**, **Adna R. Chafee**, and **Dwight D. Eisenhower**, who sought to exploit their combat potential, the army viewed tanks as simply a supporting force for the infantry.

For 20 years the U.S. Army lagged well behind other armies in the world in developing armored warfare. But, surprised by the German success with armored warfare in the invasion of Poland, the army formed the Armored Force on 10 July 1940 with Chafee as its head. The army's armored force grew to 16 armored divisions during **World War II** and played a key role in the war in Europe. Patton's Third Army exemplified the army's armored warfare as it rolled across France in 1944. In the reduction of force after the war, the army retained only one armored division. As part of the **Army Reorganization Act** of 1950, armor was designated a branch of the army. The new branch was considered a continuation of cavalry. During the **Cold War**, armor was at the core of the army's force development and doctrine designed to defeat the Soviet Union and the Warsaw Pact should they decide to invade Central Europe. After playing minor roles in the **Korean War** and the **Vietnam War**, the army's armor took center stage in the 1991 **Persian Gulf War**. During that war, the army capitalized on its Cold War preparations as it faced the Iraqi Army, trained and equipped by the Soviet Union. The Iraqi Army proved no match for the vastly superior American forces. *See also* BRANCHES OF THE ARMY.

ARMORED. A term used to designate vehicles that provide steel or aluminum protection from projectiles and shell fragments for crew, passengers, weapons systems, and other vital equipment. **Tanks** are usually heavily armored, while **infantry** fighting vehicles and self-propelled **artillery** are lightly armored. Heavily armored vehicles are capable of resisting hits from a main tank gun, while lightly armored vehicles can resist hits from small-arms fire and shell fragments. Armored personnel carriers are lightly armored vehicles with the primary function of transporting infantry troops around the battlefield with some degree of protection. They can be tracked or wheeled but are not designed for fighting. Fighting vehicles are also lightly armored, but they are tracked and provide a mobile, protected fighting platform for mechanized infantry forces on the battlefield. The army's M-2 *Bradley* fighting vehicle was designed to operate in combat with the M-1 *Abrams* tank and was used very effectively during the **Persian Gulf War**.

ARMSTRONG, JOHN (1758–1843). Secretary of war from 1813 to 1814. Armstrong was born in Pennsylvania and his education at Princeton University was interrupted by the **Revolutionary War**, when he served on the staff of **Horatio Gates**. After the war, he served in the U.S. Senate and was minister to France, before becoming secretary of war. While in this office he was instrumental in securing legislative action for a permanent **War Department** staff and in reducing the number of general officers in the army. He resigned in 1814 over the British capture of Washington, D.C., during the **War of 1812** and he returned to New York, where he engaged in agriculture until his death in 1843. *See also* Appendix 4, Secretaries of War and Secretaries of the Army.

ARMY AIR CORPS (1926–1941). Prior to 1926 American air forces were part of the Army's **Signal Corps**. From 1907 to 1914, the army's first airplanes were in the corps' Aeronautical Division. During **World War I**, it became the Aviation Section and it was designated the Army Air Service from 1918 to 1926. The Army Air Corps was established on 2 July 1926 and became the Army Air Forces in 1941. The **National Security Act of 1947** established the U.S. Air Force as a separate service. Those aircraft deemed essential to ground forces operations remained in the army after the 1947 agreement, and in 1983 **aviation** became a separate branch of the army. *See also* BRANCHES OF THE ARMY.

ARMY ART COLLECTION. The army art collection started in **World War I**, when the army sent eight artists to record the activities of the American Expeditionary Forces. Most of the art created by that team is now in the Smithsonian Institution in Washington, D.C. In 1942, the Army **Corps of Engineers** established a War Art Unit and the War Art Advisory Committee nominated 42 military and civilian artists for the new organization. In 1943 Congress withdrew funding for the program, but two civilian programs maintained the effort to create a visual record of **World War II**. *Life* magazine and Abbott Laboratories provided resources for separate programs to send artists into the combat zones. In June 1944 Congress authorized the War Art Unit to once again use military artists. By the end of the war the army had acquired more than 2,000 pieces of art, not including the work done by the Life and Abbott artists. In June 1945 the army established a Historical Properties Section to maintain and exhibit the collection. The Abbott collections became the army's property in 1946 and in 1960 the Time-Life corporation donated its paintings. There was no organized effort to send artists to cover the **Korean War**, but between 1966 and 1969 a total of 42 soldier and 10 civilian artists created their impressions of the **Vietnam War**. Since then the army has continued to use both soldiers and civilians to record its activities in peace and war, including the **Persian Gulf War** and the peace support operations in the Balkans. The collection, numbering more than 10,000 pieces of art, is located in Washington, D.C., and is under the care and supervision of the U.S. Army **Center of Military History**.

ARMY BIRTHDAY. The U.S. Army celebrates its birthday each year on 14 June. On that date in 1775 the Continental Congress passed a resolution adopting the formation of the **Continental Army**. The army is therefore one year older than the nation it is sworn to protect. *See also* Appendix 1, Resolution of the Continental Congress Adopting the Continental Army.

ARMY FLAG. The army flag is made of white silk, with the original War Office seal embroidered in blue in the center. "United States Army" is inscribed in white letters on a scarlet scroll with the year "1775" in blue numerals below. Measuring four feet, four inches by five feet, six inches, the flag was dedicated on 14 June 1956 at Independence Hall, Philadelphia, on the 181st anniversary of the army's birthday. Today it carries 174 **campaign streamers**. *See also* ARMY BIRTHDAY; WAR DEPARTMENT.

ARMY MEDICAL DEPARTMENT. Branch of the army. The Army Medical Department and the Medical Corps trace their origins to 27 July 1775, when the Continental Congress established the army hospital. In 1777, **George Washington** ordered the inoculation of all **Continental Army** recruits to prevent smallpox. The successful program was the first time an entire army had been immunized. In 1812 the army replaced smallpox inoculation with Jenner's safer cowpox vaccination. Congress provided a medical organization of the army only in time of war or emergency, until 1818, which marked the inception of a permanent and continuous Medical Department. Joseph Lovell, the army's first permanent surgeon general, ordered army surgeons to keep weather records and investigate the relation of disease to climate. This first nationwide collection of weather data was the precursor to the U.S. Weather Bureau.

In 1862, the surgeon general directed army doctors to keep detailed medical records during the **Civil War**. The records were later compiled into five volumes and became the first detailed history of wartime medicine. In 1893 the Army Medical School opened, with four part-time teachers. One of the teachers was **Walter Reed**, who later headed the 1900–1901 yellow fever commission in Cuba, which discovered the *Aedes aegypti* mosquito carried yellow fever, a discovery that changed life in the tropics. Another army physician, **William Gorgas**, used Reed's research to fight malaria and made building the Panama Canal possible.

The preventive medicine practiced by army doctors during **World War I** made this the first major war in which mortality from communicable disease was less than mortality from battle wounds. During the war, the motor ambulance added a new level of mobility to the evacuation of wounded soldiers from the battlefield. In **World War II**, American troops fought all over the globe, exposed to every climate, disease, and weapon known to man. Psychiatric problems such as shell shock and battle fatigue received unprecedented study during the war, with emphasis on outpatient care. Research laboratories studied the effects of climate and developed clothing and behavior rules to protect soldiers from cold and heat injuries. Penicillin was mass produced and the lifesaving miracles of antibiotics were first proven on North African battlefields in 1943. Army doctors developed new methods of providing fast treatment for wounds and shock.

In 1951, the first **helicopter** ambulance unit began operations during the **Korean War**. With the helicopter, wounded soldiers could reach a sterile, fully equipped hospital in minutes. By the end of the war in 1953, more than 17,000 casualties had been airlifted by helicopter. This spawned improvement in helicopters and further refinement of aeromedical battlefield evacuation in the **Vietnam War**. In December 1989, during the campaign in **Panama**, some of the wounded soldiers were flown straight from the battlefield to army hospitals in the United States and arrived still wearing their battle uniforms.

Over the years, the Army Medical Department has expanded. The **Army Nurse Corps** was established as part of the department in 1901. The army was authorized to appoint contract dentists that same year, dentists were admitted to the medical department in 1908, and a separate Dental Corps was created in 1911. Other divisions of the medical department created in the twentieth century include the Veterinary Corps in 1916, the Medical Service Corps in 1917, and the Army Medical Specialist Corps in 1947. The **Army Reorganization Act** of 1950 renamed the department the Army Medical Service, but on 4 June 1968 it was redesignated the Army Medical Department. *See also* BRANCHES OF THE ARMY.

ARMY MUSEUMS. The army has a broad system of museums that includes some 61 collections located on installations throughout the world, including a number of **Army National Guard** and **U.S. Army Reserve** holdings. The Army **Center of Military History** maintains these historical collections as visual and tangible representations of the army's mission and uses the military artifacts and art to enhance the soldier's understanding of the profession of arms. Although its large historical collection is closely related to the history of the nation, the army was long America's only armed service without a national museum. That situation changed in October 2001, when the **secretary of the army** announced that a National Museum of the United States Army would be built at Fort Belvoir, Virginia. Upon completion, this facility will contain exhibits of the army's history that will be open to soldiers, veterans, and the American public. *See also* ARMY ART COLLECTION.

ARMY NATIONAL GUARD. The Army National Guard predates the U.S. Army by almost a century and a half. America's first permanent militia regiments were organized by the Massachusetts Bay Colony in 1636. Today, the oldest units in the entire army belong to the Massachusetts Army National Guard and trace their heritage to those first militia units. Today's National Guard is the direct descendant of the militias of the 13 original English colonies.

The first colonists in Virginia and Massachusetts provided their own defense from the thousands of Native Americans whose land they occupied. Although relations with the Indians were peaceful, as the colonists took more land the two sides were soon at war. At the beginning of the French and Indian War in 1754, the British recruited regiments of militia. Their frontier experience left the militia poised to play a crucial role in the **Revolutionary War**. Most of the regiments of the **Continental Army**, which was commanded by **George Washington**, a former militia colonel, were recruited from the militia.

After the Revolutionary War the nation's founders debated the militia's role in the new government. Federalists wanted a large standing army with a militia controlled by the federal government; anti-federalists preferred a small or nonexistent **regular army** and state-controlled militias. The two sides agreed on a compromise in which the president controlled all military forces as commander in chief, but Congress had the power to raise the taxes to pay for military forces and the right to declare war. Control of the militia was divided. States received the right to appoint officers and supervise training, while the federal government was given the authority to impose standards. In 1792, Congress passed a law that required males between the ages of 18 and 45 to enroll in the militia. But law did not require inspections by the federal government or penalties for noncompliance, so the militia went into a long decline in many states with once-a-year musters often poorly organized and ineffective. During the **War of 1812**, however, the militia provided the infant republic's main defense against the British invaders.

In the **Mexican War**, militia units made up 70 percent of the U.S. Army forces. During the war, there was considerable friction between regular army officers and militia volunteers, as the regulars resented it when militia officers outranked them and at times the regulars complained that the volunteer troops were sloppy and poorly disciplined. In spite of the friction, the Mexican War set a pattern for the army: regular officers provided military know-how and leadership, while citizen-soldiers provided most of the fighting troops. When the **Civil War** began in 1861, both Northern and Southern militia units rushed to join their respective armies. Both sides thought the war would be short, but after the first battle it was apparent the war would be a long one. President **Abraham Lincoln** called for 400,000 volunteers from state militias to serve in the Union Army for three years. Many of the most famous Civil War units in the Union Army were militia units and today the largest percentage of Civil War **campaign streamers** are carried on Army National Guard unit colors.

The late nineteenth century was a growth period for American militia forces. Labor unrest in the industrializing Northeast and Midwest caused states in those areas to examine their need for a military force. Many states built large and elaborate armories to house their militia units and began to refer to them as the National Guard, a name first used by New York State's militia in honor of the **Marquis de Lafayette**, the hero of the American Revolution who also commanded the Garde Nationale in the early days of the French Revolution. During the **Spanish–American War**, National Guard units distinguished themselves. One of the most famous units in the war, the Rough Riders led by Colonel **Theodore Roosevelt**, was a **cavalry** unit partly recruited from Texas, New Mexico, and Arizona Guardsmen. Because most of the regular army was in the Caribbean, three quarters of the first U.S. troops to fight in the Philippines were from the National Guard.

As a result of the problems that surfaced during the Spanish–American War, many politicians and army officers advocated a much larger full-time force, but the country had never had a large standing army in peacetime. States-rights advocates in Congress defeated plans for a totally federal reserve force in favor of reforming the militia, or National Guard. In 1903, legislation increased federal funding for the National Guard, but units had to maintain minimum strengths, be inspected by regular army officers, and conduct regular training. The **National Defense Act of 1916** required all states to designate their militia National Guard; prescribed qualifications for National Guard officers and allowed them to attend U.S. Army schools; required that each National Guard unit would be inspected and recognized by the **War Department**; and directed the National Guard to be organized like regular army units. During the campaign in **Mexico** in 1916, the entire National Guard was called to active duty and, within four months, 158,000 Guardsmen were in place along the Mexican border.

The National Guard played a major role in **World War I**. Its units were organized into divisions by state and provided 40 percent of the combat strength of the American Expeditionary Force. Three of the first five U.S. Army divisions to enter combat were from the National Guard, while the 30th Division, consisting of National Guardsmen from the Carolinas and Tennessee, had the war's highest number of **Medal of Honor** recipients. The years between the world wars were quiet for the National Guard, but in 1940 the National Guard was again called to active duty. All 18 National Guard divisions saw combat in **World War II**. Guardsmen fought in both the Pacific and European theaters. National Guard units participated in the defense of Bataan in the **Philippine Islands**, while at **Guadalcanal** North Dakota's 164th **Infantry** became the first large body of army troops to fight offensively in the war. In the European theater, the 34th Division, composed of Minnesota, Iowa, and South Dakota Guardsmen, was the first unit to arrive overseas.

The **Korean War** began in June 1950. The first of 138,600 National Guardsmen were mobilized within two months and Guard units were in South Korea by January 1951. The 1960s began with a partial mobilization of the National Guard in response to the Berlin Wall crisis. Although none left the United States, nearly 45,000 Army Guardsmen spent a year on active duty. The army's **reserve components** were not mobilized for the **Vietnam War**, but during the 1968 **Tet Counteroffensive** campaign 34 Army National Guard units were alerted for active duty and eight served in South Vietnam. By the end of the 1980s, Army National Guard units had been supplied with the latest weaponry and equipment, and in August 1990 the **Persian Gulf War** prompted the largest mobilization of the National Guard since the Korean War. More than 60,000 Army National Guard soldiers were called to active duty for the war and two thirds of those mobilized would eventually see service in the war's main theater of operations. *See also* UNITED STATES ARMY RESERVE; MILITIA ACTS.

ARMY NURSE CORPS. Branch of the army. Women have long cared for U.S. soldiers. The 1775 law that created the medical department allowed the army to employ female nurses. Although most of them were soldiers' untrained relatives, they filled an important role. During the **Civil War**, women served in the hospitals of both armies and Dorothea Dix, famed for work with the mentally ill, was superintendent of women nurses for the Union Army. The distinguished service of women contract nurses during the **Spanish–American War** resulted in the creation of the Army Nurse Corps on 2 February 1901 as part of the **Army Medical Corps**, although the women in the Army Nurse Corps had no military rank.

The army entered **World War I** with only 403 nurses on active duty, but by November 1918 it had 21,460, almost half of whom were serving overseas. In 1922 Congress authorized "relative rank." Nurses wore officer insignia, but legally were still not commissioned officers. More than 57,000 army nurses saw service in **World War II**. In the Pacific theater 67 nurses became prisoners of war and continued to care for the ill and injured during their 37 months of Japanese captivity. During the **Algeria–French Morocco** campaign in North Africa nurses landed with army troops, while at **Anzio** they waded ashore five days after the initial assault. About 550 nurses served in the **Korean War**, more than 5,000 saw service in the **Vietnam War**, and there were approximately 2,200 in the **Persian Gulf War**. On 11 June 1970, Colonel Anna Mae Hays, chief of the Army Nurse Corps, was promoted to the grade of brigadier general, becoming the first woman in the history of the U.S. Army to attain general officer rank. *See also* BRANCHES OF THE ARMY.

ARMY REORGANIZATION ACT (1950). This act reorganized the army in accordance with the **National Security Act of 1947**. It removed limits on the size of the general staff and established an undersecretary of the army and four assistant secretaries, although that number was reduced to three after 1958. The act also recognized **infantry**, **artillery**, and **armor** as the component arms of the army while it eliminated the Coast Artillery as a **branch of the army**. At the same time, it merged the **air defense artillery** with the **field artillery** as a single arm.

ARMY RESERVE. *See* UNITED STATES ARMY RESERVE.

ARMY SCHOOLS. Prior to 1900 the army had no system for educating its soldiers and officers. Individual training was accomplished primarily in units. Notable exceptions were some of the schools of application that were forerunners of the later combat arms schools: the **Artillery School of Practice** at Fort Monroe, Virginia, was established in 1824; the Engineer School of Application in Washington Barracks, D.C., was founded in 1866; and the Infantry and Cavalry School at Fort Leavenworth, Kansas, began classes in 1886. During the **Spanish–American War**, officers in the lower echelons demonstrated that they knew their basic jobs, but those at higher levels did not react well to the problems of rapid mobilization, training, and deployment of relatively large military forces.

Elihu Root became **secretary of war** in 1899 and soon discovered that one-third of **regular army** officers had no formal military education. He believed that the **U.S. Military Academy** and the schools of application were inadequate to prepare army officers for the challenges the United States would soon face as a growing world power. He saw the Military Academy as the initial training ground for army officers and was able to increase the cadet corps, modernize its curriculum, and improve the physical plant. In 1901 he announced a comprehensive system of officer education. The Military Academy, five special service schools, and the General Service and Staff College at Fort Leavenworth trained officers in combined arms and staff positions, while the **Army War College** conducted advanced planning at Washington Barracks, D.C. The special service schools were the Artillery School at Fort Monroe; the Engineer School of Application, Washington Barracks, D.C.; the School of Submarine Defense, Fort Totten, New York; the School of Application for Cavalry and Field Artillery at Fort Riley, Kansas; and the Army Medical School, Washington, D.C. All of the army's schools for officers except the Army War College admitted **Army National Guard** officers and civilian graduates of land-grant college military training programs who were earmarked for **U.S. Volunteers** commissions. In 1904 the army added schools for the academic and technical instruction of **enlisted** soldiers.

From 1901 to 1917 the army expanded its system of military education. In 1907 Congress approved separating the **artillery** branch into the Coast Artillery Corps and the **field artillery**, which led to the opening of the School of Fire for Field Artillery at Fort Sill, Oklahoma, in 1911. The Infantry and Cavalry School at Fort Leavenworth became the School of the Line in 1910. The **Army Medical Department** redefined its specialized corps into Medical, Hospital, Army Nurse, Dental, and Medical Reserve. In 1915 **Leonard Wood**, a former chief of staff, organized a summer camp at Plattsburg, New York, to provide military training for business and professional men. While serving as **chief of staff of the army** in 1913, Wood had begun similar camps for college students. The **National Defense Act of 1916** continued the student military training and the businessmen's summer camps and placed them on a firmer legal basis by authorizing a **Reserve Officers' Training Corps** (ROTC) and an Officers' Reserve Corps. *See also* COMMAND AND GENERAL STAFF COLLEGE.

ARMY VALUES. The U.S. Army has always considered itself to be a values-based institution and in 1999 it adopted seven specific values as part of its basic **doctrine**:

Loyalty: Bear true faith and allegiance to the U.S. Constitution, the Army, your unit, and other soldiers.

Duty: Fulfill your obligations.

Respect: Treat people as they should be treated.

Selfless Service: Put the welfare of the nation, the Army, and your subordinates before your own.

Honor: Live up to all the Army values.

Integrity: Do what's right, legally and morally.

Personal Courage: Face fear, danger, or adversity (physical or moral).

ARMY WAR COLLEGE. The college was first established in November 1901 as a direct result of the poor staff work in the **Spanish–American War**, although **Emory Upton** had proposed the concept years earlier. In 1901 **Secretary of War Elihu Root** appointed a War College Board that included five officers detailed for limited terms plus the chief of engineers, the chief of artillery, the superintendent of the **U.S. Military Academy**, and the commanding officer of the **Infantry** and **Cavalry** School at Fort Leavenworth, Kansas. In 1903, with the creation of the army's **general staff**, the War College Board evolved into the Army War College, which performed some of the general staff functions and served as a capstone for a reorganized military education system. The college closed during **World War I**, but it opened again in 1919 with a curriculum that included strategy, command and management of large forces, and military history. It closed again in 1940, after having educated the officers who would hold the most senior commands in **World War II**. After opening again in 1950 at Fort Leavenworth, Kansas, it moved to Carlisle Barracks, Pennsylvania, the next year and has remained there ever since.

Today the college focuses on national military policy and is a center for strategic and international peacekeeping. The Army War College includes the Army Peacekeeping Institute, the Army Physical Fitness Research Institute, the Center for Strategic Leadership, the **Military History Institute**, and the Strategic Studies Institute. Each year, more than 300 students from all branches of the military, U.S. government, and about 40 nations attend a 10-month course of instruction at the college. The college hosts almost 7,000 temporary students, program participants, and senior leaders annually. Participants at the college's war gaming exercises and strategic leadership conferences include senior military leaders, government agency managers, foreign leaders, and academic representatives from throughout the world. *See also* ARMY SCHOOLS; COMMAND AND GENERAL STAFF COLLEGE.

ARNOLD, BENEDICT (1741–1801). American soldier and traitor. Born in Norwich, Connecticut, in 1741, Arnold joined the provincial army of New York in 1755 at age 16 and deserted shortly thereafter, as he did after a second enlistment in 1760. In April 1775, however, he led his company of militia to Massachusetts, where he was commissioned a colonel, and helped lead the expedition that captured Fort **Ticonderoga**. He participated in the unsuccessful siege of **Quebec** and was wounded during the fighting at **Saratoga**. In 1799 he received a reprimand from **George Washington** for corruption, but he was still given command of West Point, New York, on the Hudson River, where he plotted with the British to betray the garrison. He fled to the British Army when the conspiracy was uncovered and received command of a corps of American deserters. He led raids in Virginia and Connecticut before going to England in 1781 and living in London until his death in 1801. The name Benedict Arnold has become a symbol of treason in American history.

ARNOLD, HENRY HARLEY (1886–1950). Army general who commanded the Army Air Forces in **World War II** and was the first chief of staff of the U.S. Air Force. Born in Pennsylvania, Arnold graduated from the **U.S. Military Academy**

in 1907 and learned to fly with the Wright Brothers. During **World War I** he headed flight training for the army and supported the cause of army aviation. In 1925 he testified for **William Mitchell** at Mitchell's court-martial. Arnold became the chief of the **Army Air Corps** in 1838 and during World War II supervised the creation of the world's most powerful air force. He was instrumental in the Air Force becoming a separate service in the **National Security Act of 1947**, and he served as its first chief of staff.

ARTILLERY. A combat element of the army since 17 November 1775, when the Continental Congress unanimously elected **Henry Knox** colonel of the Regiment of Artillery. The regiment formally entered service on 1 January 1776. The army has long relied on the firepower provided by its artillery, known as the "King of Battle," to reduce enemy positions rather than expend the lives of its soldiers. In 1968, in recognition of their significantly different missions, **field artillery** and **air defense artillery** became separate **branches of the army**.

Artillery provides the means for delivering indirect fire support to ground forces. It uses both guns and rocket launchers. Tube artillery includes any gun or howitzer that throws a ballistic projectile with a fuse that detonates the explosive on or near the target. Towed artillery refers to guns and howitzers used by ground forces that do not have the capability to move under their own power. Usually a truck or tractor moves towed artillery, although light artillery can be lifted by **helicopters**. Self-propelled artillery guns and howitzers are mounted on automotive chassis that are capable of moving under their own power. Self-propelled artillery pieces are usually tracked vehicles and can be confused with **tanks**. But self-propelled artillery is a lightly **armored** indirect fire weapon that usually remains to the rear of the battle, while the tank is a heavily armored direct-fire weapon capable of close combat. Armored forces are supported by self-propelled artillery that has comparable mobility designed to keep up during rapid advances. Rocket artillery launches a self-propelled round that travels to the target. Rockets generally can carry a larger warhead than tube artillery. Artillery ammunition can be high explosive (HE), chemical, or biological. The larger rocket warheads can be filled with hundreds of submunitions, such as small grenades or mines that can be scattered over a wide area. The army's Multiple Launched Rocket System (MLRS) launcher weighs about 27 tons, has a speed of 35 miles an hour, and carries a crew of three. The missiles have a range in excess of 60 miles and carry a combination of antiarmor and antipersonnel bomblets. The MLRS provided devastating fire support during the **Persian Gulf War**.

ARTILLERY SCHOOL OF PRACTICE. John C. Calhoun, the **secretary of war**, established the school in April 1824 at Fort Monroe, Virginia, to teach basic tactics and administration to the army's artillery units. Under the leadership of **Emory Upton**, superintendent from 1877 and 1880, the school became the model for other army branch schools. *See also* ARMY SCHOOLS; ARTILLERY.

ATLANTA (7 May to 2 September 1864). Civil War campaign streamer. Beginning in May 1864, General **William Tecumseh Sherman** began a march through southern Georgia toward Atlanta as part of the strategy devised by **Ulysses S. Grant**, commanding general of the Union armies, to destroy the Confederacy's capability to wage war. Sherman moved south out of **Chattanooga**, Tennessee, at the head of three armies and four divisions of cavalry, a total of about 105,000 men. Opposing him was General **Joseph E. Johnston** with two corps of the Army of Tennessee, Leonidas Polk's Army of Mississippi, and Joseph W. Wheeler's cavalry, a total of about 65,000 men. Johnston adopted defensive tactics, fighting delaying actions that forced Sherman to repeatedly halt, deploy, and maneuver. In 74 days Sherman was able to advance only 100 miles toward **Atlanta**. On 27 June Sherman attempted a direct assault against prepared positions at Kenesaw Mountain, but was repulsed, suffering 2,000 casualties to only 270 for the Confederates. He then returned to a war of maneuver, forcing Johnston back to positions in front of Atlanta.

Confederate president **Jefferson Davis**, dissatisfied with Johnston's delaying tactics, replaced him with Major General John B. Hood, a more aggressive commander. On 20 July, and again on 22 July, Hood led attacks outside the Atlanta fortifications, but was repulsed both times with heavy losses. Having dissipated his striking power, Hood moved his forces out of Atlanta to begin a roundabout march to northwest Alabama. Sherman then marched his army into Atlanta unopposed on 1–2 September 1864. During the four-month campaign, the losses in killed and wounded had been more than 26,000 for the Federals and 23,000 for the Confederates.

After occupying Atlanta, Sherman sent about 30,000 men to reinforce the Union forces at **Nashville**, Tennessee, and then proposed to take four corps of about 62,000 men and march to the coast, laying waste to all Confederate resources in his path. President **Abraham Lincoln** and Grant hesitantly agreed to the plan and Sherman marched out of the ruins of Atlanta on 12 November 1864, cut a 60-mile wide path of destruction through the heart of the South, and arrived at Savannah on 10 December. The city surrendered 11 days later.

AVIATION. Branch of the army. The army's use of aviation began with the **Signal Corps** in 1907, before the establishment of the **Army Air Corps** in 1926 and the U.S. Air Force in 1947. What is now known as the army aviation branch has its origins in 1942 with the War Department's approval of a program that put artillery observers in light aircraft to observe and adjust fire. In 1945, based on the success of the air observer program in **World War II**, the army created the Army Ground Forces light aviation and the concept received legislative sanction in the **National Security Act of 1947**, which established an independent air force from the Army Air Forces. In the late 1940s the army acquired **helicopters** in addition to its fleet of light, fixed-wing aircraft. Helicopters were widely used in the **Korean War** to evacuate wounded soldiers from the battlefield. After the war the army began to experiment with armed helicopters and developed the concept of airmobile warfare. The army relied heavily on helicopters during the **Vietnam War** for a wide variety of missions, including tactical mobility, close fire support, medical evacuation, resupply, and aerial command posts. Aviation was established as a separate branch of the army on 12 April 1983. Further development of equipment and techniques led to the adoption of the army's AirLand Battle **doctrine**, which proved itself during the **Persian Gulf War**. *See also* BRANCHES OF THE ARMY.

— **B** —

BADGE OF MILITARY MERIT. The first U.S. military decoration. On 7 August 1782, **George Washington** devised two distinctive badges for **enlisted** men and **noncommissioned officers**. One was a chevron to be worn on the left sleeve of the uniform coat for soldiers who had completed three years of duty "with bravery, fidelity, and good conduct"; two chevrons signified six years of service. The other, to be awarded for "any singularly meritorious Action," was the "Figure of a Heart in Purple Cloth or Silk edged with narrow Lace or Binding." Known as the Badge of Military Merit, the device was to be affixed to the uniform coat above the left breast and permitted the recipient to pass guards and sentinels without challenge. It specifically honored the lower ranks, a concept then unknown in European armies. Only three badges were awarded, all in 1783 during the waning days of the Revolutionary War, and all to volunteers from Connecticut. Sergeants Elijah Churchill and William Brown received badges on 3 May and Sergeant Daniel Bissell Jr. received the award on 10 June. Although the badge was never officially abolished, it was not awarded again until 1932, when the **War Department**, on the 200th anniversary of George Washington's birthday, designated it the **Purple Heart**. *See also* DISTINGUISHED SERVICE CROSS; MEDAL OF HONOR; SILVER STAR.

BAINBRIDGE, WILLIAM G. (1925–). Sergeant major of the army from 1975 to 1979. Born in Illinois, Bainbridge attended rural district schools. After graduation from Williamsburg High School in 1943 he was inducted into the army and assigned to the 106th Infantry Division, the last division organized for service in **World War II**. During the **Ardennes–Alsace** campaign, he became a prisoner of war, which he remained until liberated on Good Friday in 1945. After the war he returned to civilian life, but he was soon recalled to active service, enlisted in the **regular army** in 1958, and saw service in the **Vietnam War**. He was selected in 1968 to be one of the first **command sergeants major** in the army and was instrumental in establishing the **Sergeants Major Academy** at Fort Bliss, Texas. On 1 July 1975 he became the sergeant major of the army. He retired on 18 June 1979. *See also* Appendix 5, Sergeants Major of the Army; COMMAND SERGEANT MAJOR.

BAKER, NEWTON DIEHL (1871–1937). Secretary of war from 1916 to 1921. Born in West Virginia, Baker was educated at Johns Hopkins University and received a law degree from Washington and Lee University in 1894. After moving to Cleveland, Ohio, to practice law, he was mayor of the city before becoming the secretary of war. While secretary he issued orders for the **Mexican Expedition**, administered **World War I** conscription, chaired the Council of National Defense, maintained a policy of keeping professional command free of political influence, and refined the **general staff** concept developed by **Elihu Root**. Baker returned to private law practice in 1921 and in 1928 was appointed a member of the Permanent Court of Arbitration at The Hague. He died in Cleveland on 25 December 1937. *See also* Appendix 4, Secretaries of War and Secretaries of the Army.

BANNOCKS (1878). Indian wars campaign streamer. The Bannock, Paiute, and other tribes of southern Idaho threatened rebellion in 1878, because they were unhappy with their land allotments. When many left their reservations, army regulars pursued them. On 13 July, Captain Evan Miles very effectively dispersed a large band near the Umatilla Agency, causing most of the Indians to return to their reservations within a few months.

BARBOUR, JAMES (1775–1842). Secretary of war from 1825 to 1828. Born in Virginia, Barbour was admitted to the Virginia bar in 1794 after private study while serving as a deputy sheriff. He served in the Virginia House of Delegates, was governor of Virginia, and served in the U.S. Senate before becoming secretary of war. While secretary, he established the Infantry School of Practice. After leaving office, he was minister to Great Britain until 1829 and he again served briefly in the House of Delegates before losing his seat in a disputed election. After retiring to private life, Barbour chaired the 1839 Whig convention, which nominated **William Henry Harrison** for president, and was active in the Orange County Humane Society to educate children of the poor. He died in Barboursville, Virginia, in 1842. *See also* Appendix 4, Secretaries of War and Secretaries of the Army.

BATAAN (1942). *See* PHILIPPINE ISLANDS.

BATES, JOHN COALTER (1842–1919). Chief of staff of the army for three months in 1906. Born in Missouri, Bates attended the University of St. Louis and was commissioned a second lieutenant in 1861. He served in the **infantry** during the **Civil War** and saw extended field duty on the Indian frontier after the war. He was promoted to brigadier general during the **Spanish–American War** and commanded a division during the **Philippine Insurrection**. He retired from active duty in 1906 after a brief stint as chief of staff. *See also* Appendix 3, Commanding Generals and Chiefs of Staff of the Army.

BATTALION. A unit that consists of two or more companies or batteries. Most battalions are organized by function and consist of a number of operational companies and a headquarters element that performs administrative and logistics functions. Typically, battalions have three to five companies or batteries, in addition to the headquarters. Battalions are commanded by a lieutenant colonel and are tactically and administratively self-sufficient. Two or more combat battalions make up a **brigade**. A U.S. Army **infantry** battalion may contain 900 officers and **enlisted** soldiers while an **artillery** or **armor** battalion could be half that size. **Cavalry** equivalents are called squadrons. *See also* BATTERY; COMPANY.

BATTLE OF THE BULGE. *See* ARDENNES–ALSACE.

BATTERY. The basic unit of **field artillery** and **air defense artillery** battalions. A firing battery generally consists of several howitzers, guns, or rocket launchers and supporting equipment. The organization is usually fixed, although the exact composition depends on the type of **artillery**. Generally, the larger the artillery piece, the fewer pieces will be in the battery. It is usually commanded by a captain and consists of about 100 officers and **enlisted** soldiers. *See also* BATTALION.

BELKNAP, WILLIAM WORTH (1829–1890). Secretary of war from 1869 to 1876. Born in New York, Belknap graduated from Princeton University in 1848 and studied law at Georgetown University in Washington, D.C. After being admitted to the bar he moved to Iowa to practice law. He served in the state legislature before being commissioned a major in the 14th Iowa **Infantry** at the beginning of the **Civil War**. He commanded a division during the **Atlanta** campaign and left the army at the end of the war a major general. After the war, he was collector of internal revenue in Iowa and became secretary of war on 25 October 1869. While secretary he initiated the preparation of historical reports by post commanders and proposed actions to preserve Yellowstone Park. Belknap resigned after being impeached by the House of Representatives for allegedly receiving money in return for post trader appointments. In his trial by the Senate the vote fell short of the two thirds required for conviction. He returned to the practice of law in Washington, D.C., and died there on 13 October 1890. *See also* Appendix 4, Secretaries of War and Secretaries of the Army.

BELL, JAMES FRANKLIN (1856–1919). Chief of staff of the army from 1906 to 1910. Born in Kentucky, Bell graduated from the **U.S. Military Academy** in 1878. While serving as professor of military science and tactics at Southern Illinois University, he earned a law degree and was admitted to the bar. He served in Luzon during the **Philippine Insurrection** and became chief of staff in 1910, serving for four years. During his tenure he installed and commanded the Army of Cuban Pacification and supervised the development of Army aviation. Bell also reorganized the army's **general staff**, placing greater emphasis on intelligence gathering and strategic planning, and advanced the idea of increasing the general staff's power over the War Department's long-standing and firmly entrenched administrative bureaus. After leaving office, he held various command positions in the army. He died in 1919 while commanding the Eastern Department. *See also* Appendix 3, Commanding Generals and Chiefs of Staff of the Army; ARMY AIR CORPS.

BELL, JOHN (1797–1869). Secretary of war from March to September 1841. Born on his father's farm in Tennessee, Bell graduated from Cumberland College in 1814, was admitted to the bar, and began practicing law. He represented Tennessee in the House of Representatives for 14 years before becoming secretary of war. After leaving office, he served in the Senate for another 12 years. He was the Constitutional Union candidate for president in the four-way race won by Abraham Lincoln in 1860. He died near Bear Spring Furnace, Stewart County, Tennessee, on 10 September 1869. *See also* Appendix 4, Secretaries of War and Secretaries of the Army.

BISMARCK ARCHIPELAGO (15 December 1943 to 27 November 1944). **World War II** campaign streamer. As 1943 drew to a close, the Allies in the Pacific had stopped the Japanese advances in the region. They now turned their attention to taking the offensive along two mutually supporting lines of advance, one in the Central Pacific and the other in the Southwest Pacific Area. The former was primarily naval, commanded by Admiral Chester Nimitz, while the latter, commanded by General **Douglas MacArthur,** featured a series of amphibious operations along the **New Guinea** coast that were the first steps in MacArthur's drive to make good his pledge to return to the **Philippine Islands.** But before MacArthur could begin operations against New Guinea, he needed to capture the Bismarck Archipelago, a group of islands off the eastern coast of New Guinea. The Japanese had their main supply base for supporting operations in the South Pacific at Rabaul, located on the eastern end of the island of New Britain in the Bismarck Archipelago. Following up on Admiral William Halsey's successes in the **Northern Solomons** campaign as he advanced on Rabaul from the southeast, MacArthur prepared plans that would complete the encirclement of the Japanese base and give the Allies operational and logistics bases to support operations in New Guinea. For these operations, Halsey would take strategic direction from MacArthur, although he reported to Nimitz.

Operations in the Bismarck Archipelago opened with an amphibious assault on the western end of New Britain by forces from the U.S. Sixth Army, commanded by Lieutenant General Walter Krueger. The landings at Arawe were initially challenged by the Japanese, but superior Allied firepower forced the defenders to retreat from the beaches, only to retaliate with air attacks, thus it was not until 16 January that the beachhead was cleared of Japanese. On 26 December, U.S. Marines landed at Cape Gloucester on the western tip of New Britain to seize the Japanese airfield there. By the middle of January 1944, MacArthur's forces controlled the western end of the island and the straits between the islands of New Britain and New Guinea. In February, Halsey's forces seized Green Island, north of the island of Bougainville, as part of the continued Allied efforts to surround Rabaul. Following the capture of Green Island, the Sixth Army initiated operations against the Admiralty Islands, located northwest of New Britain, with the aim of completing the isolation of Rabaul. Landings on Los Negros Island, the second largest island in the Admiralties, on 29 February initially met relatively light resistance, but it took a month of fighting to finally secure the islands. Although the campaign did not officially end until November 1944, its primary objectives had been attained by March. In four months Allies had converted the island chain from a barrier to a stepping stone in the advance against the Japanese.

BLACK HAWK (ca. 1767–1838). Sauk Indian warrior and leader from Illinois. Black Hawk was never a village chief, but his bravery and leadership made him a respected leader. He fought for the British during the **War of 1812** and after the war tried to resume normal peacetime activities. By 1830 he was a leader in the Sauks' fight to reoccupy their traditional lands in Illinois. His encouragement to a loose coalition of Sauks, Mesquakies, and Kickapoos to return to Illinois precipitated the **Black Hawk** campaign. After his capture in 1832, Black Hawk was imprisoned until his death in 1838.

BLACK HAWK (26 April 1767 to 20 September 1832). Indian wars campaign. Led by **Black Hawk**, an Illinois Sauk leader, a faction of Sauk and Mesquakie Indians in eastern Iowa threatened to go to war in 1832 when squatters occupied Illinois lands formerly held by the two tribes. The Indians believed cession of the lands to the federal government in 1804 had been illegal. When Black Hawk's followers, including some 500 warriors, crossed the Mississippi into Illinois in April 1832 and refused to return to Iowa, Brigadier General Henry Atkinson, with a force of regulars and Illinois militia, pursued the Indians up the Rock River. After a skirmish on 14 May 1832, when militia attacked Indians attempting to parley, Atkinson paused to recruit new militia. Most of the summer passed with the army forces hunting for the fleeing Indians. A volunteer force attacked Black Hawk's band at Madison, Wisconsin, on 21 July 1832 and Atkinson completely defeated what remained of it at the mouth of Bad Axe River on 2 August, capturing Black Hawk and killing 150 of his warriors. The rest of the campaign consisted of small Indian raids with militia in pursuit. Black Hawk's defeat persuaded other tribes to move west.

BLADENSBURG (17–29 August 1814). War of 1812 campaign streamer. After Napoleon surrendered in Europe, the British were able to reinforce their army in America, and on 27 June 1814 Major General Robert Ross departed from France with 4,000 veterans to raid key points on the American coast. He landed at the mouth of the Patuxent River in Maryland on 19 August and with Washington, D.C., as his objective, then marched as far as Upper Marlboro by the 22d without meeting American resistance. Brigadier General William Winder, commanding the American forces in the Potomac District, assembled a mixed force of about 5,000 men near Bladensburg. Although the Americans had an advantage in position and numbers, they were routed by Ross's force. British losses were about 249 killed and wounded; the Americans lost about 100 killed and wounded, with 100 captured. With American defenders out of the way, British detachments entered Washington and burned the Capitol and other public buildings on 24 and 25 August in what was later announced as retaliation for the American destruction at York during the campaign in **Canada**.

BLISS, TASKER HOWARD (1853–1930). Chief of staff of the army from 1917 to 1918. Born in Pennsylvania, Bliss graduated from the **U.S. Military Academy** in 1875. He served in various positions until 1888, when he became an aide to **John McAllister Schofield**, who was then the **commanding general of the**

army. Bliss was a corps chief of staff during the **Spanish–American War** and he served in a number of command positions in the Philippines during the **Philippine Insurrection**. He headed the **Army War College** and commanded military departments in the United States before becoming chief of staff in 1917. While in office, Bliss twice visited Europe, to observe conditions at the front in **World War I** and represent the War Department at Versailles. After leaving office, he was a delegate to the Paris Peace Conference and he was later governor of the Soldiers' Home before retiring from active service in 1930. *See also* Appendix 3, Commanding Generals and Chiefs of Staff of the Army.

BONUS ARMY (1932). In 1924 Congress voted to adjust the compensation promised to veterans of **World War I**, holding it until 1945, at which time a bonus would be paid. In May 1932, with the Great Depression descending on the country, one thousand veterans arrived in Washington, D.C., to urge Congress to authorize immediate payment of the bonus. By June there were almost 20,000 veterans in the city. The House of Representatives passed a bill providing for full payment, but the Senate did not. While most of the veterans departed after the Senate vote, a significant number remained in Washington to press their demands. After two deaths occurred, President Herbert Hoover ordered the army to disperse the veterans. The **chief of staff of the army**, General **Douglas MacArthur**, used tanks and tear gas to move the protestors out of the city. In 1936, Congress overrode President Franklin Roosevelt's veto and paid the promised bonus ahead of schedule, costing the federal government $3.9 billion of its $8.4 billion dollar budget.

BOSTON (17 June 1775 to 17 March 1776). Revolutionary War campaign streamer. On the night of 16–17 June 1775 about 1,200 men of the American force besieging Boston moved to the Charlestown isthmus, planning to build entrenchments on Bunker Hill, overlooking the city, but in the dark mistakenly occupied Breed's Hill. The next day the British commander, William Howe, led 2,200 troops to the isthmus and stormed the American positions on Breed's Hill. In the ensuing battle, mistakenly named Bunker Hill, the British drove the Americans from the isthmus after three assaults. The battle cost the British about 1,000 killed and wounded. American losses were approximately 400 killed and wounded. This was the only major engagement of the prolonged American siege of Boston. After **George Washington** took formal command of the army on 3 July, he devoted the next several months to building up the American force and solving its logistical difficulties. In March 1776 Washington, with an army of 14,000 men, emplaced artillery on Dorchester Heights and Nook's Hill, positions that dominated Boston from the south. Howe now recognized the difficulty of his position and evacuated the city, sailing for Nova Scotia on 26 March with about 9,000 men.

BOXER REBELLION. *See* CHINA RELIEF EXPEDITION.

BRADLEY, OMAR NELSON (1893–1981). Chief of staff of the army from 1948 to 1949. Born in Missouri, Bradley graduated from the **U.S. Military Acad-**

emy in 1915. After graduation he spent most of his time as an instructor or student in various army schools. In 1942 he successively commanded the 82d and 28th Infantry Divisions, training them for **World War II**, and in 1943 he took command of II Corps, leading it through the **Tunisia** and **Sicily** campaigns. He commanded the U.S. First Army during the **Normandy** invasion and led the 12th Army Group in the final campaigns of World War II in Western Europe. The army group included four U.S. armies with a total of 43 divisions. Bradley has been criticized for using close-in bombing for the breakout at St. Lo during the Normandy campaign and for failing to anticipate the German offensive that led to the Battle of the Bulge during the **Ardennes–Alsace** campaign.

After the war, Bradley was administrator of veterans affairs until 1947. He was the chief of staff of the army from 7 February 1948 to 16 August 1949. In response to the **National Security Act of 1947**, he initiated a study of army organization that led to consolidation of the technical services under the director of logistics, administrative services under the director of personnel and administration, and financial and management functions under the comptroller of the army. In August 1949 he became the first chairman of the Joint Chiefs of Staff and he also was the first chairman of the Military Staff Committee of the North Atlantic Treaty Organization (NATO). He died in New York City on 8 April 1981 while attending an Army Association meeting. *See also* Appendix 3, Commanding Generals and Chiefs of Staff of the Army.

BRANCHES OF THE ARMY. All soldiers in the U.S. Army are assigned to a branch of the army according to the functions they perform in combat or in support of the combat units. The branches are grouped as to whether their primary mission is to engage in combat, directly support the combat elements, or provide combat service support or administration to the army as a whole. The branches of the army have changed during its history in accordance with the demands of warfare. As of 1999, the U.S. Army included the combat and combat support branches of **Infantry, Armor, Field Artillery, Air Defense Artillery, Special Forces**, the **Corps of Engineers, Chemical Corps, Military Intelligence, Military Police, Signal Corps, Aviation**, and **Civil Affairs**. The combat service support branches include the **Ordnance Corps**, the **Quartermaster Corps**, the **Transportation Corps, Adjutant General, Chaplain, Finance, Judge Advocate General, Inspector General**, and the **Army Medical Department**.

BRANDYWINE (11 September 1777). Revolutionary War campaign streamer. The British campaign to seize the American capital in Philadelphia began in late July 1777, about one month after the **Saratoga** campaign in New York. About 15,000 British troops under **William Howe**'s command sailed from New York in July and landed at Head of Elk (now Elkton) in Maryland, about a month later. **George Washington**, with about 11,000 men, took up a defensive position blocking the way to Philadelphia at Chad's Ford on the eastern side of Brandywine Creek in Pennsylvania. Howe attacked on 11 September, sending Lord **Charles Cornwallis** across the creek around the American right, while Hessian troops demonstrated opposite Chad's Ford. **Nathanael Greene**'s troops stopped Cornwallis's threatened envelopment, but the Americans fell back to Chester with the British in close pursuit. American losses totaled about 1,000 killed, wounded, and taken prisoner. British casualties were less than 600. Howe moved on to Philadelphia, occupied the city on 21 September, and established his primary encampment in **Germantown**.

BREED'S HILL. *See* BOSTON.

BREVET. A temporary rank generally awarded during wartime for conspicuous service. It was frequently used in the nineteenth century. When awarded a brevet, the officer was allowed to wear the rank insignia of the higher grade, but he was not authorized any increase in pay or allowances. It was not uncommon for individuals to receive more than one brevet, thus allowing them to wear a rank insignia much higher than their actual grade.

BRIGADE. In the U.S. Army, brigades are flexible organizations that can be tailored according to their mission. Maneuver brigades consist of two or more **battalions** and are the major combat units of divisions. In the nineteenth century, all of the battalions in a brigade would be of the same type, such as an **infantry** brigade. Today, however, the army's brigades may be organized with a combination of maneuver battalions. Their capabilities for self-support and independent action vary considerably depending on the type of brigade. Normally there are three maneuver brigades in a division. Separate brigades, such as **field artillery**, engineer, or **aviation**, have a fixed organization and are usually employed as units when attached to **divisions** or **corps**. Brigades may be commanded by colonels or brigadier generals.

BROWN, JACOB JENNINGS (1775–1828). Commanding general of the army from 1815 to 1828. Born in Bucks County, Pennsylvania, Brown pursued various pursuits until he was appointed a colonel of militia in 1802. Appointed a brigadier general in the **regular army**, he defeated the British at **Chippewa** and **Lundy's Lane** during the **War of 1812**. While in office he recommended pay incentives to encourage enlistments and pay increases for **noncommissioned officers** and he encouraged centralized unit training. He died while in office. *See also* Appendix 3, Commanding Generals and Chiefs of Staff of the Army.

BRUCKER, WILBER MARION (1894–1968). Secretary of the army from 1955 to 1961. Born in Michigan, Brucker graduated from the University of Michigan in 1916 and enlisted in the Michigan National Guard. He served in the campaign in **Mexico** and was a second lieutenant in France during **World War I**. After the war he returned to Michigan, where he was governor from 1930 to 1932. He was the general counsel of the Department of Defense, before becoming the secretary of the army. Under his direction the army developed the pentomic **division** and established a Strategic Army Corps for quick reaction to crises. He returned to Michigan in 1961 to practice law and serve on the board of directors of the Freedom Foundation. He died at Grosse Pointe Farms, Michigan, on 28 December 1968. *See also* Appendix 4, Secretaries of War and Secretaries of the Army; ARMY NATIONAL GUARD.

BUENA VISTA (22–23 February 1847). Mexican War campaign streamer. After the Mexican defeat at **Monterrey**, General **Antonio Lopez de Santa Anna**, president of Mexico, took the field personally and assembled an army at San Luis Potosi. Learning of the weakness of the forces near Saltillo, Santa Anna moved in February with about 15,000 men to attack the Americans where they were encamped near Saltillo. In response to the Mexican move, American commander **Zachary Taylor**, whose army had been reduced to about 5,000 men when many of his troops were assigned to **Winfield Scott** for the proposed attack on the coastal town of **Vera Cruz**, redeployed his force to Buena Vista, where the terrain offered better defensive positions. On 22 February, after Taylor refused Santa Anna's invitation to surrender, the Mexican Army used French tactics to attack the defensive positions, attempting to overwhelm the Americans with dense columns of men. Massing the fire of **infantry** and **artillery** proved effective against the attacking columns and, after two days of severe fighting, Santa Anna withdrew his dispirited army to San Luis Potosi having lost more than 3,000 men killed and wounded. The Americans, too exhausted to pursue, lost 264 killed, 450 wounded, and 26 missing.

BUFFALO SOLDIERS. Term for black cavalry soldiers in the nineteenth century. After the **Civil War** the army had six regiments of black soldiers, two **cavalry** and four **infantry**. Although most of the regiments' officers were white, in 1877 **Henry O. Flipper**, the first **African American** to graduate from the **U.S. Military Academy**, was assigned to one of the units, the 10th Cavalry. Until the 1890s these regiments served almost exclusively at remote western posts and all saw action against hostile Indian tribes. They also saw service in the **Santiago** campaign of the **Spanish–American War**, the **Philippine Insurrection**, and the **Mexican Expedition**. The term "Buffalo Soldiers" was first applied to the 10th Cavalry around 1870, when it was commanded by Colonel **Henry B. Grierson**. It apparently originated with the Cheyenne Indians, who saw a similarity between the curly hair and dark skin of the soldiers and the buffalo. The name was soon applied to both cavalry regiments and eventually the infantry was also known as Buffalo Soldiers. Some authorities contend that the name indicated a sign of respect by the Indians, but Native American sources do not necessarily concur with that interpretation. *See also* AFRICAN AMERICANS.

BULL RUN (16–22 July 1861). Civil War campaign streamer. Also known as the First Battle of Bull Run and First Manassas. In April 1861 the Confederate shelling of the Union garrison at Fort **Sumter** prompted both sides to prepare for war. On the Union side, public opinion demanded immediate action, as Confederate moves to defend the approaches to Richmond, Virginia, the capital of the Confederacy, located 100 miles south of Washington, were interpreted as preparations for an attack on the U.S. capital. Some 50,000 Federal troops known as the Army of the Potomac were assembled in the Washington area under the command of Brigadier General Irwin A. McDowell to defend the city. Another force of 18,000 troops commanded by Brigadier General Robert E. Patterson was stationed in the nearby Shenandoah Valley of Virginia. On the Confederate side, there were 20,000 soldiers under Brigadier General Pierre G. T. Beauregard at Manassas, a town located about 30 miles southwest of Washington, and about 11,000 more commanded by Brigadier General **Joseph E. Johnston** in the Shenandoah Valley.

In late June 1861, with the three-month enlistments for militia nearing an end, President **Abraham Lincoln** decided to attack. McDowell left Washington on 16 July with around 35,000 troops and slowly moved 20 miles west to Centreville, Virginia. Learning of the movement, Johnston slipped away from Patterson in the Shenandoah Valley and sent 9,000 troops by rail to join Beauregard, who had deployed his army along a stream north of Manassas known as Bull Run. McDowell opened the attack on 21 July 1861. The main body of the attacking force crossed Bull Run at Sudley Springs and rolled back Beauregard's left flank. But the retreating Confederates rallied on a low ridge behind a brigade led by Brigadier General **Thomas J. Jackson**, whose stout defense earned him the name "Stonewall." After two hours of fighting, Beauregard counterattacked and drove the Federals back to Washington in retreat. Only about 18,500 Federals and possibly 18,000 Confederates actually participated in the fight. The estimated number of casualties is about 500 killed, 1,000 wounded, and 1,200 missing on the Union side and 400 killed, 1,600 wounded, and 13 missing for the Confederates.

The results sobered the optimism of the North while encouraging the South. After the battle, both sides spent the remainder of 1861 preparing for a long war. The confusion caused by the wide variety of uniforms worn by both sides in the battle led to the adoption of a gray uniform for Confederate troops and blue for the Federals. In the months following the battle, Lincoln made some changes in the senior leadership of the U.S. Army. Major General **George B. McClellan** replaced McDowell as commander of the Army of the Potomac and later in the year became **commanding general of the army**, replacing the aging Lieutenant General **Winfield Scott**. In January 1862 Lincoln dismissed **Simon Cameron** as **secretary of war** and named **Edwin Stanton** to replace him.

BUNKER HILL. *See* BOSTON.

BURGOYNE, JOHN (1723–1792). British general in the **Revolutionary War**. Born in England, Burgoyne entered the British army in 1740, saw extensive military service in Europe, and held a seat in Parliament before coming to America. In June 1777 he led an expedition from Canada into New York, intending to meet another British force moving north. He captured Ticonderoga but lost contact with his base in Canada when he crossed the Hudson River in September. Instead of joining with Sir **Henry Clinton**'s forces as planned, Burgoyne confronted **Horatio Gates**' Americans, who forced the British to surrender at **Saratoga** in October. After the surrender, Burgoyne was allowed to go back to England, where he returned to Parliament and wrote plays. Like many British officers, he was an experienced soldier and commander, but he underestimated the Americans' resolve on the battlefield.

BURMA 1942 (7 December 1941 to 26 May 1942). World War II campaign streamer. For some months prior to the Japanese attack on Pearl Harbor in December 1941, the United States had been supporting China's war against Japan with money and materiel. The United States was shipping lend-lease materiel by sea to Burma and then overland by rail and, finally, truck, along the Burma Road into China. Because the American support to the Chinese Army kept a considerable number of Japanese troops tied down in China, Japan wanted to cut the Burma Road lifeline to free their scarce forces for use elsewhere in the Pacific. On 12 December 1941, small Japanese units began to infiltrate into Burma to begin an offensive against the British forces occupying the country. The only American combat force even remotely available was the American Volunteer Group, which was preparing to provide air support to the Chinese Army against Japan. With the outbreak of war in the Pacific, the group began flying missions in support of the British.

Prompted by the string of Japanese successes throughout the Pacific, U.S. president Franklin D. Roosevelt convinced the British prime minister, Winston Churchill, that China would be a useful ally in the war. In February 1942, General **Joseph Stilwell** was dispatched to China, where he found the situation rapidly deteriorating. On 15 February the British surrendered Singapore and eight days later the British-Indian brigades in Burma were crushed by the Japanese. In March, China agreed to send two divisions under Stilwell's command to help defend Burma. In spite of the Chinese reinforcements, however, the Japanese advance could not be stopped and on 6 May Stilwell ordered his radios and vehicles destroyed and he headed west on foot into the jungle. He was accompanied by 114 people, including what remained of his staff, a group of nurses, a Chinese general with his personal bodyguard, a number of British commandos, a collection of mechanics, a few civilians, and a newspaperman. In a remarkable display of personal leadership, Stilwell emerged from the jungle in India on 15 May without losing a single member of his party. The campaign ended a few days later, when the last of the Allied forces slipped out of the country. Undaunted, Stilwell set about training forces in India, intending to return to Burma. Japanese occupation of Burma cut off the last land route by which the Allies could deliver aid to the Chinese government of Chiang Kai-shek. The only supply route available was the costly and dangerous route over the Himalayas for transport planes known as the Hump. *See also* CENTRAL PACIFIC; INDIA–BURMA.

BURNSIDE, AMBROSE (1824–1881). Union **Civil War** general. Born in Indiana, Burnside graduated from the U.S. Military Academy in 1847 and served six years in the artillery before resigning in 1853 to manufacture a breech-loading carbine in Rhode Island, where he was a major general in the state militia. When the Civil War started in 1861, he received command of a Rhode Island regiment and was a brigadier general by the end of the year. In 1862, he was offered command of the Army of the Potomac to replace **George B. McClellan** after the **Peninsula** campaign, but he turned it down. Offered the same command after the **Manassas** campaign, he again refused. While in command of a wing of the Army of the Potomac at **Antietam**, he was faulted for not pushing the attack against the Confederate flank, but was again asked to replace McClellan. This time Burnside accepted. At **Fredericksburg**, he was unsuccessful in forcing the Confederates to withdraw and shortly thereafter was reassigned to Ohio. He later commanded a corps under **Ulysses S. Grant** during the **Wilderness** and **Spotsylvania** campaigns, in which he did not perform well. After the war he resigned from the army. He was governor of Rhode Island for three years and later represented the state in the U.S. Senate until he died in 1881. One of his more enduring legacies was his peculiar habit of wearing long whiskers, which gave rise to the term "sideburns.

— C —

CALDERA, LOUIS EDWARD (1956–). Secretary of the army from 1998 to 2001. Born in Texas and raised in California, Caldera graduated from the **U.S. Military Academy** in 1978. He left the army as a captain in 1983 and received a degree from Harvard Law School and an advanced degree from the Harvard Business School. After practicing law in Los Angeles for a number of years, he was appointed a deputy county counsel for Los Angeles County and served three terms in the California legislature. He became the **Secretary of the army** in 1998, and while he was in office, the army began its transformation into a rapidly deployable force and created the Army University Access Online distance education Internet portal for soldiers. *See also* Appendix 4, Secretaries of War and Secretaries of the Army.

CALHOUN, JOHN CALDWELL (1782–1850). Secretary of war from 1817 to 1825. Born in South Carolina, Calhoun studied at Carmel Academy in Georgia and graduated from Yale College in 1804. He was elected to the South Carolina legislature in 1808 and served from 1811 to 1817 in the House of Representatives, where he recommended a declaration of war against England in 1812. During his tenure he established the army's bureau system, formalized the lines of authority between staff and line, advocated an expandable **regular army**, created the position of **commanding general of the army**, established the **Artillery School of Practice**, and instituted reforms at the **U.S. Military Academy**. After leaving office Calhoun was vice president under John Quincy Adams and **Andrew Jackson**. He represented South Carolina in the U.S. Senate from 1832 to 1843 and became a leading spokesman for slavery and states' rights. In 1843 he became the secretary of state, before returning to the Senate in 1845 and dying in office several years later. *See also* Appendix 4, Secretaries of War and Secretaries of the Army.

CALLAWAY, HOWARD HOLLIS (1927–). Secretary of the army from 1973 to 1975. Born in Georgia, Callaway attended the Georgia Institute of Technology in Atlanta for a year before going to the **U.S. Military Academy**, where he graduated in 1949. After serving three years in the infantry, he left the army to manage a tourist resort in Georgia. He served a term in the U.S. House of Representatives and was an unsuccessful candidate for governor of Georgia in 1966. While Secretary of the army, he saw the end of the draft and the beginning of the **All-Volunteer Force**. After leaving office, Callaway managed Gerald Ford's unsuccessful campaign for president in 1976 and then returned to private business and became president of a resort in Colorado. *See also* Appendix 4, Secretaries of War and Secretaries of the Army.

CAMBRAI (20 November to 4 December 1917). World War I campaign streamer. The year America entered World War I was marked by near disaster for the Allies on all European fronts. A French offensive in April failed and was followed by widespread mutinies in the French armies. The British maintained strong pressure on their front throughout the year, but attacks on the Messines Ridge in June, at Ypres in July, and at Cambrai in November failed to capture German submarine bases and took a severe toll of British fighting strength. The first taste of war for the American Expeditionary Force came in November, when three American engineer regiments, doing construction work behind the British lines at Cambrai, were called upon to go into the front lines during an emergency.

CAMERON, JAMES DONALD (1833–1918). Secretary of war from May 1876 to March 1877. Born in Pennsylvania, Cameron graduated from Princeton University in 1852. He then worked in a bank founded by his father, **Simon Cameron**, where he eventually became president. During the **Civil War** he supervised the transportation of Union troops on the Northern Central Railroad, one of his father's enterprises, and from 1863 to 1974 he was president of the railroad. Appointed secretary of war in 1876, he resigned the next year to take his father's seat in the U.S. Senate. *See also* Appendix 4, Secretaries of War and Secretaries of the Army.

CAMERON, SIMON (1799–1889). Secretary of war from March 1861 to January 1862. Born in Pennsylvania, Cameron pursued a career in printing and became a powerful political figure in the state. He served in the U.S. Senate as a Democrat from 1845 to 1849 and again as a Republican from 1857 to 1861. A favorite-son candidate for president at the 1860 Republican convention, he gave his support to **Abraham Lincoln** after being promised a cabinet post by Lincoln's campaign managers. Lincoln was not happy with the deal, but appointed Cameron secretary of war. Widely criticized during his short tenure as secretary for favoritism in awarding contracts and making departmental appointments, Cameron resigned in January 1862 after the Union's military failures in the first year of the Civil War. He was appointed U.S. minister to Russia, where he garnered that country's support for the Union cause. He served in the Senate from 1867 to 1877 and used his political influence to have his son, **James Donald**

Cameron, appointed secretary of war in 1876 and then elected by the Pennsylvania legislature to succeed him in his Senate seat in 1877. *See also* Appendix 4, Secretaries of War and Secretaries of the Army.

CAMPAIGN. A phase of a war. A campaign is usually a connected series of battles directed toward a strategic objective of a war. In longer wars, campaigns may be designated to identify a phase of the war rather than identifying the attainment of a specific objective. The planning and conduct of campaigns is known in army **doctrine** as **operational art**. Individual army units receive a streamer for each campaign in which they participate. Once awarded, the streamer is carried on the flagstaff of the unit color. *See also* Appendix 6, Campaigns of the United States Army; CAMPAIGN STREAMER.

CAMPAIGN STREAMER. The **army flag** currently carries 174 campaign streamers dating back to the **Revolutionary War**. Individual army unit colors also carry a streamer for each campaign in which the unit has participated. The tradition of awarding streamers began in 1861, when John Charles Frémont commended troops from Iowa, Kansas, and Missouri for their service at the battle of Wilson's Creek near Springfield, Missouri, and ordered the word "Springfield" to be embroidered on the national colors of the units that participated in the fighting. Congress confirmed Frémont's order and the **War Department** instructed all regiments and batteries in the army to inscribe the names of battles in which they had participated. By 1890 some units claimed credit for so many battles that it was impossible to inscribe all the names on the national color, so the War Department directed that the names of battles be engraved on silver bands that were attached to the staff of the regimental color.

At the end of **World War I**, General **John Joseph Pershing**, commander of the American Expeditionary Force, directed that because of a shortage of time, units departing France for the United States be given ribbons in lieu of the silver bands. The use of silver bands was suspended in 1919 because of a shortage of silver and the War Department adopted campaign streamers in 1920. In 1921 the Historical Section of the **Army War College** developed a standard list of battles and campaigns to be recognized by having their names embroidered on streamers in the color of the campaign medal awarded for each war. That system has remained essentially the same since then, with streamers added as necessary, the latest having been added after the **Kosovo Air Campaign** in 1999. Ironically, there is no streamer for Springfield, the battle that inspired the tradition. *See also* Appendix 6, Campaigns of the United States Army.

CANADA (18 June 1812 to 17 February 1815). War of 1812 campaign streamer. This campaign includes all operations that occurred in the Canadian-American border region, except for the campaigns of **Chippewa** and **Lundy's Lane**. The invasion and conquest of Canada was a major objective of the United States in the war. The campaign started badly and the United States suffered a series of reverses in 1812. Fort Michilimackinac fell to the British on 6 August, Fort Dearborn was evacuated on 15 August, and Fort Detroit surrendered without a fight on 16 August. American attempts to invade Canada across the Niagara River in October and move toward Montreal in November failed completely.

The Americans fared better in the next year. **William Henry Harrison**'s move to recapture Detroit was repulsed in January 1813, but he stopped British efforts to penetrate deeper into the region at the west end of Lake Erie during the summer. In April, an expedition led by **Henry Dearborn** captured Fort Toronto and partially burned York, the capital of Upper Canada, and on 27 May **Jacob Jennings Brown** repelled a British assault on Sackett's Harbor. **Winfield Scott** led an American force that seized Fort George and the town of Queenston across the Niagara during May and June, but the British regained control of this area in December. A two-pronged American drive on Montreal from Sackett's Harbor and Plattsburg in the fall of 1813 ended in failure. Commodore Oliver Hazard Perry defeated the British fleet on Lake Erie on 10 September 1813, opening the way for Harrison's victory at the Thames River in October, which reestablished American control over the Detroit Area.

CASS, LEWIS (1782–1866). Secretary of war from 1831 to 1836. Born in New Hampshire, Cass attended Exeter Academy and taught school briefly before moving to Ohio to practice law. He served with the Ohio militia in the **War of 1812** and became a brigadier general in the **regular army** in 1813. From 1813 to 1831 he was the governor of Michigan Territory and at the same time was superintendent of Indian affairs for the region. Appointed **secretary of war** in 1831, he oversaw removing the eastern Indians to land west of the Mississippi River and in 1836 resigned to become minister to France. Cass served in the U.S. Senate from 1845 to 1848 and again from 1849 to 1857, when he was appointed secretary of state. He held this position until 1860, when he resigned in protest over the government's decision not to reinforce Fort **Sumter** in Charleston, South Carolina. *See also* Appendix 4, Secretaries of War and Secretaries of the Army.

CAVALRY. Branch of the army. Established as a branch on 12 December 1776. On 12 December 1776, the Continental Congress authorized a **regiment** of cavalry. Although mounted units were raised at various times after the **Revolutionary War**, the cavalry was eliminated from the **regular army** in 1802 in a cost-cutting measure. The branch was reinstated in 1808 as war with England threatened, but in the 1815 reorganization of the army, the cavalry was once again removed from the army's roles. In 1833, Congress authorized a regiment of **dragoons** to be trained and equipped to fight both mounted and on foot. Three years later, a second regiment of dragoons was added to the army and during the **Mexican War** the Regiment of Mounted Riflemen was formed. In 1855 the 1st and 2d Cavalry regiments were organized, giving the army a mounted force of dragoons, mounted riflemen, and cavalry. At the beginning of the **Civil War**, the army added a third regiment of cavalry and in August 1861 all six mounted units were designated cavalry and renumbered, beginning with the oldest. Thus, the 1st Dragoons became the 1st Cavalry, the 2d Dragoons the 2d Cavalry, the mounted riflemen the 3d Cavalry, and the three cavalry regiments the 4th through 6th

Cavalry. The number and strength of the cavalry regiments continued to fluctuate throughout the remainder of the nineteenth century and horse-mounted units stayed on the army's roles until after **World War II**. The branch was abolished in 1947, but as the army made the transition to modern **armored** warfare, many of the units retained the cavalry designation. Today's armored cavalry regiments are direct descendants of the nineteenth-century mounted regiments. *See also* ARMOR; BRANCHES OF THE ARMY.

CAVITE (7–13 October 1899, 4 January to 9 February 1900). Philippine Insurrection campaign streamer. This streamer represents two separate campaigns. In October 1899, U.S. Army forces under the command of Brigadier Generals Lloyd Wheaton and Theodore Schwan destroyed organized resistance by the followers of Emilio Aguinaldo in Cavite and adjacent provinces. In the same month, Major General Elwell S. Otis launched a three-pronged offensive in North Luzon directed at Aguinaldo's remaining forces. Fighting again occurred in Cavite in early 1990, and the forces under Wheaton and Schwan finally subdued the insurgents in February. *See also* MANILA (31 July to 13 August 1898); MANILA (4 February to 17 March 1899).

CCF (CHINESE COMMUNIST FORCES) INTERVENTION (3 November 1950 to 24 January 1951). Korean War campaign streamer. As the United Nations (UN) offensive moved into North Korea in late 1950, General **Douglas MacArthur**, commander of UN forces in Korea, ordered the Eighth Army and the X Corps to continue the attack toward the Manchurian border and restore peace in Korea before the onset of winter. On 1 November, as those forces moved forward, they encountered Chinese soldiers south of the Changjin (Chosin) Reservoir, and within ten days had identified 12 divisions of Chinese Communist Forces (CCF). By 10 November, the Eighth Army and the X Corps were conducting only small-scale operations, but in the latter part of the month, brief clashes with Chinese troops posed a new threat. Chinese participation in the conflict caused MacArthur to reconsider, but not abandon, his plans for an attack to the Yalu River. The Eighth Army launched the planned offensive on 24 November and for the first 24 hours met little enemy opposition. But on the second day enemy troops initiated a violent counterattack against the Eighth Army in the mountainous territory of central North Korea. The bulk of the enemy forces were well-organized CCF units. The Chinese had moved two large armies into North Korea from Manchuria under cover of darkness and camouflaged them during the day. The strength of the attacking Chinese forces surprised most of the UN Command in Korea. On 5 December the Eighth Army fell back to positions about 25 miles south of P'yongyang and by the middle of December they had withdrawn below the 38th parallel to form a defensive perimeter north and east of Seoul.

On 27 November the Chinese began their offensive against X Corps. MacArthur ordered the corps to concentrate its forces and withdraw to South Korea by water. Most of the corps reached the port of Hungnam without serious incident. However, 14,000 men of the First Marine and Seventh Infantry Divisions were trapped in the Hagaru-Kot'o area and were forced to fight their way to the coast along a narrow escape route, while a provisional battalion of marines and soldiers, aided by close and efficient air support, cleared the CCF from the high ground that dominated the road. U.S. Air Force, Navy, and Marine cargo planes parachuted ammunition, food, and medicines to the column and combat aircraft bombed and strafed enemy-held mountainsides and troop concentrations. On 9 December the two forces met in the mountains a few miles south of Kot'o and moved toward Hamhung to be evacuated. Evacuation began on 11 December and was completed on 24 December. On 23 December, General Walton H. Walker, commander of the Eighth Army, was killed in an auto accident north of Seoul and two days later he was replaced by Lieutenant General **Matthew B. Ridgway**.

With his forces under pressure, MacArthur warned the U.S. Joint Chiefs of Staff that the Chinese Communist could drive the UN forces out of Korea. The Joint Chiefs directed MacArthur to defend his positions, to inflict as much damage as possible on the enemy, and to maintain his units intact. If necessary to avoid severe losses, he was authorized to retire as far back as the former Pusan perimeter and even withdraw to Japan. MacArthur gave Ridgway authority to plan and execute operations in Korea. In late December, Ridgway established a defensive line along the 38th parallel, and at daybreak on 1 January 1951, after a night of mortar and artillery bombardment, the enemy launched an attack all along the UN line. A force of seven Chinese armies and two North Korean corps pushed toward Seoul and Wonju.

As the offensive gained momentum, Ridgway ordered his forces to fall back to the frozen Han River. A delaying force remained around Seoul to deny the enemy use of the Han bridges, but when it became clear that the Seoul bridgehead could not be held any longer, Ridgway decided to withdraw south to a line in the vicinity of the 37th parallel. Seoul fell on 4 January and the port of Inchon was evacuated. After the fall of Seoul, Chinese attacks tapered off in the west. By the third week of January 1951, the situation had eased somewhat and pressure on the UN troops was gradually decreasing. Air reconnaissance, however, revealed that the Chinese Communists were establishing reserves of supplies and bringing up thousands of replacements. *See also* UN OFFENSIVE.

CCF (CHINESE COMMUNIST FORCES) SPRING OFFENSIVE (22 April to 8 July 1951). Korean War campaign streamer. As the United Nations (UN) forces in Korea were advancing on their first offensive, enemy activity across the front suddenly increased on 22 April 1951 and the advance halted abruptly. The expected Chinese Communist Forces (CCF) spring offensive was at hand. Following a four-hour artillery bombardment, three Communist armies attacked the UN line and forced UN units to pull back to within four miles of Seoul. By the end of April, UN forces had stopped the CCF short of Seoul and the Han River and held a strong, continuous defense line. UN forces quickly renewed the offensive and, by 31 May, South Korea was virtually cleared of the enemy. At that point, the U.S. Joint Chiefs of Staff directed that the Eighth Army conduct only those tactical operations necessary to protect its forces and harass the enemy. This established the pattern of UN military operations for the rest of the war. *See also* FIRST UN COUNTEROFFENSIVE.

CEASE-FIRE (30 March 1972 to 28 January 1973). Vietnam War campaign streamer. On 30 March 1972 the North Vietnamese Army launched its greatest offensive of the entire war and deployed its troops with modern weapons in a major effort to end the war. The offensive concentrated on the northern provinces of South Vietnam, the central highlands, and the area northwest of Saigon. The South Vietnamese Army received support from U.S. B-52 bombers to stem the offensive. In October, the United States and the North Vietnamese government, negotiating in Paris, agreed to a cease-fire, but the South Vietnamese government objected to the terms and the talks stopped. In December, the United States repeatedly bombed North Vietnam in an effort to bring North Vietnam back to the peace table. On 27 January the United States, North Vietnam, South Vietnam, and the Provisional Revolutionary Government, which was North Vietnam's political organization in South Vietnam, signed the "Paris Peace Agreement Ending the War and Restoring Peace in Vietnam." By April 1973, U.S. forces were out of Vietnam. Reacting to the end of the war, in November 1973, the U.S. Congress passed the War Powers Resolution, which limited the power of the president to commit U.S. forces to hostile action without congressional approval.

CEASE-FIRE (12 April 1991 to 30 November 1995). Persian Gulf War campaign streamer. Fighting in the war ended on 11 April 1991, just over four days after the ground invasion began, but it took another four years to finally end the campaign. On the battlefield the results of the war appeared quite clear: the Iraqi Army had been forced out of Kuwait in a shattering defeat. But while Iraq was bloodied and bowed, it was not knocked out. **Saddam Hussein**, the president of Iraq, retained his elite Republican Guard forces relatively intact and challenged the United Nations (UN) cease-fire inspection teams at every opportunity. Although Iraq appeared to be a big loser in the war, Saddam Hussein continued to control the country. He never admitted defeat and acted like he had won the war.

Although the Gulf War was a stunning display of the capabilities of the U.S. Army, which had led the ground forces to victory, it did not remove Saddam Hussein from power or eliminate Iraq as a threat to the stability of the Middle East. As a result the cease-fire campaign dragged on for more than four years, while Saddam Hussein defied world opinion in a variety of ways. When the fighting ended, dramatic television footage showed the world what appeared to be a badly beaten Iraqi Army burning in the desert, and there were widespread hopes that the rule of Saddam Hussein would finally end as a result of the apparently humiliating defeat. But in October 1995, in a presidential referendum in which he was the only candidate, he received 99.96 percent of the votes to remain in office for another seven years.

Although the fighting ended in 1991, the United States continued to respond to Saddam Hussein's belligerent taunts and threats. In 1992 the army deployed **air defense artillery** missile systems to Kuwait and Bahrain, while U.S. planes periodically attacked Iraqi missile sites and ground radars challenged patrolling aircraft. In 1994, when Iraq moved 20,000 Republican Guard troops close to the Kuwait border, the army deployed some 40,000 troops to Kuwait and alerted 100,000 more. In August 1995, the Iraqi government announced its air force was conducting defensive exercises in anticipation of an attack by the United States, and the U.S. moved ships carrying army tanks and other supplies into the Persian Gulf as a precautionary move taken in response to what it termed unusual training activities conducted by Iraqi ground forces near Baghdad. The cease-fire campaign was officially terminated in November 1995, but the United States still had forces in the Persian Gulf in 2001, ten years after the end of the war. *See also* LIBERATION AND DEFENSE OF KUWAIT.

CENTER OF MILITARY HISTORY. The U.S. Army Center of Military History, located in Washington, D.C., has the mission of recording the official history of the army in both war and peace and advising the army staff on relevant historical matters. The center traces its lineage from the work of the historians who compiled the *Official Records of the Rebellion*, which documents the **Civil War**, and to a similar work on **World War I** prepared by historians in the historical section of the **Army War College**. The modern organization of the center dates from the creation of the historical section of the **general staff** in July 1943. This section formed the nucleus of a large team of professional historians, translators, editors, and cartographers who recorded the official history of the army in **World War II**. The team produced the United States Army in World War II series (popularly known as the green books), which now numbers 78 volumes. The center has also published a series of books on the army's role in the **Korean War** and the **Vietnam War** and has started work on a **Cold War** series. These works, supplemented by hundreds of monographs and books on a wide range of military subjects of interest to the army, have made the center a major publisher of military history. Under the direction of the chief of military history, the center also oversees the management of the army's museum system and art collection. *See also* ARMY ART COLLECTION; ARMY MUSEUMS; MILITARY HISTORY INSTITUTE.

CENTRAL BURMA (29 January to 15 July 1945). World War II campaign streamer. The campaign in Burma during the last year of World War II was largely a British show. Except for five Chinese divisions and a mixed American and Chinese brigade known as the Mars Task Force, which replaced Merrill's Marauders, Allied forces in Burma consisted of British and British Commonwealth troops. The British were really more interested in recovering Singapore than in taking Burma or helping China, but American control of lend-lease, combined with an American policy that continued to back Chiang Kai-shek, more or less dictated that the Allies would try to recapture Burma. After opening the Burma Road in January 1945, the next step was to push the Japanese out of Central Burma.

The British preferred to occupy Burma from the south, beginning with a seaborne assault on Rangoon, but demands on shipping for European and Pacific operations precluded such a plan, so they attacked from India, across the Irrawaddy River to Mandalay, and then south to Rangoon. The rugged terrain and tenacious resistance of crack Japanese troops made it a tremendously difficult task complicated by the fact that ground forces had to be supplied by air. Mandalay was captured after a prolonged fight in mid-March 1945, and from then on progress was relatively fast. With the capture of Rangoon on 3 May 1945, the occupation of Burma was essentially complete. Isolated fighting continued for some months, until the final surrender of all Japanese forces at Singapore in September. *See also* BURMA 1942; INDIA–BURMA.

CENTRAL EUROPE (22 March to 11 May 1945). World War II campaign streamer. By March 1945, German forces in the west could no longer halt a new Allied drive to the Rhine River on a broad front. The German Army had been exhausted by its ambitious counteroffensive in the **Ardennes–Alsace** campaign and further weakened by transfers of troops to meet the new Soviet threat in the east. On 7 March 1945 elements of the U.S. Ninth Armored Division seized an opportunity to cross a bridge at Remagen that the Germans had inadvertently left undestroyed, and Allied forces were able to gain a firm foothold on the eastern bank of the Rhine River. Two weeks later, troops of the U.S. Third Army staged a surprise crossing of the Rhine south of Remagen using assault boats. At about the same time, in the north, British and American troops crossed the Rhine in an **airborne** assault. During the last week of March, both the U.S. Seventh and First French Armies crossed the Rhine, setting the stage for the final campaign of the war in Europe.

Following the Rhine crossings, the Allies fanned out with massive columns of **armor** and motorized **infantry** and were soon making spectacular advances through Germany. Resistance was staunch at some points, but Allied strength was by now overwhelming. The U.S. Ninth and First Armies, with the help of the new U.S. Fifteenth Army, encircled the Ruhr Valley and captured more than 325,000 prisoners. Allied forces in the north and center made rapid advances against slight opposition and by mid-April they had reached the Elbe and Mulde Rivers, where they waited for the rapidly approaching Soviet Army. In the south, other Allied columns penetrated into Czechoslovakia and Austria.

In the east, the Soviets began the final drive on Berlin on 17 April, and by 25 April they had completely encircled the German capital. On the same day, leading elements of the Soviet forces came in contact with American troops at Torgau on the Elbe River. Fierce street fighting broke out in Berlin, Hitler committed suicide on 30 April, and what remained of the German garrison in Berlin surrendered two days later. Mussolini had been killed by Italian partisans on 28 April 1945 while attempting to escape into Switzerland. On 7 May, Admiral Karl Doenitz, Hitler's successor, granted his representative, General Alfred Jodl, permission to surrender on all fronts and the surrender became effective the next day. Except for some scattered resistance from a few isolated units, the war in Europe was over.

CENTRAL PACIFIC (7 December 1941 to 6 December 1943). World War II
campaign streamer. In 1941 Japanese military leaders recognized American naval
strength as the chief deterrent to war with the United States. Late that year they
completed plans for assaults against Malaya, the Philippines, and the Netherlands
East Indies, to be coordinated with a crushing blow on the Pacific Fleet at Pearl
Harbor in the Hawaiian Island of Oahu. The Japanese assumption was that, before the United States could recover from such a surprise blow, the Japanese
would be able to seize all their objectives in the Far East and could then hold out
indefinitely. In November a Japanese naval force of some 30 ships, including six
aircraft carriers with about 430 planes, set sail for Hawaii. On the night of 6–7
December, five midget submarines carried on larger submarines cast off and began converging on Pearl Harbor. The main task force arrived undetected about
200 miles north of Oahu at 0600 on 7 December and launched about 360 planes
toward Hawaii.

The U.S. Navy had 96 vessels, which included eight battleships and was the
bulk of the Pacific Fleet, moored in Pearl Harbor. But the aircraft carriers were all
at sea. There were about 390 navy and army planes of all types located on several

1. *Army troops wading ashore at Makin Atoll in November 1943 during the Central Pacific campaign.*

airfields. The Japanese air attack began at 0755 and ended shortly before 1000. The Americans fought back vigorously with antiaircraft fire but devastation of the airfields was so quick and thorough that only a few planes were able to counterattack. The attack crippled the Pacific Fleet, sinking three battleships, capsizing another, and severely damaging the other four. The Japanese sank or severely damaged 18 ships, including the eight battleships, three light cruisers, and three destroyers, while destroying 161 American airplanes (74 army, 87 navy) and seriously damaging another 102 (71 army, 31 navy). The navy and marines suffered 2,896 casualties, of which 2,117 were killed and 779 wounded; the army lost 228 killed, 113 seriously wounded, and 346 slightly wounded; and 57 civilians were killed and nearly as many were seriously injured. The Japanese lost 29 planes, one large submarine, and all five midget submarines. According to Japanese sources, they lost 55 airmen, 9 crewmen on the midget submarines, and an unknown number on the large submarine. The Japanese carrier task force sailed away undetected and unscathed. Japan won the first round of the war. The United States was knocked down but not out.

The day after the attack on Pearl Harbor, the United States declared war on Japan, and four days later Germany and Italy declared war on America. With the United States now at war in Europe and the Pacific, American strategic planners envisioned rapidly moving forces across the Atlantic to defeat Germany and Italy, thus relegating the Pacific to a defensive theater. But a defensive strategy did not mean inaction, and by the spring of 1942 the U.S. Navy was beginning to make some inroads against the Japanese. The Japanese suffered their first major setback when they attempted an invasion by sea of Port Moresby on the southeastern coast of New Guinea. Allied naval units intercepted the invading Japanese naval force in the Coral Sea on 7–8 May 1942. After two days of fighting, the Japanese task force broke off the engagement and withdrew northward. The most significant losses were the U.S. carrier *Lexington* and the Japanese carrier *Shoho*, while both sides suffered heavy losses in planes. At the Battle of Midway in early June, the U.S. Navy destroyed four Japanese aircraft carriers, along with a heavy cruiser, three destroyers, some 275 planes, and about 4,800 men with the loss of only a single aircraft carrier, about 150 planes, and 307 men. After the Japanese broke off the engagement, part of their task force moved northward and seized three of the **Aleutian Islands**. Japan's losses in the Battles of the Coral Sea and Midway restored the balance of naval power in the Pacific and the Japanese never fully recovered from the loss of many of their best naval pilots.

Most of the Central Pacific campaign centered on naval action, as the United States moved west across the vast ocean spaces. The army's only battle came late in the campaign, when troops of the 27th Infantry Division landed on Makin Atoll in the Gilbert Islands. Although the army had superiority in men and weapons, it took four days to finally subdue the island's small defensive force, due mainly to coordination difficulties in executing a complex plan involving two separate landings. While the army was struggling at Makin, the U.S. Marine Corps was locked in a deadly struggle at Tarawa, in one of the toughest fights in corps history. Both amphibious assaults captured their respective objectives and the Central Pacific campaign ended on 6 December 1943. The occupation of Makin and Tarawa gave the United States advance bases in the Gilbert Islands, which facilitated later operations against the Marshall Islands during the **Eastern Mandates** campaign in 1944. *See also* PAPUA.

CERRO GORDO (17 April 1847). Mexican War campaign streamer. As **Winfield Scott** began his advance from **Vera Cruz** toward Mexico City on 8 April 1847, the first resistance his army encountered was near the small village of Cerro Gordo, about 50 miles from Mexico City. General **Antonio Lopez de Santa Anna**, the president of Mexico and commander of its army, had strongly entrenched about 12,000 men in the mountain passes. Scott, using information gained by his engineers, including **Robert E. Lee** and **George B. McClellan**, maneuvered his army around the Mexicans, forcing Santa Anna to withdraw his army into the mountains. Mexican casualties were about 1,000 killed and about 3,000 taken prisoner who were later paroled. American losses were 64 killed and 353 wounded.

CHAFFEE, ADNA ROMANZA (1842–1914). Chief of staff of the army from 1904 to 1906. Born in Ohio, Chaffee enlisted in the **regular army** in 1861 and was commissioned a second lieutenant in 1863. Twice wounded during the **Civil War**, he stayed in the army after the war and served on the western frontier. He commanded a brigade in the **Spanish–American War** and the American contingent in the **China Relief Expedition**. In 1904 he became chief of staff of the army, in which capacity he established territorial divisions to supervise field operations and served on an army-navy board intended to improve cooperation between the two services. He retired from active service in 1906. *See also* Appendix 3, Commanding Generals and Chiefs of Staff of the Army.

CHAMBERLAIN, JOSHUA LAWRENCE (1828–1914). Civil War Union general. A professor at Bowdoin College before volunteering his services, Chamberlain commanded the 20th Maine, an **infantry** regiment organized in 1862. He and his regiment held the Union left flank during a critical period on the first day of **Gettysburg**. During the course of the war he was wounded six times and suffered from malaria, but he continued to return to his regiment. He was promoted to brigadier general by special order of **Ulysses S. Grant** for heroism at **Petersburg**. Later Grant selected Chamberlain to receive the formal surrender of the Confederates after the **Appomattox** campaign. After the war, Chamberlain went on to become the governor of Maine and president of Bowdoin College.

CHAMPAGNE–MARNE (15–18 July 1918). World War I campaign streamer. In their four offensives from 21 March to 13 June 1918, the Germans gained considerable ground, but failed to achieve a decisive advantage anywhere on the Allied front. Their success cost more than 600,000 irreplaceable casualties, while the arrival of the American Expeditionary Force compensated for the Allied losses of some 800,000 men. By July 1918, Allied troops outnumbered the Germans on the

Western Front and the Allied blockade and propaganda campaign was depleting German morale both at the front and at home. But the Germans planned two more offensives for July. The first was designed to capture Rheims and secure supply lines to the Merge salient and draw in Allied reserves. The second, which never happened, was to be another strike at the British in Flanders. When the German assault began on 15 July the Allies were ready. Plans for the attack had leaked out of Berlin and Allied aircraft had detected German preparations behind their front lines. As a result, the German drive east of Rheims fell short of its objective, although the attack west of the city pushed across the Marne River near Chateau-Thierry before it was checked there by French and American units. American Expeditionary Forces participated in the campaign and the 38th Infantry of the 3d Division earned its famous motto, "Rock of the Marne" for its defensive actions at Chateau-Thierry. By 17 July, the Champagne–Marne offensive was over and the initiative passed to the Allies. The German people had great hopes for the offensive and its failure dealt a tremendous psychological blow to the nation.

CHANCELLORSVILLE (27 April to 6 May 1863). Civil War campaign streamer. After the Fredericksburg campaign, President **Abraham Lincoln** named Major General Joseph Hooker commander of the Army of the Potomac, replacing **Ambrose E. Burnside** on 25 January 1863. Hooker made some changes in the army and by late April was ready to assume the offensive with about 134,000 men. Hooker's objective was to destroy **Robert E. Lee**'s Army of Northern Virginia of about 60,000 men, which was still holding **Fredericksburg**. Hooker planned a double envelopment to place strong Union forces on each of Lee's flanks. The campaign began on 29 April with the movement of five Union corps up the Rappahannock River to Chancellorsville, while two more corps under Major General John Sedgwick crossed the river below Fredericksburg. At the same time, Union **cavalry** made a diversionary raid on Lee's rear. When Lee recognized the Union intent, he sent General **Thomas J. Jackson** to attack toward Chancellorsville, leaving only a small force to defend Fredericksburg. When the two forces met, Hooker faltered and stayed on the defensive. When Lee turned his attention to Chancellorsville, Hooker believed the Confederates were retreating and ignored rumors of an impending flanking movement.

On 2 May, Jackson attacked the Union right flank and began rolling up Hooker's defensive line. At nightfall the Confederate attack slowed and Jackson moved forward to find the Federals. After locating the Union line, Jackson started back to join his forces but he and his staff were mistaken for Federal cavalry and fired on by a North Carolina regiment. Jackson was mortally wounded and died on 10 May. The Confederates attempted to renew the attack on 3 May, but Sedgwick occupied Fredericksburg, causing Lee to move 25,000 men to stop the Union threat. Sedgwick moved back across the Rappahannock on 4 May and Hooker, although outnumbering the Confederates by two to one, followed the next day. The campaign was a Confederate victory, but came at the cost of one of Lee's most valuable generals, Jackson. Federal casualties were 1,575 killed,

9,594 wounded, and 5,676 missing; Confederate losses were 1,665 killed, 9,081 wounded, and 2,018 missing.

CHAPLAIN. Branch of the army. The origin of army chaplains was in a resolution of the Continental Congress, adopted 29 July 1775, that provided for the pay of chaplains. The office of the chief of chaplains was created by the National Defense Act of 1920. *See also* BRANCHES OF THE ARMY.

CHAPULTEPEC (13 September 1847). Mexican War campaign streamer. After reducing the outworks at **Molino del Rey**, the American army, led by **Winfield Scott**, continued the attack on Chapultepec, the citadel protecting Mexico City. Scott ordered part of his force to move south of the city to attract the attention of Mexican general **Antonio Lopez de Santa Anna** and his 15,000 troops, while American **artillery** pounded Chapultepec. On 13 September U.S. **infantry** scaled the summit and overran the castle. American losses were 138 killed and 673 wounded during the siege of the fortress. Mexican losses totaled about 1,800, including 100 boy cadets who were defending their college and Mexican honor. After the fall of the citadel, some U.S. soldiers moved onto the causeway that led to the gates at the southwest corner of the city, while others assaulted the gateway at the northwest corner. The Mexican defenders put up a strong fight, but when night came U.S. troops were inside Mexico City. Santa Anna withdrew his army in the darkness and the next day Scott entered the city. American casualties were about 860, while Mexican losses were estimated at about twice that number. After the city surrendered, Santa Anna abdicated the presidency; the last remnant of his army, about 1,500 volunteers, was defeated about a month later while attempting to capture an American supply train.

CHARLESTON (28–29 June 1776; 29 March to 12 May 1780). Revolutionary War campaign streamer. A single streamer reflects the two engagements at Charleston, South Carolina, during the war. In the first engagement, a British expedition led by **Henry Clinton** failed to seize the city. The result blunted the British threat in the southern theater for three years. In the second engagement, four years later, a successful invasion by 8,000 British from New York, again led by Clinton, forced the American garrison in Charleston to surrender on 12 May 1780. That defeat, however, did not end the war in the south. American guerrillas led by **Francis Marion** harried British posts and lines of communications. The British, commanded by Lord **Charles Cornwallis**, were unable to maintain control of the region. The grassroots strength of the rebellion denied victory to the British and eventually caused Cornwallis to withdraw to Virginia, where his forces were trapped at **Yorktown.**

CHATTANOOGA (23–27 November 1863). Civil War campaign streamer. At the end of the **Chickamauga** campaign, Confederate General **Braxton Bragg** occupied positions south and east of Chattanooga, Tennessee, on Lookout Mountain and along Missionary Ridge, trapping the Union forces under General William Rosecrans, who were cut off from direct supply by rail. Washington authorities moved to help Rosecrans, dispatching by rail two corps of about 20,000 men under General Joseph Hooker from the Army of the Potomac at the end of September. Hooker's troops eventually attacked the Confederate forces southwest of Chattanooga and opened the rail supply line to the city in late October. During that month General **Ulysses S. Grant** took overall charge of the operation in his capacity as newly appointed commander of the Military Division of the Mississippi. At about the same time, General **William T. Sherman** took over Grant's Army of the Tennessee and General George H. Thomas replaced Rosecrans in Chattanooga.

Early in November, Bragg sent part of his army under General **James Longstreet** in pursuit of Union forces in eastern Tennessee, which reduced the Confederate force besieging Chattanooga to little more than 40,000 men. Shortly thereafter, Sherman arrived in Chattanooga, bringing Grant's strength there to about 60,000 men. Grant took the offensive in the latter part of November. Hooker's force took Lookout Mountain on 24 November and Thomas's and Sherman's troops took Missionary Ridge the next day. Bragg was forced to retreat south, one of his divisions skillfully halting Grant's attempted pursuit. Federal losses were 753 killed, 4,722 wounded, and 349 missing; Confederate losses were 361 killed, 2,160 wounded, and 4,165 missing. Shortly after Bragg's retreat, Longstreet returned to Virginia, leaving Tennessee clear of Confederate forces. With Chattanooga available as a base of operations, the way was open for a Union invasion of the lower South.

CHEMICAL CORPS. Branch of the army. The Chemical Warfare Service was established on 28 June 1918 and combined activities that until then had been dispersed among five separate agencies of the U.S. government. The Chemical Warfare Service was made a permanent branch of the army by the National Defense Act of 1920 and in 1945 it was redesignated the Chemical Corps. *See also* BRANCHES OF THE ARMY.

CHEYENNES (1878–1879). Indian wars campaign streamer. On 1 July 1878, the army held more than 940 hostile Northern Cheyenne at the Indian agency at Fort Reno in Indian Territory. While they were there, many of the Northern Cheyenne found friends among the more peaceful Southern Cheyenne. But about 375 of the Northern Cheyenne, led by Dull Knife, Wild Hog, Little Wolf, and others, remained together and would not affiliate with the Southern Cheyenne. Unhappy with agency life, 89 warriors accompanied by almost 250 women and children surprised their army watchers by abandoning their lodges and escaping on 9 September 1878. The army dispatched troops from several posts to intercept and return them to the agency, but the Indians eluded their pursuers and continued north, raiding settlements for stock. On 21 September a minor skirmish took place and six days later the army troops overtook the Cheyenne on the Punished Woman's Fork of the Smoky Hill River in Kansas. The Indians were waiting for their pursuers in strong, entrenched positions. The army commander and one Indian were killed and three **enlisted** men were wounded in the attack. The Cheyenne escaped and continued moving north.

On 23 October 1878, army troops captured 149 Indians and 140 head of stock, including the leaders Dull Knife, Old Crow, and Wild Hog, but Little Wolf and some of his followers escaped. In January 1879 a number of Cheyenne escaped and joined Little Wolf after a skirmish with troops near Fort Robinson, Nebraska. The army intercepted the Indians near the telegraph line from Fort Robinson to Hat Creek, where they were entrenched in a gully. Refusing to surrender, the army attacked and killed or captured the entire party, including the leader, Dull Knife. On 25 March a large army force found Little Wolf and his band near Box Elder. The Indians were persuaded to surrender without fighting and gave up all their arms and about 250 ponies. The 33 men, 43 women, and 38 children marched with the troops to Fort Keogh, Montana.

CHICKAMAUGA (16 August to 22 September 1863). Civil War campaign streamer. After the successes at **Gettysburg** and **Vicksburg** the Union focused on **Chattanooga**, Tennessee, an important Confederate communications center. In July 1863 Union general William S. Rosecrans moved his Army of the Cumberland, numbering about 65,000 men, southeast out of Murfreesboro. By 4 September, Rosecrans had crossed the Tennessee River near Stevenson, Alabama, and was moving northeast toward Chattanooga. The Chattanooga area was defended by General Braxton Bragg's Army of Tennessee. In mid-September, General **James Longstreet** joined Bragg with 10,000 men and six **field artillery** brigades, giving the Confederate force a strength of about 62,000 men.

Rosecrans planned to march south of Chattanooga to cut off Bragg's potential southern escape route and then attack the city. When Bragg learned of the approaching Federals, he moved his army out of the city to make a stand along Chickamauga Creek near Lafayette, Georgia, about 15 miles south of Chattanooga. Rosecrans changed his direction of march to intercept Bragg. Moving across mountainous terrain, Rosecrans made contact sooner than expected and had difficulty concentrating his forces. Bragg waited until 18 September, when Longstreet's force began to arrive, before launching his attack across Chickamauga Creek. The battle raged throughout 19 September without a decision. The next day, a Confederate assault pierced the Union line and drove about a third of the Federals, Rosecrans among them, northward in retreat. Rosecrans conceded the victory and moved on to Chattanooga, but the remaining Federals, under Major General George E. Thomas, stood fast under repeated attacks. Thomas retired his force from the field that night and the next day joined Rosecrans in Chattanooga. Although the Confederates were successful in winning the field, it was a hollow victory, because the Federal Army of the Cumberland remained intact. Federal losses were 1,657 killed, 9,756 wounded, and 4,757 missing; the Confederates lost 2,312 killed, 14,674 wounded, and 1,468 missing.

CHIEF JOSEPH (Himmahton-Yahlaktit; Thunder Rolling Over the Mountains) (1840–1904). Nez Perce Indian chief. Leader of a band living in Wallowa Valley in eastern Oregon, Chief Joseph complied when the U.S. government ordered the Nez Perce to settle on a reservation, but in 1877 he was one of a number of chiefs who led 800 Nez Perce in a desperate attempt to reach Canada. Although other chiefs played a larger military role in the final battle in the Bear Paw Mountains of Montana, he surrendered with the famous speech on 5 October 1877 that ended, "From where the sun now stands, I will fight no more forever." The words endeared him to the American people as a humane chief and, although he and his people were sent to Indian Territory, he was later allowed to move to a reservation in Washington State, where he lived until his death.

CHIEF OF STAFF OF THE ARMY. On 15 August 1903 Major General **Samuel B. M. Young** became the first chief of staff of the army, a position that replaced that of **commanding general of the army**. The change was the result of efforts by **Elihu Root** while he was the **secretary of war** to resolve long-standing differences between the army's senior military and civil officials. An officer with the title of commanding general expected to command, but that proved impossible, because the president was the constitutional commander of the army and the secretary of war was responsible to the president for supervising the army's activities. Consequently, the secretary of war and the commanding general of the army were frequently in conflict in attempting to carry out what they saw as their duties and responsibilities. Designating the senior officer as the chief of staff made the position one of managing the army and presiding over a general staff that supervised current operations and planned for future contingencies. The chief of staff of the army has no command authority, but exercises managerial functions over the Department of the Army and is a member of the Joint Chiefs of Staff, which also includes the uniformed heads of the air force, marine corps, and navy. *See also* Appendix 3, Commanding Generals and Chiefs of Staff of the Army.

CHIEF WARRANT OFFICER. *See* WARRANT OFFICER.

CHINA DEFENSIVE (4 July 1942 to 4 May 1945). World War II campaign streamer. The United States faced two problems in China during World War II, one political, the other logistical. On the political front, tensions within China precluded a truly unified war effort against Japan. Logistically, there were enormous distances involved with moving supplies in support of the Chinese Army, the Allied war effort in the China–Burma–India (CBI) theater had a low priority, and the theater was the most remote from the United States. Initially, securing a port and establishing airfields in southeastern China for launching bombing raids against the Japanese home islands was considered essential for defeating Japan. Opening a land supply route to China across Burma to equip Chinese Nationalist troops was the first step to that end.

To facilitate Allied support to the Chinese, General **Joseph Stilwell** was named commander of the CBI. He concurrently served as chief of staff to Generalissimo Chiang Kai-shek, head of the Nationalist Chinese government, and commander of the combined Allied forces. When Stilwell arrived in China in March 1942, he found himself in a political and military quagmire. He was dismayed at the Chinese war effort. Chiang Kai-shek's Nationalist government did not have a strong military force and was engrossed with the revolt of China's Communists, led by

Mao Tse-tung, who had gained control in North China. With the Japanese threatening to cut the Allied supply lines, Stilwell turned his attention to Burma, but even with nine Chinese divisions at his disposal, he was unable to prevent losing the Burma Road, the last land route into China.

Stilwell wanted to go on the offensive, but Chiang Kai-shek was unwilling to use Chinese divisions to help the British regain control of Burma and questioned the sincerity of the U.S. lend-lease effort for China. Stilwell had a rocky relationship with Chiang Kai-shek during his tenure as chief of staff, as American patience with the lack of progress by Chinese forces to initiate offensive operations eventually grew thin. President Franklin D. Roosevelt lost interest in China following his meeting with Chiang Kai-shek at Cairo in November 1943 and the grandiose lend-lease plans for equipping and training 30 Chinese divisions gradually evaporated.

In September 1944, Japanese forces in China overran the airfields in South China, but by that time it was evident that islands in the Pacific that the Allies were capturing could be used to greater advantage than China as springboards for an effective attack on Japan. Ongoing differences with Stilwell caused Chiang Kai-shek to ask that he be relieved as his chief of staff in early October 1944. By May 1945, the United States and China were ready to go on the offensive. In spite of the political and logistical difficulties, however, the campaign did succeed in diverting between 600,000 and 800,000 Japanese from the Pacific campaigns, a not insignificant accomplishment.

The army's primary role in the campaign was to keep China in the war by providing advice and material assistance. Keeping China in the war tied up hundreds of thousands of Japanese troops who could otherwise be used to defend the Pacific islands. The major failure in China was logistical. The United States simply could not meet the Chinese requirements in the face of other pressing Allied demands, while the loss of the Burma Road in 1942 made it impossible to deliver sufficient weapons, munitions, and equipment to build an effective Chinese Army. *See also* BURMA 1942; CHINA OFFENSIVE; INDIA–BURMA.

CHINA OFFENSIVE (5 May to 2 September 1945). World War II campaign streamer. As Allied victory in Europe appeared increasingly probable in early 1945, the Allies allocated more military resources to the war against Japan. By 1944 Allied forces had driven the Japanese from numerous Pacific islands, invaded the Philippines, and reoccupied Burma, but the bulk of Japan's land forces were on the Chinese mainland. General William Wedemeyer replaced **Joseph Stilwell** as the commander of the China–Burma–India theater in late 1944, when Stilwell was recalled to the United States. During the long China defensive campaign, Stilwell had managed to keep China in the war, even though he was faced with considerable political and logistical difficulties in doing so. When Wedemeyer arrived, he was able to convince the Chinese leader Chiang Kai-shek, that he needed U.S. advisers to train the Chinese Army and create a more effective command-and-control organization. Building on the foundation laid by Stilwell, an American cadre revitalized the Chinese Army, although they were aided in

January 1945 by the reopening of the Burma Road, which provided a growing stream of supplies and weapons to the Chinese.

On 5 May 1945 a Chinese division successfully attacked and defeated a Japanese detachment near Wu-yang. Over the next few days, Chinese forces repeatedly outflanked the Japanese and forced them north, while two Chinese armies moved into the Japanese rear. Frequent airdrops of ammunition and food kept Chinese morale high and American advisers were impressed with how well the Chinese soldiers fought. The operation demonstrated that Chinese troops could defeat the Japanese. Had the war lasted longer, the Japanese would have faced a difficult task defending against the Chinese, but success in China was the product of victories won in other battles in the Pacific. *See also* CHINA DEFENSIVE.

CHINA RELIEF EXPEDITION. The Boxer movement in China gained momentum in the final years of the nineteenth century. The Boxers were fanatical members of a Chinese secret society who wished to drive all foreigners from the country and eradicate foreign influences. In June 1900 foreigners in China, especially those in **Peking** (Beijing), found themselves in grave danger. The movement against Westerners in Peking reached a climax on 20 June 1900, when the German minister was murdered. About 3,500 foreigners and Chinese Christians, fearing for their safety, took refuge in the foreign legation compound, where they were besieged by thousands of Chinese. A composite military force of 407 men (including 56 Americans) plus about 200 civilians defended the compound. The Great Powers responded with the China Relief Expedition, organized under British command to stamp out what came to be known as the Boxer Rebellion. After successfully rescuing the hostages, most of the U.S. Army units in the expedition withdrew to Manila before winter, leaving mop-up operations in the provinces to other national forces. A few American soldiers remained as part of an allied occupation force and as a small guard for the U.S. legation in Peking. The Boxer Protocol of 7 September 1901, negotiated by the Great Powers with China, included provisions for a fortified legation quarter, foreign garrisons along the Tientsin-Peking railway, and a large indemnity. In 1908 the United States remitted a portion of its share of the indemnity, most of which was used to educate Chinese students in America. *See also* TIENTSIN; YANG-TSUN.

CHIPPEWA (5 July 1814). War of 1812 campaign streamer. In March 1814, the British halted an American advance led by **James Wilkinson** just after it crossed the Canadian border. But on 3 July, 3,500 men under **Jacob Jennings Brown** seized Fort Erie in a coordinated attack with Commodore Isaac Chauncey's fleet in which the Americans took control of Lake Ontario. Operating in the Niagara River region, **Winfield Scott**'s brigade, about 1,300 men and part of Brown's command, was unexpectedly confronted by a large British force on 5 July 1814 while the Americans were preparing for an Independence Day parade near the Chippewa River. Scott's well-trained troops broke the British line with a skillfully executed charge, sending the survivors into a hasty retreat. The British commander, astonished at the American soldiers' ability to stand their ground, is alleged to have exclaimed, "Those are regulars by God." British losses were 137 killed and 304 wounded; American, 48 killed and 227 wounded. Tradition has it that the cadets at the **U.S. Military Academy** wear their traditional gray uniforms in honor of the American victory at Chippewa. *See also* LUNDY'S LANE.

CHURUBUSCO (20 August 1847). Mexican War campaign streamer. After the battle at **Contreras, Winfield Scott**, the American commander, continued his move toward Mexico City. General **Antonio Lopez de Santa Anna**, the Mexican commander, made another stand on Churubusco, where he suffered a disastrous defeat. Scott estimated the Mexican losses at 4,297 killed and wounded, and he took 2,637 prisoners. Of the 8,497 Americans engaged in the almost continuous battles of Contreras and Churubusco, 131 were killed, 865 were wounded, and about 40 were missing.

CIVIL AFFAIRS. Branch of the army. The Civil Affairs/Military Government branch of the **U.S. Army Reserve** was established on 17 August 1955. It was redesignated the Civil Affairs branch on 2 October 1959 and has continued its mission to provide guidance to commanders in a broad spectrum of activities ranging from host-guest relationships to the assumption of executive, legislative, and judicial processes in occupied or liberated areas. *See also* BRANCHES OF THE ARMY.

CIVILIAN CONSERVATION CORPS. In March 1933 Congress established the Civilian Conservation Corps (CCC) as a means to put large numbers of young men to work on reforestation, flood control, soil erosion control, and road construction projects during the Great Depression. President Franklin Roosevelt directed the army to organize and run the camps without making it a military program. Within three weeks there were 310,000 men in 1,315 camps, making this the fastest and most orderly mobilization in the army's history. About 3,000 **regular army** officers ran the program, which stripped tactical units of leadership and virtually halted training, until the **War Department** called a large number of **U.S. Army Reserve** officers to active duty in late 1934. The program gave thousands of reserve officers valuable experience dealing with young men and provided nonmilitary but disciplined training to hundreds of thousands of the future soldiers and sailors who fought **World War II**.

CIVIL WAR (1861–1865). When **Abraham Lincoln** was elected president of the United States in 1860, his commitment to prohibiting the expansion of slavery was seen as intolerable by the South, where the agriculture-based economy depended heavily on the practice. Lincoln's election had virtually no base of support in the South and secessionists eagerly pursued a course of establishing an independent nation. South Carolina left the Union in December 1860, setting the stage for the first military confrontation of the war at Fort **Sumter** in Charleston harbor. Other states in the deep South followed South Carolina's lead and together they formed the Confederate States of America. After his inauguration in March 1861, Lincoln decided to resupply the garrison at Fort Sumter, the most visible Southern military installation held by the Union. **Jefferson Davis**, president of the Confederacy, did not want the fort to remain in Union hands and demanded its surrender in early April. Confederate batteries in Charleston began bombarding the fort on 12 April and the garrison surrendered on 14 April. The

U.S. Army Military History Institute.

2. *Company F, 3d Massachusetts Heavy Artillery at Fort Devens in the District of Columbia in 1865.*

next day, Lincoln called for 75,000 state militia to defend the Union and within five weeks five more states joined the Confederacy.

In its first efforts to restore the Union in 1861 the Union Army achieved mixed results. It secured Washington, D.C., and the border states, provided aid and comfort to Union supporters in the western portion of Virginia, occupied most of Tennessee, secured almost all of the Mississippi River, and cooperated with the navy to seize key points along the Southern coast. But in the first major battle of the war, at **Bull Run** in July, the Confederates forced Union troops from the field in disarray.

In 1862 the Union met with some success in the west during the **Henry and Donelson** campaign, but in eastern Virginia, the area nearest the capitals of both the United States and the Confederacy and the most visible theater of the war, the Union Army of the Potomac made little progress against the Confederate Army of Northern Virginia, commanded by **Robert E. Lee**. After stopping **George B. McClellan** during the **Peninsula** campaign and defeating the Army of the Potomac at **Manassas**, Lee invaded Maryland in the hope of encouraging European intervention. The Union victory at **Antietam** forced Lee back to Virginia, but a subsequent defeat at **Fredericksburg** brought the Union effort in the east no closer to success than it had been at the beginning of the year.

The third year of the war, 1863, saw Union fortunes start to turn around. In early July, **Ulysses S. Grant** triumphed at **Vicksburg**, giving the North control of the entire Mississippi River. At the same time, the Union victory at **Gettysburg** turned back Lee's second invasion of the North, while later in the year the capture of **Chattanooga**, Tennessee, opened the way for a Union invasion of the Southern heartland. Assuming command of all Union armies in 1863 after his success at Vicksburg, Grant coordinated the operations of all Northern armies toward the strategic goal of destroying the South's capability to wage war.

By 1864, Civil War battles exhibited the characteristics of industrial warfare, in which the strategic goal became destroying an opponent's ability to wage war rather than directly attacking its armies. In this style of war, the Union, with its larger population and superior industrial capability, had a significant advantage over the agriculturally based South, but success took a commander who understood that war had changed. A single, decisive battle could not end a war against a determined nation in arms. War had to be prosecuted using firepower to relentlessly wear down the opponent in annihilation operations, and Grant understood this. Accompanying **George G. Meade** and the Army of the Potomac, he pursued a grinding style of war, wearing down Lee's Army of Northern Virginia during the **Wilderness**, **Spotsylvania**, and **Petersburg** campaigns of 1864 and 1865. In the west, **William T. Sherman** drove through Georgia and the Carolinas, burning crops, dismantling railroads, and destroying the South's economic infrastructure. Cavalry raids and other Union operations also carried out Grant's goal of destroying the economic and moral basis for resistance. The Civil War ended in 1865. Lee surrendered his army to Grant at the end of the **Appomattox** campaign in April and the remaining Confederate forces surrendered by the end of May.

The **U.S. Military Academy** produced most of the generals who conducted active operations during the Civil War. Of the 60 major battles fought in the war, 55 had academy graduates commanding both sides and the remaining five had a graduate commanding on at least one side. While they were cadets, these commanders learned the Napoleonic style of conducting large land operations. Napoleon inspired the rise of theoretical literature of war in Europe in the early nineteenth century with his approach to war. His objective was to crush the main body of the opposing army, believing that would end a campaign quickly and decisively in his favor. One of the most prominent Napoleonic writers in the nineteenth century was **Antoine-Henri Jomini**, a Swiss officer who had served in Napoleon's army. The basic tenet of Jomini's theories of war was bringing superior forces to bear on the enemy's inferior force, and he stressed that offensive operations were absolutely essential to attain victory. At the Military Academy, **Dennis Hart Mahan** taught Jomini's theory of strategy to America's future Civil War generals and Mahan's students learned their lessons well.

During the war, commanders on both sides initially emulated the Napoleonic style of operations as they conducted offensive campaigns in search of the big, decisive battle that would end the war. **Artillery** became an essential element of conducting operations, but **infantry** had a significant capability to retaliate. In

1855 the army had received a new standard shoulder arm, the .58 caliber Springfield rifle, with improved range and accuracy. The new rifle forced the artillery to stand back so far that it lost much of its effectiveness against infantry in defensive positions. Infantry assaults had to face a higher rate of fire from the defenders. The defense grew stronger as commanders learned the value of field fortifications to protect their troops from artillery and rifle fire. Increased firepower favored tactical defensive operations, while other technological innovations encouraged offensive strategic operations. The railroad allowed commanders to rapidly concentrate combat power at a decisive point, while the telegraph gave them the capability to coordinate operations across long distances. The combination of rapid strategic offensive operations with massive firepower at the tactical defense often resulted in elegantly planned campaigns ending in bloody, indecisive battles. *See also* Civil War campaigns listed in Appendix 6, Campaigns of the United States Army.

CLARK, MARK WAYNE (1896–1984). U.S. Army general who commanded the U.S. Fifth Army in Italy in **World War II** and the United Nations (UN) forces during the **Korean War** from 1952 to 1953. Born in New York to a military family, Clark graduated from the **U.S. Military Academy** in 1917 and served in **World War I**, where he was wounded in France. He attended the **Command and General Staff College** between World War I and World War II and played a key role in preparations for the Allied invasion of North Africa during the **Algeria–French Morocco** campaign, when he led a secret mission to gain the cooperation of Vichy French officials to reduce resistance to the landings. He commanded the U.S. Fifth Army during the successful **Sicily** campaign, but was criticized over the **Anzio** landings for choosing to capture Rome rather than encircling the German armies in Italy. In 1952 Clark succeeded **Matthew Ridgway** as commander of the UN forces in Korea, where he signed the armistice in 1953. After retiring that year, he became president of the Citadel military college in South Carolina and became an advocate for continued conscription and expanded U.S. efforts during the **Vietnam War**.

CLARK, WILLIAM (1770–1838). Army officer and explorer. Born in Virginia, Clark moved west in 1785 with his family and followed his older brother, a **Revolutionary War** general, into military service. He received a commission as a lieutenant in 1792 and served with **Anthony Wayne** at the battle of Fallen Timbers in the **Miami** Indian campaign. He resigned from the army in 1796, but in 1803 **Meriwether Lewis**, who had served under Clark for a time, invited him to accompany Lewis on an expedition to explore the west. For the next three years Clark and Lewis led the Corps of Discovery from Saint Louis to the Pacific Ocean and back. After the expedition, Clark became a brigadier general and superintendent of Indian affairs for the Louisiana Territory. He led several volunteer military campaigns during the **War of 1812** and remained involved in U.S. dealings with the Indians after the war.

CLAUSEWITZ, CARL PHILIP GOTTLIEB VON (1780–1831). Prussian general and military theorist in the nineteenth century. Clausewitz's *On War* is one of the most influential studies of war ever written. Although incomplete and needing revision at the time of his death, the work continues to have considerable influence on U.S. Army **doctrine**. The book was first translated into English in 1873 and its theories gained widespread attention after 1914, as they were studied for insights into the German conduct of **World War I**. In 1976 a new English translation of *On War* appeared and Clausewitz's ideas on the political nature of war gained widespread attention as the army struggled to understand what went wrong during the **Vietnam War**. By the end of the twentieth century, Clausewitz had permeated the army's education of its officers.

CLAY, LUCIUS DUBIGNON (1897–1978). Army general who commanded U.S. forces in Europe during **World War II** and was military governor of the U.S. zone of occupation from 1947 to 1949. Born in Georgia, Clay graduated from the **U.S. Military Academy** in 1918 as an engineer officer. After serving in a variety of engineering assignments, he attended the International Naval Conference in Brussels and served on **Douglas MacArthur**'s staff in the Philippines in the 1930s. During World War II, he oversaw the army's production and procurement programs, before serving as **Dwight D. Eisenhower**'s deputy in Europe for a brief period. Clay was appointed deputy military governor of the U.S. zone of occupation in Germany in 1945 and served as the military governor and commander of U.S. forces in Europe from 1947 to 1949. He was widely praised for his role in the Berlin airlift during 1948–1949, which supplied the city when the Soviets cut off ground access. He retired in May 1949 to pursue a successful business career. During the Berlin crisis of 1961, when the Soviets encircled the city with a wall to keep East Germans from reaching the West, President John F. Kennedy recalled Clay to active service as his personal representative to the city. Clay was later chairman of Radio Free Europe, from 1965 to 1974. *See also* COLD WAR.

CLINTON, HENRY, SIR (1730–1795). British **Revolutionary War** general. Born in Canada, the son of the Newfoundland governor, Clinton served in the British army in Europe before being sent to America in 1775 as a major general. He fought in the **Boston** campaign, forced the Americans to surrender at **Charleston** in 1776, and assumed overall command of British forces in the colonies in 1778 from Sir **William Howe**. Although Clinton had grand plans to crush the Revolution, his caution led to the naming of a more aggressive commander, Lord **Charles Cornwallis**, as second in command. When he was blamed for Cornwallis's defeat at **Yorktown** in 1781, Clinton resigned and returned to England to defend his reputation.

COCHISE (ca. 1812–1874). Chiricahua Apache Indian chief. Born in the area of what is now Arizona and New Mexico, Cochise was initially friendly toward white settlers, but became hostile after being imprisoned over false accusations of kidnapping a white child. After the death of his father, Mangas Colorado, in

1863, Cochise became the main war chief for the Apaches and for many years led them in a series of violent raids against white settlers and the army. After keeping the army at bay in his stronghold in the Chiricahua Mountains, he received assurances that he and his tribe could remain in their traditional homeland and he surrendered to **George Crook** in 1872.

CODE OF CONDUCT (1955). After the **Korean War**, 21 American prisoners of war (POWs) refused to return home. The news came as a shock to the American public and commissions were assembled to determine why any American soldier would elect to remain in a Communist country. Postwar interviews with former U.S. POWs revealed many charges of collaboration with the enemy among the returning soldiers. The department of defense investigated more than 500 repatriated soldiers, but only a few were convicted of misconduct. An advisory committee on POWs to the department recommended that U.S. armed forces personnel receive training in resistance to enemy interrogation and drafted a code of conduct that provided a standard of behavior whereby American POWs should resist the enemy and keep faith with their fellow prisoners. On 17 August 1955, President **Dwight D. Eisenhower** signed Executive Order 10631, approving the code. The code contains six articles and was amended in 1988 to incorporate gender-neutral language.

Article I – I am an American, fighting for the forces which guard my country and our way of life. I am prepared to give my life in their defense.

Article II – I will never surrender of my own free will. If in command, I will never surrender my men while they still have the means to resist.

Article III – If I am captured I will continue to resist by all means available. I will make every effort to escape and aid others to escape. I will accept neither parole nor special favors from the enemy.

Article IV – If I become a prisoner of war, I will keep faith with my fellow prisoners. I will give no information nor take part in any action which might be harmful to my comrades. If I am senior, I will take command. If not, I will obey lawful orders of those appointed over me and will back them up in every way.

Article V – When questioned, should I become a prisoner of war, I am required to give name, rank, service number, and date of birth. I will evade answering further questions to the utmost of my ability. I will make no oral or written statements disloyal to my country and its allies or harmful to their cause.

Article VI – I will never forget that I am an American, fighting for freedom, responsible for my actions, and dedicated to the principles which made my country free. I will trust in my God and in the United States of America.

COLD HARBOR (22 May to 3 June 1864). Civil War campaign streamer. While Union forces under **Ulysses S. Grant** engaged **Robert E. Lee**'s Confederates during the **Wilderness** and **Spotsylvania** campaigns, General Benjamin Franklin Butler marched his Army of the James up the peninsula, but he was outmaneuvered and bottled up at Bermuda Hundred by General P. G. T. Beauregard. This allowed Lee to fall back to the Richmond defenses, where he placed his right flank on the Chickahominy River and his center at Cold Harbor. Grant's forces took position along six to eight miles of front facing the entrenched Confederates. On 3 June, Grant launched a heavy assault at Cold Harbor. The Union forces were repulsed with a loss of some 12,000 killed and wounded. By the end of the Cold Harbor campaign, fighting in the eastern theater had resulted in some 25,000 to 30,000 Confederate casualties, while Union losses were between 55,000 and 60,000. Although Grant had not achieved a single major objective, he had dealt a nearly fatal blow to the South, which was rapidly running out of men to fill its depleted ranks. The North, even though it suffered even greater losses, had a large reservoir of manpower available for its armies.

COLD WAR. At the end of **World War II**, the alliance of the United States, Great Britain, and the Soviet Union, bound together mainly to defeat Nazi Germany, began to show signs of strain and began to unravel. Competing security and economic demands introduced the Cold War, a period of marked distrust between the former allies that was characterized by a bipolar world with competing coalitions led by the United States and the Soviet Union. Relations between the former allies deteriorated rapidly, and in June 1948, the Soviet Union shut off all ground access to the American, British, and French sectors of Berlin. The action prompted what became known as the Berlin airlift—a massive air operation by the United States and Great Britain to deliver the 4,500 tons of supplies West Berlin needed every day. When the Soviets finally lifted the blockade, 1,783,000 tons had been delivered to the city at a cost of 31 U.S. lives. The airlift demonstrated the U.S. resolve to stand by Europe.

The airlift spurred 12 Western powers, including the United States, to create the North Atlantic Treaty Organization (NATO) in 1949. NATO was a military alliance designed to deter the Soviet Union from widening its sphere of influence in Western Europe. In 1951, with the formation of the Supreme Headquarters Allied Powers Europe (SHAPE), U.S. president **Harry S. Truman** brought **Dwight D. Eisenhower** out of retirement to become the Supreme Allied Commander in Europe. The Soviet Union strongly objected to NATO and in 1955 organized its own military alliance, the Warsaw Pact. For the next 34 years, the two military alliances faced each other in Europe. In 1961, in an effort to stem the flood of refugees through Berlin, East Germany built a wall around the western part of the city, the West German enclave in East Germany. The Berlin Wall became a symbol of the confrontation between the two superpowers, the United States and the Soviet Union, and with its fall in 1989 the Cold War ended.

During the Cold War, the army focused on Europe, preparing to fight a major land war against the Warsaw Pact. Although the army fought both the **Korean War** and the **Vietnam War** during that time, its doctrine, organization, and equipment centered on fighting the Soviets in Europe. In 1991, as the world adjusted to the end of the Cold War, the army found itself fighting the Iraqi Army during the **Persian Gulf War**. The decisive victory in the desert against a foe trained and equipped by the Soviets demonstrated that the U.S. Army had prepared well for the war in Europe that never came. Since then, the army has seen its force structure reduced, even as it has had to contend with a wider variety of missions. In many respects, the tensions and confrontations of the Cold War, with its clearly discernable threat, presented the army with a clearer focus for preparing for war than it has had at almost any time in its history.

COLLINS, JOSEPH LAWTON (1896–1987). Chief of staff of the army from 1949 to 1953. Born in Louisiana, Collins graduated from the **U.S. Army Military Academy** in 1917. He served in France during **World War I** and afterward held a variety of command and staff positions and attended a number of army schools, including the **Army War College.** During **World War II**, he participated in campaigns in both the Pacific and European theaters of operations. He became chief of staff in 1949, in which position he was closely associated with developing the army's contribution to the newly established North Atlantic Treaty Organization (NATO), and he was the army's senior officer during the **Korean War.** He was the U.S. representative to NATO's Military Committee after leaving office as chief of staff, and he retired from active service in 1956. *See also* Appendix 3, Commanding Generals and Chiefs of Staff of the Army.

COMANCHES (1867–1875). Indian wars campaign streamer. Major General **Philip Sheridan**, commanding the Department of the Missouri, instituted winter campaigning in 1868 as a means of locating the Indians living in the southern Great Plains, among whom the dominant group was the Comanches. The campaign included battles with a number of tribes, including the nine-day defense of Beecher's Island against Roman Nose's band of Cheyennes in September 1868 by Major General George A. Forsyth; the defeat of Black Kettle on the Washita River in Oklahoma on 27 November 1868 by Lieutenant **George Armstrong Custer** and the 7th Cavalry; and the crushing of the Cheyenne under Tall Bull at Summit Spring in Colorado on 13 May 1869. The most significant battle of the campaign was the 28 September 1875 assault on a large encampment of Comanche, Cheyenne, and Kiowa bands in Palo Duro Canyon, Texas, on 27 September 1875 by troops under Colonel Ronald S. Mackenzie. The camps were located over a wide area and the Indians were unable to mount a united defense. Only three Indian warriors and one soldier were killed during the scattered skirmishes, but Mackenzie's troops captured villages, most of the Indians' possessions, and more than 1,400 ponies. With no horses or supplies for the winter, the Indians were forced to surrender to reservation life. The battle effectively ended any further resistance to white settlers by the Comanches and other tribes on the southern Plains.

COMMAND AND GENERAL STAFF COLLEGE. In 1882, at the direction of **William T. Sherman, commanding general of the army**, a School of Application for **Cavalry** and **Infantry** was established at Fort Leavenworth, Kansas. Over the years, the name of the school changed several times to include the names U.S. Infantry and Cavalry School, the Army School of the Line, the General Staff School, the Command and General Staff School, and the Command and General Staff College. During its early years, the school prepared lieutenants for duty at the company level, but between 1890 and 1910 Arthur L. Wagner and

Eben Swift transformed the college. Convinced the army needed officers educated in both the theory and practical aspects of warfare, they introduced the systematic study of **strategy** and **tactics**, and the use of military history under the so-called applicatory method, which stressed active student learning by using map studies, indoor war games, and outdoor exercises known as tactical rides rather than emphasizing passive lectures.

In 1887, the best graduates were selected for a second year of study that evolved into the Command and General Staff College, so designated in 1928. Between the two world wars, the college thrived and is now frequently credited with being the principal educational influence on the men who led the army to victory in **World War II**. During the war, the school shortened and accelerated the courses that prepared officers for leadership at the division level. Special courses were given to officers designated to command divisions and their staffs.

In 1980 the college added the Combined Arms and Services Staff School, known as CAS3 or "cass-cubed," to prepare company-grade officers for battalion and brigade staff positions. Three years later, the Advanced Military Studies Program added a second year of study for selected graduates of the college. Today, the college is the army's senior tactical educational institution, teaching field grade officers war-fighting skills and preparing them for duty at corps and division levels. The student body includes army and other U.S. armed forces officers, department of the army civilians, and about 100 international officers from some 70 nations. *See also* ARMY SCHOOLS; ARMY WAR COLLEGE.

COMMAND SERGEANT MAJOR. Both a rank and a position, it is the senior **enlisted** soldier in units and organizations at battalion and higher levels. The command sergeant major, or CSM, advises the commander on matters pertaining to enlisted solders in the command. *See also* SERGEANT MAJOR; SERGEANT MAJOR OF THE ARMY; SERGEANTS MAJOR ACADEMY.

COMMANDING GENERAL OF THE ARMY. George **Washington** was the first commanding general of the army, but after he resigned the post in 1783, changes in the size of the army, the rank and location of the senior officer, and the views of the incumbent **secretary of war** all influenced the designation used for the senior officer in the army. Designations varied between 1775, when Washington was appointed, and 1903, when the title for the senior officer became **chief of staff of the army**. The various titles included commander in chief, general in chief, major general commanding in chief, commanding general of the army, lieutenant general of the army, and general of the army.

While the duties and responsibilities of the secretary of war, the civilian official who headed the **War Department**, were generally accepted and understood, the role of the senior military officer in the army was not clear at all. In 1821, John C. Calhoun, the secretary of war, formalized the title as commanding general, but his action failed to fully resolve organizational problems. The commanding general theoretically headed the line, but he did not in fact or law command the army. There was no direct, vertical, integrated chain of command. The administrative, technical, and supply bureau chiefs in Washington dealt directly with their own officers in the field at all levels of command. Most of the time, the men who held the posts of secretary of war and commanding general worked out a reasonable division of labor, although there were periods of antagonism between the incumbents, as the leaders of the nation's military establishment developed procedures for maintaining an American Army under civilian control. Military business was conducted by correspondence and personal visits between the secretary and the commanding general. Depending on personalities, the relationship between the secretary of war and the commanding general was in a constant state of flux for the century and a quarter between Washington's appointment as commanding general of the **Continental Army** and the establishment of the position of chief of staff of the army in 1903. *See also* Appendix 3, Commanding Generals and Chiefs of Staff; CHIEF OF STAFF OF THE ARMY.

COMMISSIONED OFFICER. An army officer holding rank by a commission issued by the president. The commission is the officer's authority. All army ranks from second lieutenant to general are commissioned officers, and they are all senior to **warrant officers** and **noncommissioned officers**. Commissioned officers command or lead virtually every organization in the army, from platoon and above. There are three categories of commissioned officer. Company grade officers are lieutenants and captains; they generally lead platoons, command companies, and serve on lower staffs. Field grade officers are majors, lieutenant colonels, and colonels; they generally command battalions and brigades and serve as primary staff officers in organizations up to corps level. General officers include all grades from brigadier general and above and, with the exception of some specialists, such as chaplains, doctors, or lawyers, general officers do not have a specific branch identity. General officers command divisions and above and serve as primary staff officers on major army and joint headquarters. *See also* Appendix 8, United States Army Rank Insignia; NONCOMMISSIONED OFFICER; WARRANT OFFICER.

COMPANY. Units that consist of two or more platoons, usually of the same type, with a headquarters. Companies are the basic elements of **battalions** and can be separate units in brigades and larger organizations. They are commanded by captains and usually consist of 150 to 220 soldiers. An **artillery** unit of this size is a **battery**; a comparable **cavalry** unit is a troop. Normally, four or five companies constitute a battalion.

CONCORD. *See* LEXINGTON.

CONNELLY, WILLIAM A. (1931–). Sergeant major of the army from 1979 to 1983. Born in Georgia, Connelly attended Georgia Southwestern College and enlisted in the Georgia National Guard in 1949 to pay his college tuition. After two years of college, he volunteered for the **regular army** in 1954. After serving a variety of armor units in the United States and Germany, he served as first sergeant of a hand-picked company of tanks that deployed to the **Dominican Republic** in

1965. In 1966 he returned to Georgia as an **Army National Guard** adviser. He served in the **Vietnam War** and was a **first sergeant** for ten years before being promoted to **sergeant major** in 1970. Connelly graduated from the **Sergeants Major Academy** in 1973 and became the sergeant major of the army in July 1979. While in the job, he wrote a regulation for a **noncommissioned officer** development program and pushed for improvements in the quality of life for soldiers. He retired from active service on 30 June 1983. *See also* Appendix 5, Sergeants Major of the Army.

CONRAD, CHARLES MAGILL (1804–1878). Secretary of war from 1850 to 1853. Born in Virginia, Conrad moved with his family to Louisiana, where he studied law and was admitted to the bar in New Orleans. During the course of his law studies, he fought a duel in which he killed his opponent. He served in the Louisiana legislature for two terms before being appointed to fill a U.S. Senate seat in 1842. Defeated for the seat the next year, he was elected to the House of Representatives in 1848, but resigned to become secretary of war in 1850. While in office he proposed that local militias be armed by the government to meet Indian threats and urged that Indians who took up farming be fed by the government. Leaving office in 1853, he was active in state politics and represented Louisiana in the Confederate Congress during the **Civil War**. *See also* Appendix 4, Secretaries of War and Secretaries of the Army.

CONSOLIDATION I (1 July to 30 November 1971). Vietnam War campaign streamer. During this campaign, there was continued progress in turning over the ground war to South Vietnam and sustaining the withdrawal of U.S. troops. South Vietnam assumed full control of defending the area immediately below the demilitarized zone on 11 July, and the U.S. relinquished all ground combat responsibilities to the Republic of Vietnam on 11 August. But U.S. maneuver battalions still participated in operations. The U.S. Army's 101st Airborne Division took part in Jefferson Glen, a South Vietnamese operation that took place in Thua Thien Province in October. It was the last major combat operation in Vietnam for U.S. ground forces, as the 101st began stand-down procedures on 8 October and became the last U.S. division in Vietnam. By November, U.S. troop totals dropped to 191,000, the lowest level since December 1965. In early November, U.S. president Richard M. Nixon announced that American troops had reverted to a defensive role in Vietnam.

CONSOLIDATION II (1 December 1971 to 29 March 1972). Vietnam War campaign streamer. The United States continued to reduce its ground presence in South Vietnam during late 1971 and early 1972, even as American air attacks increased and both sides exchanged peace proposals. In early January 1972, U.S. president Richard M. Nixon confirmed that U.S. troop withdrawals would continue, but promised that a force of 25,000–30,000 would remain in Vietnam until all American prisoners of war were released. On 25 January, Nixon announced an eight-part program to end the war that included agreement to remove all U.S.

and foreign allied troops from South Vietnam no later than six months after a peace agreement was reached. The North Vietnamese and Viet Cong delegates to the peace talks rejected the proposal and insisted upon complete withdrawal of all foreign troops from Indochina and cessation of all forms of U.S. aid to South Vietnam. U.S. troop strength in Vietnam dropped to 95,500 by the end of March 1972.

CONTINENTAL ARMY. The designation "Continental Army" is most closely associated with the forces led by **George Washington** from early July 1775 through the fall of 1783. In 1775, after American militia forces had their first confrontations with the British army, the Second Continental Congress recognized that a regular military force was necessary if their revolution was to be successful. On 14 June 1775, therefore, Congress adopted the army of 36 regiments of New England militia that was besieging **Boston** and authorized recruiting and financing of 10 companies of riflemen, six from Pennsylvania and two each from Maryland and Virginia. This small force provided the permanent nucleus of an American army that would be supplemented by militia units as necessary. Each state raised a portion of the new army, referring to them as the Continental Line, because they were to be trained to employ European linear tactics. Discipline was based largely on mutual agreement among the individual soldiers of the line. Legislators selected commissioned officers with proven leadership abilities and who had experience from the French and Indian War.

In perhaps its most important military decision, Congress named Washington to command the new army. His leadership proved key to the ultimate success of the army. At one time or another during the **Revolutionary War**, regiments from every state except South Carolina served under Washington's command. One of the biggest challenges facing Washington was manning the force. He wanted soldiers to stay in the army long enough to become proficient in linear tactics and capable of standing up to British regulars, but it was not until late 1776 that he was able to persuade Congress to raise the term of enlistment for Continental Army soldiers beyond one year. Congress authorized the states to raise a total of 88 regiments for three years. During the course of the Revolutionary War, some states raised more regiments than others, with the New England states and Pennsylvania making the largest contributions to the army.

It is virtually impossible to know with any exactitude how many men served in the Continental Army. Congress considered military service by individual enlistments, and terms of service varied from those serving one day in the militia to Continental soldiers who were in for the duration of the war. It was not uncommon for soldiers to have multiple enlistments, moving from Continental units to militia and back as circumstances changed. Also, record keeping left much to be desired during the most intense fighting and muster rolls were occasionally lost when America suffered reverses during the war. Perhaps as many as 120,000 men served in the Continental Army during the war. It was probably at its largest in late 1778, when there were about 32,000 men on the rolls, although only 21,500 were fit for duty. The core of the army, men who enlisted repeatedly and officers who served several consecutive years, was probably something less than 15,000.

The fluctuating strength of the army and the multitude of enlistment options made recruiting difficult and gave Washington serious problems maintaining an effective fighting force, but it did provide individual soldiers great flexibility in supporting the cause while seeing to their obligations at home. In spite of the constant turnover, Washington was able to make the Continental Army an effective fighting force that eventually prevailed over the British. By the end of the Revolutionary War, this force had become a uniquely American army that had accomplished what the fledgling nation demanded of it.

Having won independence for America, the Continental Army made perhaps its most important contribution to the nation, deference to civilian authority. Throughout the Revolutionary War, Congress had lacked the funds to properly maintain the army. The irregular pay, lack of compensation after disbandment, and general neglect fomented considerable discontent among American soldiers. When an officer delegation presented its grievances to Congress during the winter of 1782–1783, Washington called his own meeting, warning the officers against impulsiveness, arguing that an attempted coup would open the way to civil discord, and recalling their sacrifices. Heeding his words, the officers reaffirmed their loyalty and confirmed the American policy of civilian authority over the military. *See also* Appendix 1, Resolution of the Continental Congress Adopting the Continental Army.

CONTRERAS (18–20 August 1847). Mexican War campaign streamer. After the battle at **Cerro Gordo, Winfield Scott** pushed on to Jalapa, but wounds and sickness had put 3,200 men in the hospital, while some 3,700 volunteers departed for home when their enlistments expired. Scott had only about 7,000 effective soldiers by the end of May, when he halted at Pueblo to await the arrival of reinforcements and to build up supplies. To conserve his force, Scott decided not to garrison the lines of communications with **Vera Cruz**. In so doing, he cut off his supplies from the coast and lived off the land. It was a bold move that rendered his army vulnerable, but his good relations with local residents served him well. Other than a few guerrilla attacks on the edges of its camps, the army did not suffer appreciably. Scott once again began advancing toward Mexico City on 7 August, by which time reinforcements had increased his army to almost 10,000 men. General **Antonio Lopez de Santa Anna**, the Mexican president and army commander, had disposed his forces in and around Mexico City, strongly fortifying the many natural obstacles that lay in the way of the Americans. In the first encounter, Scott met stiff resistance at Contreras, where the Mexicans were put to flight after suffering an estimated 700 casualties and the loss of 800 prisoners. *See also* CHURUBUSCO.

COPELAND, SILAS L. (1922–2001). Sergeant major of the army from 1970 to 1973. Born in Texas, Copeland attended a one-room school through high school. He was inducted into the army in 1942 and assigned to the **Army Air Corps**, where he spent three years as a refueling specialist at Biggs Army Airfield near El Paso, Texas. After retraining, he became a tank commander and fought the closing days of **World War II** in Europe. He was wounded during the **Korean War** and in 1951 declined an officer's commission because he believed he was too old to be a second lieutenant. Copeland left the army in 1954, but soon returned to active service and was promoted to sergeant major in 1962. He was the **command sergeant major** of four different divisions and saw service in the **Vietnam War** before becoming the sergeant major of the army in 1970. While in that position, he was involved in the army's move to an all-volunteer force and its reduction in strength from 1.3 million soldiers in 1970 to 788,000 in 1973. Copeland retired in June 1973 with 30 years of active service. *See also* Appendix 5, Sergeants Major of the Army.

CORNWALLIS, LORD CHARLES (1738–1805). British **Revolutionary War** general. Born in London, Cornwallis studied at the Military Academy of Turin and served in the Seven Years' War before accepting a command in America in 1776, although he was opposed to taxing the colonists. He served with **William Howe** during the **Long Island** campaign and under Sir **Henry Clinton** when the British captured **Charleston**, after which he assumed command in the South. He was unable to gain control of the area and Clinton ordered him to Virginia, where he and his army were trapped at **Yorktown** and forced to surrender to **George Washington** in 1781. Returning to England after Yorktown, he blamed Clinton for his defeat. In 1786, Cornwallis became governor-general of India, where he served with distinction and regained his reputation. He was lord-lieutenant of Ireland from 1798 to 1801 and returned to India as governor-general in 1804.

CORPS. The U.S. Army's largest tactical unit. A corps is tailored for the theater and mission for which it is deployed. It contains the necessary combat, combat support, and combat service support to conduct sustained operations. A corps usually consists of two or more **divisions** with necessary supporting forces and is usually commanded by a lieutenant general. Until the early twentieth century, the corps was a temporary command. With the rapid expansion of the army in **World War I**, the corps became a permanent part of the force structure. Traditionally, a corps is designated with roman numerals.

CORPS OF ENGINEERS. Branch of the army. The corps is the branch responsible for facilitating military movement by constructing roads, bridges, and bases. Engineers supervise construction of bases and fortifications. The Continental Congress authorized a chief engineer for the army on 16 June 1775 and a Corps of Engineers for the United States on 11 March 1779. On 16 March 1802 Congress authorized President Thomas Jefferson to organize a Corps of Engineers to be stationed at West Point, New York, where it established the **U.S. Military Academy.** For more than a quarter century, the academy, popularly known as West Point, was the only engineering school in the United States and, until 1866, its superintendent was an engineer.

Engineers have supported the army in every war it has fought. During the **Petersburg** campaign in the **Civil War**, engineers built a 2,170-foot-long pontoon bridge across the James River, the longest such structure until **World War II**. In

World War II, engineers served around the world. Some of their most celebrated accomplishments included clearing mines and obstacles from the beaches at **Normandy** and building roads through the mountains and jungles of Asia. During the **Korean War**, engineers destroyed bridges over the Naktong River and constructed fortifications that helped stop the North Korean invasion during the **UN Defensive** campaign. In the **Vietnam War**, they cut through jungles to support search-and-destroy missions, while in the deserts of Iraq during the **Persian Gulf War** engineers conducted breaching operations through the Iraqi defenses during the **Liberation and Defense of Kuwait** in 1991.

In addition to its battlefield support of military operations, the Corps of Engineers has played a large role in civil engineering. During the nineteenth century, the corps supervised construction of extensive coastal fortifications and built lighthouses, piers, and jetties. The General Survey Act of 1824 led to the corps being assigned to survey routes for roads and maps. Later the same year, it was authorized to make improvements on the nation's waterways, including dredging, which eventually resulted in a series of regional and local district offices supervised by the chief of engineers. The Corps of Topographical Engineers, authorized on 4 July 1838, was merged with the Corps of Engineers in March 1863. During its existence, the topographical engineers explored, surveyed, and mapped large portions of the American West. In 1907, **George Washington Goethals**, an army engineer, was given responsibility for completing the Panama Canal. The Flood Control Act of 1936 authorized the engineers to build and supervise construction of levees, dams, and reservoirs on major rivers, while the Flood Control Act of 1944 authorized the corps to construct multipurpose dams for such things as flood control, irrigation, navigation, water supply, hydroelectric power, and recreation. In 1986, however, the Water Resources Act reduced federal involvement in civil works and provided the Corps of Engineers a smaller role in such projects. *See also* BRANCHES OF THE ARMY.

CORREGIDOR. *See* PHILIPPINE ISLANDS.

COUNTEROFFENSIVE (25 December 1965 to 30 June 1966). Vietnam War campaign streamer. Following the U.S. victory in the Ia Drang Valley, American forces sought to keep the enemy off balance while building base camps and logistical installations. This involved search-and-destroy operations to protect the logistical bases under construction along the coast and the base camps for incoming U.S. units in the provinces near Saigon. Part of the American military mission was protecting the government and people of South Vietnam. U.S. efforts were concentrated in the most vital and heavily populated regions. The U.S. Army's I **Field Force** supported the central region and the II Field Force supported the area around Saigon. During February and March 1966, U.S. intelligence reported heavy North Vietnamese Army infiltration from Laos and across the demilitarized zone into Quang Tri Province. To defend against this threatened invasion, the bulk of the U.S. Third Marine Division and the U.S. Army's 173d

Airborne Brigade moved into the northern provinces. Throughout the campaign, the enemy continued to take refuge in Laos, Cambodia, and North Vietnam.

COUNTEROFFENSIVE, PHASE II (1 July 1966 to 31 May 1967). Vietnam War campaign streamer. After 1 July 1966, U.S. military operations were a continuation of the earlier counteroffensive campaign. Recognizing the interdependence of political, economic, sociological, and military factors, the U.S. Joint Chiefs of Staff directed that American military objectives be to stop North Vietnam's control and support of the insurgency in South Vietnam and Laos, to assist South Vietnam in defeating Viet Cong (VC) and North Vietnamese forces in South Vietnam, and to assist South Vietnam in extending control over its territory. North Vietnam continued to build its own forces inside South Vietnam. U.S. air elements conducted reconnaissance bombing raids and tactical air strikes into North Vietnam, just north of the demilitarized zone (DMZ), but ground forces were not permitted to conduct reconnaissance patrols in the northern portion of the DMZ and inside North Vietnam. Confined to South Vietnamese territory, U.S. ground forces fought a war of attrition against the enemy, relying for a time on body counts as an indicator of progress.

The largest operation of 1966 took place northwest of Saigon in Operation Attleboro and involved 22,000 American and South Vietnamese troops pitted against the VC Ninth Division and a North Vietnamese Army (NVA) regiment. The Americans and South Vietnamese forced the VC and NVA into havens in Cambodia and Laos. By 31 December 1966, U.S. military personnel in South Vietnam numbered 385,300, while enemy strength was in excess of 282,000, in addition to an estimated 80,000 political cadres. On 8 January 1967, U.S. and South Vietnamese troops launched separate drives against two major VC strongholds in the Iron Triangle, about 25 miles northwest of Saigon. For years this area had been under development as a VC logistics base and headquarters to control enemy activity in and around Saigon. The operations resulted in the capture of huge caches of rice and other foodstuffs, destruction of an extensive system of tunnels, and the seizure of documents with considerable intelligence value. In February, the same U.S. forces that had cleared the Iron Triangle were committed with other units in the largest allied operation of the war to date, Junction City, in which more than 22 U.S. and four South Vietnamese Army battalions engaged the enemy, killing 2,728. By June 1967, U.S. forces in Vietnam had increased to 448,800, but enemy strength went up as well.

COUNTEROFFENSIVE, PHASE III (1 June 1967 to 29 January 1968). Vietnam War campaign streamer. As Operation Junction City, conducted during the **Counteroffensive, Phase II**, campaign, ended, elements of the U.S. Army's 1st and 25th Infantry Divisions, the 11th Armored Cavalry Regiment, and forces of the Army of the Republic of Vietnam moved back toward Saigon to conduct another clearing operation known as Manhattan, that took place in the Long Nguyen base area just north of the Iron Triangle. South Vietnamese armed forces became more active and capable under U.S. advisers in 1967. During that year, the Vietnamese Army **Special Forces** assumed responsibility for several camps and for the Civilian Irregular Defense Group companies manning them. In each case, all of the U.S. advisers withdrew. With their increased responsibility, the South Vietnamese conducted a number of successful major operations during 1967.

Despite the success of U.S. and South Vietnamese Army operations, there were indications in the fall of 1967 of another enemy buildup in areas close to Laos and Cambodia. In late October, the Viet Cong (VC) struck the Special Forces camp at Loc Ninh, but Vietnamese reinforcements prevented the camp from being overrun. At about the same time, approximately 12,000 VC troops converged on an American Special Forces camp at Dak To, located in northern Kontum Province, where the borders of Laos, Cambodia, and South Vietnam meet. The U.S. and South Vietnam Armies committed 16 battalions to the region to counter the enemy resurgence at Kontum and Loc Ninh.

COUNTEROFFENSIVE, PHASE IV (2 April to 30 June 1968). Vietnam War campaign streamer. After the 1968 **Tet Counteroffensive**, U.S. and South Vietnamese forces conducted a number of battalion-size operations against the enemy. On 5 April, Operation Pegasus-Lam Son 207 relieved the Khe Sanh combat base and opened Route 9 for the first time since August 1967. This operation restricted the North Vietnamese Army's use of western Quang Tri Province and inflicted a number of casualties on the remnants of two North Vietnamese divisions withdrawing from the area. This success was followed by a spoiling operation in the A Shau Valley known as Delaware-Lam Son. These two operations prevented the enemy from further attacks on population centers in the northern part of South Vietnam and forced the enemy to shift activities further south. During 5–12 May, the Viet Cong (VC) launched an offensive against Saigon, but the city's defenders stopped the attack well short of its objectives. The small number of VC units that made it into the outskirts of the city were driven out with high losses. By the end of June, friendly forces had decisively blunted the enemy's attacks, inflicted very heavy casualties, and hindered attacks on urban areas throughout the Republic of Vietnam. The strength of the U.S. Army in Vietnam stood at nearly 360,000 soldiers during this campaign.

COUNTEROFFENSIVE, PHASE V (1 July to 1 November 1968). Vietnam War campaign streamer. During this campaign, there was a countrywide effort to restore government control of territory lost to the enemy since the 1968 **Tet Counteroffensive**. The enemy attempted another such offensive on 17–18 August, but those efforts were comparatively feeble and quickly overwhelmed by U.S. and South Vietnamese forces. In the fall, the South Vietnamese government, with major U.S. support, launched an accelerated pacification campaign. All friendly forces were coordinated and brought to bear on the Communist forces. During the pacification operations, friendly units secured a target area, then Vietnamese government units, regional and popular forces, police, and civil authorities screened the inhabitants, seeking to identify members of the Viet Cong (VC) infrastructure. This technique was so successful against the political apparatus that it became the basis for subsequent friendly operations and helped expand South Vietnamese government influence into areas of the countryside previously dominated by the VC.

COUNTEROFFENSIVE, PHASE VI (2 November 1968–22 February 1969). **Vietnam War** campaign streamer. In November 1968, the South Vietnamese government, with American support, began a concentrated effort to expand security in the countryside, although the campaign was characterized as marking time in preparation for a change in American policy. The United States elected Richard M. Nixon president in November 1968 and in early 1969 he announced a new policy that aimed to eventually end combat in Southeast Asia while strengthening South Vietnam's ability to defend itself. Formal truce negotiations began in Paris on 25 January 1969. In spite of the impending policy and peace talks, U.S. and South Vietnamese forces conducted 47 ground combat operations during the campaign.

COUNTEROFFENSIVE, PHASE VII (1 July 1970 to 30 June 1971). Vietnam War campaign streamer. Operation Lam Son 719 was the most significant operation conducted during this campaign. As the withdrawal of American forces continued, South Vietnamese troops, backed by U.S. fire and air support, sought to cut the North Vietnamese supply route known as the Ho Chi Minh Trail and destroy enemy bases in Laos. In early 1971, in preparation for the operation, a brigade of the U.S. Army's Fifth Infantry Division occupied the Khe Sanh area and cleared Route 9 up to the Laotian border, while the U.S. Army's 101st Airborne Division conducted diversionary operations in the A Shau Valley. American engineers had the mission of repairing Route 9 once it was clear. The South Vietnamese began the operation in March, but faced with mounting losses, Lieutenant General Hoang Xuan Lam, the commander of the invasion forces, decided to cut short the operation and ordered a withdrawal. Although rather less than a definite success, the operation forestalled a Communist offensive in the spring of 1971, as North Vietnamese units and replacements were diverted to the fighting.

COWPENS (17 January 1781). Revolutionary War campaign streamer. This battle in northwestern South Carolina is considered a tactical masterpiece by many authorities. **Daniel Morgan**'s 1,100 men decisively defeated a British force of 1,100 under Banastre Tarleton. Tarleton was eager to defeat the last regular American forces in the south and he pressed forward without knowing the number or location of his enemy. Morgan chose to defend a rolling meadow that seemingly would offer Tarleton an opportunity to use the British cavalry to good advantage. Morgan, anticipating that the aggressive Tarleton would attack headlong into his forces, arrayed his soldiers to make the best of their varying capabilities. He positioned his relatively untrained militia in the first two of his three lines of defense and instructed them to take three shots at British officers before falling back through the third line. Morgan's third line consisted of **Continental Army** regulars who could be relied on to hold their positions. Morgan also stationed about 100 horsemen on a small ridge to the rear. When Tarleton launched the attack, his troops moved forward as planned, but when they hit the third line Morgan sent his small force of horsemen into the British right, while the militia, which had reformed after withdrawing in good order, hit the British left. His forces in disarray, Tarleton fled the field. The victory severely reduced the British capability to continue operations in the south.

CRAIG, MALIN (1875–1945). Chief of staff of the army from 1935 to 1939. Born in Missouri, Craig graduated from the **U.S. Military Academy** in 1898. He participated in the **Santiago** campaign in the **Spanish–American War** and in the **China Relief Expedition**. After holding various command and staff positions, including being a student and faculty member at the **Army War College**, he served in the American Expeditionary Force in France during **World War I**. Craig became chief of staff in 1935 and focused attention on army planning and stressed the need for lead time for military preparedness. He retired from active service in 1939, but was recalled in 1941 to head the **secretary of war**'s personnel board. *See also* Appendix 3, Commanding Generals and Chiefs of Staff of the Army.

CRAWFORD, GEORGE WASHINGTON* (1798–1872). Secretary of war from 1849 to 1850. Born in Georgia, Crawford graduated from Princeton College in 1820, studied law, and was admitted to the bar in Augusta. He was active in state politics and was elected in 1843 to the House of Representatives, where he served about a month before resigning to conduct his successful run for governor of Georgia. He became secretary of war in 1849, but resigned the next year, upon the death of President **Zachary Taylor**. In 1861 he chaired the Georgia secession convention. Crawford's cousin, **William Harris Crawford**, also served as secretary of war, from 1815 to 1816. *See also* Appendix 4, Secretaries of War and Secretaries of the Army. (*Crawford's middle name is listed as Walker in some sources.)

CRAWFORD, WILLIAM HARRIS (1772–1834). Secretary of war from August 1815 to October 1816. Crawford was born in Virginia and his family moved to Georgia, where he studied at Carmel Academy in Augusta and eventually began practicing law. He fought two duels, killing his opponent in one and suffering a crippled wrist in the other. Active in state politics, he was elected to the U.S. Senate in 1807 and in 1813 he declined an offer to be secretary of war and served as minister to France. Accepting the position of secretary of war in 1815, he became secretary of the treasury the next year, after losing a bid to be the Republican nominee for president. He remained in that position until 1825, when he declined to remain in office after the election of John Quincy Adams. Crawford had been nominated for president by the congressional caucus in February 1824, but when no candidate received a majority of electoral votes in December, the election was decided in the House of Representatives, where Adams won by a wide margin. Crawford was appointed a judge in Georgia in 1827 and was twice reelected to the post, before dying in office in 1834. Crawford's cousin, **George Washington**

Crawford, also served as secretary of war from 1849 to 1850. *See also* Appendix 4, Secretaries of War and Secretaries of the Army.

CRAZY HORSE (Taschunka-Witko) (ca. 1849–1877). War leader of the Oglala Lakota Sioux. He gained a reputation as a warrior while waging war against other tribes and the U.S. Army. He married a Cheyenne woman and gained an alliance with that tribe. Crazy Horse was an introverted, mystical leader with a great talent for hit-and-run tactics and is best known for his role during the **Little Big Horn** campaign, when on 25 June 1876 he and other Sioux and Cheyenne warriors killed every soldier in Lieutenant Colonel **George Custer's** unit on the banks of the Little Bighorn River in Montana. The Indian victory prompted decisive retaliation and, pursued relentlessly by **Nelson Miles**, Crazy Horse and about 1,000 men, women, and children surrendered on 6 May 1877 at Camp Robinson, Nebraska. He was killed in September while resisting confinement at the post guardhouse. His was buried in an unknown grave on the Plains and is remembered as the greatest of all Sioux leaders.

CREEKS (27 July 1813 to August 1814, February 1836 to July 1837). Indian wars campaign streamer. The first Creek campaign in 1813 and 1814 was part of the **War of 1812**. The Upper Creeks, allied with the British, sacked Fort Mims in Alabama in the summer of 1813 and massacred more than 500 men, women, and children. In March 1814, **Andrew Jackson**, leading a force of about 2,000 regulars, militia, and volunteers, plus several hundred friendly Indians, defeated about 900 Upper Creek warriors at Horseshoe Bend in Alabama to end that campaign. Many Creeks were removed to Indian Territory in 1832 and those who remained in the southeast were removed in 1836–1837. This prompted the second campaign, when Creeks took up arms during the time of the Second **Seminole** War.

CROOK, GEORGE (1829–1890). Army general and Indian fighter. Born in Ohio, Crook graduated from the **U.S. Military Academy** in 1852 and served in California before the **Civil War**. By the end of the war in 1865 he was commanding a corps. He stayed in the army, serving extensively in the western part of the country, where he captured the Apache Indian chief **Cochise** in 1871. He participated in the **Little Big Horn** campaign in 1876 and was later back in Arizona for a campaign against the **Apaches**. In January 1884, the Apache chief **Geronimo** surrendered to him. When Geronimo left the reservation in 1885, Crook pursued him and induced the Apache to once again surrender in 1886. When the federal government would not agree to the terms under which Geronimo surrendered, Crook objected and was replaced by **Nelson A. Miles**. Crook stayed in the army until his death, fighting for the rights of the Apaches, especially his former scouts, whom he believed had been unjustly removed from Arizona.

CUSTER, GEORGE ARMSTRONG (1839–1876). Union **Civil War** general and Indian fighter. Graduating at the bottom of his class at the **U.S. Military Academy** in 1861, he was commissioned in the **cavalry**. He served the first two years of the Civil War as a staff officer, but he received command of a cavalry brigade in 1863. He saw action in a number of Civil War campaigns and was present during the fight at Yellow Tavern during the **Spotsylvania** campaign, when the renowned Confederate cavalry leader J. E. B. Stuart was killed. Although he received **brevet** promotions through the ranks to major general during the war, Custer reverted to his permanent rank and remained in the army as a lieutenant colonel commanding the 7th Cavalry. His introduction to Indian fighting in Kansas resulted in a one-year suspension, but he was recalled in 1868 to lead his regiment in the **Comanche** campaign. In 1876, Custer's 7th Cavalry was part of the force that attacked a large camp of Sioux and Cheyenne Indians during the **Little Big Horn** campaign. He and all the troopers in the five companies under his immediate command were killed. His actions up to and during the battle remain controversial, but his "last stand" has gained lasting fame.

— D —

DAVIS, BENJAMIN OLIVER, JR. (1912–2002). First **African American** lieutenant general in the U.S. military. Born in Washington, D.C., the son of a black Army officer, **Benjamin Oliver Davis Sr.** , the younger Davis attended the University of Chicago, before graduating from the **U.S. Military Academy** in 1936. Refused assignment to the **Army Air Corps** because there were no black aviation units, he was assigned to a black **infantry** regiment. In 1941, when the **War Department** established black aviation units, Davis set up a flight program at Tuskegee, Alabama, commanded the 99th Pursuit Squadron, the first black air unit, and as a colonel flew 60 combat missions in Italy during **World War II**. After the war, he developed the plan to desegregate the U.S. Air Force in 1948 and was promoted to brigadier general in that service in 1954. In 1959, Davis was promoted to major general and six years later he became America's first black lieutenant general. After retiring from the air force, he served in the U.S. Department of Transportation.

DAVIS, BENJAMIN OLIVER, SR. (1880–1970). First **African American** army **general officer**. Born in Washington, D.C., Davis attended Howard University and during the **Spanish–American War** he was a lieutenant in the Eighth U.S. Volunteer **Infantry**. After the war, he enlisted as a private in the 9th **Cavalry** and two years later passed a competitive examination and was commissioned a second lieutenant. As a **commissioned officer**, he served in a variety of assignments, but could not command white officers or soldiers in the segregated army of that era. In 1930, he became the army's first black colonel and a year later he was promoted to brigadier general, making him the army's first black general officer. During **World War II**, he headed a special office in the **Inspector General**'s Department that dealt with racial issues among U.S. troops. He retired in 1948 after 50 years of army service. His son, **Benjamin O. Davis Jr.**, became the U.S. military's first lieutenant general when he was promoted to that grade in the U.S. Air Force in 1965.

DAVIS, DWIGHT FILLEY (1879–1945). Secretary of war from 1925 to 1929. Born in Missouri, Davis attended Smith Academy in St. Louis and graduated from Harvard University in 1900. He established the Davis Cup as an international trophy for tennis. In 1903, he received a law degree from Washington University in St. Louis, where he became active in civic affairs. After holding a variety of municipal positions, he served on the executive committee of the National Municipal League, before attending the Plattsburg Military Camp for businessmen in 1915. He served on the Rockefeller War Relief Committee before entering the army, where he participated in the **St. Mihiel** and **Meuse–Argonne** campaigns in **World War I**. After the war, Davis was the director of the War Finance Corporation and then assistant secretary of war. Appointed secretary of war on 14 October 1925, he was in office when the army began experimenting with mechanized forces. After leaving office, he was governor general of the Philippines and he became the director general of the Army Specialist Corps in 1942. *See also* Appendix 4, Secretaries of War and Secretaries of the Army.

DAVIS, JEFFERSON (1808–1889). Secretary of war from 7 March 1853 to 6 March 1857. Born in Kentucky, Davis moved with his family to Mississippi. He graduated from the **U.S. Military Academy** in 1828 and saw service in the **Black Hawk** campaign before resigning his commission in 1835, when he eloped with the daughter of his commander, **Zachary Taylor**. She died shortly after the wedding and Davis returned to Mississippi to become a cotton planter on a plantation he received from an older brother. Davis served in the House of Representatives in 1845, but resigned the next year to become the colonel of the First Mississippi Rifles. He led the regiment in the **Mexican War**, where he was wounded at **Buena Vista**, and returned home a hero. After the war, he was appointed to fill a Senate seat, from which he resigned in 1851 for what proved to be an unsuccessful run for governor of Mississippi. President Franklin Pierce appointed him secretary of war in 1853 and he held this post during Pierce's entire presidency. During his time in office, Davis adopted improved rifled muskets for the **infantry**, sponsored army map and route surveys west of the Mississippi River, and obtained four new regiments for the **regular army**. In 1857 he was elected to the U.S. Senate from Mississippi.

In January 1861, when Mississippi announced its secession from the union, Davis resigned from the Senate and was given command of the state's militia as a major general. The next month, the provisional Confederate congress elected him president. He was elected by popular vote in November and inaugurated as president of the Confederate States of America at Richmond, Virginia, in February 1862. With his military education and experience, Davis was closely involved with the organization and strategy of the Confederate Army during the **Civil War**, and he believed that the outnumbered Southern forces should protect their territory rather than attempt to destroy opposing armies. The strategy was ultimately overwhelmed by simultaneous advances by a number of larger, better-supplied Union armies. Although some criticized Davis for defending some of the Confederacy's nonperforming generals, he showed excellent judgment in selecting **Robert E. Lee** to command the Army of Northern Virginia. When Lee surrendered at **Appomattox** in April 1865 against Davis's wishes, the president fled Richmond only to be captured in Georgia by Union forces and held prisoner at Fort Monroe, Virginia, for treason. Released in 1867, he returned to Mississippi, where he wrote his autobiography, steadfastly refusing to take an oath of allegiance to the United States. In 1978, Congress restored his U.S. citizenship. *See also* Appendix 4, Secretaries of War and Secretaries of the Army.

D-DAY. A term that designates the day on which a combat attack or operation is to be initiated when the exact date has not yet been determined or is to be kept secret. Detailed planning for large-scale operations begins long before specific dates are set, so planners designate the dates for the various phases or steps in relation to D-day, where "D" stands for the first day of the operation. When used in combination with figures and plus or minus signs, it indicates the number of days before or after D-day. For example, "D-3" means three days before the scheduled start date, while "D+3" means three days after D-day. One of the army's earliest uses of the term is in Field Order Number 9, First Army, American Expeditionary Forces, dated 7 September 1918: "The First Army will attack at H hour on D day with the object of forcing the evacuation of the **St. Mihiel** Salient." In **World War II**, D-day for the Allied invasion of **Normandy** was 6 June 1944, and since then that day has been popularly referred to as D-Day.

DEARBORN, HENRY (1715–1829). Secretary of war from 1801 to 1809 and **commanding general of the army** from 1812 to 1815. Born in New Hampshire, Dearborn studied medicine and began practice as a physician in 1772. He was elected captain of a military company in 1775 and participated in the **Boston** campaign. After serving in various military positions during the **Revolutionary War**, Dearborn returned to private life in Maine and represented the state in the U.S. House of Representatives from 1793 to 1797. While secretary, he helped plan the removal of the Indians beyond the Mississippi and founded Fort Dearborn, which became the city of Chicago. While the senior officer in the army, he commanded the northeastern theater in the **War of 1812**, where he led the expedition that captured Fort Toronto in 1813 during the **Canada** campaign. *See also* Appendix 3, Commanding Generals and Chiefs of Staff of the Army; Appendix 4, Secretaries of War and Secretaries of the Army.

DECKER, GEORGE HENRY (1902–1980). Chief of staff of the army from 1960 to 1962. Born in New York, Decker graduated from Lafayette College in Pennsylvania in 1924 and was commissioned a second lieutenant through the **Reserve Officers' Training Corps** program. He served in a variety of command and staff positions before participating in **World War II**. He became chief of staff in 1960 and while in office he supervised expansion of the army to 16 divisions. He retired from active service in 1962. *See also* Appendix 3, Commanding Generals and Chiefs of Staff of the Army.

DEFENSE (8 March to 24 December 1965). Vietnam War campaign streamer. During this early campaign of the war, the U.S. objective was to hold off the enemy while building base camps and logistical facilities. American support in the five northernmost provinces was primarily a U.S. Marine Corps responsibility, while the U.S. Army operated mainly in the central highlands, adjacent coastal regions, and the area around Saigon. South Vietnamese troops retained primary responsibility for the Mekong Delta region of the country. The most significant operation in the campaign took place in the Ia Drang Valley. In November 1965, elements of the army's 1st Cavalry Division made a helicopter assault into the valley to prevent the North Vietnamese Army (NVA) from splitting South Vietnam in two. Taking advantage of an overwhelming advantage in artillery fire and air support, the assault routed two NVA regiments and forced them back into sanctuaries in Cambodia. Although considered a success, the victory was marred when remnants of the NVA regiments ambushed a U.S. battalion and inflicted considerable casualties, including 234 killed in action. The battle marked a shift in strategy for both sides. The North Vietnamese moved from relying on the irregular Viet Cong forces to using the more conventional forces of the NVA. For the United States, it was the beginning of increased participation in combat and the widespread use of **helicopters** to prosecute the ground war.

DEFENSE OF SAUDI ARABIA (2 August 1990 to 16 January 1991). Persian Gulf War campaign streamer. Known also as Desert Shield. On 2 August 1990 Iraq, under the leadership of **Saddam Hussein**, invaded and occupied its smaller neighbor, Kuwait. As Iraq consolidated its gains in Kuwait, there was widespread fear that the attack would continue south into Saudi Arabia. There was considerable sympathy in the world over the fate of Kuwait, but because the area around the Persian Gulf contains over half of the world's known oil reserves, the industrial nations of the world saw the threat to Saudi Arabia as a greater problem. The United States moved quickly to form a coalition of nations to oppose the Iraqi action, providing both the political and military leadership for the campaign. By the end of August the first American military ground forces, U.S. Marines and the army's 82d Airborne Division, commanded by U.S. Army general **H. Norman Schwarzkopf Jr.**, were in Saudi Arabia, ready to fight, with more marines and three army divisions on the way.

The first phase of the campaign was complete by October 1990, by which time adequate combat power was in place to defend Saudi Arabia. The second phase of the campaign was to move enough combat power into the area to force Iraq out of Kuwait. By early 1991, the army had moved three more heavy divisions into the theater of operations, two of which were from its forces stationed in Germany. During the coalition's buildup of forces, Iraq made no moves against Saudi Arabia. The early decision to go on the defensive in Kuwait indicates that Saddam Hussein either had no real intentions of moving into Saudi Arabia or did not understand that it would take time for the coalition to build a viable defensive force. He gave up the military initiative and went into a passive, positional defensive, offering not the slightest challenge to the buildup going on against him. Iraq could have exacted some damage and casualties early in the coalition's buildup, which might have caused the participating nations to reconsider their support. By the end of the campaign, the army had almost 300,000 soldiers in the Persian Gulf area, ready to participate in the liberation of Kuwait. *See also* LIBERATION AND DEFENSE OF KUWAIT.

DEPARTMENT OF THE ARMY. The executive agency that controls and manages the army. The department is headed by a civilian secretary who is appointed by the president and approved by Congress. From 1789 until 1947, the **War Department** provided civilian direction to the army. When the **National Security Act of 1947** created a new military establishment for the United States, the War Department became the Department of the Army, one of the three military departments in the Department of Defense; the other two are the Department of the Navy and the Department of the Air Force. At the same time, the **secretary of war** became the **secretary of the army** and the office lost its cabinet level status when the secretary of defense assumed that role.

DERN, GEORGE HENRY (1872–1936). Secretary of war from 1933 to 1936. Born in Nebraska, Dern attended public schools before graduating from Fremont Normal College in Fremont, Nebraska, in 1888. He attended the University of Nebraska before entering the mining business, in which he became general manager of the Consolidated Mercur Gold Mines Corporation. He was instrumental in developing several important mining processes, including the Holt-Dern roaster oven. He represented Utah in the U.S. Senate and served several years as governor of the state before becoming secretary of war in 1933. While in office, he supervised the army's role in the **Civilian Conservation Corps**, approved the procurement of 2,320 airplanes, and inaugurated several projects for the **Corps of Engineers**. He died while in office. *See also* Appendix 4, Secretaries of War and Secretaries of the Army.

DESERT SHIELD. *See* DEFENSE OF SAUDI ARABIA.

DESERT STORM. *See* LIBERATION AND DEFENSE OF KUWAIT.

DEXTER, SAMUEL (1761–1816). Secretary of war from 1800 to 1801. Born in Massachusetts, Dexter studied under the Reverend Aaron Putnam before attending Harvard University, where he graduated in 1781. He studied law at Worcester, was admitted to the bar in 1784, and practiced in several locations before settling at Charlestown, Massachusetts, in 1788. He served in the U.S. House of Representatives and Senate and wrote the memorial eulogy for **George Washington** in December 1799. After serving as secretary of war, he became secretary of the treasury for about a year before returning to private life and the practice of law. Remaining active in politics, he declined a special mission to the court of Spain for President James Monroe and ran unsuccessfully for governor of Massachusetts. An ardent supporter of temperance, Dexter headed its first formal organization in Massachusetts. *See also* Appendix 4, Secretaries of War and Secretaries of the Army.

DICKINSON, JACOB McGAVOCK (1851–1928). Secretary of war from 1909 to 1911. Born in Mississippi, Dickinson enlisted in the Confederate cavalry at the age of 14. He moved with his family to Tennessee after the **Civil War** and graduated from the University of Nashville in 1871. He received a master's degree the next year and studied law at Columbia University. Continuing his studies in Europe at Leipzig and Paris, he was admitted to the Tennessee bar in 1876. He was active in bar associations and was an attorney for several railroads before becoming the secretary of war in 1909. While in office Dickinson suggested that Congress consider stopping the pay of soldiers rendered unfit for duty as a result of venereal disease or alcoholism, as a means of combating those problems. After leaving office, he helped prosecute the U.S. Steel Corporation in 1913 and was active in several labor cases. *See also* Appendix 4, Secretaries of War and Secretaries of the Army.

DISTINGUISHED SERVICE CROSS. The second highest medal for valor awarded to members of the army, recognizing bravery that falls short of that required for the **Medal of Honor**. It was established by order of President Woodrow Wilson on 2 January 1918 and confirmed by Congress 9 July 1918 to be awarded to members of the U.S. Army serving after 6 April 1917 who distinguish themselves by "extraordinary heroism in connection with military operations against an opposing armed force." *See also* PURPLE HEART; SILVER STAR.

DIVISION. The army's basic combined arms organization. A division consists of several **brigades** or **regiments** plus a number of supporting **battalions** and **companies**. The division is usually the smallest army organization designed to fight independently, and the composition and size of divisions varies depending on its intended mission. A heavy division usually has a large numbers of **tanks** and other **armored** vehicles, while a light division primarily has dismounted **infantry** forces.

The army has used divisions for more than 220 years on the battlefield, but they have been permanent parts of its force structure only since **World War I**. Although ad hoc divisions were occasionally used prior to the **Civil War**, that conflict was the first in which the nation fielded large armies. Both the Union and the Confederate armies used divisions as command-and-control headquarters. In 1916, prompted by the war in Europe, Congress passed a **National Defense Act** that authorized the formation of divisions in peacetime. The **War Department** produced tables of organization for a division in 1917 and, in May of that year, the First Expeditionary Division was formed in New York. In August, after deploying to France, it was designated the 1st Infantry Division; it remains on active duty as the army's oldest and most highly decorated division, having seen service in World War I, **World War II**, the **Vietnam War**, and the **Persian Gulf War**.

Over the years, the organization and structure of army divisions have changed periodically. In the 1950s the army developed a division with five battle groups designed to fight on a nuclear battlefield. Combining pentagon (for five) and atomic, it was known as the Pentomic division. In order to give its divisions more tactical flexibility, the army adopted the ROAD (Reorganization Objective Army Divisions) division in the 1960s. The ROAD division had three brigades that could be task organized according to the mission by changing the number and types of battalions.

The types and designations of the army's divisions have changed with the requirements of national defense, while the number of divisions has increased during periods of crisis and war and decreased in peacetime. Divisions' designations have included air assault, **airborne**, armored, **cavalry**, and infantry. At one time, the designations reflected the organization of the division, but today the designations for the active divisions are largely traditional. For example, the 1st Cavalry Division, presently structured as an armored division, has also been organized as an air assault, cavalry, and infantry division at various times in its history. *See also* CORPS.

DOCTRINE. The condensed expression of an army's approach to fighting. Doctrine must be rooted in time-tested theories and principles, but be forward looking and adaptable to changes in technology, threats, and missions. For the U.S. Army, the land force of a global power, doctrine must be definitive to guide operations, yet versatile to accommodate a wide variety of situations worldwide. To be useful, it must be uniformly known and understood by the army's soldiers and officers. The U.S. Army publishes its doctrine in field manuals known by the acronym FM. The army's principles of war, published in a number of its field manuals, are an example of doctrine. The writings of two nineteenth-century theorists, **Carl von Clausewitz** and **Antoine-Henri Jomini**, have had considerable influence on the army's doctrine and the doctrinal thinking of its officers.

The army's doctrine for planning and conducting operations is generally applicable worldwide, but it leaves room for local adaptation and individual initiative, a characteristic reminiscent of the colonial experience of learning to fight an unconventional force on unfamiliar terrain. The army's desire to use technology to best advantage stems from the American light infantry's early use of the rifle, with its spiral groves, or rifling, in the barrel (which caused the musket ball to spin, giving it greater range and accuracy), when European armies were still armed with smooth-bore muskets. The army's concern for preserving its manpower by using firepower and fortifications whenever possible stems from the earliest militia, which were composed of friends and neighbors who cared about those fighting alongside them in the ranks. In most of America's wars, firepower has been preferred over ground assaults. During the **Civil War**, entrenched positions made frontal attacks very costly in manpower. That experience impressed upon the army leadership the importance of firepower and mobile warfare,

The army entered **World War I** after the French and British had been fighting a long defensive war in which the trenches on both sides made offensive operations very deadly, in spite of **artillery** bombardments that lasted for days in some cases. Accepting the need for learning to fight in the trenches, the army also trained its soldiers with an offensive doctrine for fighting mobile warfare. While the army's offensive doctrine worked in the closing months of the war, when the Allies were fighting an exhausted and demoralized enemy, the machine gun in combination with fortified defensive positions severely restricted mobile warfare. It took the **tank** to once again open the battlefields to offensive tactics. In World War II, the army fielded **armored** forces that employed a doctrine of mobile warfare with great success in Europe. During the **Cold War**, the army continued to develop doctrine that centered on central Europe.

But the heavy forces and mobile warfare doctrine that proved so effective in World War II in Europe were of little use in the jungles that covered the battlefields of the **Vietnam War**. To cope with the dispersed enemy and difficult environment, the army used **helicopters** for transport and fire support and developed a doctrine for airmobile warfare. After the U.S. made its ignoble withdrawal from Vietnam, the army reevaluated its doctrine and once again focused on its heavy armored forces stationed in Germany. The result was AirLand Battle, doctrine designed for defeat of Soviet forces on the so-called plains of Europe, but adaptable to fighting a wide variety of opponents in many areas of the world. The doctrine was the result of 75 years of thought, experimentation, and reflection on the army's experiences in peace and war in the twentieth century. The AirLand Battle concept was used with great success during the **Persian Gulf War**. *See also* ARMY VALUES; PRINCIPLES OF WAR; OPERATIONAL ART;. STRATEGY; TACTICS.

DOMINICAN REPUBLIC (28 April 1965 to 21 September 1966). Armed forces expedition campaign streamer. In April 1965, a military revolt in the Dominican Republic attempted to overthrow the constitutional government. As the two sides battled for control, the United States monitored the situation. As the crisis escalated, U.S. president Lyndon B. Johnson sent U.S. Army and Marine forces into the country to protect American nationals and ensure that Communist forces did not gain control of the island nation. By early May, some 23,000 American soldiers and marines were in the Dominican Republic. Although the initial deployment of forces was a unilateral action, the United States put pressure on the Organization of American States to send troops and six nations—Brazil, Costa Rica, El Salvador, Honduras, Nicaragua, and Paraguay—eventually contributed forces. A Brazilian, Lieutenant General Hugo Panasco Alvim, was named commander of the multinational force, even though the largest contingent by far was from the United States. Lieutenant General **Bruce Palmer Jr.** , the American ground force commander, was named Alvim's deputy. U.S. forces began to withdraw shortly after the arrival of the Latin American troops and, by the end of 1965, only three U.S. Army battalions remained in the country. After elections in the Dominican Republic in mid-1966, all of the intervention forces departed, with the last ones leaving in September 1966.

DOUGHTY, JOHN (1754–1826). Commanding general of the army for a brief time in 1784. Born in New York City, Doughty served in various military positions from 1776 to 1798. He participated in the **Brandywine, Germantown, Monmouth**, and **Yorktown** campaigns as the commander of the New York State **artillery** company, the same unit commanded earlier by **Alexander Hamilton**. Doughty became a **brevet** major in 1784, making him the senior officer in the army when it was reduced to 80 men. He conducted negotiations with various Indian tribes, declined an appointment to lieutenant colonel, and left the army in 1791. Doughty became a brigadier general of artillery in the New Jersey militia and in 1798 was appointed a lieutenant colonel in the army when war with France threatened. He resigned shortly thereafter and returned to private life on his estate in New Jersey. *See also* Appendix 3, Commanding Generals and Chiefs of Staff of the Army.

DRAGOONS. Mounted **infantry** who rode horses but dismounted to fight on foot. The **Continental Army** had units of dragoons during the **Revolutionary War**, but it was not until 1833 that Congress authorized a mounted regiment in the army. In 1861 that regiment, the 1st Dragoons, became the 1st Cavalry as the army reorganized its mounted forces for the **Civil War**.

DUNAWAY, GEORGE W. (1922–). Sergeant major of the army from 1968 to 1970. Born in Virginia, Dunaway left school after the 10th grade to help support his family, but later earned his high-school equivalency diploma at Fort Benning, Georgia. In 1940 he joined the Virginia National Guard and in 1941 became a member of the **regular army** when his division entered federal service. He volunteered for **airborne** training in 1943 and fought in Belgium and Germany during the **Ardennes–Alsace** campaign of **World War II**. After the war, he remained in the army and by 1952 was a sergeant major. He was the **command sergeant major** in a variety of airborne units and served twice in the **Vietnam War** before becoming the sergeant major of the army in 1968. During his tenure, the army instituted the command sergeant major program and established the **Sergeants Major Academy**. Dunaway retired on 30 September 1970, after 30 years of active service in the army. *See also* Appendix 5, Sergeants Major of the Army

— E —

EAST INDIES (1 January to 22 July 1942). World War II campaign streamer. The Japanese attacks on Pearl Harbor and the **Philippine Islands** on 7 and 8 December prompted the Allies to form a new command to coordinate operations in the Pacific, the American-British-Dutch-Australian Command (ABDACOM), with Lieutenant General Sir Archibald Wavell, a British officer, commanding. In an attempt to slow the southward advance of Japanese forces, Wavell frantically transferred any available Allied units into the western Pacific. Among those forces was the U.S. Army's 26th Field Artillery Brigade, which was aboard a convoy en route to the Philippines that had departed Pearl Harbor just before the Japanese attack. The convoy changed course after the attack, heading for Australia, and arrived on

22 December in Brisbane, where the brigade's regiments and battalions were designated to occupy defensive positions along the Malay Barrier defensive line. On 11 January, the 2d Battalion, 131st Field Artillery, arrived on the island of Java in the Netherlands East Indies, where Wavell had established his headquarters.

In February 1942, the western anchor of the ABDACOM defensive line began to collapse. The British surrendered Singapore on 16 February and the Japanese were pushing British and Indian troops out of Burma. On 19 February, Japanese troops landed on Bali, just east of Java, and on the 25th Wavell disbanded ABDACOM. During the last two days of February, Japanese naval forces cleared the seas around Java of Allied ships and then landed forces at three different locations on the island. Although the Allied forces on Java mounted a spirited defense, the Japanese forces were overwhelming. On 8 March, Lieutenant General Hein ter Poorten, a Dutch officer commanding the Allied forces on Java, surrendered to the Japanese. Troops under Poorten's command included the 2d Battalion, 131st Field Artillery, from the Texas National Guard, which had entered federal service in November 1940. The Texas artillerymen were taken prisoner on Java and shipped to northern Burma, where they spent the rest of the war in heavy labor gangs working on the Burma-Thailand railway. Out of touch with Allied units, the Texas unit became known as the "Lost Battalion," until late 1945, when three hundred survivors were finally liberated by Allied forces in Thailand. The battalion was the only U.S. Army unit to participate in ground combat in the East Indies campaign. See also BURMA; CENTRAL PACIFIC; PHILIPPINE ISLANDS.

EASTERN MANDATES (31 January to 14 June 1944). World War II campaign streamer. By the end of 1943, the Allies were on the offensive against Japan in the Pacific and making progress along two routes of advance, one in the **Central Pacific** under Admiral Chester Nimitz and the other in the Southwest Pacific under General **Douglas MacArthur**. One important objective of the Central Pacific advance was to capture the Mariana Islands, from which the American long-range B-29 Superfortress bombers could strike at the heart of Japan. In November 1943 the Allies seized Tarawa and Makin in the Gilbert Islands during the Central Pacific campaign and, in January and February 1944, Nimitz took the next step toward the Marianas by moving to the Eastern Mandates, better known as the Marshall Islands, located some 565 nautical miles north of the Gilberts. After the securing of Tarawa and Makin, U.S. warplanes could now carry out combat and photographic missions deep within Japanese occupied territory. Nimitz surprised the Japanese by making the first move against Kwajalein Atoll, located inside the Marshalls, rather than beginning at the outer islands. On 1 February 1944, an army force landed on Kwajalein Island, in the southern part of the atoll, while U.S. Marines invaded the islands of Roi and Namur in the northern part. Within days, Nimitz's soldiers and marines had secured the atoll. After this early success, a naval task force moved 340 miles with one army and one marine regiment to capture a Japanese air base on Engebi in the Eniwetok Atoll on 19 February 1944. After capturing Eniwetok, the marines secured the more lightly defended islands in the Marshalls and isolated the more heavily garrisoned Japanese bases. The campaign ended on 14 June 1944, but U.S. ships and planes conducted operations against the Japanese from bases in the Marshall Islands until the end of the war. Capturing the bases also opened the way for the **Western Pacific** campaign.

EATON, JOHN HENRY (1790–1856). Secretary of war from 1829 to 1831. Born in North Carolina, Eaton attended the University of North Carolina and later studied law. He was a private soldier in the War of 1812. His first wife was a ward of **Andrew Jackson** and Eaton wrote a biography of the general that was published in 1817. In 1818 he was appointed to fill a vacant seat in the U.S. Senate from Tennessee and he was later elected in his own right and served until 1829. Eaton's appointment as secretary of war caused a stir among several cabinet wives because he had recently married the widow of a seaman and the other cabinet wives believed her unsuitable for Washington society. The controversy concerning Eaton's wife helped rupture the cabinet, and Eaton resigned from the post in 1831. While in office, Eaton made the topographical engineers a separate bureau and advocated compensation for soldiers who were discharged honorably. After leaving office, he was defeated in a reelection bid for the Senate, served a term as governor of Florida, and was minister to Spain for four years. *See also* Appendix 4, Secretaries of War and Secretaries of the Army.

EGYPT–LIBYA (11 June 1942 to 12 February 1943). World War II campaign streamer. When the United States entered World War II in December 1941, the British had been fighting the German and Italian armies in the Western Desert of Egypt and Libya for over a year. Initially, the British had enjoyed success in countering an Italian offensive in 1940, but when German forces entered North Africa in support of their Italian allies, British fortunes suffered severe reversals. Field Marshal **Erwin Rommel's** rapid and unexpected offensive in March 1941 almost drove the British out of North Africa. Recognizing that a British collapse would have far-reaching implications, American planners began preparing to send air power to the Middle East in January 1942.

In June 1942, the army moved 23 B-24D Liberator heavy bombers to Egypt. Their first mission was a surprise raid on the oil refineries in Ploesti, Rumania, to upset German preparations for their expected summer offensive against the Soviet Union. The raid did relatively little physical damage, but it was the first time American bombers hit a strategic target in Europe and it had a significant psychological impact not unlike the Doolittle raid flown against Japan in April 1942. Plans for further raids into Europe from the base in Egypt were halted when continued German successes in North Africa made it necessary for U.S. bombers to fly in Egypt in support of the British and led to the creation of the U.S. Army Forces in the Middle East in June 1942, a command that encompassed both North Africa and Iran. There were plans to send as many as 6,000 American support troops to the new command, but there were no plans to send any ground combat units. More air combat units were provided to the theater, but in late 1942, preparations for the **Algeria–French** Morocco campaign took priority and slowed the flow of American soldiers to Egypt. By the end of 1942, only about half of the planned construction projects for the Allied support infrastructure in Egypt had been completed, and by that time British combat forces had regained the initiative. With the success of the **Tunisia** campaign, the Allies drove the Germans out of Libya in February 1943, ending the Egypt–Libya campaign. Although the U.S. Army provided no ground combat troops during the campaign, the close coordination between American and British staffs set the tone for Anglo-American cooperation for the rest of the war. *See also* AIR OFFENSIVE, EUROPE; AIR OFFENSIVE, JAPAN.

EISENHOWER, DWIGHT DAVID (1890–1969). Chief of staff of the army from 1945 to 1948 and 34th president of the United States. Born in Texas, Eisenhower moved with his family to Abilene the year after he was born. He attended public schools and graduated from the **U.S. Military Academy** in 1915. During **World War I**, he commanded the army **tank** training center at Camp Colt near Gettysburg, Pennsylvania. After the war, he rose slowly through the ranks, holding staff positions under some of the army's most influential officers, including **John J. Pershing** and **Douglas MacArthur**. Eisenhower earned a reputation as a strategist and the chief of staff of the army, George C. Marshall, assigned him to the War Plans Division of the **general staff** in 1942. In June of that year Eisenhower was appointed to command U.S. forces in Europe and led the invasion forces in North Africa, **Sicily**, and Italy. He was appointed supreme commander of allied forces in Europe in January 1944 and he oversaw the landings at **Normandy** on 6 June 1944.

During **World War II**, Eisenhower was criticized by both Americans and allies. U.S. critics saw his rapid rise to high command in spite of having no combat experience as a function of his genial manner, while the British questioned his strategy for invading Germany. But Eisenhower had learned the lessons of history well, having studied the art of war under leading American strategists between the world wars. He advocated a broad advance across the Ruhr industrial heartland rather than the narrow thrust to Berlin the British preferred. Eisenhower stayed with his plan and, since the war, historians have generally agreed that it was the correct approach. While he had setbacks, most notably the American defeat at the Kasserine Pass during the **Tunisia** campaign of 1943 and during the Battle of the Bulge in the **Ardennes–Alsace** campaign in late 1944, he was extremely successful as a commander of large modern military forces during the war. Promoted to **general of the army** in December 1944, Eisenhower accepted Germany's unconditional surrender in May 1945 and returned to the United States to become chief of staff of the army.

While chief of staff, Eisenhower oversaw the army's demobilization effort, cautioned against excessive reduction in the size of the U.S. armed forces, supported the unification of the services under the Department of Defense, and reorganized the army to decentralize many functions. His best-selling memoir, *Cru-*

sade in Europe, was published in 1948, the same year he retired from the army to become president of Columbia University. In 1950, he was recalled to active duty to become the supreme allied commander Europe in the newly formed North Atlantic Treaty Organization. In May 1952, he again retired and announced his candidacy for president of the United States. Elected by a wide margin, he served two terms as president and retired to private life in 1961. During his presidency, Eisenhower was a firm believer in the traditional separation of powers for the federal government and he left most of the problems of postwar America to his designated subordinates or Congress. In retrospect, Eisenhower's is generally considered one of the most successful presidencies in the modern era. *See also* Appendix 3, Commanding Generals and Chiefs of Staff of the Army; COLD WAR.

ELKINS, STEPHEN BENTON (1841–1911). Secretary of war from 1891 to 1893. Born in Ohio, Elkins moved with his family to Missouri in the mid-1840s, graduated from the University of Missouri in 1860, and taught school. He was a captain in the Missouri militia on the Union side during the **Civil War**, when a former student, the outlaw Cole Younger, helped Elkins escape from the notorious Quantrill's Raiders. Elkins was admitted to the bar in 1864 and he moved to New Mexico to begin a practice. While there, he was active in politics and served as district attorney for the territory. He was the founder and first president of the Santa Fe National Bank and pursued business interests in land, rail, mining, and finance. In about 1890, he moved to Elkins, West Virginia, a town he had founded some time earlier and where he had considerable rail and coal interests. He served as secretary of war for about 16 months, from December 1891 to March 1893. After leaving office, he represented West Virginia in the Senate, serving from 1895 until his death in 1911. *See also* Appendix 4, Secretaries of War and Secretaries of the Army.

ENDICOTT, WILLIAM CROWNINSHIELD (1826–1900). Secretary of war from 1885 to 1889. Born in Massachusetts, Endicott attended Salem Latin School and graduated from Harvard University in 1847. He graduated from Harvard Law School in 1850 and formed a law firm. Active in local politics, he served as a justice of the Massachusetts Supreme Court from 1873 to 1882 and ran unsuccessfully for governor of Massachusetts in 1884, before becoming secretary of war in 1885. While in office, Endicott was a member of the board on fortifications, proposed legislation that would have required army officers to pass examinations to be promoted, and requested Congress to authorize the Public Printer to publish **War Department** records. After returning to private life, he remained active in various academic endeavors in Boston, until his death in 1900. *See also* Appendix 4, Secretaries of War and Secretaries of the Army.

ENGINEERS. *See* CORPS OF ENGINEERS.

ENLISTED. Soldiers who are not **commissioned officers** or **warrant officers** are enlisted. Enlisted soldiers with the rank of corporal and above are **noncommissioned**

officers. In the army's early years, enlisted soldiers generally led a physically arduous, dirty, and thankless life, with little training and virtually no opportunity for advancement. Duties during peacetime were dull and required little talent. With the rapid changes in technology since the beginning of the twentieth century, the need for technicians and maintenance personnel has greatly enhanced the lot of the enlisted soldier. In the early 1950s, the army established service schools for enlisted soldiers, giving them the opportunity to receive professional training and education throughout their career. The highest grade for enlisted soldiers is **sergeant major.** *See also* Appendix 8, United States Army Rank Insignia.

EUSTIS, WILLIAM (1753–1825). Secretary of war from 1809 to 1813. Born in Massachusetts, Eustis studied at Boston Latin School and in 1772 graduated from Harvard College. He studied medicine and helped care for the wounded at Bunker Hill during the **Boston** campaign. During the **Revolutionary War,** he served as the surgeon of an **artillery** regiment and as a hospital surgeon. After the war, Eustis entered medical practice in Boston and served as surgeon with the Shay's Rebellion expedition. He became active in politics and he served two terms in the U.S. House of Representatives, from 1801 to 1804. As secretary of war, he tried to prepare the army for the **War of 1812,** but he resigned after being severely criticized for army reverses on the battlefield. After leaving office, he became minister to Holland in 1814 and returned home because of poor health in 1818. He served again in the House of Representatives and was governor of Massachusetts for two terms before his death while in office. *See also* Appendix 4, Secretaries of War and Secretaries of the Army.

— F —

FIELD ARTILLERY. Branch of the army. In 1968 the traditional **artillery** branch was separated into field artillery and air defense artillery. Although cannons first came to America with the earliest colonial settlers, it was the **Revolutionary War** that spurred interest in exploiting their capabilities. The field artillery traces its origins to the Continental Army when, under the leadership of **Henry Knox,** the army used a wide variety of artillery pieces, including light cannons as field artillery and heavier pieces for garrison and coastal defense. Today, the oldest unit in the active army is the 1st Battalion, 5th Field Artillery, which perpetuates the artillery company **Alexander Hamilton** commanded during the Revolutionary War.

Although the majority of the **War of 1812** was fought on water, Americans used artillery in several ground engagements. In July 1814, American artillery, supporting the charge of General **Winfield Scott's** brigade at **Chippewa,** was faster and more accurate than the British artillery. By the **Mexican War,** American artillery was much more developed than that of the Mexican Army and it therefore played a key role in most of the major battles of that conflict, with the artillery frequently firing from the front lines. During the Battle of **Palo Alto**, the U.S. Army, facing a Mexican Army twice its size, won the day through the use of its superior artillery. The American artillery outranged the Mexicans, while the Mexican cavalry found itself exposed to grape and canister shot and cannonball, with no support from the Mexican guns. Artillery played a vital role in the battles of **Monterrey** and **Buena Vista**. The field artillery's nickname "Redlegs" came from this era, when artillery uniforms had a two-inch stripe on the trousers and horse artillerymen wore red canvas leggings.

With the appearance of the rifled musket, artillery became more of a defensive weapon during the **Civil War** as the infantry could easily outrange the cannons. As their cannons were forced off the front lines, artillerymen developed techniques for massing fires from positions to the rear of the infantry. Artillery played an important role in many Civil War battles. Union field artillery devastated Confederate forces at **Gettysburg**. In the three-day battle, the two sides suffered a total of 51,000 casualties, the bulk of which were caused by Union artillery. The Civil War fostered a change for employment of artillery. In the latter part of the nineteenth century, technology dramatically improved artillery effectiveness with such innovations as smokeless powder, cartridge ammunition, and breech-loading cannons. Smokeless powder increased ranges over black powder, while cartridge ammunition and breech-loading gave the guns a higher rate of fire.

World War I introduced the U.S. Army to the famous "French 75," a 75-mm cannon provided by the French in exchange for raw materials. The war raised artillery to a new level of importance on the battlefield with the development of a variety of new techniques and devices of destruction. Preparation fires before the ground assault lasted anywhere from four hours to 16 days. The **St. Mihiel** salient, which the Germans had held for years, was sealed off by American troops, as some 3,000 guns of 26 calibers and 46 models poured 74 types of ammunition into the salient for almost five hours before the attack. Altogether, 838,019 rounds of ammunition, including high explosives, smoke, and nonpersistent gas, were expended in a single battle. The introduction of the chemical shell, the appearance of massive and effectively controlled artillery barrages, and aerial observation were among the most significant artillery advances of World War I. Artillery established itself as the greatest killer on the battlefield, inflicting more than 75 percent of the casualties.

During the interwar years, the army developed a variety of towed and self-propelled artillery, and the American industrial base was able to produce the vast numbers needed for **World War II**. There were numerous improvements in artillery weapons during the war. Some improvements were based upon experiences of World War I, while others were the natural outcome of scientific progress. The new 155-mm howitzer appeared in 1942. The 8-inch howitzer was in action and the 240-mm howitzer soon followed. The introduction of self-propelled artillery increased the mobility and changed the employment tactics of artillery on the battlefield. The 1950s brought continued improvements as the army added long-range cannon, rocket, and guided missile artillery capable of firing nuclear and conventional warheads at longer ranges with greater accuracy. The **Korean War** was a chaotic and difficult environment for American artillery. Classical front lines disappeared and artillery units often found themselves surrounded, as artillerymen were called upon to fight side by side with the infantry. Artillery was used to perform rear-guard actions. To make up for their lack of artillery, the Chinese made American battery positions their prime targets. Batteries had to fight off invaders in close combat and still fire their guns in support of the combat operations.

The **Vietnam War** saw another change in artillery tactics. Front lines common in previous wars were replaced by perimeter defenses, while the **helicopter** gave artillery increased mobility. Artillery units occupied fire-support bases and could fire 360 degrees in support of operations. The ability of the artillery to provide rapid and devastating fire support at critical times often spelled the difference between victory and defeat. During the **Persian Gulf War**, the army's multiple launched rocket system provided overwhelming fire support during the ground campaign. Artillery advances in target acquisition, weapon design, fire direction by computer, and laser locators also made significant contributions to the coalition victory. *See also* BRANCHES OF THE ARMY.

FIELD FORCE. The designation for a **corps** equivalent headquarters used during the **Vietnam War**.

FINANCE CORPS. Branch of the army. It originated on 16 June 1775, when the Second Continental Congress appointed a paymaster general of the army. In 1816, the pay department became a separate department and paymasters, usually with the rank of major, had the principal duty of paying soldiers in the regiments. The department remained unchanged until 1912, when it joined the quartermaster corps. During **World War I**, the quartermaster corps had difficulty controlling disbursing and logistical activities, so in October 1918 Congress authorized the Finance Service, which became the Finance Department in June 1920. The department handled military pay and travel expenses as well as centralized disbursing, auditing, and budgeting for the **War Department**. In 1933, the Finance Department assumed the role of paying the **Civilian Conservation Corps**. The department remained a separate entity until **World War II**, when it assumed a number of additional responsibilities, such as the sale of war bonds and the promotion of National Service Life Insurance. In 1950, the **Army Reorganization Act** designated the Finance Department a basic branch of the army, the Finance Corps. *See also* BRANCHES OF THE ARMY.

FIRST SERGEANT. Both a rank and a position. The first sergeant is the senior **noncommissioned officer** in a company, battery, troop, or equivalent-size unit.

FIRST MANASSAS. *See* BULL RUN.

FIRST UN COUNTEROFFENSIVE (25 January to 21 April 1951). Korean War campaign streamer. On 22 January 1951, a reconnaissance by elements of the

First Cavalry Division revealed that the Chinese Communists facing the United Nations (UN) forces in Korea had withdrawn from frontline positions. General **Matthew Ridgway**, commanding the U.S. Eighth Army, scheduled an operation that began on 25 January and advanced slowly against light resistance for the rest of the month. By 10 February, UN forces secured the port of Inchon and Kimpo Airfield. Ridgway was determined to give the North Koreans and Chinese Communists no chance to rest and reorganize. On 21 February, he launched a general advance to deny important positions and to destroy as many enemy troops as could be found. Advances were slow and unspectacular. The spring thaw and heavy rains produced swollen streams and deep mud, which greatly hampered military operations. By 28 February, the Communist foothold south of the Han River had collapsed and the Eighth Army line was relatively stable.

By the end of March, Ridgway's forces had reached the 38th parallel and the UN forces were again faced with the problem of moving into North Korea. Ridgway, with the approval of President **Harry Truman** and General **Douglas MacArthur**, commander of the UN forces, elected to continue the advance, with the hope of achieving maximum destruction of enemy forces. UN commanders made their plans to advance, with the knowledge that the enemy was engaged in a full-scale buildup of troops and materiel for its expected spring offensive. On 5 April, Ridgway opened a general advance toward a new objective line. Six days later, Truman relieved MacArthur of all his commands because of differences over national policy and military strategy and he replaced him with Ridgway. By 17 April, UN units were no longer in contact with the enemy and the general advance was virtually unopposed. But there was fresh evidence of enemy preparations for a counterattack. *See also* CHINESE COMMUNIST FORCES INTERVENTION.

FIVE STAR GENERAL. *See* GENERAL OF THE ARMY.

FLIPPER, HENRY OSSIAN (1856–1940). First **African-American** to graduate from the **U.S. Military Academy**. Born in Thomasville, Georgia, on 21 March 1856 into slavery, Flipper spent his formative years in Georgia. Following the **Civil War**, he attended the American Missionary Association Schools in his home state. In 1873, Flipper was appointed to the Military Academy. He graduated in 1877 and was commissioned a second lieutenant in the 10th Cavalry, a black regiment known as the **Buffalo Soldiers**, in which he saw frontier duty in various installations in the Southwest. In 1881, Flipper's commanding officer accused him of "embezzling funds and of conduct unbecoming an officer and a gentleman." Flipper was acquitted of the embezzlement charge, but a general court-martial found him guilty of conduct unbecoming an officer and he was dismissed from the army in 1882. Flipper maintained his innocence for the rest of his life.

Flipper distinguished himself in a variety of governmental and private engineering positions as a civilian, including special agent of the Justice Department, special assistant to the secretary of the interior with the Alaskan Engineering Commission, and aide to the Senate Committee on Foreign Relations. He died in

Georgia in 1940. In 1976 his descendants and supporters applied to the Army Board for the Correction of Military Records on his behalf. The board recommended commuting Flipper's dismissal to a good conduct discharge. In 1997 a private law firm filed an application of pardon with the secretary of the army on Flipper's behalf and President Bill Clinton issued the desired pardon on 19 February 1999.

FLOYD, JOHN BUCHANAN (1806–1863). Secretary of war from 1857 to 1860. Born in Virginia, Floyd was educated at home by gifted parents and was probably a student at Georgetown College in Washington, D.C., before transferring to South Carolina College, where he graduated in 1829. He started a law practice in Wytheville, Virginia, before moving to Arkansas to become a cotton planter. Stricken by fever, he returned to Virginia, where he became active in politics and served in the state legislature and for a term as governor before becoming secretary of war. His tenure as secretary was marked by controversy. There were questions of misusing funds that were supposed to go to the Indians and of accepting drafts by government contractors for future services. In 1860, Floyd disagreed with the president's decision to sustain the federal garrison at Fort **Sumter** and he resigned in December amid charges that he had transferred arms to Southern arsenals in anticipation of the coming war. He raised a brigade for the Confederate Army during the **Civil War**, but in his first independent command in western Virginia, he displayed an uncanny ability to disagree with his fellow commanders. He was in command of Fort Donelson when that post came under federal attack in 1862 but, just before the garrison surrendered, he put Gideon J. Pillow in charge and escaped with his troops. Shortly thereafter, **Jefferson Davis**, president of the Confederacy, summarily relieved Floyd of his commission. Floyd managed to secure a commission as a major general in the Virginia militia two months later, but his health failed and he died shortly thereafter. *See also* Appendix 4, Secretaries of War and Secretaries of the Army; HENRY AND DONELSON.

FORREST, NATHAN BEDFORD (1821–1877). Civil War Confederate general. Born in Tennessee, Forrest received little formal education. He was a successful slave trader and planter who enlisted in the Confederate Army as a private in 1861, before raising a mounted battalion at his own expense. When the Confederates failed to break out of Fort Donelson in early 1862, he led his battalion out just before the surrender. He was severely wounded at **Shilo** a few months later. He led his cavalry through the rest of the war, feuding periodically with senior commanders and consistently outmaneuvering larger Union forces. In 1864, during the capture of Fort Pillow, his men killed a number of black Union soldiers when they attempted to surrender. After the war Forrest joined the Ku Klux Klan and became its first grand wizard. With no military training, he was an excellent leader of a semi-independent force, although his hot temper marred his reputation. His alleged advice to commanders that the key to success in war was to "Get there first with the most men," or as sometimes seen in its more colloquial version, "Get there firstest with the mostest," has come to be widely quoted in U.S. Army **doctrine**. *See also* HENRY AND DONELSON.

FORT MCHENRY (13 September 1814). War of 1812 campaign streamer. While the British marched on Washington, D.C., during the **Bladensburg** campaign, Baltimore had time to hastily strengthen its defenses. Major General Samuel Smith had about 9,000 militia, including 1,000 in Fort McHenry guarding the harbor. On 12 September, the British landed at North Point, about 14 miles below the city, where their advance was momentarily checked by 3,200 Maryland militiamen. The British commander, Major General Robert Ross, and 38 of his soldiers were killed in the engagement and 251 were wounded. The fight cost the Americans 24 killed, 139 wounded, and 50 taken prisoner. When a British naval bombardment and boat attack during the night of 13–14 September failed to reduce Fort McHenry, the British decided that a land attack on the very formidable fortifications defending the city would be too costly, so they sailed for Jamaica on 14 October. The unsuccessful British bombardment of Fort McHenry prompted Francis Scott Key to write the verses of "The Star Spangled Banner," which became the U.S. national anthem.

FORT SUMTER. *See* SUMTER.

FORTS HENRY AND DONELSON. *See* HENRY AND DONELSON.

FRANKLIN (17–30 November 1864). Civil War campaign streamer. After occupying **Atlanta** in September, General **William T. Sherman** sent two infantry corps under Major General **John M. Schofield** to reinforce General George H. Thomas at **Nashville** on the chance that General John B. Hood would attempt to lead his Confederates into Tennessee. Before Schofield could reach Nashville, however, Hood and 30,000 Confederates attacked his force of 30,000 men on 30 November at Franklin, Tennessee. In a short, furious engagement, Schofield defeated Hood. Union losses were 189 killed, 1,033 wounded, and 1,104 missing; Confederate losses were 1,750 killed, 3,800 wounded, and 702 missing.

FREDERICKSBURG (9 November to 15 December 1862). Civil War campaign streamer. After replacing **George B. McClellan** as commander of the Army of the Potomac in November 1862, Major General **Ambrose Burnside** prepared to make a move against Richmond. His first goal was to cross the Rappahannock River at Fredericksburg and get between **Robert E. Lee**'s Army of Northern Virginia and Richmond. Success depended on speed, because Burnside wanted to seize high ground southwest of Fredericksburg before Lee could get there. Moving more than 40 miles in two days, Union forces leading the drive reached Falmouth, across the Rappahannock from Fredericksburg, on 17 November, but it was another week before the pontoons necessary for bridging the river finally arrived. By the time Burnside was finally ready to attack, Lee had 78,500 Confederates dug in and waiting on the high ground behind Fredericksburg. Burnside's engineers started building the bridge on 11 December and, during the night,

Union forces attacked across the river and occupied the city. On 13 December the Federals launched an assault on the well-defended Confederate positions. After heavy fighting, the Confederates finally repulsed the attacks, inflicting heavy Federal casualties. As Burnside was preparing for yet another assault, several of his corps commanders persuaded him to withdraw. By 16 December, Burnside had moved his forces back across the Rappahannock. Of nearly 114,000 Federals engaged at Fredericksburg, 1,284 were killed, 9,600 were wounded, and 1,769 were missing; of some 72,500 Confederates engaged, 595 were killed, 4,061 were wounded, and 653 were missing.

FROEHLKE, ROBERT FREDERICK (1922–). Secretary of the army from 1971 to 1973. Born in Wisconsin, Froehlke enlisted in the army in 1943 and during **World War II** served in the **infantry** in the European theater. After leaving the army in 1946 as a captain, he attended the University of Wisconsin Law School and in 1949 received his degree. He began practicing law in Madison, Wisconsin, worked for the Sentry Insurance Company until 1969, when he became the assistant secretary of defense for administration, and was appointed secretary of the army in 1971. During his tenure, the last army forces returned from the **Vietnam War** and the **All-Volunteer Force** concept was introduced. He resigned in 1973 to resume his association with the Sentry Insurance Company. *See also* Appendix 4, Secretaries of War and Secretaries of the Army.

— G —

GARRISON, LINDLEY MILLER (1864–1932). Secretary of war from 1913 to 1916. Born in New Jersey, Garrison went to public schools, attended the Protestant Episcopal Academy, and studied at the Phillips Exeter Academy before entering Harvard University as a special student for a year. After serving as clerk at a law firm in Philadelphia, he received a law degree from the University of Pennsylvania and was admitted to the bar in 1886. He practiced law in New Jersey and was vice chancellor of the state before becoming secretary of war in 1913. While in office, Garrison directed his efforts toward preparing the army for a possible war in Europe. He resigned in 1916 because of differences with the president over military policies and returned to practicing law in New Jersey. *See also* Appendix 4, Secretaries of War and Secretaries of the Army.

GATES, HORATIO (1728–1806). American **Revolutionary War** general. Born in England, Gates served in the British army in Nova Scotia and participated in the French and Indian War. After living in England for a short time, he returned to America and received a commission in the **Continental Army**, where he became the first **adjutant general** of the army. He commanded the American forces that defeated the British at **Saratoga** and from 1777 to 1778 was the president of the short-lived Board of War, predecessor to the **War Department**.

GATES, JULIUS W. (1941–). Sergeant major of the army from 1987 to 1991. Born in North Carolina, Gates attended high school in Chapel Hill, but dropped out after three years to enlist in the army in 1958. He later earned his high school diploma by taking and passing the General Educational Development tests. When his enlistment ended in 1961, he left the army for a short time to sell cars in his hometown, but he soon reenlisted, became a paratrooper, and attended **ranger** school, graduating as the top student in his class. Gates twice served combat tours of duty during the **Vietnam War** and in 1973 was a chief instructor at the army's ranger school. After attending the **Sergeants Major Academy**, he was promoted to **sergeant major** in 1978 and became the sergeant major of the army in 1987. While in that position, he worked hard to make training the army's number one priority and was instrumental in establishing the Army Career and Alumni Program to assist soldiers leaving the service prior to retirement. He retired on 30 June 1991. *See also* Appendix 5, Sergeants Major of the Army.

GENERAL OF THE ARMIES. In September 1919, Congress made **John J. Pershing** general of the armies for his service in **World War I**. He retired with that rank on 13 September 1924 and held it until his death in 1948, although he continued to wear only four stars. No other officer held the title until 1978, when Congress posthumously appointed **George Washington** to be general of the armies and specified that he would rank first among all officers of the U.S. Army, past and present. *See also* GENERAL OF THE ARMY.

GENERAL OF THE ARMY. A temporary grade of general officer designated by five stars. It was established by Congress on 14 December 1944. Five officers have been awarded the rank: **George C. Marshall**, on 16 December 1944; **Douglas MacArthur**, on 18 December 1944; **Dwight D. Eisenhower**, on 20 December 1944; **Henry H. Arnold**, on 21 December 1944; and **Omar N. Bradley** on 20 September 1950. Arnold's rank was changed to general of the air force on 7 May 1949. Army regulations prescribed the insignia to be five stars. The similar-sounding rank of **general of the armies** applies to **George Washington** and **John J. Pershing**.

GENERAL STAFF. Established in 1903 by the **General Staff Act**, the general staff was the result of Secretary of War **Elihu Root**'s analysis of the problems the army had in preparing for and conducting the **Spanish–American War**. The staff was made responsible for preparing plans for the nation's defense and mobilization in time of war, investigating and reporting on the army's efficiency and its readiness to conduct military operations, and providing assistance to the **secretary of war**, army general officers, and other commanders.

The formation of the general staff was not without problems. The well-established and tradition-minded bureau chiefs, led by the very powerful **adjutant general**, were opposed to the concept of a general staff, while influential congressmen remained protective of their long-established connections with the bureau chiefs. Opposition continued even after the staff was formed. In 1912, Congress passed legislation that reduced the number of general staff officers to 36 and tightened restrictions on detached service by line officers, making it more difficult for them to serve on the staff. The **National Defense Act of 1916** increased the number of general staff officers to 54, but limited the number that could serve in Washington, D.C.

GENERAL STAFF ACT (1903). Prompted by the chaotic preparations for the **Spanish–American War** in 1898, the act established a **general staff** that would come to be the central planning agency for the army. After the Franco-Prussian War in 1870–1871, all the major military powers of the world had developed some variant of the German general staff, which had planned and conducted that war. Following that lead and with the impetus of **Elihu Root**, the act created a small general staff corps of 44 officers assigned to the **War Department** on a four-year detail. It also changed the position of **commanding general of the army** to **chief of staff of the army**, which held the responsibility for supervising the general staff and serving as principal adviser to the **secretary of war**. In passing the act, Congress limited the chief of staff's term of office to four years and required that general staff officers rotate out of Washington to serve in the field. The act also formalized the **Army War College**, a planning body Root established in 1901.

GERMANTOWN (4 October 1777). Revolutionary War campaign streamer. At the end of the **Brandywine** campaign, British forces under William Howe occupied Philadelphia on 26 September. Howe established a large encampment in nearby Germantown with about 9,000 men. **George Washington** moved to attack the garrison on the night of 3–4 October. Columns were to move into Germantown from four different directions and begin the assault at dawn, but two of the columns, both militia forces, failed to take part in the attack. The other two columns met with initial success, until a dense early morning fog caused confusion in the American ranks, while the better-disciplined British reformed for a successful counterattack. Howe pursued the Americans as they fell back in disorder, but failed to exploit his victory. American losses were 673 killed and wounded and about 400 taken prisoner. British losses were approximately 533 killed and wounded.

GERONIMO (Jerome; Goyathly) (1829–1909). Apache Indian leader and warrior. Born in what is now Arizona, Geronimo grew up in a period of raiding by various Chiricahua chiefs, including **Cochise**. After his family was killed by Mexican irregular troops in 1858, Geronimo led a series of raids of revenge against the Mexicans, who gave him the name by which he is now known. He became a skilled and courageous leader and for 15 years his fame increased as a war leader always ready to lead a raid into Mexico. Arrested in 1877, he was confined to a reservation. For the next few years, Geronimo and his small band of followers alternated between reservation life and raiding into Mexico. American and Mexican troops were unable to cope with his cunning, stealth, endurance, perseverance, fortitude, and command of the harsh conditions of his homeland. In 1882, **George Crook**, with a contingent of Apache scouts, tracked Geronimo into the Sierra Madre and persuaded him to surrender; but in 1885 he once again left the reservation. Crook captured him again, but the captivity was short-lived, as Geronimo fled back to the mountains. Under fire from Washington for his methods, Crook resigned and was replaced by **Nelson A. Miles**. With 5,000 troops, Miles took 18 months to finally capture Geronimo in 1886. Geronimo and his followers were sent to Florida, then Alabama, and finally Fort Sill, Oklahoma, where he lived until his death from pneumonia in 1909. While at Fort Sill, the Apache leader became something of a celebrity, appearing at the 1904 Louisiana Purchase Exposition in St. Louis and taking part in President **Theodore Roosevelt**'s inaugural procession in 1905.

GETTYSBURG (29 June to 3 July 1863). Civil War campaign streamer. Encouraged by the Confederate success during the **Chancellorsville** campaign in May 1863, General **Robert E. Lee** decided to attempt an invasion of the North to threaten Harrisburg (Pennsylvania), Baltimore, and Washington, and to relieve some of the pressure **Ulysses S. Grant**'s Union forces were putting on **Vicksburg**. In early June, Lee began moving his Army of Northern Virginia with 75,000 men up the Shenandoah and Cumberland Valleys into Pennsylvania. When Union general **Joseph Hooker** became aware of Lee's intentions, he started north with 88,000 men and crossed the Potomac River near Leesburg on 25 and 26 June. As he moved north with his Army of the Potomac, Hooker was replaced by Major General **George G. Meade** on 28 June. The two armies met near Gettysburg, while the Confederates were looking for shoes and other supplies and the Federals were looking for Confederates.

The fighting started on 1 July, when Confederate infantry encountered Federal cavalry. Reinforcements arrived rapidly on both sides and, by late afternoon, Lee held the town of Gettysburg while Meade was pouring troops onto Cemetery Ridge. By daylight on 2 July, the two armies faced each other across open country. Lee ordered General **James Longstreet** to attack the Federal left, which was not strongly defended in the morning. But after much delay and countermarching, the Confederate attack did not begin until afternoon, by which time the Federals had strengthened their lines, thus allowing them to repulse repeated assaults. Neither side gained a significant advantage on the day, although Meade prepared for another attack on the center of the Federal line. The next day, 3 July, Lee opted to renew the assault with a frontal attack against a mile-long section of the center of Meade's line. Federal **artillery** swept across the 12,000 to 15,000 Confederates making the attack, now known as Pickett's charge after the general who commanded the attacking forces, and the assault failed to penetrate the Federal line. The 5,000 or so survivors of Pickett's shattered command retired, ending the fighting. Meade did not counterattack and, two days later, Lee retreated with a seven-mile long column of wounded.

Although criticized for not pursuing Lee, Meade did stop the Confederate invasion of the North. Coupled with the Union victory at Vicksburg on 4 July, the two campaigns mark the turning point of the Civil War. The cost was high on both sides. Federal casualties amounted to more than 3,155 dead, 14,529 wounded, and 5,365 missing, for a total of about one fourth of Meade's force. Confederate losses were more than 2,500 dead, almost 13,000 wounded, and some 5,500 missing, together nearly one third of Lee's army.

GOOD, JAMES WILLIAM (1866–1929). Secretary of the army for about eight months in 1929. Born in Iowa, Good graduated from Coe College, received his degree from the University of Michigan Law School in 1893, and was admitted to the bar. He served in the U.S. House of Representatives from 1909 to 1921 and then returned to the practice of law. He was the western campaign manager for Calvin Coolidge in 1924 and Herbert Hoover in 1928. After being appointed secretary in March 1929, he died in November of that year. *See also* Appendix 4, Secretaries of War and Secretaries of the Army.

GOETHALS, GEORGE WASHINGTON (1858–1928). Army engineer. Born in New York, Goethals attended public schools and the College of the City of New York before transferring to the **U.S. Military Academy**, where he graduated in 1880. As an army engineer, he worked on a number of lock and dam projects and taught engineering at the Military Academy. In 1907 President **Theodore Roosevelt** appointed Goethals chief engineer for the Panama Canal, when his predecessor resigned because of the construction difficulties he had encountered on the project. Goethals supervised nearly all the major excavation and all construction for the canal. He had virtually absolute control over all aspects of the project and was responsible for providing food, shelter, medicine, and recreation for almost 30,000 civilian employees of various nationalities. Goethals organized a highly regimented structure, with engineers and designers at the top and workers at the bottom, to finish the canal in 1914, ahead of schedule, under budget, and with most of the original equipment still in use. He was appointed to be the first governor of the Canal Zone and was promoted to major general. He retired from the army in 1916, but was recalled in 1917 to work with the **War Department** supply agencies during **World War I**. He retired again in 1919 to head his own engineering firm. *See also* CORPS OF ENGINEERS.

GORGAS, WILLIAM CRAWFORD (1854–1920). Army medical officer. Born in Alabama, Gorgas graduated from the University of the South in Tennessee. He wanted a military career, but when he was unable to gain entrance to the **U.S. Military Academy**, he entered Bellevue Medical College in New York City, where he graduated in 1879, and entered the army as a surgeon in 1880. He served in a variety of assignments before in 1898 becoming head of sanitation in Havana, Cuba, where he improved sanitation conditions in the city. After **Walter Reed** discovered that yellow fever was transmitted by a species of mosquito, Gorgas quickly took advantage of the new knowledge to destroy mosquito breeding grounds and rid Havana of the disease, bringing him international fame. In 1904, he became the chief sanitary officer for the Panama Canal project, where he duplicated his success in Cuba, significantly reducing malaria outbreaks among the canal workers. He later applied his techniques in other parts of the world, including South America and Africa. In 1914, Gorgas became surgeon general of the army and in **World War I** he administered the **Army Medical De-**

partment. He retired with the rank of major general in 1919 and died of a stroke in London in 1920.

GRANT, ULYSSES SIMPSON (HIRAM ULYSSES) (1822–1885). Command-ing general of the army from 1864 to 1869 and 18th president of the United States. Born in Ohio, Grant was educated at local schools and graduated in 1843 from the **U.S. Military Academy**, where he was mistakenly registered as Ulysses Simpson rather than by his given name of Hiram Ulysses. During most of his ser-vice in the **Mexican War**, he was a regimental quartermaster, but he earned a **brevet** to captain at **Chapultepec**. After the war, he was stationed in California, where he was separated from his family and very unhappy. Surrounded by rumors of heavy drinking, he resigned in 1854 and returned to Ohio to farm his father-in-law's estate. The farm failed in 1857 and Grant moved to Galena, Illinois, to work in his father's leather goods store.

When the **Civil War** started, he offered his services to the **War Department** and General **George B. McClellan** with no success. He finally received com-mand of an Illinois regiment, but before he saw any fighting he was promoted to brigadier general and put in command of the Union forces at Cairo, Illinois. When the Confederates occupied Kentucky, Grant moved to take Paducah, at the mouth of the Tennessee River. He then moved on to take Belmont, Missouri, where an early success was soon turned into defeat, when the Confederates launched an unexpected counterattack. During the **Henry and Donelson** cam-paign, he stopped an attempted Confederate breakout at Fort Donelson. When the Confederate commander asked for surrender terms, Grant replied "unconditional surrender," which matched his initials and gave him a popular nickname. Grant was promoted to major general as a result of his success at Donelson and his counterattack on the second day at Shiloh furthered his reputation as a fighter, al-though questions about high casualty rates left him second in command under General **Henry W. Halleck**. When Halleck was called to Washington, D.C., to become commanding general of the army, Grant succeeded him and went on to capture Vicksburg and open the Mississippi River for the Union. He sealed his reputation as the Union's finest commander with a singular victory at Chat-tanooga in November 1863 and was made commanding general of the army the following March.

When he became commanding general, Grant made his predecessor, Halleck, his chief of staff. Grant then accompanied General **George G. Meade**, com-manding the Army of the Potomac, on the final campaigns of the Civil War, while planning and executing a coordinated strategic movement against Richmond and **Atlanta**. While Grant remained with Meade, putting pressure on **Robert E. Lee**'s Army of Northern Virginia and the Confederate capital of Richmond, General **William T. Sherman** moved against Atlanta. Grant fought Lee in the **Wilder-ness, Spotsylvania**, and **Cold Harbor** campaigns and finally pushed the Con-federates into **Petersburg**, where the Union army instituted siege operations. In March 1865 Grant launched a final campaign against Lee and in April forced him to surrender at **Appomattox**. Grant's victories came at a high cost in casualties and earned him a reputation as a butcher, but his success ended the long and bloody war in favor of the Union. In Grant, after a succession of disappointments, President **Abraham Lincoln** finally found the general he had sought and he left him to handle military matters.

After the war, Grant was **secretary of war** ad interim for a brief period before becoming the successful Republican candidate for president. After two terms as president (1869–1877), he engaged in several unsuccessful business endeavors that left him without financial resources. He wrote his highly acclaimed biography as he was dying of cancer of the throat to raise funds to support his wife. Shortly before he died, the army placed him on the retired list as a general to help ease his financial difficulties. *See also* Appendix 3, Commanding Generals and Chiefs of Staff of the Army.

GRAY, GORDON (1909–1982). Secretary of the army from 1949 to 1950. Born in Maryland, Gray graduated from the University of North Carolina in 1930 and received a law degree from Yale Law School three years later. He practiced law, was president of the Piedmont Publishing Company, and served in the North Carolina state senate until 1942, when he enlisted as a private in the army. He was commissioned in 1943 and served in Europe from 1944 to 1945, when he left the army as a captain and returned to private life in North Carolina. Gray served successively as assistant secretary and then undersecretary of the army before becoming secretary in 1949. During his tenure, the army ended its military government in Germany. Leaving office after ten months, he was a special assistant to the president on foreign economic policy. After five years as president of the University of North Carolina, he served in a variety of positions in the federal government involving the nation's defense. *See also* Appendix 4, Secretaries of War and Secretaries of the Army.

GREEN BERETS. *See* SPECIAL FORCES.

GREENE, NATHANAEL (1742–1786). American **Revolutionary War** general. Born in Rhode Island, Greene helped manage his father's iron foundry and served for a while in the colonial legislature. Raised a Quaker, he was expelled from the group for taking too great an interest in military matters and in 1774 he helped organize a company of militia. Commissioned a brigadier general in the **Continental Army**, he served in the **Boston** campaign and was commander in Boston for a brief time after the British departed. One of **George Washington**'s favorite commanders, Greene fought at **Trenton**, **Brandywine**, and **Princeton** and was often in command when Washington was absent. As the quartermaster general of the army in 1778, he reorganized the supply system after **Valley Forge** and established the first depot system. In 1780 he accepted command of the Southern Department, where Georgia and North Carolina had fallen to the British. He organized an efficient and dependable supply system in the South and restored the troops' morale. He boldly divided his small force by sending **Daniel Morgan** into the South Carolina backcountry and **Henry Lee**'s cavalry to join **Francis Marion**'s forces on the coast. The move recaptured the strategic initiative for the

Americans. After Morgan's victory at **Cowpens**, Greene united his forces and fought an engagement with the British general, **Charles Cornwallis**, at **Guilford Court House**. The fight was a Pyrrhic victory for the British and Cornwallis retired to Virginia, where he subsequently met Washington at **Yorktown**. Remaining in the South, Greene eventually won control of most of the area before leaving the army in 1783. A brilliant and innovative leader, Greene proved extremely capable in guerilla warfare. He died of sunstroke at his estate in Georgia.

GRENADA (23 October to 21 November 1983). Armed forces expedition campaign streamer. In 1979 a Communist-led coup overthrew the government of Grenada. Shortly after coming to power, the new government began construction of a 9,800-foot airstrip that the United States saw as a potential threat to the Caribbean sea lanes and the Panama Canal that could be used for staging Soviet and Cuban military flights to Latin America and Africa. In 1983, another, more violent coup left the country in disorder and prompted Grenada's governor general, Sir Paul Scoon, to ask the Organization of Eastern Caribbean States for help in restoring order. U.S. president Ronald Reagan, a staunch anti-Communist, promptly approved intervention by American forces. The United States also expressed concern for some 1,000 medical students, the majority of whom were American, living in Grenada.

The American invasion, Operation Urgent Fury, overwhelmed the Grenadian defenders, who consisted of 500 to 600 soldiers, between 2,000 and 2,500 militia, and 750 to 800 Cubans, mostly construction workers. The U.S. forces were drawn from all four services in the armed forces and included two army **ranger** battalions and a brigade from the 82d **Airborne** Division. The U.S. forces began landing on 25 October. They quickly seized the airstrip, destroyed Radio Free Grenada, and ensured the safety of the medical students. Twelve U.S. Army soldiers were killed and 120 were wounded during the brief fighting to take control of the island. Reagan declared the operation a success, but the services drew considerable criticism. Although it accomplished all of its assigned missions, the campaign had some serious flaws. Intelligence was inadequate and poorly disseminated and there were problems with communications and coordination among the army, navy, and marine units in the operation.

GRIERSON, HENRY BENJAMIN (1826–1911). Union **Civil War** general. Entering the Union Army early in the Civil War without pay, this former music teacher and merchant was a staff officer until given command of a mounted unit. In 1863, Grierson led three regiments of **cavalry** and a battery of light **artillery** on an 800-mile raid from LaGrange, Tennessee, across Mississippi to Baton Rouge, Louisiana, to distract Confederate attention from General **Ulysses S. Grant**'s river crossing below **Vicksburg**. With the loss of only three killed, seven wounded, nine missing, and seven left behind sick or tending to wounded, the raiders killed an estimated 100 Confederates and paroled 500 more, captured 1,000 mules, and destroyed more than 50 miles of railroad lines and 3,000 stands of arms. Mustered out of volunteer service as a major general, Grierson received command of one of two newly created regiments for black soldiers. He commanded the 10th Cavalry from 1866 to 1888, molding it into a highly regarded frontier unit known as the **Buffalo Soldiers**. Grierson retired in 1890 as a brigadier general.

GUADALCANAL (7 August 1942 to 21 February 1943). World War II campaign streamer. After the attack at Pearl Harbor in December 1941, the Japanese advanced throughout the Pacific, establishing bases and threatening Australia and New Zealand. Naval action in early 1942 gave Allied ground forces an opportunity to open an offensive in the South Pacific. With the U.S. Navy victories in the Battles of the Coral Sea and Midway, Japanese sea power was seriously damaged, bringing the balance of naval power close enough to make an amphibious assault a realistic option. The Joint Chiefs of Staff therefore proposed a two-pronged offensive, one toward the Solomon Islands and the other from Port Moresby on the island of New Guinea. The island of Guadalcanal, standing between Australia and the Solomons, was the first objective.

Initially, the Guadalcanal campaign was primarily a U.S. Navy and Marine Corps effort commanded by Vice Admiral Robert L. Ghormley. On 7 August 1942, a U.S. Marine division landed on Guadalcanal and nearby islands and provoked a vigorous Japanese defense. In a three-month operation, the Marines took the airfield and established a beachhead some six miles wide and three miles deep. On 13 October, the first army units landed on the island to reinforce the marines. In December, the First Marine Division was withdrawn and responsibility for clearing the island passed to the army. During the last weeks of 1942 and the first weeks of 1943, the army strengthened its forces on Guadalcanal. Before the island was finally secured in February 1943, the United States had committed two marine divisions, two army divisions, and an additional army regiment to the fight.

Victory on Guadalcanal brought important strategic gains, but at a cost. The Americans lost 1,592 killed and 4,183 wounded, with thousands more disabled by disease, while the Japanese lost 14,800 killed in battle, 9,000 dead from disease, and 1,000 taken prisoner. The greatest single factor reducing troop effectiveness during the campaign was disease. For each combat casualty, there were five cases of malaria. The campaign made it clear that future Allied success in the Pacific depended on cooperation between land and sea forces. Although the early stages of the campaign were dominated by the navy and marines, the army eventually secured the victory. As the Allies moved from island to island on their way to defeating Japan, the army would play an increasingly large role in amphibious operations in the Pacific. With Guadalcanal in hand, the Allies were ready to continue into the Solomons. *See also* CENTRAL PACIFIC; NORTHERN SOLOMONS; PAPUA.

GUILFORD COURT HOUSE (15 March 1781). Revolutionary War campaign streamer. In December 1780, **Nathanael Greene** received command of a small, demoralized portion of the **Continental Army** in South Carolina that was awaiting an invasion by British forces under **Charles Cornwallis**. Greene restored morale, instilled discipline in his force, and went on the initiative. After the British defeat at **Cowpens** in January 1781, Cornwallis set out after Greene, who led his enemy into North Carolina until he reached Guilford Court House, where he prepared for battle. Greene emulated Daniel Morgan's tactics at Cowpens: militia in front with regulars behind them and **cavalry** in reserve. Unlike in the battle at Cowpens, however, the American militia at Guilford Court House fled the field in the face of a frontal assault by Cornwallis. But the Continentals from Maryland and Delaware held their positions, driving Cornwallis to unleash his **artillery**, which fired indiscriminately at both friend and foe. Green withdrew with 261 casualties, but it was a hollow victory for Cornwallis, who suffered 532 casualties. The battle was the culmination of Greene's campaign against Cornwallis, who retreated to the coast and from there moved to **Yorktown**, Virginia. Greene moved south and within six months had confined the British to two seacoast strongholds in Savannah and Charleston.

— H —

HALL, ROBERT E. (1947–). Sergeant major of the army from to 1997 to 2000. Born in South Carolina, Hall entered the army in 1968 and attended basic training at Fort Bragg, North Carolina. During his career, he held every key **noncommissioned officer** leadership position from squad leader to **command sergeant major**. He served in the **Persian Gulf War** and, prior to becoming sergeant major of the army, was the command sergeant major of the U.S. Central Command. As sergeant major of the army, Hall devoted most of his time to observing training and talking to soldiers and their families so he could provide sound advice to the **chief of staff of the army** on **enlisted** matters. He retired on 23 June 2000 with more than 32 years of active service. *See also* Appendix 5, Sergeants Major of the Army.

HALLECK, HENRY WAGER (1815–1872). Commanding general of the army from 1862 to 1864. Born in Westernville, New York, Halleck graduated from the **U.S. Military Academy** in 1839. Considered an intellectual, he visited Europe, wrote a report on French fortifications, published the *Elements of Military Art and Science*, and translated **Henri Jomini**'s *Vie politique et militaire de Napoleon*. Halleck served in California during the **Mexican War**, where he held a variety of staff positions. In 1854, he resigned from the army to practice law. He held a number of civilian management positions and published treatises on mining and international law. In 1861, at the beginning of the **Civil War**, he was appointed a major general in the **regular army** and commanded the departments of Missouri and Mississippi, before becoming the commanding general of the army. In this position, he proved himself an able administrator and champion of discipline. When **Ulysses S. Grant** replaced Halleck as commanding general of the army, he made Halleck his chief of staff, a post Halleck held until 1865, when he received command of the Division of the James. Halleck then successively commanded the Division of the Pacific and the Division of the South. He died at his headquarters while he held the latter post. *See also* Appendix 3, Commanding Generals and Chiefs of Staff of the Army.

HAMBURGER HILL (1969). Battle during the **Vietnam War**. For 10 days in May 1969, units of the U.S. Army's 101st Airborne Division and soldiers of the Republic of Vietnam Army attacked the well-defended, fortified positions of North Vietnamese Army units on a mountain named Dong Ap Bia in the A Shau Valley. The bloody battle ground out heavy casualties on both sides, causing the mountain to be dubbed "Hamburger Hill." Coming shortly after the United States had announced a policy of turning the war over to the South Vietnamese, the battle was widely criticized for wasting the lives of American soldiers on what appeared to be useless terrain. *See also* TET 69 COUNTEROFFENSIVE.

HAMILTON, ALEXANDER (1757–1804). Commanding general of the army from 1799 to 1800. Born in the West Indies, Hamilton attended King's College at Columbia University and wrote articles and pamphlets supporting the colonists' cause. In 1776, he commanded the New York Provincial Company of **Artillery**, a unit that became known as "Alexander Hamilton's battery" and that continues in existence as the 1st Battalion, 5th **Field Artillery**. Hamilton was appointed a captain in the **Continental Army** and rose to command a regiment under the Marquis de **Lafayette** at **Yorktown**. He was a New York delegate to the Constitutional Convention and was one of the chief advocates of the new Constitution. Hamilton was the secretary of the treasury from 1789 to 1795 and was responsible for the establishment of the Bank of the United States. While commanding general of the army, he supervised the preparation of new drill regulations. He died of wounds received in a duel with Aaron Burr at Weehawken Heights, New Jersey. *See also* Appendix 3, Commanding Generals and Chiefs of Staff of the Army.

HARMAR, JOSIAH (1753–1813). Commanding general of the army from 1784 to 1791. Born in Philadelphia, Harmar served in various military positions from 1775 to 1792. While the senior officer in the army, he was twice defeated by Indians during the **Miami** campaign. He was adjutant general of Pennsylvania from 1793 to 1799, after which he entered the mercantile business in Philadelphia. *See also* Appendix 3, Commanding Generals and Chiefs of Staff of the Army.

HARRISON, WILLIAM HENRY (1773–1841). Army general and 23d president of the United States. Born in Virginia, Harrison studied at Hampden-Sidney College and moved in 1790 to Philadelphia, where he attended the College of Physicians and Surgeons before joining the army in 1791. As an aide-de-camp to **Anthony Wayne**, he participated in the campaign against the **Miami** Indians. Harrison resigned as a captain in 1798 and became secretary of the Northwest Territory. Two years later, he became governor of the Indiana Territory, a post he held until 1812. He lead the successful **Tippecanoe** campaign against **Tecumseh** in 1811 and led the American attack on Detroit during the **Canada** campaign of the **War of 1812**. He again resigned from the army in 1814 and became active in politics. In 1840, he ran successfully for president, using the slogan "Tippecanoe and Tyler too!," which referred to his 1811 victory and to his running mate, John Tyler. Exhausted by the campaign, Harrison contracted pneumonia and died after one month in office.

HELICOPTER. First introduced at the end of **World War II**, where they were used primarily for air rescue, helicopters have become an integral part of the army's fighting and support forces. During the **Korean War**, the army used the helicopter for evacuating casualties from the battlefield and started to experiment with arming them for fire support. Helicopters also saw service transporting troops and supplies and were used for observation. After the war, the army developed a variety of helicopters for a wide range of uses. In the **Vietnam War**, they were used in large numbers, with entire **divisions** equipped with helicopters. The UH-1 utility helicopter, known as the "Huey," was produced in a variety of models that were used for aerial fire support, resupply, command and control, airmobile assaults, and medical evacuation. The Vietnam experience made the helicopter a permanent fixture of the army and played a key role in the AirLand Battle **doctrine** developed after the war. By the time of the **Persian Gulf War**, the UH-60 Blackhawk was the army's primary utility helicopter. Used for air assault, cargo transport, aeromedical evacuation, search and rescue, and electronic warfare, it could carry 11 combat-equipped infantry soldiers or an M-102 105-mm artillery piece with 30 rounds of ammunition and a crew of six cannoneers. Fighting alongside the Blackhawk was the AH-64 Apache, the army's principal attack helicopter. The Apache was able to operate day or night in adverse weather conditions, could achieve a speed of 227 miles per hour, and had a range of 200 miles. Its armaments included antitank missiles, high explosive rockets, and a 30-mm high-speed machine gun.

HENRY AND DONELSON (6–16 February 1862). Civil War campaign streamer. Early in 1862, the second year of the war, Confederate general Albert Sidney Johnston, with 43,000 troops, occupied a line of forts and camps that extended from the Cumberland Gap in Virginia through Bowling Green, Kentucky, to New Madrid and Island No. 10 on the Mississippi River. As part of that line, the Confederates built Fort Henry on the Tennessee River and Fort Donelson on the Cumberland River to protect a lateral railroad vital to their lines of communications. The two forts were located 10 miles apart on the northern border of Tennessee. In February 1862, Federal troops under Brigadier General **Ulysses S. Grant** moved up the Tennessee River, landed near Fort Henry, and marched overland to seize the fort. Brigadier General Lloyd Tilghman, commanding Fort Henry, sent most of the garrison to Fort Donelson before surrendering on 6 February. The loss of Fort Henry had rendered the Confederate position at Bowling Green untenable, so Johnston sent 12,000 men to reinforce Fort Donelson. Grant then moved against Fort Donelson, which he invested on 12 February with more than 25,000 men. Donelson was a strong position and Grant prepared to lay siege, but when a Confederate sortie failed, he took the opportunity to attack. The fort, along with 11,500 Confederate troops, surrendered on 16 February, but not before a number of Confederate units led by **Nathan Bedford Forrest** and including **John B. Floyd**, a former U.S. **secretary of war**, escaped. Union losses at Donelson were 500 killed, 2,108 wounded, and 224 missing. Confederate losses, aside from prisoners, were about 2,000 killed and wounded.

HINES, JOHN LEONARD (1868–1968). Chief of staff of the army from 1924 to 1926. Born in West Virginia, Hines graduated from the **U.S. Military Academy** and was commissioned a second lieutenant in 1891. He served a number of years on the frontier in Nebraska and Montana and participated in the **Santiago** campaign of the **Spanish–American War**. He served in the **Philippine Insurrection** and **World War I**. He became chief of staff in 1924 and, while in office, he stressed the need for balancing funding and personnel. After leaving office, Hines remained on active service in various command positions, until retiring in 1932. He died in 1968 at the age of 100. *See also* Appendix 3, Commanding Generals and Chiefs of Staff of the Army.

HOBBY, OVETA CULP (1905–1995). First director of the **Women's Army Corps** (WAC). Born and raised in Texas, Hobby accompanied her father when he was elected to the state house of representatives. She served as parliamentarian of the house for a number of years and later held a number of positions on the *Houston Post*, a Texas newspaper. Hobby was the first director of the Women's Auxiliary Army Corps when it was formed in 1942, and she became the first director of the WAC when it became part of the army in 1943. She held the post until 1945. Her rank was limited to colonel, even though there were more than 100,000 WACs on active duty by the end of World War II. In 1953, she became the first secretary of the Department of Health, Education, and Welfare, making her the second woman to hold a cabinet post. She resigned in 1955 to become editor of the *Houston Post*, assuming her husband's position when he became ill. *See also* WOMEN IN THE ARMY.

HOFFMAN, MARTIN RICHARD (1932–). Secretary of the army from 1975 to 1977. Born in Massachusetts, Hoffman graduated from Princeton University in 1954 and that same year enlisted in the army, where he attended the **Field Artillery** Officer Candidate School. He left active service in 1956, but stayed in the **U.S. Army Reserve**. Graduating from the University of Virginia Law School in 1961, he pursued a law career in government service and was appointed secretary of the army in 1975. During his tenure, the army struggled with the problems left from the **Vietnam War**. Leaving office in 1977, he entered private law practice. *See also* Appendix 4, Secretaries of War and Secretaries of the Army.

HOLT, JOSEPH (1807–1875). Secretary of war for about two months in early 1861. Born in Kentucky, Holt was educated at St. Joseph's College and Centre College before practicing law. He was the U.S. commissioner of patents and postmaster general before serving briefly as secretary of war. In 1862, he became the **judge advocate general** of the army and in this position he prosecuted the John Wilkes Booth conspirators for their role in the assassination of President **Abraham Lincoln**. Holt resigned the post in 1875. *See also* Appendix 4, Secretaries of War and Secretaries of the Army.

HURLEY, PATRICK JAY (1883–1963). Secretary of war from 1929 to 1933. Born in the Choctaw Nation, Indian Territory, Hurley graduated from Indian University in 1905 and received a degree from the National University of Law in 1908. He practiced law in Tulsa, Oklahoma, was admitted to the bar of the Supreme Court, and was national attorney for the Choctaw Nation. He served in the Indian Territorial Volunteer Militia and the Oklahoma National Guard, before seeing service in France during the **Aisne–Marne, Meuse–Argonne**, and **St. Mihiel** campaigns of **World War I** and rising to the rank of lieutenant colonel. Hurley was assistant secretary of war for about nine months in 1929 before becoming secretary of war. While secretary, he issued the order to **Douglas MacArthur** to evict the **Bonus Army** from Washington, D.C., in 1932. He was recalled to active duty as a brigadier general in 1942 to undertake a special mission to Australia and he later became the first U.S. minister to New Zealand. He was a personal representative of the president to various countries around the world until 1944, when he returned to private life in New Mexico. *See also* Appendix 4, Secretaries of War and Secretaries of the Army.

HUSSEIN, SADDAM (1937–). President of Iraq during the **Persian Gulf War.** Hussein was born in Takrit, Iraq. His life has been one of violence and his career has been marked by potentially disastrous international miscalculations, including a costly and bloody war with Iran from 1980 to 1988. He was the supreme commander of all Iraqi forces during the Persian Gulf War and his conduct of the war was marked by miscalculations. He misread the world's reaction to the invasion of Kuwait, he overestimated his ability to manipulate public opinion outside Iraq, he underestimated the strength of playing Israel against the Arabs in the coalition, and he misjudged his ability to stand up to the military might of the United Nations coalition aligned against him. Although he had no prior military service, he personally managed the deployment of troops in the Kuwait invasion. Contrary to expectations immediately after the war, the Iraqi defeat did not remove Saddam Hussein from power. He took advantage of the decision to stop the ground war by portraying it as the result of a brilliant delaying action that prevented an enemy from crossing the Euphrates River and entering Baghdad. He boasted that his army and country were still intact, in spite of having been under attack from half a million troops.

— I —

ILOILO (8–12 February 1899). Philippine Insurrection campaign streamer. After suppressing an attempted uprising in Manila in early February 1899, Major General Elwell S. Otis, the commander of U.S. Army forces in the Philippines, sent several columns of troops into the countryside to split the insurgent forces and capture key positions. Control of Luzon was the principal military objective for the United States in 1899, but the army also took measures to establish American control over other important islands. American forces occupied Iloilo on 11 February and Cebu on 26 February, on the island of Panay; Bacolod on 10 March, on Negros Island; and **Jolo** Island on May 19, in the Sulu Archipelago.

INCHON. *See* UN OFFENSIVE.

INDIA–BURMA (2 April 1942 to 28 January 1945). World War II campaign streamer. When General **Joseph Stilwell** emerged from his trek through the jungle in May 1942 at the end of the **Burma 1942** campaign, he announced that "We got a hell of a beating. We got run out of Burma and it is humiliating as hell." With the Allied failure to keep Burma out of Japanese hands went the last overland route for supplying the Chinese: the Burma Road. Reopening that road became the major American goal of the India–Burma campaign and Stilwell, serving in multiple capacities—chief of Chiang Kai-shek's joint Allied staff, the personal representative of the U.S. president to China, administrator of the American lend-lease program, and commanding officer of the China–Burma–India, or CBI, theater of operations—was the motivating force behind it. With the theater's low priority in the overall Allied war effort and the long distances and extraordinary terrain involved, it took a long time to do almost everything in the CBI.

In March 1942, the first American troops began to arrive in the theater, including the first elements of what would become the 10th Air Force, along with logistical units to provide services and supplies to the theater. Late in the year, American engineers began to build a road to restore land communications to China. During 1943, the United States managed to provide minimal support to Major General Claire L. Chennault's 14th Army Air Force in China, train two Chinese divisions in India, fly supplies over the Himalayas (the Hump, as the route was popularly known), and send a combat team of U.S. ground forces to support the Chinese in a projected plan to recapture Burma.

In the spring of 1944, the Allies were ready to reoccupy Burma and launched multiple offensives into the country. A Chinese–American force under Stilwell fought down the Hukawang Valley and reached the area north of Myitkyina, a key communications center and Japanese stronghold, in May. Meanwhile, the 5307th Composite Unit (Provisional), a reinforced U.S. Army regiment better known as Merrill's Marauders, had marched through some of the most rugged terrain in the world, including a 65-mile stretch over the 6,000-foot Kumon range, to outflank the Japanese, attack Myitkyina from the south, and capture the airfield there on 17 May. However, Japanese resistance and the onset of the monsoon season in June delayed capture of the city until August. The fall of Myitkyina was Stilwell's greatest triumph, but within three months he was recalled to the United States at the request of Chiang Kai-shek.

While the Americans focused on Myitkyina, an Allied offensive by a British force known as the Chindits under Major General Orde C. Wingate made a successful airdrop near Kotha in March and proceeded to disrupt Japanese communications in central Burma. Farther to the south, a British Commonwealth force inflicted a considerable defeat on Japanese forces defending against a drive on Akyab, a port of the Bay of Bengal. Meanwhile, in western Burma, the Japanese had launched a powerful, and very nearly successful, counterattack toward Imphal and Kohima in eastern India. The British made a last-ditch stand in the vicinity of Kohima and, when reserves arrived, won a decisive victory at the end of June 1944. As the monsoon broke, the decimated Japanese force was in disorderly retreat back into the jungles of Burma.

By October 1944, the Allies had cleared northern Burma of Japanese and were ready to open the Burma Road. Two Chinese divisions moved along the Ledo Road, which engineers had pushed to within 80 miles of joining the Burma Road at Bhamo, while an American–Chinese force advanced up the Burma Road toward China, forcing the Japanese out of Burma. At the same time, another Chinese force moved from the Chinese end of the Burma Road. The two forces linked up on 20 January and eight days later the first convoy from Ledo moved into China, ending the campaign after almost three years. *See also* SPECIAL OPERATIONS FORCES.

INDIAN WARS (1790–1891). In the early years of the nation, the army occupied western forts as British garrisons withdrew under the terms of the treaty that ended the **Revolutionary War**. The **War Department**, the federal agency with the most contact with the Native Americans who lived in the area, was responsible for the conduct of Indian affairs. Army officers served as agents and commissioners, negotiating treaties of trade and friendship. When that failed and hostilities ensued, army expeditions subdued the Indian nations.

The Indian wars began early in the nation's history. In 1790 and 1791, after two expeditions of largely militia failed to pacify the **Miami** Indians in the Ohio Valley, **Anthony Wayne** led a force of regulars on a third attempt and was successful at Fallen Timbers in August 1794. Some years later, the Indian leader **Tecumseh** attempted to revive resistance in the region, but a force of regulars and militia under **William Henry Harrison** dealt a fatal blow to Indian hopes at **Tippecanoe** in 1811. With the collapse of **Tecumseh's** confederacy, Indians in that part of the nation posed no further significant obstacle to expansion.

After the **War of 1812**, the army frequently found itself caught between restless settlers moving to the frontier in search of new lands and Indians trying to defend their homelands. When directed by the federal government, the army fought tribes that refused to turn over their lands to the settlers and they moved the tribes from their lands by force when necessary. The removal of the Cherokees from their ancestral homeland in the Southeast to present-day Oklahoma is a tragic example of that policy. In Florida, regular army soldiers and militia achieved only partial success in driving the **Seminoles** from their homelands in a series of campaigns between 1817 and 1858 known as the Seminole Wars.

During the **Civil War**, the army's efforts were focused on keeping the nation together. After the war, a greatly reduced army returned to the western frontier. Army officers negotiated treaties with the Sioux, **Cheyenne**, and other tribes, as the army tried to maintain order between the Indians and the white prospectors, hunters, ranchers, and farmers who were flooding into the West. When the inevitable hostilities erupted, soldiers forced the Indians onto reservations. The campaigns against the Indians generally took the form of converging columns invading hostile territory in an attempt to bring the enemy to battle. Most of the time, the tribes lacked the numbers or inclination to challenge an army unit of any size. At the **Little Big Horn** in June 1876, however, the Indians had both superior numbers and the desire to fight. Led by **Crazy Horse**, the Sioux and Cheyenne warriors killed **George A. Custer** and all of the Seventh Cavalry soldiers with him. In the Southwest, the Apache Indians resisted the army's efforts to keep them on reservations until 1886, when **Geronimo** was finally persuaded to surrender. The final tragic encounter between Indians and the army came at Wounded Knee, South Dakota, in December 1890. *See also* Indian wars campaigns listed in Appendix 6, Campaigns of the United States Army.

INFANTRY. Branch of the army. The branch that fights close battles with fire and maneuver. The oldest branch of the army, the infantry was established on 14 June 1775, when the Continental Congress authorized formation of 10 companies of riflemen to be part of the **Continental Army**. The Congress continued to authorize infantry units and, by December 1775, there were 49 **battalions** or **regiments** (the terms were virtually synonymous at the time) and several unattached **companies** in the American military establishment. A year later, there were a total of 82 battalions of foot soldiers in service. During the **Revolutionary War**, infantry companies were organized into regiments, which remained the infantry's tactical and administrative unit for 181 years. During that time, the number and designation of regiments fluctuated greatly as the United States increased the size of its military establishment during wartime and then sent the troops home as soon as the fighting stopped, reflecting the nation's unease with maintaining a large peacetime army.

In 1815, as part of the reduction in the size of the army after the **War of 1812**, 46 infantry regiments were consolidated into 10, with no consideration to retaining the numerical designations. The new regimental numbers were based on the seniority of the colonels commanding the new units, with the senior officer commanding the 1st regiment. As part of the reorganization, the 1st Infantry, the oldest regiment in the army at the time, was merged with the 2d, 3d, 4th, 6th, and 7th, while the new organization was designated the 3d Infantry, which today is considered the oldest regiment in the army.

The regimental structure changed several times, but the basic structure was 10 companies grouped under a headquarters. In 1898, regiments were organized into two battalions, each with four companies. The battalion became the tactical headquarters, while the regiment retained administrative responsibilities. At the beginning of **World War I**, a third battalion was added to each regiment. Each battalion had four companies. This organization remained unchanged until 1956, when the regimental structure was replaced by the Pentomic battle group, a unit smaller than a regiment but larger than a battalion. The Pentomic concept was based on the need for smaller, more flexible units that could cope with the potential threat of atomic and chemical weapons on the battlefield. The concept lasted only a few years and in 1961 the Reorganized Objective Army **Division** replaced the battle groups with battalions as the infantry's primary tactical and administrative headquarters. The regimental headquarters was not included in the reorganization, although the army has attempted to perpetuate the history and honors of infantry units through the regimental designations.

The infantry was the largest single branch in the army until recently and it has suffered the greatest number of casualties on the battlefield. Largely for that reason, it has never been considered choice duty for soldiers. It was not until 1918 that the army established a training center and school for infantry. Until that time, infantry officers and soldiers received no special training for their critical role on the battlefield.

Although the infantry was originally organized as foot soldiers, modern infantrymen arrive on the battlefield in a variety of ways, but their fundamental function remains dismounted ground combat. The basic weapon is the rifle and bayonet, although infantrymen have carried a wide variety of other weaponry, including grenade launchers, machine guns, mortars, flame throwers, and antitank rockets, to enhance their fighting capabilities. Over the years, the army has organized various types of infantry to keep pace with changes in warfare. These types include light, **airborne**, air assault, and mechanized, making infantry one of the most versatile branches in the army. Light infantry is organized to fight on foot, but it can move into combat a variety of ways. Airborne infantry consists of paratroopers who jump from aircraft into battle, while air assault infantry use helicopters. Mechanized infantry use **armored** vehicles and personnel carriers to move around the battlefield and are task organized to fight in a mutually supporting role with **tanks**, dismounting when it is necessary to fight. *See also* Appendix 1, Resolution of the Continental Congress Adopting the Continental Army; BRANCHES OF THE ARMY.

INSPECTOR GENERAL. The office of inspector general of the army was established on 13 December 1776. The first officer to hold the post was **Friedrich Wilhelm von Steuben**, a Prussian engineer who had served as an aide-de-camp to Frederick the Great. Von Steuben received the **brevet** rank of captain from Congress and joined **George Washington** and the **Continental Army** at **Valley Forge** in February 1778. There he drilled the troops, training them to execute battlefield maneuvers in preparation for facing the British. The office has been part of the army ever since. During the 1790s the inspector general was second in command of the army and for a period after 1800 the inspector general's duties were relegated to the **adjutant general**. The influence of the inspector general changed frequently during the nineteenth century along with army strength fluctuations, different personalities of the incumbent, and philosophical approaches of senior army policymakers. On several occasions the position was eliminated altogether. In 1876 the **secretary of war** directed the inspector general to report to the commanding general of the army on all subjects pertaining to military control and discipline, and all inspectors general in the field were to report directly to their respective commanding generals. This directive placed inspectors general under local commanders' control for all matters, and this relationship continues today. *See also* BRANCHES OF THE ARMY.

— J —

JACKSON, ANDREW (1767–1845). Army general and seventh president of the United States. Jackson first saw service in the **Revolutionary War**, at the battle of Hanging Rock, South Carolina in 1780, where at the age of 13 he was captured by the British. In 1802 he was elected a major general in the Tennessee militia and commanded the Tennessee troops that fought against the **Creeks** in 1813. During the **War of 1812**, he was commissioned a major general in the U.S. Army and defeated the British at **New Orleans** in 1815. After the war, he once again was fighting Indians as he pursued the **Seminoles** in Spanish Florida. He was one of the first field commanders in the army to challenge the **War Department** on the chain of command when one of his attached technical service officers was reassigned by the **secretary of war** without his knowledge or approval. Although he had no formal schooling in warfare, Jackson was an excellent general who could command militia and volunteers as well as regulars. He skillfully conducted both conventional operations against British regulars and unconventional warfare against Indians.

JACKSON, THOMAS JONATHAN (1824–1863). Confederate **Civil War** general. Born in what is now West Virginia Jackson had very little formal schooling, but received an appointment to the **U.S. Military Academy**, where he graduated in 1846. He fought in the **Mexican War**, earning **brevet** promotions to major. In 1852 he resigned from the army to take a position teaching at the Virginia Military Institute at Lexington. In 1861, at the start of the Civil War, he received a commission as colonel in the Confederate Army and received command of a brigade. During the **Bull Run** campaign, he earned his famous nickname, "Stonewall," when Brigadier General Bernard E. Bee rallied his troops by calling out words to the effect of "there stands Jackson like a stone wall." Contrary to the name, however, Jackson was one of the South's most aggressive generals, preferring to maneuver rather than remain in a static defense.

In 1862, with his success against superior Union forces in the **Valley** campaign, he received wide recognition as an able, independent commander. Commanding a corps in **Robert E. Lee**'s Army of Northern Virginia, Jackson was a loyal and bold general who, unlike many Civil War generals, did not seek to aggrandize himself. After his brilliant 1862 campaign in the Shenandoah Valley, he added to his reputation at **Manassas**, **Antietam**, and **Fredericksburg**, before his untimely death at **Chancellorsville**, when he was accidentally shot and killed by his own troops.

JOHNSON, HAROLD KEITH (1912–1983). Chief of staff of the army from 1964 to 1968. Born in North Dakota, Johnson graduated from the **U.S. Military**

Academy in 1933. He was a battalion commander in the Philippines in 1941, was captured during the **Philippine Island** campaign in **World War II**, and survived the infamous Bataan death march and imprisonment by his Japanese captors. After liberation in 1945, he held a variety of command and staff positions, before becoming chief of staff in 1964. While in office, Johnson supervised the army's expansion during the **Vietnam War** and sent forces to the **Dominican Republic**. After he retired from active service in 1968, he expressed regret in not having taken a stand against the commitment of U.S. forces to Vietnam. *See also* Appendix 3, Commanding Generals and Chiefs of Staff of the Army.

JOHNSTON, JOSEPH E. (1807–1891). Confederate **Civil War** general. Born in Virginia, Johnston graduated from the **U.S. Military Academy** in 1829. He saw active service against the **Seminoles** and during the **Mexican War**, where he received a **brevet** for gallantry. In 1860, he became the quartermaster general of the army. But when the Civil War broke out in 1861, he became the highest-ranking officer to resign, when he accepted a commission as a brigadier general in the Confederate Army. In July 1861, he eluded Federal forces in the Shenandoah Valley and moved his troops to join General Pierre G. T. Beauregard to defeat the Union Army at **Bull Run**. In 1862, he commanded the Confederate Army opposing General **George B. McClellan**'s move against Richmond in the **Peninsula** campaign. After being wounded during that campaign, Johnston took command of Confederate forces in the west, where he suffered defeat at **Vicksburg**. In late 1863, he engineered a successful strategic withdrawal of his army to **Atlanta**, saving it from destruction by **William Tecumseh Sherman**. The retreat, however, displeased Confederate president **Jefferson Davis**, who relieved Johnston of his command in 1864. Recalled to active duty in February 1865, Johnston was unable to stop Sherman's advance and surrendered at Durham Station, North Carolina, in April. After the war, he published a book on the operations he directed and, from 1879 to 1881, represented Virginia in Congress. He became U.S. commissioner of railroads in 1885 and died in March 1891 from a cold he apparently caught while marching in Sherman's funeral procession.

JOLO (1–24 May 1905, 6–8 March 1906, 6 August 1906, 11–15 June 1913). **Philippine Insurrection** campaign streamer. This streamer represents three separate campaigns against the Moros in the Philippine Islands. In May 1905, March 1906, and June 1913, **regular army** soldiers had to cope with disorders too extensive to be handled by the local constabulary and Philippine scouts on the island of Jolo, a Moro stronghold. During May 1905, Moro leader Pala and some of his followers were killed in fighting against U.S. forces. The remainder gathered in a volcanic crater, where they surrendered to the Americans. On 6–8 March 1906, U.S. Army forces defeated the Moros at the battle of Bud Dajo, but resistance did not end until the Moros were beaten at Bagsac in mid-June 1913. *See also* MINDANAO.

JOMINI, ANTOINE-HENRI (1779–1869). Nineteenth-century Swiss authority on the art of war. Jomini served in Napoleon's army as chief of staff to Marshal

Michel Ney and was a later general officer in the Russian Army (for a time, he held general's commissions in both the French and Russian armies, with the consent of both sovereigns). His interpretations and analyses of the campaigns of Frederick the Great, the French Revolution, and the Napoleonic wars emphasized offensive warfare. Jomini's ideas were very popular among British and American officers in the nineteenth century. **Dennis Hart Mahan**, a professor at the **U.S. Military Academy** beginning in 1832, popularized Jomini as a source of military theory for army officers.

JUDGE ADVOCATE GENERAL CORPS. The Continental Congress adopted the Articles of War, on the model of the British Articles of War, on 30 June 1775, and created the office of judge advocate on 29 July. In 1802, the judge advocate was abolished and most legal functions were transferred to the state militias, but Congress reestablished the position in 1849 and authorized a corps of judge advocates in 1862. During the **Civil War**, 33 judge advocates were appointed. **Joseph Holt**, who served briefly as the secretary of war and was the army's judge advocate during the Civil War, served as coprosecutor in the trials that followed President Abraham Lincoln's assassination. The Judge Advocate General's Department was established in 1884 and received its present designation as a corps in 1948. Today, lawyers from the department continue to support army commanders around the world. *See also* BRANCHES OF THE ARMY.

— **K** —

KEARNY, STEPHEN WATTS (1794–1848). Army general who occupied the territory of New Mexico at the beginning of the **Mexican War** and became the American commander in California later in 1846. Born in New Jersey to a prominent family, Kearny served with distinction in the **War of 1812**. After the war, he joined several expeditions to the western frontier. In June 1846, he led the 1,800 men of the Army of the West 700 miles from Fort Leavenworth, Kansas, to Santa Fe, New Mexico, where he established a U.S. civilian government, before moving on to California with 700 men in September. Upon learning that California had already been occupied, he sent half his troops back to Santa Fe, but by the time he arrived near Los Angeles the city had been retaken by the Mexicans. Joining forces with Commodore Robert F. Stockton's sailors and marines, he defeated a 600-man Mexican detachment at San Gabriel and reoccupied Los Angeles. After a feud with Stockton over who was in charge, Kearny was recognized as the military governor. He died of yellow fever in 1848.

KEY WEST AGREEMENT (1948). The **National Security Act of 1947**, which established the air force as a separate service, was not clear on service functions, so in March 1948 the chiefs of the four armed services (army, navy, marine corps, and air force) met in Key West, Florida, to resolve their differences in roles and missions. The compromise that came out of the meeting was known as the Key

West Agreement and became the official statement of functions of the services until 1954, when an updated agreement replaced it.

KIDD, RICHARD A. (1943–). Sergeant major of the army from 1991 to 1995. Born in Kentucky, Kidd grew up in a military family, living at many different posts in the United States and Germany. He enlisted in the army in 1962, intending to remain in uniform only three years. He became a member of a paratrooper unit before reporting for duty in Germany, where he met a platoon sergeant who inspired him to make the army a career. After service in the **Vietnam War**, he joined the army's **Special Forces**. He returned to Vietnam in 1970 as a light weapons **infantry** adviser to South Vietnamese units. He graduated from the **Sergeants Major Academy** in 1977 and was a **battalion, brigade, division,** and **corps command sergeant major** before becoming the sergeant major of the army in 1991. While in office, Kidd helped enlisted soldiers and their families cope with the army's reductions in force that came at the end of the **Cold War**. He retired in 1995. *See also* Appendix 5, Sergeants Major of the Army.

KNOX, HENRY (1750–1806). Commanding general of the army from 1783 to 1784; **secretary at war** from 1785 to 1789; and **secretary of war** from 1789 to 1794. Born in Boston, Knox opened a bookstore there and was present at the Boston Massacre in 1770, when he tried to restrain British grenadiers from firing on the crowd. He joined the local grenadier corps and became a student of military science and engineering. After taking up the patriot cause, he was appointed colonel of the Continental Regiment of **Artillery** and became a close friend and adviser to **George Washington**. An active participant in the **Revolutionary War**, he became the chief of artillery for the **Continental Army** in 1776 and fought at **Trenton, Princeton, Brandywine, Germantown,** and **Monmouth**. He was in charge of positioning the American artillery at **Yorktown** and he commanded the post at West Point from 1782 to 1783. Knox has the distinction of being the only person to have served as both as the senior military officer and the senior civilian official of the army. While secretary, he initiated the establishment of a series of coastal fortifications and advocated the formation of a regular U.S. Navy. *See also* Appendix 3, Commanding Generals and Chiefs of Staff of the Army.

KOREAN WAR (1950–1953). At 0400, Sunday, 25 June 1950, North Korean forces attacked across the 38th parallel into the Republic of Korea. The main attack quickly moved toward the capital city of Seoul. The United Nations (UN) Security Council passed resolutions that condemned the invasion and encouraged member nations to render assistance to South Korea. On 27 June, President **Harry S. Truman** sent American naval and air forces to the aid of South Korea and, when they failed to stop the North Korean tide, he ordered in ground troops. Shortly thereafter, a Security Council resolution recommended a unified command and the UN asked the United States to provide the commander. The next day, Truman appointed General **Douglas MacArthur** to the post.

The first army unit into Korea, **Task Force Smith**, was quickly swept aside, but the buildup of American ground forces continued. UN member nations

U.S. Army Military History Institute.

3. A gun crew from the 159th Field Artillery provides supporting fire during the UN Defensive campaign of 1950.

quickly began sending forces to Korea and by mid-September these forces had stabilized the front along a perimeter enclosing the southeast Korean port of Pusan. During the **UN Offensive** campaign, MacArthur surprised the North Koreans with an amphibious landing at Inchon that severed the lines of communication supporting the North Korean invasion. As a result, the North Koreans quickly withdrew across the 38th parallel and moved north toward the Yalu River at the border of North Korea and Communist China. Bolstered by the success at Inchon, the UN expanded its objective from preserving South Korea from occupation to reunifying the peninsula, despite warnings from the Communist Chinese government that they would intervene should UN troops approach their border with Korea. In November, MacArthur's advance to the Yalu met an overwhelming counterattack by Communist Chinese forces. When the U.S. Eighth Army commander, Walton H. Walker, was killed in an automobile accident, **Matthew B. Ridgway** replaced him and rallied the demoralized UN forces to stop the Chinese advance.

With the situation stabilized, the United States and its allies limited their objective to preserving South Korea. The army became the primary instrument of this limited war strategy, which was a significant change to the American tradition of overwhelming victory. As cease-fire negotiations dragged on, army troops concentrated on maintaining a coherent defensive line while limiting friendly casualties. In so doing, they built fortifications and made liberal use of artillery. The concept of limited war was frustrating, but when MacArthur exceeded his authority in an attempt to pursue policies that might have widened the conflict, Truman, supported by the U.S. Joint Chiefs of Staff, relieved the general of command. After two years of stalemate and tedious negotiations, the two sides finally agreed to an armistice in July 1953. The agreement was signed on 27 July at Panmunjon and the cease-fire line became the border between North and South Korea. The war did not reunify the two Koreas, but it preserved the independence of South Korea. While the limited result strengthened the credibility of the American containment policy against communism, it left many Americans with the feeling that Korea was the first war the United States had not won. See also Korean War campaigns in Appendix 6, Campaigns of the United States Army.

KOREA, SUMMER 1953 (1 May to 27 July 1953). Korean War campaign streamer. The armistice negotiations between North Korea and the United Nations (UN), which had stalled in late 1952, resumed in April. On 18 June, the terms of the armistice had been all but completed, when the president of South Korea, Syngman Rhee, unilaterally ordered the release of 27,000 anti-Communist North Korean prisoners of war to protest armistice terms that left Korea divided. UN officials disclaimed any responsibility for this action, but the North Korean delegates denounced it as a serious breach of faith and delayed the final armistice agreement for another month. Communist forces on the battlefield took advantage of this delay and launched a three-division attack on 13 July, forcing the UN forces to withdraw about eight miles. By 20 July, UN forces had counterattacked and established a new main line of resistance. There was no attempt to restore the original line, as it was believed that the armistice would be signed at any time. By 19 July, the negotiators at Panmunjon had reached an accord on all points. Details were worked out within a week and the Korean Armistice Agreement was signed at 1000 hours on 27 July 1953. See also THIRD KOREAN WINTER.

KOREA, SUMMER–FALL 1952 (1 May to 30 November 1952). Korean War campaign streamer. In May 1952, the Communist forces in Korea became bolder, increasing probing attacks and patrols, intensifying artillery fire, and aggressively interrupting United Nations (UN) patrols. In May 1952, an estimated 102,000 artillery and mortar rounds fell in the U.S. Eighth Army positions. During the first half of 1952, UN forces waged a war of containment, while front-line soldiers hoped that the armistice negotiators would soon reach an agreement. In June, as the war went into its third year, the deadlock continued. July began with a series of small-scale attacks by both sides, but torrential rains restricted activity in the last week of July and for most of August. A series of Communist attacks in October 1952 produced some of the heaviest fighting in more than a year. The attacks began on 6 October with the largest volume of mortar and artillery fire received by the Eighth Army during the war, but on 15 October the disputed ground remained firmly in UN hands and the enemy withdrew.

By the end of 1952, armistice talks in Korea had stalled over several issues. The disagreements centered on the exchange of prisoners of war. The UN delegates proposed to give captives a choice of repatriation, so that those who did not wish to return to Communist control could be repatriated elsewhere. North Korea protested vigorously, insisting that all captives held by the Eighth Army be returned to their side. When North Korea failed to respond to UN efforts to settle the question, the UN delegation called an indefinite recess in the armistice negotiations on 7 October. Both military operations and armistice talks remained stalemated and, as the year 1952 ended, peace prospects seemed as remote as they had at the year's beginning. *See also* SECOND KOREAN WINTER.

KOSOVO AIR CAMPAIGN (24 March to 10 June 1999). Campaign streamer. In 1999, the nations of the North Atlantic Treaty Organization (NATO) conducted extensive air operations against Yugoslavia in an effort to stop the fighting in the province of Kosovo. U.S. Army forces, known as Task Force Hawk, deployed to the area from Germany and the United States in anticipation of conducting a ground invasion. There was no ground invasion during the campaign, but the army troops that had moved to the area formed the nucleus of the NATO occupation force.

— L —

LAFAYETTE, MARIE JOSEPH, MARQUIS DE (1757–1834). French **Revolutionary War** general. Born in Chavagnac, France, Lafayette joined the **Continental Army** in 1777 with a commission as a brigadier general, but without pay. He participated in the **Brandywine** campaign, where his performance impressed **George Washington**. In 1781, Lafayette received a command in the Southern Department, where his troops helped force **Charles Cornwallis**'s army to the Virginia coast, where Cornwallis was trapped by Washington at **Yorktown**. Lafayette returned to France, where he continued to support the United States during the French Revolution, in spite of the risks to him and his family.

LAGUNA DE BAY (8–17 April 1899). Philippine Insurrection campaign streamer. After suppressing an uprising in **Manila**, Major General Elwell S. Otis, commanding U.S. Army forces in the Philippines, sent several columns of troops into the countryside to split the insurgent forces and capture key positions. Major General Arthur MacArthur's column moved out of the city to capture the rebel capital of **Malolos**, while Major General Henry W. Lawton led a column south to capture Santa Cruz in the Laguna de Bay area on 10 April, before returning to Manila a week later.

LAMONT, DANIEL SCOTT (1851–1905). Secretary of war from 1893 to 1897. Born in New York, Lamont attended Union College but did not graduate. He became a clerk at the state capitol and rose to chief clerk by 1875. In 1883, he became military secretary with the rank of colonel to the governor of New York, Grover Cleveland. Cleveland later appointed Lamont secretary of war during Cleveland's second term as U.S. president. While in office, Lamont urged the adoption of a three-battalion **regiment** and recommended that the land being used for Apache Indian prisoners at Fort Sill, Oklahoma, be acquired for their permanent use and that their prisoner status be terminated. After leaving office, he was vice president of the Pacific Railway Company and sat on numerous boards of directors for banks and corporations. *See also* Appendix 4, Secretaries of War and Secretaries of the Army.

LEE, HENRY (1756–1818). American **Revolutionary War** officer. Born in Virginia, Lee graduated from the College of New Jersey in 1773. He was an exceptional horseman and during the Revolutionary War he led a mixed formation of **dragoons** and light **infantry**, earning the name "Light-Horse Harry." Lee believed that liberty in America required a strong federal government. In 1799, speaking in the House of Representatives, he memorialized **George Washington** as "first in war, first in peace, and first in the hearts of his countrymen." His son was **Robert E. Lee.**

LEE, ROBERT EDWARD (1807–1870). Confederate **Civil War** general. Born of a prominent family in Virginia, Lee's father was **Henry Lee,** a **Revolutionary War** hero. The younger Lee graduated from the **U.S. Military Academy** in 1829 and was commissioned an engineer. In 1831, he married Mary Custis, daughter of Martha Washington's grandson. The Lees made their home at Arlington, the Custis estate that overlooked Washington, D.C. Lee served under Winfield Scott in the **Mexican War,** where he observed how Scott handled a large army operating in hostile territory. By the end of the war, he had received **brevet** promotions to the rank of colonel. He remained in the army after the war, and his service included a number of years as superintendent of the Military Academy, before he accepted a position as second in command of one of the army's two new **cavalry** regiments formed in 1855.

When the state of Virginia seceded from the Union to join the Confederacy in 1861, Lee resigned from the U.S. Army, citing allegiance to his home state as taking precedence over allegiance to the Union. At the beginning of the **Civil War,** he received command of the Virginia militia, but **Jefferson Davis** made Lee the commander of the Army of Northern Virginia in 1862, when **Joseph E. Johnston** was wounded during the **Peninsula** campaign. Lee believed that the Confederacy had to defeat the Union militarily, so he assumed the offensive whenever possible, although his two invasions of Northern territory—**Antietam** in 1862 and **Gettysburg** a year later—both ended in failure. Remaining in command of the army until the end of the war, he surrendered to **Ulysses S. Grant** at **Appomattox** Courthouse in April 1865. Declining the numerous business opportunities he was offered after the war, Lee became president of Washington College in Lexington, Virginia, where he served quietly until his death in 1870. The institution subsequently became known as Washington and Lee University.

Lee ended the war as the Confederacy's greatest hero and is widely considered one of America's greatest generals. He was a man of high personal character and a natural leader whose presence inspired officers and soldiers alike. His subordinates were fiercely loyal to him and he returned that loyalty almost to a fault, rarely uttering a harsh word or rendering punishment for those who made mistakes. Declining to write his memoirs, Lee preferred to let others record his accomplishments. Since his death, Lee's reputation has reached legendary proportions.

LEMNITZER, LYMAN LOUIS (1899–1988). Chief of staff of the army from 1959 to 1960. Born in Pennsylvania, Lemnitzer graduated from the **U.S. Military Academy** in 1920. After being commissioned, he served in the coast artillery and taught natural and experimental philosophy at the Military Academy. Lemnitzer graduated from the **Command and Staff College** in 1936 and the **Army War College** in 1940. During **World War II**, he was a planner for the **Algeria–French Morocco and Sicily** campaigns in 1942 and 1943. He assumed command of U.S. forces in North Africa in 1944 and was one of the Allied negotiators for the German surrender in 1945. From 1945 to 1950, he was a military representative to the negotiations that led to the creation of the North Atlantic Treaty Organization (NATO). In the 1950s, Lemnitzer commanded various army forces before becoming the chief of staff of the army in 1959. He served in this position only about a year before being named the chairman of the Joint Chiefs of Staff. He was appointed to be NATO's supreme Allied commander Europe in 1963 and remained in that post until his retirement from active service in 1969. *See also* Appendix 3, Commanding Generals and Chiefs of Staff of the Army.

LEWIS AND CLARK EXPEDITION (May 1804 to 23 September 1806). In 1803, President Thomas Jefferson asked his secretary, **Meriwether Lewis**, to organize and lead an expedition to explore what is now the northwest United States. Lewis named **William Clark** coleader of the expedition and the two men left St. Louis in May 1804 with three sergeants and 22 **enlisted** men, as well as a number of volunteers and interpreters. Known as the Corps of Discovery, the expedition followed the Missouri River to its headwaters, crossed the Continental Divide, and followed the Columbia River to the Pacific Ocean. They returned on generally the same route and reached St. Louis on 23 September 1806, after a journey of 8,000 miles. While the exploration revealed there was no transcontinental water route to the Pacific Ocean, it provided a wealth of information on the environment as well as maps of the area.

LEWIS, MERIWETHER (1774–1809). Army officer and explorer. Born in Virginia, Lewis grew up among the aristocracy there and was educated by private tutors. As a member of the local militia, he participated in the suppression of the Whiskey Rebellion in 1794, joined the army a year later, and served briefly under **William Clark**, his future partner in the Corps of Discovery. In 1801, President Thomas Jefferson asked Lewis to be his private secretary, and for the next two years Lewis lived in the White House in Washington, D.C. In anticipation of the expedition, Jefferson sent Lewis to Philadelphia to learn mapmaking and other scientific skills. In 1803, with monies appropriated by Congress, Lewis began to organize the Corps of Discovery. He asked Clark to be his co-commander and the two men set out from St. Louis in May 1804. Their return to that city in 1806, after traveling overland to the Pacific Ocean, made them national figures. That same year, Lewis was appointed governor of the Louisiana Territory and he served in that post for two years. In October 1809, on his way to Washington, D.C., to clear up some financial matters, he died under mysterious circumstances near Nashville, Tennessee. *See also* LEWIS AND CLARK EXPEDITION.

LEXINGTON (19 April 1775). Revolutionary War campaign streamer. Hostilities between the British and the colonists in the war opened at Lexington and Concord in Massachusetts on 19 April 1775, when Minutemen and militia, alerted by Paul Revere, fired on a column of British troops moving to seize rebel military stores at Concord. The resistance forced the British to retreat back to **Boston**, while Massachusetts militia forces fired sporadically from behind the stone walls that lined the roads along the way back, then subsequently placed the British forces in Boston under siege. Shortly after the engagement, Americans began planning an expedition against the British at Fort **Ticonderoga** on Lake Champlain, a strategic post stocked with **artillery** and other military stores.

LEYTE (17 October 1944 to 1 July 1945). World War II campaign streamer. By the summer of 1944, the Allies were within 300 miles of Mindanao, the southernmost island in the Philippines. Admiral Chester Nimitz, directing the Allied move across the **Central Pacific**, had captured the Gilbert, Marshall, and Caroline Islands, while General **Douglas MacArthur** in the Southwest Pacific had blocked the Japanese move toward Australia and recaptured New Guinea and the Solomon Islands. The next strategic step was the Philippine Islands, a compelling political objective. The Philippines had been a special concern for the United States since 1898 and MacArthur, when he departed the islands under pressure in 1942, had made a very public promise to return. The principal objective in the Philippines was the island of **Luzon**, where the capital of Manila was located. Allied planners assumed that the Japanese had massed their principal ground, air, and naval strength on the island, so initial planning focused on first gaining a foothold in southernmost Mindanao Island, well away from Japanese strength. Once established on Mindanao, the Allies would move against Leyte and Luzon.

In September 1944, naval reconnaissance revealed relatively little Japanese activity in the Philippines, so Admiral William F. Halsey, commanding the naval forces supporting MacArthur, proposed bypassing Mindanao and landing directly on Leyte. The change was quickly approved by the U.S. chiefs of staff and an amphibious assault took place on 20 October 1944 with four divisions of Lieutenant General Walter Krueger's U.S. Sixth Army going in abreast. Initial opposition was light and by early afternoon the beach in the 24th Infantry Division's sector was deemed secure enough for MacArthur to wade ashore and declare "People of the Philippines, I have returned!"

In the days that followed, American forces made steady progress inland against the Japanese, who resisted tenaciously but were unable to coordinate an overall defensive effort. The Japanese used what air and naval forces they could muster against the Allies. On 24 October, between 150 and 200 Japanese bombers approached the beachhead from the north, while some 50 American fighters based on Leyte rose to intercept them and downed between 66 and 84 of them. Japanese air attacks continued until 28 October, when conventional raids ceased to be a major threat. But as their air strength diminished, the Japanese introduced a new and deadly weapon, a corps of pilots who deliberately crashed their bomb-laden planes directly into American ships. Termed *kamikaze*, or divine wind, after a thirteenth century typhoon that scattered a Mongol invasion fleet off Japan, the suicide pilots attacked the transport and escort vessels in Leyte Gulf supporting the landings. In addition to the kamikaze threat, a naval fleet with virtually all of Japan's surface forces converged on Leyte Gulf in three columns and for a time threatened the landing. But in a series of engagements at sea lasting from 23 to 26 October, the Japanese fleet was almost completely destroyed, giving Allied naval forces virtual control of the Pacific Ocean.

It took the Allies two months of fighting to finally secure the island. Japanese defenders continued to fight as units until 31 December. Although Japanese stragglers were no longer a threat to American units, the mop up of the stragglers continued until 8 May 1945. The campaign cost American forces 15,584 casualties. The Japanese lost an estimated 49,000 troops, mostly combat forces, in their unsuccessful defense. Although there were some 255,000 Japanese troops on Luzon, the loss of air and naval forces during the Leyte campaign put Japan into a defensive posture in the rest of the Philippines, and even before the fighting ended on Leyte Americans landed on Luzon. The loss of Leyte in effect cost Japan the Philippines. *See also* PHILIPPINE ISLANDS.

LIBERATION AND DEFENSE OF KUWAIT (17 January to 11 April 1991). **Persian Gulf War** campaign streamer. Known also as Desert Storm. The campaign for liberating Kuwait from the August 1990 occupation by the Iraqi Army was conducted by a United Nations (UN) coalition military force commanded by U.S. Army general **H. Norman Schwarzkopf.** Planning for the campaign centered on the U.S. Army forces that had deployed to the Persian Gulf during the **Defense of Saudi Arabia** campaign. Two army corps held the left and center of the coalition line, while a combined force of U.S. Marine and Arab units were on the right. The XVIII Airborne Corps, with three U.S. Army divisions and a French division, was on the left flank, while the VII Corps, with four U.S. Army divisions and a British division, was in the center. During the campaign, the VII Corps moved north into Iraq after the coalition left and right flanks had been secured, made a sharp turn to the right, and pushed into Kuwait from the west.

The ground campaign lasted only four days and was far more successful and suffered fewer coalition casualties than expected. The attack began on the far right of the coalition line on Sunday, 24 February, as U.S. Marines moved on

Kuwait City. Iraqi resistance was light and on 27 February the Kuwaiti 35th Brigade entered the capital and began mopping up large numbers of disorganized Iraqi soldiers in and around the city. At about the same time, as the Marines started their operations on the right, the French division advanced into Iraq to cover the left flank of the coalition's advance into the desert. By 27 February, as Kuwaiti forces were entering Kuwait City, U.S. Army forces slammed into elements of **Saddam Hussein**'s elite Republican Guards north of Kuwait and forced the Iraqis to fall back toward Baghdad. In the center, a heavily armored U.S. Army corps advanced with more than 2,000 armored vehicles. Within hours, it achieved a breakthrough and the offensive moved north and then east into Kuwait. Low visibility caused by a combination of poor weather and smoke from oil wells set ablaze by fleeing Iraqi forces gave the advantage to the U.S. forces. Equipped with thermal sights, the army's Abrams **tanks** saw through the rain and smoke, while the Iraqis, with no such devices, were fighting blind.

The coalition's ground campaign was a bold plan that succeeded like no other ground campaign in the history of warfare. However, its initial military success led to a political decision to stop the ground campaign before it could completely trap and destroy the Republican Guard, thus three divisions were allowed to escape essentially intact, giving Saddam Hussein a loyal fighting force to use against internal rebellion. The Persian Gulf War saw the attainment of the UN goal of removing the Iraqis from Kuwait, while the terms of the cease-fire allowed UN inspection teams into Iraq to seek out weapons of mass destruction, although Saddam Hussein remained in power. At the end of the war, while Iraq was no longer the most dominant military power in the area, it was not rendered impotent by any means. In spite of the overwhelming defeat of his military forces in battle, Saddam Hussein retained control of the Iraqi government and appeared to have lost little of his prestige among the civilian population in Iraq. Even as the coalition began withdrawing their military forces and the UN began to impose the terms of the cease-fire, Hussein began to obstruct inspection teams and ruthlessly suppress internal uprisings opposing his continued rule. *See also* CEASE-FIRE (12 April 1991 to 30 November 1995).

LINCOLN, ABRAHAM (1809–1865). President of the United States during the **Civil War**. Born in Kentucky, Lincoln was raised there and in Illinois. Self-educated, he served in the Illinois legislature and was admitted to the Illinois bar in 1836. He served a term in the House of Representatives from 1847 to 1849, when he was critical of the **Mexican War**; ran unsuccessfully for the Senate in 1858; and was the Republican candidate for president in 1860. Lincoln narrowly won the election and his victory prompted seven states to secede from the Union by the end of 1860, as more were preparing to follow suit. Lincoln took office in March 1861 with the country in crisis. In April, the fall of Fort **Sumter** opened hostilities in the Civil War.

Lincoln was directly involved in running the war and naming the commanders of the Union Army. He tried to explain to his generals the necessity of having specific objectives and a plan to attain them, but the first two years of the war produced a succession of disappointments, until Lincoln named **Ulysses S. Grant** to the post of commanding general, after Grant's victory at **Vicksburg** in 1863. With Grant handling the military side of things, Lincoln concentrated on the political aspects of the war. Five days after **Robert E. Lee** surrendered to Grant at **Appomattox**, Lincoln was shot while attending a play at Ford's theater and he died the next day. His son, **Robert Todd Lincoln**, became secretary of war in 1881.

LINCOLN, BENJAMIN (1733–1810). Secretary at war from 1781 to 1783. Born in Hingham, Massachusetts, Lincoln was a farmer who commanded the Vermont militia in 1776 and 1777 and was wounded at **Saratoga**. He later commanded American forces in South Carolina, where he was forced to surrender to the British. After returning in a prisoner exchange, he participated in the **Yorktown** campaign, where he accepted the formal British surrender. He was one of the two men who served as secretary at war; **Henry Knox** was the other. While Knox held the post, the title became the "**secretary of war.**" Lincoln worked closely with **George Washington**, commander of the **Continental Army**, to develop the operational relationship between the army's senior civil official and its military leader. *See also* Appendix 4, Secretaries of War and Secretaries of the Army.

LINCOLN, ROBERT TODD (1843–1929). Secretary of war from 1881 to 1885. Born in Illinois, Lincoln attended local schools and the Phillips Exeter Academy, before attending Harvard University from 1859 until 1864. His father, **Abraham Lincoln**, was elected president of the United States in 1860. The younger Lincoln entered Harvard Law School but left after four months to join the army, where he served on **Ulysses S. Grant**'s staff until the end of the **Civil War**. After the war, he studied law in Chicago and was admitted to the bar in 1867. He was a representative to the 1880 Republican Convention and was appointed secretary of war the next year. While in office, Lincoln made recommendations to punish white intrusion onto Indian lands, separate the weather bureau from the army, and provide appropriations to the states to support volunteer militia organizations. After leaving office, he resumed his private law practice, but served as minister to Great Britain from 1889 to 1893. Again resuming his legal practice, he was legal counsel to the Pullman Company and became its president in 1897. He resigned as president of the company in 1911, but remained chairman of its board of directors. *See also* Appendix 4, Secretaries of War and Secretaries of the Army.

LITTLE BIG HORN (1876–1877). Indian wars campaign streamer. The influx of whites following discovery of gold in the Black Hills of South Dakota in 1874 triggered renewed unrest among the Indians, prompting many to leave their reservations. When the Indians refused to return, the army sent a small expedition into the Powder River country of present-day Montana and Wyoming in March 1876 with negligible results, so Lieutenant General **Philip Sheridan** embarked on a larger operation in the summer. The plan was for several columns to converge on the Yellowstone River to trap the Indians and force their return to the reservations. One column, under Major General **George Crook**, moved north from Fort Fetterman in Wyoming in late May 1876 with about 1,000 troops. At the same time, two columns under Brigadier General Alfred H. Terry marched up the Yellowstone. Terry moved from Fort Abraham Lincoln in North Dakota with one column of more than 1,000 men to the mouth of Powder River. The second of Terry's columns, about 450 men under Colonel John Gibbon, moved from Fort Ellis in Montana to the mouth of the Bighorn River.

On 17 June 1876, Crook's troops fought an indecisive engagement on the Rosebud River with a large band of Sioux and **Cheyennes** under **Crazy Horse** and **Sitting Bull** and then moved back to the Tongue River to wait for reinforcements. Meanwhile, Terry was on the trail of the same Indian band. He sent Lieutenant Colonel **George Custer** with the 7th Cavalry up the Rosebud to locate the war party and move south of it. Terry, with the rest of his command, continued up the Yellowstone to meet Gibbon and close on the Indians from the north. On 25 June, the 7th Cavalry, proceeding up the Rosebud, discovered 4,000 to 5,000 Indians, including about 2,500 warriors, camped along the banks of the Little Bighorn River. Custer divided his forces to strike the camp from several directions. Major Marcus A. Reno's detachment attacked first and surprised the Indians, who quickly rallied and drove the soldiers off, inflicting heavy losses. With Reno's withdrawal, the Indians were able to concentrate on Custer's command. The Indians surrounded Custer on broken terrain east of the Little Bighorn and killed the entire force of 211 men. When the Indians learned of Terry's approach from the north, they moved south. The disaster touched off a debate that continues today over Custer's decisions that led to the battle. But with his crushing defeat, Custer gained a place in army history a victory would not have provided.

The campaign continued until September 1877. Crook and Terry joined forces on the Rosebud on 10 August 1876. Most of the Indians slipped past the troops, although many did return to the agencies. Fighting in the fall and winter of 1876–77 consisted mostly of skirmishes and raids, including Crook's capture of American Horse's village at Slim Buttes in South Dakota on 9 September and of Dull Knife's village in the Bighorn Mountains on 26 November. On 8 January 1877, Colonel **Nelson A. Miles** attacked Crazy Horse's camp in the Wolf Mountains. By the summer of 1877, most of the Sioux were back on the reservations. Crazy Horse came in and was killed resisting arrest at Camp Robinson, Nebraska, in September. Sitting Bull, with a small band of Sioux, escaped to Canada, but surrendered at Fort Buford, Montana, in July 1881.

LOGISTICS. The practical art of moving armies and keeping them supplied. Logistics is said to make up as much as nine-tenths of the business of war. No matter how grand or clever, the operational plan can only be accomplished if it can be supported logistically. One of the army's **armored** divisions can use up to 600,000 gallons of fuel, 75 tons of food, 108,000 gallons of water, and 3,500 rounds of ammunition in a day of combat. Logistics encompasses the materiel and services needed to sustain military operations. Materiel includes organizational items such as unit equipment, ammunition, spare parts, fuel, and lubricants, as well as individual items such as food, water, clothing, and personal equipment. Services include equipment repair and maintenance, transportation of people and supplies, medical treatment and evacuation, construction, and individual services such as mail delivery and sanitation facilities.

LONG ISLAND (26–29 August 1776). Revolutionary War campaign streamer. After the British evacuation of **Boston** in March 1776, **George Washington** moved his army, minus the militia, to New York in anticipation of a British invasion. During July and August 1776, British commander William Howe, supported by a British fleet, landed an army of 32,000 British and Hessian regulars on Staten Island. By late August, Washington had a force of over 20,000 Continentals and militia and a system of defenses on and around Manhattan Island. About half of his troops were deployed in fortifications on Brooklyn Heights and at forward positions at the western end of Long Island, under command of Major General Israel Putnam. Between 22 and 25 August, Howe landed about 20,000 men on Long Island. In the evening of the 26th, the British conducted a wide flanking movement around the American left. The next day, Howe attacked and the American front crumbled. Remnants of the American forces fell back into entrenchments on Brooklyn Heights and two nights later evacuated to Manhattan, unobserved by the British. Estimates place American losses at 300–400 killed and wounded and 700–1,200 taken prisoner, while Howe listed his losses as 367. The British followed up their success on Long Island with a series of landings on Manhattan Island that compelled Washington to retire north to avoid entrapment.

LONGSTREET, JAMES (1821–1904). Confederate **Civil War** general. Born in South Carolina, Longstreet graduated from the **U.S. Military Academy** in 1842. He served in the **Mexican War**, where he received **brevet** promotions to major. At the beginning of the Civil War in 1861, he resigned and offered his services to the Confederacy. He was commissioned a brigadier general and, except for missing **Chancellorsville** while on medical leave after being wounded in the **Wilderness** campaign, he fought in every major battle in the eastern theater of the war. As **Robert E. Lee**'s second in command, Longstreet was an excellent corps commander and one of the most modern-thinking soldiers in the Civil War. Although not generally considered a student of war, he was among the first to see the advantages of using fortifications in the defense, and of using maneuver instead of frontal attacks, against a prepared enemy. At **Gettysburg**, he disagreed with Lee's handling of the battle and was subsequently unfairly accused of delaying his attack on the second day. As a result, his postwar reputation suffered. After the war, he became a Republican and held a variety of political posts.

LUNDY'S LANE (25 July 1814). War of 1812 campaign streamer. After the **Chippewa** campaign, **Jacob Jenning Brown**'s force advanced to Queenston, but abandoned plans for an attack on Forts George and Niagara when the American fleet on Lake Erie failed to cooperate in the operation. On 24 and 25 July 1814, Brown moved back to the Chippewa River to prepare for a cross-country march along Lundy's Lane to the west end of Lake Ontario. The British, however, had concentrated about 2,200 troops in the vicinity of Lundy's Lane and had some 1,500 more men in Forts George and Niagara. On 25 July, **Winfield Scott's** brigade, moving toward Queenston to distract a British detachment threatening the American line of communications on the American side of the Niagara, ran into an enemy force at the junction of Queenston Road and Lundy's Lane. The ensuing battle, which eventually involved all of Brown's 2,900 men and some 3,000 British soldiers, was fiercely fought, but did not result in a clear-cut victory for either side. The Americans retired to the Chippewa unmolested, but the battle terminated Brown's invasion of Canada. Casualties were heavy on both sides, the British losing 878 and the Americans 854 in killed and wounded; both Brown and Scott were wounded and the British commander was wounded and captured.

LUZON (15 December 1944 to 4 July 1945). World War II campaign streamer. With the successful landing and occupation of **Leyte** in late 1944, the Allies had gained a foothold in the **Philippine Islands**. The primary objective, however, was the island of Luzon, which had some 255,000 Japanese defenders. General **Douglas MacArthur** had already kept his promise of returning to the Philippines when he waded ashore at Leyte in October 1944, but he was anxious to complete the recapture of the islands. Even before the fighting stopped on Leyte, MacArthur landed troops on Mindoro, an island with minimal Japanese defenders just south of Luzon. From the airfields on Mindoro, Allied aircraft could provide close air support to the landings on Luzon. American forces invaded the small island on 15 December 1944 and by the end of the day army engineers were preparing airfields. They had one ready in five days and a second one ready eight days after that.

Although there were a quarter million Japanese on Luzon, Japan's air and naval forces were largely gone by the end of 1944. With few modern weapons and little equipment, the Japanese commander, General Tomoyuki Yamashita, knew his troops could not hope to defeat the well-equipped and well-armed American invaders in the open field, so he put his main forces into mountain strongholds and opted for a campaign of attrition. On 9 January, the U.S. Sixth Army made a massive amphibious assault on Luzon along the shores of the Lingayen Gulf. The Japanese did not intend to defend the Central Plains and the area around Manila Bay, but Japanese forces, primarily naval, disregarded Yamashita's plan and held out in **Manila**. Directed by MacArthur to get to Manila, a powerful American force moved rapidly down the central valley from the Gulf of Manila, with units racing at speeds up to 50 miles an hour to get the honor of reaching the city first. On 3 February, the leading elements of the 1st Cavalry Division reached the outskirts of Manila. The next day, MacArthur announced the imminent capture of the city, but it was another month before Japanese resistance in Manila ceased. The Japanese forces in the mountain strongholds conducted a protracted defense, but except for one strong pocket in the mountains of north-central Luzon, where fighting continued until the end of the war on 15 August, organized Japanese resistance in Luzon ceased by the end of May.

The loss of Luzon was a severe blow to the Japanese and placed the Allies one step closer to ultimate victory, but Japan did not admit defeat. The Allies were planning for an invasion of the Japanese home islands when President **Harry S. Truman** decided to use the atomic bomb in an attempt to end the war quickly. The devastating effects of the two atomic bombs dropped on Hiroshima and Nagasaki persuaded the Japanese to surrender in August, negating the need for what would surely have been a costly amphibious assault of the Japanese homeland. *See also* AIR OFFENSIVE, JAPAN.

LYS (9–27 April 1918). World War I campaign streamer. After their attack on the Somme, the Germans still hoped to destroy the hard-hit British army before it had a chance to recover. In an attack launched on 9 April 1918, the Germans committed 46 divisions to the assault and quickly scored a breakthrough. The British appealed to the French for reinforcements, but the Allied supreme commander, convinced that the British could hold, would not release the reserves he was hold-

4. The machine gun battalion from the 26th Infantry moving toward the front in April 1918, during the Lys campaign.

U.S. Army Military History Institute.

ing for a renewed Allied offensive. The British held and the Germans called off the offensive on 29 April. About 500 Americans participated in the campaign. *See also* SOMME DEFENSIVE.

— M —

MACARTHUR, DOUGLAS (1880–1964). Chief of staff of the army from 1930 to 1935. Born in Arkansas and raised on army posts as the son of General Arthur MacArthur, the younger MacArthur graduated from the **U.S. Military Academy** in 1903. Commissioned an engineer, he received a number of engineering assignments and was an aide to the commander of the Pacific Division and to President **Theodore Roosevelt**, before being assigned to the army's **general staff** in 1913. During **World War I**, MacArthur was chief of staff of the 42d Infantry Division and commanded a brigade during the **St. Mihiel** and **Meuse–Argonne** campaigns. From 1919 to 1922, he was superintendent of the Military Academy and then served in the Philippines until becoming chief of staff of the army in 1930. While in office, he administered the army's participation in the **Civilian Conservation Corps** and dispersed the World War I veterans who had gathered in Washington, D.C., during the **Bonus Army** March. In 1935, President Franklin Roosevelt sent him to the Philippines to organize the island's defense forces and two years later he retired from the army to become an adviser to the Philippine government.

MacArthur was recalled to active duty in July 1941 amid rising tensions and placed in command of all U.S. forces in the Far East. When the Japanese attacked the American bases in the Philippines on 7 December, MacArthur and his men retreated to the Bataan peninsula and eventually to the island of Corregidor. He led the defense until Roosevelt ordered him to Australia in March 1942 to command the Southwest Pacific Area. Upon his departure from the Philippines, he promised "I shall return." He took the offensive late in 1942 and began his island-hopping campaign strategy, which used air, land, and sea forces in a series of flanking movements that took him back to the Philippines in October 1944. Two months later, he was promoted to **general of the army**. In September 1945, he accepted the Japanese surrender on the deck of the battleship USS *Missouri* and was appointed commander of the Allied occupation of Japan, where he implemented generally liberal economic, social, and political reforms.

When North Korea invaded South Korea in June 1950 to start the **Korean War**, President **Harry S. Truman** named MacArthur commander of the U.S. and United Nations (UN) forces that rushed to defend the beleaguered country. MacArthur surprised the invaders with a strategic flanking attack by landing forces at Inchon during the **UN Offensive** campaign and cutting the supply lines for the North Korean armies in the south. Taking advantage of the confusion created by the landing, he pushed his UN force beyond the 38th parallel, the boundary between the two Koreas, and by November his force was nearing the Yalu

River, the North Korean border with China. MacArthur dismissed a warning issued by the Chinese that they were prepared to intervene and he ordered his forces to push on to the Yalu. In late November, the Chinese sent massive forces across the river and pushed the UN back to the 38th parallel. MacArthur advocated carrying the war into China by air and publicly disagreed with Truman's proposed cease-fire. When a letter MacArthur wrote to a Republican senator, branding Truman's position appeasement, appeared in the press, the president, with the support of the joint chiefs of staff, relieved the general from command in April 1951. MacArthur was hailed as a hero when he returned to the United States, but Senate investigations revealed that his position was generally opposed by most experts. He returned to private life but retained his rank and active status in the army until his death in 1964. *See also* Appendix 3, Commanding Generals and Chiefs of Staff of the Army.

MACOMB, ALEXANDER (1782–1841). Commanding general of the army from 1828 to 1841. Born in British-held Detroit, Macomb moved with his parents to New York and was educated at an academy in New Jersey. He joined a New York militia company at age 16 and was commissioned a first lieutenant in the **Corps of Engineers** in 1802. He was one of the first officers to receive formal training at the **U.S. Military Academy**, established at West Point that same year. Rising through the ranks as an engineer, he was promoted to major general in 1828 and became commanding general of the army. Macomb believed that the commanding general should have authority over the entire army and only loose supervision by the **secretary of war**. While in office, he recommended doubling the size of the army, increasing enlisted pay to reduce desertion, and developing a system of officer retirement and replacement. He died while in office. *See also* Appendix 3, Commanding Generals and Chiefs of Staff of the Army.

MAHAN, DENNIS HART (1802–1871). U.S. Military Academy professor. Born in New York, Mahan graduated from the Military Academy at the head of his class in 1824. After studying in France, he resigned as a first lieutenant to become a professor at the academy, where he taught engineering and the science of war. He taught strategy using European interpretations of Napoleonic warfare, particularly the writings of **Antoine-Henri Jomini**, a Swiss officer who had served in those wars. Through Mahan, Jomini became a popular source of military history and theory for American officers interested in pursuing the study of war in the nineteenth century.

MALOLOS (24 March to 16 August 1899). Philippine Insurrection campaign streamer. After suppressing an attempted uprising in **Manila** during February 1899, Major General Elwell S. Otis, the commander of U.S. Army forces in the Philippine Islands, sent several columns of troops into the countryside to split the insurgent forces and capture key positions. Major General Arthur MacArthur led a column along the railroad to the north of Manila. Malolos, the insurgent capitol, was his first objective. En route, MacArthur's column seized Calocan on 10 February 1899, Malolos on 31 March, and San Fernando, Pampanga, on 5 May.

The troops also took the stronghold of San Isidro on 15 May, but held it only temporarily. The Americans quickly took advantage of the capture of Malolos and rapidly advanced to Angeles, which they captured on 16 August.

MANASSAS (7 August to 2 September 1862). Civil War campaign streamer. Known also as the Second Battle of Bull Run or Second Manassas. In July 1862, Confederate General **Robert E. Lee** withdrew the Army of Northern Virginia to Richmond after thwarting Union forces led by General **George B. McClellan** during the **Peninsula** campaign. On 13 July, General **Thomas J. Jackson** marched northwest out of Richmond with a corps of Lee's army, some 24,000 men, to strike advance elements of General John Pope's army, which was moving to join McClellan. Jackson met and defeated a Federal corps at Cedar Mountain on 9 August, but did not follow up the victory because Pope's main body was nearby. Lee followed Jackson out of Richmond with the remainder of the Army of Northern Virginia, intending to outflank and cut off Pope before he and McClellan could join forces. Lee conducted a series of maneuvers that caused Pope to withdraw to the northern bank of the Rappahannock River.

While General **James Longstreet** and his corps held the Federals on the Rappahannock, Lee sent Jackson around the Union right flank. Jackson got behind Pope on 26 August at Manassas, where he captured extensive Federal military stores. Pope moved northeast and clashed with Jackson at Groveton on 28 August, after which Jackson established defensive positions in the vicinity of the 1861 **Bull Run** battlefield. On 29 August, as McClellan's troops began to arrive on the scene, Pope moved to attack Jackson. A two-day engagement ensued, during which Longstreet's divisions arrived and turned the tide against the Federals. Pope retired to Washington, fighting off a Confederate force at Chantilly on the way and ending the campaign with the Confederates holding the battlefield. After the campaign, Pope was relieved of command of his army and his forces were combined with McClellan's Army of the Potomac. On the Confederate side, the success emboldened Lee to attempt an invasion of Maryland. During the Manassas campaign, 48,527 Confederates engaged 75,696 Federals. The Confederates lost 1,481 killed, 7,627 wounded, and 89 missing; the Federals lost 1,724 killed, 8,372 wounded, and 5,958 missing.

MANILA (31 July to 13 August 1898). Spanish–American War campaign streamer. The ground campaign was a sequel to the first naval engagement of the war. On 1 May 1898, a small American squadron under Commodore George Dewey destroyed a Spanish naval force in Manila Bay. Dewey then blockaded the port and requested 5,000 men to take the city of Manila. While waiting for the ground forces to arrive, he encouraged Filipino insurgents, led by Emilio Aguinaldo, whom Dewey had brought from exile in China, to besiege the city. Aguinaldo, who had previously led an insurrection against Spanish rule, hoped to gain recognition of a Philippine Republic. The **War Department** sent about 11,300 troops to Manila under the command of Major General Wesley Merritt. The Spaniards in Manila indicated a willingness to surrender to the Americans, but not to the Filipinos, because they did not want the city exposed to undisciplined native insurgents after capitulation. The United States agreed and Dewey persuaded the Filipinos to let only Americans make the final assault on Manila. At the same time, he and Merritt made arrangements with the Spanish for a noisy but bloodless capture of the city. The operation began on 12 August, but some Filipinos became mixed with the advancing troops, resulting in fighting that killed 5 Americans and wounded 35. Eventually, the Spaniards surrendered to the Americans and signed the formal articles of capitulation on 14 August. American losses during the operations in the Philippines were 18 killed and 109 wounded. Filipino units that had entered Manila were persuaded to leave, but subsequently Aguinaldo led a rebellion against American rule during the **Philippine Insurrection**. See also MANILA (4 February to 17 March 1899).

MANILA (4 February to 17 March 1899). Philippine Insurrection campaign streamer. On 21 January 1899, Filipino nationalists, disappointed when Spain ceded the Philippines to the United States at the end of the **Spanish–American War**, declared the formation of a Philippine Republic with Emilio Aguinaldo as president. The nationalist fervor led to a clash with U.S. Army troops near Manila on 4 February. The Americans, numbering about 12,000 combat troops under Major General Elwell S. Otis, the commander of U.S. Army forces in the Philippines, defeated Aguinaldo's force of some 40,000 men and suppressed the attempted uprising in Manila. Otis then dispatched army columns north, east, and south from Manila to split the insurgent forces and seize key towns. Brigadier General Lloyd Wheaton's column pushed out of Manila and gained control of the Pasig River in March, permanently interrupting communications between insurgent forces in north and south Luzon. During operations in the Philippines, the insurgent forces generally fought bravely, but they were poorly equipped and led. Aguinaldo was an indifferent field commander and had trouble keeping his subordinates in line. See also MANILA (31 July to 13 August 1898).

MARCH, PEYTON CONWAY (1864–1955). Chief of staff of the army from 1918 to 1921. Born in Pennsylvania, March graduated from the **U.S. Military Academy** in 1888. He served in various positions until 1898, when he commanded an **artillery** battery in the **Manila** campaign during the **Spanish–American War**, and later participated in the suppression of the **Philippine Insurrection**. He commanded an artillery regiment during the campaign in **Mexico** and was an artillery commander with the American Expeditionary Force in **World War I**, before becoming chief of staff in 1918. While in office, March oversaw the buildup of army forces for World War I; established the air service, tank corps, and chemical warfare service; and supervised the army's demobilization at the end of the war. He retired from active service in 1921. See also Appendix 3, Commanding Generals and Chiefs of Staff of the Army.

MARCY, WILLIAM LEARNED (1786–1857). Secretary of war from 1845 to 1849. Born in Massachusetts, Marcy was educated at Leicester and Woodstock

Academies and in 1808 graduated from Brown University. He studied law at Troy, New York, and was admitted to the bar in 1811. He served in the New York militia and saw action during the **War of 1812**. Becoming active in state politics, he was elected to the U.S. Senate before serving three terms as governor of New York. Marcy became secretary of war in 1845 and, while in office, proposed establishing an Indian agency in Oregon Territory and played a key role in settling the 1846 Oregon boundary dispute with Great Britain. After leaving office, he was U.S. secretary of state from 1853 to 1857 and in this position negotiated the Gadsden Treaty, which added almost 30,000 square miles to the Southwestern United States. *See also* Appendix 4, Secretaries of War and Secretaries of the Army.

MARION, FRANCIS (1732–1795). Revolutionary War partisan leader. Born in South Carolina, Marion was a planter who gained experience fighting the Cherokee Indians in 1759 and 1761. A regimental commander in the Revolutionary War, he escaped the British siege of **Charleston** in 1780, raised a band of irregular forces, and conducted small, surprise raids against the British forces in the Southern theater. He and his **rangers** cooperated with **Nathanael Greene**, the theater commander, as he denied the British a secure base and prevented their regulars from concentrating against Greene. After the war, Marion served in the South Carolina Senate.

MARSH, JOHN OTTO, JR. (1926–). Secretary of the army from 1981 to 1989. Born in Virginia, Marsh attended public schools and joined the army in 1944. Commissioned in the **infantry**, he served with the army's occupation forces in Germany after **World War II**. He remained in the **U.S. Army Reserve** until 1951, at which time he entered the **Army National Guard** in Virginia. He graduated from Washington and Lee University that same year and was admitted to the bar a year later. Becoming active in politics, he served four terms in the U.S. House of Representatives before becoming assistant secretary of defense for legislative affairs and serving as counselor to President Gerald Ford for three years. He became secretary of the army in 1981 and held the office longer than any previous secretary. While Marsh was in office, the army observed the 200th anniversary of the nation and implemented legislative provisions facilitating joint operations among all military services. *See also* Appendix 4, Secretaries of War and Secretaries of the Army.

MARSHALL, GEORGE CATLETT (1880–1959). Chief of staff of the army from 1939 to 1945. Born in Pennsylvania, Marshall graduated from the Virginia Military Institute in 1901 and was commissioned a second lieutenant the next year. After service in the Philippines, he attended the **Command and General Staff College** and was on **John J. Pershing**'s staff during **World War I**, when he had a major part in planning the **St. Mihiel** and **Meuse–Argonne** campaigns. With his reputation as an exceptional planner and organizer, Marshall was denied his request for a command so that he could remain on the staff. After the war, he was an aide to Pershing for five years, served three years in China, and in 1927 became the assistant commandant of the army's **infantry** school, where he mentored many of the lieutenants who would become the army's senior commanders in **World War II**. Finally promoted to brigadier general in 1936, after 34 years of active service, he rose rapidly to become chief of staff of the army in 1939, being selected over several officers more senior to him.

In his first years as chief of staff, Marshall concentrated on building a modern army, in anticipation of the U.S. entry into World War II. During the building process, he gained a reputation for honesty and impressed Congress with his military expertise. He was responsible for organizing, training, supplying, and deploying American soldiers to theaters of war all over the world. He was also a principal adviser to President Franklin D. Roosevelt on strategy and attended all the major Allied planning conferences from Casablanca to Yalta. Marshall was the leading figure in the U.S. Joint Chiefs of Staff and the British-American Combined Chiefs of Staff (CSC), both created to coordinate Allied efforts during World War II. When Allied planning began for the cross-channel invasion of **Normandy**, it was widely expected that Marshall would be given command of the operation, but he was deemed indispensable in Washington and he chose not to request the position. The command went to **Dwight D. Eisenhower**.

Marshall was promoted to **general of the army** in 1944. After the war, he retired and was a special emissary to China before becoming secretary of state in 1947. In this position, he developed the successful plan for economic recovery in Europe that came to be known as the Marshall Plan. He received a Nobel Peace Prize in 1953 for his work as secretary of state. He became secretary of defense in 1950, in which position he rebuilt U.S. forces during the **Korean War** and played a key role in President **Harry S. Truman**'s relief of **Douglas MacArthur** in 1951. Since his death in 1959, his reputation for integrity and selfless public service has grown and he is widely considered one of the world's greatest soldier-statesmen. *See also* Appendix 3, Commanding Generals and Chiefs of Staff of the Army.

MARSHALL, S. L. A. (1900–1977). Army officer and author. Born in New York, Marshall joined the army in 1917 and earned a commission in France during **World War I**. After the war, he became a journalist and covered wars for the next 40 years. He pioneered the combat history technique of interviewing survivors of a battle individually and in groups immediately after a battle to get their reactions. By concentrating on **enlisted** soldiers and junior officers, he elicited details of the action and was able to compare the stories of various participants. Marshall wrote his accounts in a narrative style using anecdotes from the interviews. He was promoted to brigadier general during the **Korean War** and assigned to the U.S. Eighth Army, where he continued to use his interview techniques to write combat history. Years later, he defended the army's role in the **Vietnam War**. During his long writing career, he wrote a number of books. His most influential work was the 1947 *Men against Fire*, in which he asserted that only 25 or 30 percent of infantry soldiers fired their weapons in combat, a claim challenged by several authorities over the years. In spite of the controversy that surrounded that claim, Marshall's writings have had a significant influence on how the army and public viewed combat.

MAULDIN, WILLIAM HENRY (1921–). Editorial cartoonist. Born in New Mexico, Mauldin studied cartooning in Chicago in 1939 and trained with the army's 45th Infantry Division in 1940, when he became a cartoonist for the division newspaper. He joined the *Stars and Stripes* in 1944 and developed the characters Willie and Joe to depict the life of the American soldier in **World War II** in Europe. The cartoons were featured in more than a hundred newspapers in the United States and Willie and Joe became two of the most recognized symbols of the American combat infantryman. Mauldin received the Pulitzer Prize in 1945 and his book *Up Front* was an instant best-seller. After the war, he continued as an editorial cartoonist and during the **Korean War** he visited the front and reported his impressions of the war.

McCAULEY, MARY LUDWIG HAYS (1744?–1832). Revolutionary War heroine. Born of German immigrants who settled in New Jersey, McCauley was the servant of Dr. William Irvine in Carlisle, Pennsylvania, in 1769, when she married a local barber, John Casper Hays. While her husband was serving in 1777 in the regiment commanded by Irvine, now a colonel, she joined her husband in camp. When Private Hays, an artilleryman, was wounded during the **Monmouth** campaign, Mary Hays took his place at the cannon and helped serve the gun for the remainder of the battle. She had been carrying water in pitchers, or buckets, to the gun crew and gained the nickname Molly Pitcher. When Hays died some years later, she married another veteran of the war, John (or George) McCauley. When McCauley died, she petitioned for a widow's pension, but the state of Pennsylvania awarded her a $40 annuity in recognition of her own services during the war. *See also* WOMEN IN THE ARMY.

McCLELLAN, GEORGE BRINTON (1826–1885). Commanding general of the army from 1861 to 1862. Born in Pennsylvania, McClellan graduated from the **U.S. Military Academy** in 1846 and was shortly on his way to the **Mexican War** as a member of the Company of Engineers and became part of the **Vera Cruz** campaign, led by General **Winfield Scott**. Receiving a **brevet** to captain during the war, he participated in a variety of expeditions and surveys before transferring to the **cavalry** to join one of two new regiments formed in 1853. Before joining his new command, however, he visited Europe as part of a U.S. Army team to observe the Crimean War and study military developments. After completing his report of the tour, he resigned to go into railroading.

When the **Civil War** started, McClellan, who had a reputation as one of the nation's finest soldiers, was offered command of the militias of New York, Pennsylvania, and Ohio. He accepted Ohio, because it was the first offer to reach him. His allegiance was to preserving the Union rather than to a particular state. McClellan led the first major Union force into western Virginia in 1861 and his success in the mountains attracted the attention of President **Abraham Lincoln** shortly after the disastrous Union defeat in the **Bull Run** campaign. Lincoln appointed McClellan to command the Army of the Potomac in July and named him to replace Scott as commanding general of the army in November. In 1862, McClellan set out to capture Richmond, Virginia, the Confederate capital, but his hesitation during the **Peninsula** campaign led Lincoln to abandon the campaign and transfer most of McClellan's soldiers to General John Pope in northern Virginia. After Pope's defeat at **Manassas**, however, McClellan's command was restored and he was off to confront **Robert E. Lee** at **Antietam**. Unable to take full advantage of finding a copy of Lee's plans, McClellan failed to destroy the Confederates at Antietam and Lincoln; his patience gone, he sent the general home to await orders that never came. In 1864, he ran for president against Lincoln as the Democratic nominee and lost, then went to Europe for three years. From 1878 to 1881, he was governor of New Jersey.

McClellan was a brilliant organizer and inspired the soldiers who served under him, but he was reluctant to advance aggressively against well-defended positions. His reputation reached its zenith in 1861, when his victories in western Virginia led the nation to proclaim him the "Young Napoleon." With a reputation for vanity and arrogance, he continues to be one of the most controversial figures of the Civil War. *See also* Appendix 3, Commanding Generals and Chiefs of Staff of the Army.

McCRARY, GEORGE WASHINGTON (1835–1890). Secretary of war from 1877 to 1879. Born in Indiana, McCrary moved to Iowa with his family and was educated in regional schools. He studied law in Keokuk, Iowa, and was admitted to the bar in 1856. Active in politics, he served in the U.S. House of Representatives for eight years before becoming secretary of war in 1877. After leaving office, he was a federal judge for four years and then general counsel for the Atchison, Topeka & Santa Fe Railroad. *See also* Appendix 4, Secretaries of War and Secretaries of the Army.

McHENRY, JAMES (1753–1816). Secretary of war from 1796 to 1800. Born in Ireland, McHenry attended Dublin University and in 1771 emigrated to the United States, where he attended the Newark Academy in Delaware and studied medicine in Philadelphia. He volunteered for military service in 1775 and became a military surgeon at a hospital in Cambridge, Massachusetts. During the **Revolutionary War**, McHenry served on the staffs of **George Washington** and the **Marquis de Lafayette**. After the war, he was a delegate to the constitutional conventions of 1783 and 1787 and served in the Maryland legislature, before becoming secretary of war in 1796. While in office, he continued work on coastal fortifications. *See also* Appendix 4, Secretaries of War and Secretaries of the Army.

McKINNEY, GENE C. (1950–). Sergeant major of the army from 1995 to 1997. Born in Florida, McKinney entered the army in 1968 and served in every **enlisted** leadership position from squad leader to **sergeant major**. Prior to becoming the sergeant major of the army, he was the **command sergeant major** of the U.S.

Army, Europe. On 10 February 1997, he was suspended from his duties after charges of sexual misconduct were made against him. He was reassigned as of 9 October 1997, one day after the case was referred to court-martial. In 1998 he was found guilty of only one of the 19 charges he faced. *See also* Appendix 5, Sergeants Major of the Army.

MEADE, GEORGE GORDON (1815–1872). Union **Civil War** general. Born in Cadiz, Spain, the son of an American naval agent, Meade graduated from the **U.S. Military Academy** in 1835 and resigned from the army a year later. In 1842, he rejoined the army and earned a **brevet** promotion during the **Mexican War**. He was appointed a brigadier general when the **Civil War** started in 1861 and led a brigade during the **Bull Run** campaign. A corps commander during the **Chancellorsville** campaign, he was given command of the Army of the Potomac shortly before **Gettysburg** and led it for the rest of the war. At Gettysburg, Meade stopped **Robert E. Lee**'s second invasion of the North, but was criticized when he let the Confederate Army escape to Virginia. When **Ulysses S. Grant** was appointed **commanding general of the army** in 1864, he accompanied Meade's army and the two generals worked well together in the final campaigns of the war. After the war, Meade remained in the army and died while in command of the Division of the Atlantic.

MEDAL OF HONOR. The highest award for valor the United States can bestow on members of the army. It is awarded "for conspicuous gallantry and intrepidity at the risk of life, above and beyond the call of duty, in action involving actual conflict with an opposing armed force." A Senate resolution of 17 February 1862 authorized presenting Medals of Honor to "such non-commissioned officers and privates as shall most distinguish themselves by their gallantry in action and other soldier-like qualities, during the **Civil War**." Congress changed the resolution in March 1863 to include officers and to make "gallantry in action" the only qualification for the medal. President **Abraham Lincoln** signed the resolution into law in July. In April 1904, Congress authorized a new design for the medal and President **Theodore Roosevelt** subsequently ordered that "The recipient of a Medal of Honor will, whenever practicable, be ordered to Washington and the presentation will be made by the President." *See also* DISTINGUISHED SERVICE CROSS; PURPLE HEART; SILVER STAR.

MEDICAL CORPS. *See* ARMY MEDICAL DEPARTMENT.

MEIGS, MONTGOMERY (1816–1892). Union **Civil War** general. An 1836 graduate of the **U.S. Military Academy**, Meigs was an accomplished engineer, having been in charge of expanding the U.S. Capitol and constructing its dome and of building a 12-mile aqueduct for Washington, D.C. In 1861, he replaced **Joseph E. Johnston** as quartermaster general of the army when Johnston resigned to accept a commission in the Confederate Army. Meigs's responsibilities for the Union Army during the Civil War included housing, clothing, equipping, and feeding more than a million soldiers. His recommendation that property owned by **Robert E. Lee** in Arlington, Virginia, be used as a military burial ground led to the creation of the Arlington National Cemetery in 1864. Meigs's efforts to organize the North's economic potential toward maintaining the military effort was a significant factor in the Union victory. After the war, he remained in office until 1882.

MEUSE–ARGONNE (26 September to 11 November 1918). World War I campaign streamer. At the end of August 1918, the Allied commander in chief submitted plans to the national commanders for a final offensive along the entire Western Front, with the objective of driving the Germans out of France before winter and ending the war in the spring of 1919. Allied attacks met with success all along the front in August and there were active operations already underway between the Moselle and Meuse Rivers, between the Oise and Aisne Rivers, and on the Somme and Lys Rivers. Because the Germans could stave off immediate defeat by an orderly evacuation and the destruction of materiel and communications, the overall aim of the fall offensive was to prevent a methodical retirement. The offensive, planned to begin in the last week in September, called for a gigantic pincers movement with the objective of capturing Aulnoye and Mézières, two key rail junctions, behind the German front. Loss of either junction would seriously hamper an orderly German withdrawal. A mainly British army had the task of driving toward Aulnoye, while the U.S. First Army made the thrust on Mézières.

John J. Pershing, the U.S. First Army commander, decided to make the main attack in a zone about 20 miles wide between the heights of the Meuse on the east and the western edge of the densely wooded Argonne Forest. Elaborate German defenses consisted of a fortified system of three main defense lines backed up by a fourth, less well-constructed line extending along the entire front. Pershing hoped to launch the attack with enough momentum to drive through the German defenses and into the open area beyond, where his troops could then strike at the exposed German flanks. As preparations for the offensive began, many American units were still engaged at **St. Mihiel** and some 600,000 Americans had to be moved into the Argonne sector as 220,000 French soldiers departed. **George C. Marshall**, a First Army staff officer, had the task of solving this tricky logistical problem. The troop movements were accomplished on time and in good order, but many untried divisions found themselves in the vanguard of the attacking forces. Pershing's forces included nearly 4,000 guns, two-thirds manned by American artillerymen; 190 light French **tanks** manned mostly by Americans; and some 820 aircraft, of which 600 were flown by Americans.

The campaign had three phases. From 26 September to 3 October, the First Army advanced through most of the southern Meuse–Argonne region, captured enemy strong points, and seized the first two German defense lines, before it stalled in front of the third line. Inadequate tank support, a difficult supply situation, and inexperienced American troops were factors in stopping the advance. After replacing the inexperienced divisions with veteran units, the First Army slowly ground its way through the third German line from 4 to 31 October. Facing a stubborn German defense, the Americans made limited progress and suffered severe casualties. In response to the Germans' newly devised tactic of attacking frontline troops with airplanes, American air units conducted bombing raids that broke up German preparations for counterattacks. By the end of October, the Germans had been cleared from the Argonne and First Army troops were through the German main positions. At the end of this phase, the First Army replaced many of its exhausted divisions, built and repaired roads, improved supply, and withdrew most of the Allied units serving with the American Expeditionary Force. In mid-October, the U.S. Second Army completed its organization at Toul in the St. Mihiel salient, providing better control of the lengthening American front. Pershing assumed command of the new army group thus formed. During this phase of the campaign, **Alvin C. York** captured 132 German soldiers and killed as many as 28 during a patrol on 8 October.

On 1 November, the third phase of the offensive got underway as First Army units began the assault of the German fourth line of defense, now significantly stronger. But the American penetration was rapid and spectacular. V Corps, in the center, advanced about six miles the first day; on 4 November, III Corps forced a crossing of the Meuse and advanced northeast toward Montmédy; on 7 November, elements of V Corps occupied the heights opposite Sedan, denying the Sedan-Mézières railroad to the Germans; and on 11 November, when the war ended, American units were closing up along the Meuse River and advancing toward Montmédy, Briny, and Metz. During the 47-day campaign, the First Army lost about 117,000 of its soldiers in killed and wounded, while it captured 26,000 prisoners, 847 cannon, 3,000 machine guns, and large quantities of material. More than 1,200,000 Americans participated in the campaign.

MEXICAN EXPEDITION. *See* MEXICO.

MEXICAN WAR (1846–1848). When Texas became part of the United States in 1845, Mexico claimed that one of its provinces had been seized. Mexico also disputed the U.S. and Texas position that the Rio Grande was the border between the two countries. The Mexican government argued that the Nueces River, further to the north, was the proper boundary. In April 1846, President James K. Polk stationed **Zachary Taylor**, with an army of about 4,000 men, near the Rio Grande to pressure Mexico into accepting the Rio Grande as the border. The president of Mexico responded by declaring that a state of defensive war existed between it and the United States. When Taylor built a fort on the Rio Grande opposite the Mexican town of Matamoros, the Mexican Army forces there challenged the American position. Taylor deployed his forces and won battles at **Palo Alto** and **Reseca de la Palma** in May. He then went on to capture **Monterrey** in September and in early 1847 defeated the Mexican general and president, **Antonio Lopez de Santa Anna**, at **Buena Vista**. While Taylor was fighting along the Rio Grande, **Stephen W. Kearney** and his Army of the West secured California and the future states of Arizona and New Mexico for the United States.

With the Mexican government showing no signs of agreeing to any changes in the border, American leaders decided to invade Mexico, with the ultimate objective of capturing the capital, Mexico City. In preparation for the expedition, **Winfield Scott, commanding general of the army**, detached about 8,000 men from Taylor's command in early 1847 to join other army forces assembling for the invasion. Under Scott, army forces landed at **Vera Cruz** and moved overland to Mexican City. Along the way, American soldiers again displayed their fighting qualities at **Cerro Gordo** and **Churubusco**, where Scott won victories over the Mexican Army as it fell back to defend the capital. In August, Scott's army reached the outskirts of the city and began attacking Mexican defensive positions. The fighting culminated with the American capture of **Chapultepec**, the citadel that protected Mexico City, and victorious U.S. forces entered the central plaza. Scott occupied the city for several months, until the Treaty of Guadalupe Hidalgo brought the war to its official end on 2 February 1848. The U.S. Senate ratified the treaty on 10 March, the Mexican Congress approved it in May, and on 1 August the last American soldiers departed for home.

In the opening battles of the Mexican War, the army's **enlisted** soldiers demonstrated their toughness and resiliency and the officer corps provided skillful leadership. The volunteer regiments that had grown out of the militia system also generally served with distinction. Although there were disputes between the **regular army** and the militia, the army overall performed well during the war. Many officers educated at the **U.S. Military Academy** distinguished themselves during the war as scouts, engineers, staff officers, military governors, and combat leaders. Many of them, including **Robert E. Lee, Joseph E. Johnston, Thomas J. Jackson, Ulysses S. Grant**, and **George B. McClellan**, later commanded the armies that faced each other 14 years later, during the **Civil War**. *See also* Mexican War campaigns in Appendix 6, Campaigns of the United States Army.

MEXICO (14 March 1916 to 7 February 1917). Mexican Expedition campaign streamer. In 1916, a number of incidents along the U.S. border with Mexico culminated in an invasion of American territory, when **Francisco "Pancho" Villa** and his band of 500 men raided Columbus, New Mexico, on 8 March. U.S. Army **cavalry** repulsed the attack, but there were 24 American casualties,14 military and 10 civilian. The United States quickly organized a punitive expedition of about 12,000 men commanded by **John J. Pershing** to capture Villa. In mid-March, the expedition crossed the border into Mexico, where resentment by the Mexican people caused Villa's forces to increase almost tenfold, from about 500 to some 5,000. Advance elements of the Mexican Expedition penetrated as far as Parral, some 400 miles south of the border, meeting only sporadic resistance. The campaign consisted primarily of minor skirmishes with small bands of Villa's supporters. There were some clashes with Mexican Army units, the most serious of which was on 21 June 1916 at Carrizal, where a detachment of U.S. cavalry was nearly destroyed.

Villa was never captured. The United States recalled the expedition in January 1917, when its relations with Germany worsened and drew its attention to **World**

War I in Europe. American troops left Mexico in February 1917 and the tension was resolved by diplomatic negotiation, although minor clashes with Mexican irregulars continued to disturb the border until 1919. The expedition involved virtually the entire **regular army**, while some 100,000 soldiers of the **Army National Guard** were federalized and concentrated on the border. This was the first time that the army used motor transportation on a large scale. To support the expedition, the **quartermaster corps** shipped over 3,000 trucks and operators by train to Columbus, New Mexico.

MEYER, EDWARD CHARLES (1928–). Chief of staff of the army from 1979 to 1983. Born in Pennsylvania, Meyer graduated from the **U.S. Military Academy** in 1951. He served in the **Korean War** and commanded a battalion in the **Vietnam War**. In 1979, he became the chief of staff and pursued an armywide modernization program that emphasized quality and the need for a long-term investment in weapons and equipment. He retired from active service in 1983. *See also* Appendix 3, Commanding Generals and Chiefs of Staff of the Army.

MIAMI (January 1790 to August 1795). Indian wars campaign streamer. In the late 1780s a confederacy of hostile Indians, chiefly Miamis, in the northern part of present-day Ohio and Indiana restricted settlement in the area. In 1790, the army responded by sending a force of 320 **regular army** soldiers and 1,000 Kentucky and Pennsylvania militiamen under Brigadier General **Josiah Harmar** north from Fort Washington (Cincinnati). Harmer was badly defeated in engagements on 18 and 22 October 1790 near present-day Fort Wayne, Indiana. Congress reacted by making **Arthur St. Clair** a major general and sending him to the region. In September 1791, St. Clair led a force of about 2,000 regulars and militia north from Fort Washington, the army force building a road and forts as it progressed. On the night of 3–4 November, some 1,000 Indians surrounded 1,400 of St. Clair's men near the headwaters of the Wabash River and routed them. St. Clair, having lost 637 killed and 263 wounded, returned to Fort Washington. In 1792, Congress doubled the authorized strength of the regular army and appointed **Anthony Wayne** to replace St. Clair. Wayne set about reorganizing and training his troops near Pittsburgh, before moving to Fort Washington in the spring of 1793.

When peace negotiations failed in October 1793, Wayne's troops advanced along St. Clair's route toward Fort Miami, a new British post on the present site of Toledo, Ohio, building fortifications along the way. After wintering at Greenville, a detachment of 150 men moved to the site of St. Clair's defeat and built Fort Recovery in the spring of 1794. At the end of June, more than 1,000 Indian warriors assaulted the fort for 10 days, but failed to dislodge the defenders and withdrew. Wayne moved forward in July with a force of some 3,000 men, paused to build Fort Defiance at the junction of the Glaize and Maumee Rivers, and resumed the pursuit on 15 August. At Fallen Timbers, an area near Fort Miami where a tornado had hit, the Indians made a stand among the uprooted trees. On 20 August 1794, they were finally defeated in a two-hour fight characterized by Wayne's excellent tactics and the performance of his well-trained troops. The Treaty of Greenville ended the campaign in August 1795. The tribes of the region ceded their lands in southern and eastern Ohio, opening the Northwest Territory for further settlement.

MILES, NELSON APPLETON (1839–1925). Commanding general of the army from 1895 to 1903. Born in Massachusetts, Miles attended John R. Galt's academy in Westminster, before moving to Boston, where he was a clerk. He attended night school, read military history, and paid a French veteran officer to tutor him in military drill and principles. In 1861, at the beginning of the **Civil War**, he recruited a company of volunteers and received a commission as a captain. He served in various positions during the war, was wounded several times, and received the **Medal of Honor** for his gallantry at **Chancellorsville**. After the war, he continued to serve in the army, seeing duty in the western United States against the Indians. He fought the Sioux in 1877, accepted the surrender of **Geronimo** in 1886, and was responsible for operations during the **Pine Ridge** campaign that resulted in the massacre at **Wounded Knee** in 1890, the army's last major battle against the Indians. While serving as commanding general of the army, Miles led an expedition to **Puerto Rico** during the **Spanish–American War** and after that war opposed the efforts of **Elihu Root**, the **secretary of war**, to institute a **general staff** and change the position of commanding general to chief of staff. Upon Miles's retirement in 1903, **Samuel B. M. Young** became commanding general for one week, before becoming the first **chief of staff of the army** under the provisions of the **General Staff Act**. *See also* Appendix 3, Commanding Generals and Chiefs of Staff of the Army.

MILITARY HISTORY INSTITUTE. Located at Carlisle Barracks, Pennsylvania, the U.S. Army Military History Institute seeks to preserve the army's history by ensuring access to historical research materials. The institute is the primary research facility for the historical study of the U.S. Army. It collects, organizes, and preserves source materials on American military history and makes them available to the defense community, researchers, and scholars. Its holdings include more than nine million items relating to military history, including books, periodicals, photographs, manuscripts (diaries, letter, memoirs), military publications and manuals, maps, and oral histories, making the institute one of the finest military research libraries in the world. The institute accepts donations of papers, letters, scrapbooks, diaries, photographs, and other materials representing military service from all eras. All donated items are cataloged, inventoried, stored, cross-referenced, and preserved as important contributions to the nation's military heritage. *See also* CENTER OF MILITARY HISTORY.

MILITARY INTELLIGENCE. Branch of the army. Intelligence has been an essential element of army operations during war as well as during periods of peace. To meet its increased requirement for national and tactical intelligence, the army established an Intelligence and Security Branch on 1 July 1962. Five years later, on 1 July 1967, the branch was redesignated Military Intelligence. *See also* BRANCHES OF THE ARMY.

MILITARY POLICE. Branch of the army. A Provost Marshal General's Office and Corps of Military Police were established on 26 September 1941. Prior to that time, except during the **Civil War** and **World War I**, there was no regularly appointed provost marshal general or regularly constituted Military Police Corps, although there are references in army documents to a provost marshal as early as January 1776 and a Provost Corps in 1778. *See also* BRANCHES OF THE ARMY.

MILITIA. *See* ARMY NATIONAL GUARD.

MILITIA ACTS. Between 1792 and 1916, the U.S. Congress sought to develop a policy that would make America's traditional citizen–soldier a useful part of the U.S. defense establishment. The challenge was to balance the militia's prerogatives established in the Constitution with the army's need for a disciplined force that could augment its forces in national emergencies quickly and effectively. The Militia Act of 1792 left the militia, which theoretically included all able-bodied men between the ages of 18 and 45, under state control and barred **African Americans** from serving in state militias. Congress provided $200,000 in 1808 for weapons to be shared among the states and doubled the amount in 1887, but there were no provisions for a trained and organized national reserve. The Militia Act of 1903, known also as the Dick Act and amended in 1906 and again in 1908, increased federal aid to $4 million annually and reorganized the National Guard as the Organized Militia. It aligned the National Guard's training program, organization, and equipment in line with that of the **regular army**, but control over Guard personnel remained with the state governments. The president was authorized to call the Guard into federal service in case of invasion or insurrection or to enforce the laws of the nation, but federal service was limited to nine months. The **National Defense Act of 1916**, amended in 1920, gave the army more control over the National Guard. *See also* ARMY NATIONAL GUARD.

MINDANAO (4 July 1902 to 31 December 1904, 22 October 1905). Philippine Insurrection campaign streamer. In 1902, serious trouble began with the Moros in Mindanao and the Sulu Archipelago, who had never been completely subjugated by the Spanish when they controlled the Philippine Islands. When the U.S. Army occupied former Spanish garrison points during the Philippine Insurrection, the Moros began to raid villages, attack soldiers, and otherwise resist American jurisdiction. Between July 1902 and December 1904, and again late in 1905, the army dispatched a series of expeditions into the interior of Mindanao to destroy Moro strongholds. Colonel Frank D. Baldwin, with some 1,000 men, invaded the territory of the sultan of Bayan near Lake Lanao and defeated the sultan's forces in the hotly contested Battle of Bayan on 2 May 1902. Captain **John J. Pershing** headed a similar expedition into the Lanao country in 1903 and Captain Frank R.

McCoy finally killed the notorious Moro outlaw, Dato Ali, in the Cotabato district in October 1905. *See also* JOLO.

MISSISSIPPI RIVER (6 February 1862 to 9 July 1863). **Civil War** campaign streamer. The Union capture of Forts Henry and Donelson marked the beginning of the Mississippi River campaign. After the **Henry and Donelson** campaign, President **Abraham Lincoln** unified command of the Union's western armies under Major General **Henry W. Halleck**. The new command had a total strength of more than 100,000 men and consisted of Major General Samuel Curtis's Army of the Southwest in Missouri and Arkansas, **Ulysses S. Grant's** Army of the Tennessee, Brigadier General Don Carlos Buell's Army of the Ohio, and Major General John Pope's Army of the Mississippi. The strategic goal of the campaign was for the Union to gain control of the Mississippi River and split the Confederacy in two, isolating its western armies. The campaign came to a successful conclusion for the Union with the capture of **Vicksburg** on 4 July 1863 and of Port Hudson four days later.

MITCHELL, WILLIAM (1879–1936). Army officer and airpower proponent known as "Billy." Born in Nice, France, where his parents were vacationing, Mitchell enlisted as a private and was commissioned a lieutenant in the **signal corps** when his influential father, a U.S. senator, appealed to the army. Billy Mitchell headed the army's Air Service, a part of the signal corps, during **World War I** and was the first American officer to fly over enemy lines, in May 1918. After the war, he proposed the **airborne** concept of using parachutes for soldiers to jump from airplanes into battle and campaigned for a large independent air force, correctly foreseeing the potential of strategic air bombardment and massive air strikes. In prearranged tests off the Virginia coast, his planes sank captured ships to demonstrate the capabilities of air power. Mitchell's outspokenness led to a 1925 court-martial in which he was suspended from active duty for five years. He resigned the next year to air his views as a civilian and became even more strident in his opinions, writing articles and books to make his point.

MODOCS (1872–1873). **Indian wars** campaign streamer. When the Modocs, a small and restless tribe, were placed on a reservation with the Klamaths, their traditional enemies, the situation was intolerable and most of the Modocs left the reservation. Led by a chief known as Captain Jack, they returned to their old lands. A cavalry troop under Captain James Jackson skirmished with these Indians along the Lost River on 29 November 1872 when the soldiers attempted to disarm the Indians and arrest the leaders. Following the skirmish, Captain Jack and about 120 well-supplied warriors retreated to the Lava Beds, a naturally fortified area east of Mount Shasta. On 17 January 1873, Colonel Alvan Gillem, with some 400 men, half of them regulars, attacked the Modoc positions, but the troops could make no progress in the almost impassable terrain and suffered losses of 10 killed and 28 wounded. By the spring of 1873, Brigadier General Edward R. S. Canby, commander of the Department of the Pacific, with about 1,000 men moved to besiege the Modocs. On 11 April, Canby and three civilian commissioners arranged a parley with Modoc representatives, but the Indians violated the truce. After Captain Jack killed Canby and other Indians killed one commissioner and wounded another, the siege was resumed. Brigadier General Jefferson C. Davis replaced Canby in May and pushed columns deep into the Lava Beds, harassing the Indians day and night with mortar and rifle fire. When their source of water was cut off, the Indians were finally forced into the open and all were captured by 1 June 1873. Captain Jack and two others were hanged and the rest of the Indians were moved to Indian Territory.

MOLINO DEL REY (8 September 1847). Mexican War campaign streamer. After the battle at **Churubusco, Winfield Scott**, the American commander, proposed an armistice to discuss peace terms. The commander of the Mexican Army, General **Antonio Lopez de Santa Anna**, agreed, but after two weeks of negotiations it became apparent that the Mexicans were using the armistice to gain a respite from the fighting. On 6 September, Scott broke off discussions and prepared to attack Mexico City. The first step was to take the citadel of **Chapultepec**, a massive stone fortress on a hill about a mile outside the city. Defending Mexico City were 18,000 to 20,000 troops and the Mexicans were confident of victory; they knew Scott had barely 8,000 men and was far from his base of supply. On 8 September 1847, the Americans launched an assault on Molino del Rey, the most important outwork of Chapultepec. Molino del Rey was taken after a bloody fight in which the Mexicans suffered an estimated 2,000 casualties and lost 700 as prisoners, while perhaps as many as 2,000 deserted. The small American force had sustained comparatively serious losses, 124 killed and 582 wounded.

MONMOUTH (28 June 1778). Revolutionary War campaign streamer. After France allied itself with the American cause in February 1778, the British forces in America had to consider the threat created by the powerful French fleet. **Henry Clinton**, who relieved William Howe as British commander in America on 8 May 1778, decided to shift the main body of his troops from Philadelphia to a point nearer the coast so he could maintain close communications with the British Fleet. The 10,000-man Philadelphia garrison started moving in mid-June. As these troops set out through New Jersey toward New York, **George Washington** left his winter headquarters in **Valley Forge** and began pursuit of Clinton with an army of about 13,500 men. An advance element of about 5,000 troops under the command of Charles Lee launched the initial attack on the British column as it marched out of Monmouth Courthouse (now Freehold, New Jersey) on 28 June. When British reinforcements arrived on the scene, Lee ordered a retreat. Thus encouraged, Clinton attacked with his main force. After an angry exchange with Lee, Washington assumed personal direction of the battle, which continued until dark without either side retiring from the field. During the night, the British slipped away to the coast, where their fleet took them to New York City. The British reported losses of 65 killed, 155 wounded, and 64 missing; the Americans listed 69 killed, 161 wounded, and 130 missing. Washington's army moved northward, crossed the Hudson, and occupied positions at White Plains, New

York. Lee was later found guilty of disobedience, disrespect, and misbehavior before the enemy and dismissed from the army.

MONROE, JAMES (1758–1831). Secretary of war from 1814 to 1815. Born in Virginia, Monroe attended private school, entered William and Mary College, but left in 1776 to become an officer in the **Continental Army**, where he participated in the **Trenton, Brandywine, Germantown,** and **Monmouth** campaigns. After the war, he studied law under Thomas Jefferson, then the governor of Virginia. After practicing law in Fredericksburg, Monroe was elected to the U.S. Senate, was minister to France, and served as governor of Virginia. In 1803, he participated in negotiations for the Louisiana Purchase and was minister to Great Britain for four years. After declining an offer to be governor of Upper Louisiana in 1809, he served in the Virginia legislature and was governor for a second time. He was U.S. secretary of state from 1811 to 1817. From September 1814 to March 1815, he was also the secretary of war. Elected president in 1816, he served two terms (1817–1825), during which he announced the Monroe Doctrine, which restrained European countries from intruding into affairs in the Americas. *See also* Appendix 4, Secretaries of War and Secretaries of the Army.

MONTDIDIER–NOYON (9–13 June 1918). World War I campaign streamer. The Germans followed up their stalled **Aisne** offensive with a small-scale drive in the Montdidier–Noyon sector on 9 June 1918, when 21 German divisions attacked the French on a 23-mile front extending from Montdidier to the Oise River. The French, anticipating the assault, contained it after a nine-mile penetration by the Germans and quickly counterattacked. The fighting was over by 12 June and the enemy had little to show for the heavy losses incurred. No large American units were in the immediate vicinity of the action, but the U.S. Army's 1st Division at Cantigny did receive some artillery fire and diversionary raids.

MONTERREY (20–24 September 1846). Mexican War campaign streamer. After the **Palo Alto** and **Resaca de la Palma** campaigns in 1846, **Zachary Taylor's** forces left the Mexican town of Camargo at the end of August and launched an attack on Monterrey on 21 September. The city was defended by between 7,300 and 9,000 Mexican troops, but in three days of hard fighting the Americans drove the enemy from the streets to the central plaza. On 24 September, the Mexicans offered to surrender the city on the condition that the troops be allowed to withdraw unimpeded and that an eight-week armistice go into effect. Taylor, believing that his mission was simply to hold northern Mexico, accepted the terms and the Mexican troops evacuated the city the following day. The Mexicans reported 367 casualties in the three-day fight and the Americans suffered 120 killed and 368 wounded. Taylor was severely criticized in Washington, D.C., for agreeing to the Mexican terms and the United States repudiated the armistice, although it had almost expired by the time the news reached Monterrey.

MORGAN, DANIEL (ca. 1735–1802). American Revolutionary War general. Born of Welsh farmers, Morgan grew up along the Pennsylvania–New Jersey border, before settling in Virginia. With experience fighting Indians with the British, he received command of one of the companies raised for the **Continental Army** at the beginning of the Revolutionary War. He led his company during **Benedict Arnold**'s ill-fated **Quebec** campaign. An expert in guerilla tactics, Morgan led a regiment of **rangers** during the **Saratoga** campaign, before transferring to the Southern Department, where he defeated the British at **Cowpens**. After the war, he served a single term in the U.S. House of Representatives.

MORRELL, GLEN E. (1936–). Sergeant major of the army from 1983 to 1987. Born in West Virginia, Morrell attended a one-room public school, graduated from high school in 1954, and enlisted in the army to become a paratrooper. He left the army at the end of his enlistment, but shortly returned and was sent to Germany, where he joined the army's **Special Forces**. He served with the Special Forces in the United States and Panama as well as in the **Vietnam War**. In 1976, after attending the **Sergeants Major Academy**, he became the **command sergeant major** of a ranger battalion. Before reporting for duty, Morrell attended ranger school, where at the age of 41 he was the distinguished honor graduate. He became sergeant major of the army in 1983 and while in that position visited the People's Republic of China as part of a delegation to reestablish an American military presence there. He retired on 30 June 1987, after 33 years of active service. *See also* Appendix 5, Sergeants Major of the Army; AIRBORNE.

MURFREESBOROUGH (26 December 1862 to 4 January 1863). Civil War campaign streamer. In November 1862, Confederate general Braxton Bragg moved his Army of Tennessee with 35,000 soldiers toward Murfeesboro, Tennessee (the current name of the town), to protect the railroad line that ran from Nashville into the heart of the Confederacy. Union general William S. Rosecrans advanced from Nashville to meet Bragg with about 45,000 Federals in the Army of the Cumberland. The two forces clashed at Stone's River on the last day of the year. Both generals planned to attack, but Bragg's early morning move surprised the Federals. Rosecrans managed to cobble together a defense by nightfall and the two armies spent the next day facing each other in the bitter cold. On 2 January 1863, Rosecrans attacked the Confederate right, but a counterattack negated the Federal attempt to break the stalemate. Believing that Rosecrans was receiving reinforcements, Bragg retreated on 3 January. Rosecrans opted to fortify the Union positions and did not pursue. The battle was considered a Union victory, but both armies were so exhausted by the effort that they halted active operations for the next six months. Rosecrans lost 1,677 killed, 7,543 wounded, and 3,686 missing; Bragg's losses were 1,294 killed, 7,945 wounded, and about 2,500 missing.

MURPHY, AUDIE (1924–1971). World War II hero. Born in Texas, Murphy joined the army in 1942 at the age of 17. He demonstrated his bravery on numerous occasions while fighting in Sicily and the mainland of Italy, winning a number of medals and declining a battlefield commission to second lieutenant. During the 1944 invasion of southern France, he received the **Distinguished Service Cross** and was wounded shortly thereafter. Murphy accepted a commission when it was offered again and, in January 1945, he received the **Medal of Honor** for mounting a burning **tank** destroyer and single-handedly stopping an attacking German battalion supported by tanks. He was decorated a total of 29 times during the war and was credited with killing, wounding, or capturing 240 Germany soldiers. Returning home a genuine hero, he wrote his best-selling autobiography, *To Hell and Back*, and starred in the motion picture version of the book. He pursued a successful acting career and was killed in a plane crash in 1971.

MY LAI (1968). Vietnam War incident. In March 1968, during the **Tet Counteroffensive**, a company of American soldiers attacked the hamlet of My Lai, a Viet Cong (VC) stronghold. Prior to the assault, the company commander, Captain Ernest L. Medina, ordered his troops to burn and destroy the hamlet. Even though there was no enemy contact, the company systematically killed all the inhabitants, men, women, and children. The massacre was successfully covered up through all levels of command within the American Division, until a letter sent by a soldier not connected with the incident but who had heard rumors of a massacre brought it to the attention of U.S. government officials. As a result, the secretary of the army appointed a board of inquiry, which implicated 30 people, five of whom were tried by court-martial. Only one, First Lieutenant William L. Calley, was found guilty. It was a controversial result. Many Americans disagreed with the verdict, believing that the war without fronts in Vietnam created an environment in which atrocities were to be expected and believed Calley was unfairly singled out for blame. The majority of American soldiers in Vietnam did not intentionally shoot civilians and My Lai was an unusual event. Since the incident, the army has emphasized to its soldiers that acting under a superior's orders is not a defense to a charge of murder or other war crimes.

— N —

NAPLES–FOGGIA (18 August 1943 to 21 January 1944 [Air]; 9 September 1943 to 21 January 1944 [Ground]). World War II campaign streamer. After the Allied victory in **Sicily**, the Italian government of Benito Mussolini fell and the Allies announced an armistice on 8 September. After Italy's surrender, the Germans evacuated the islands of Sardinia and Corsica and the Allies controlled the Italian Navy. The surrender effectively made Italy a cobelligerent against Germany, but German forces maintained a firm hold on the country.

The Allied invasion of the Italian mainland had a number of objectives: take advantage of the collapse of Italian resistance, make immediate use of available Allied strength, engage German forces that might otherwise be available in Russia and northern France, secure airfields for bombing Germany and the Balkans, and consolidate control of the Mediterranean. On 3 September 1943, elements of the British Eighth Army landed on the toe of Italy to place Allied troops on the European mainland for the first time. Six days after the British landings, the U.S.

Fifth Army, under Lieutenant General **Mark W. Clark**, landed on beaches along the Gulf of Salerno, while a British fleet placed a division of troops at Taranto in the arch of the boot. Heavy fighting developed at Salerno, where German armored counterattacks jeopardized the Allied position, and it was six days before the Americans secured the beachhead. On 16 September, the British Eighth and the U.S. Fifth Armies joined forces southeast of Salerno. The British captured the airfields of Foggia near the Adriatic coast on 27 September and took the port city of Naples on 7 October. By mid-October they had moved north to a line extending from Larino west to Campobasso, where they were abreast of the Americans on their left.

Under strategic priorities decided upon by the Combined Chiefs of Staff (CCS) at the Quebec Conference in August 1943, Allied forces in the Mediterranean were reduced by seven divisions (four U.S. and three British) that were withdrawn to Great Britain to prepare for the **Normandy** campaign. Shipping limitations precluded large-scale Allied reinforcements in the Mediterranean and, by October 1943, the U.S. Fifth and British Eighth Armies had a total of only 11 divisions. This force tied down some 20 German divisions. The mountainous terrain and the narrow peninsula favored the German defenders, but the Allied force continued to press northward until the end of the war. A few days after taking Naples and Foggia, the Allies renewed the offensive in late October. This drive penetrated a strong German position at the Volturno River and carried the Allies as far as the so-called Winter Line, or Gustav Line, a defensive position the Germans prepared about 75 miles south of Rome.

NASHVILLE (1–16 December 1864). Civil War campaign streamer. After defeating General John B. Hood at **Franklin**, Tennessee, **John M. Schofield** moved on to Nashville, where his arrival brought the Union forces to a total strength of about 50,000. Under the command of General George Thomas, the Federals made slow, careful preparations to attack and destroy Hood. In a two-day battle that began on 15 December, Thomas struck hard and drove Hood's forces from the field in complete disorder, inflicting heavy losses and taking 4,462 prisoners. Thomas lost 387 killed and 2,949 wounded. Hood's losses are not accurately known, but his command was shattered and never again posed an offensive threat.

NATIONAL DEFENSE ACT (1916). Prompted by the Mexican Expedition, which concentrated virtually the entire army along the border with **Mexico**, this act provided that the army of the United States would consist of the **regular army**, the volunteer army, the Officer's Reserve Corps, the Enlisted Reserve Corps, the National Guard in the service of the United States, and the **Reserve Officers' Training Corps** (ROTC). The act also provided that the regular army and National Guard be organized into permanent brigades and divisions. It increased federal funding, made state forces available for service overseas, and gave the army more control over National Guard officers and units. The act, as amended in 1920, continues to govern the essential relations between state and federal military organizations. *See also* ARMY NATIONAL GUARD; MILITIA ACTS; RESERVE COMPONENTS; UNITED STATES ARMY RESERVE.

NATIONAL GUARD. *See* ARMY NATIONAL GUARD.

NATIONAL SECURITY ACT (1947). Among other changes to the national defense establishment, this act created the Department of Defense, with subordinate departments for each service. The **War Department** became the **Department of the Army** and the Army Air Forces became the U.S. Air Force, a separate service. At the same time, the post of **secretary of war** became the **secretary of the army** and lost its cabinet-level status, which was taken by the secretary of defense. Subsequent to this legislation, the service chiefs developed the **Key West Agreement** in 1948 to clarify the functions of each service. In 1950, the **Army Reorganization Act** implemented changes in the army.

NEW GUINEA (24 January 1943 to 31 December 1944). World War II campaign streamer. New Guinea is the second-largest island in the world, behind only Greenland. Its terrain provides a tactical nightmare and the climate is worse. Disease thrived on the island and a host of tropical sicknesses awaited the American soldiers who served there in World War II. With the success of the **Papua** and **Guadalcanal** campaigns, New Guinea was the next objective of the Allied drive to push the Japanese out of the Southwest Pacific Area. In January 1943, the American forces on the island were exhausted after the rigors of the Papua campaign. It was six months before they were ready to tackle the Japanese again.

In June 1943, in conjunction with operations by Admiral William F. Halsey's South Pacific forces in the **Northern Solomons** campaign, General **Douglas MacArthur** landed forces at Nassau Bay on the New Guinea coast, northwest of Buna. These forces moved along the coast, while an Australian division moved overland from the town of Wau, further inland. The Australian advance through the jungle, and the capture of Salamaua on 11 September 1943, took 75 days. Meanwhile, the Ninth Australian Division and a U.S. Army Engineer Special Brigade had landed east of Lae on 4 September. The next day, a regiment of U.S. Army paratroopers, conducting the first American **airborne** operation in the Pacific, flew from Port Moresby, jumped, and captured Nadzab, northwest of Lae, after which the Seventh Australian Division was flown into Nadzab. A coordinated attack by the Seventh and Ninth Australian Divisions resulted in the fall of Lae on 16 September. The Allies developed a forward naval base at Lae, while Nadzab became a major air base. Allied forces next moved on Finschhafen on the eastern end of the Huon Peninsula. Australian forces arrived there on 22 September and quickly cleared the area. In mid-October, the Japanese launched a combined land and amphibious counterattack, which the Australians defeated. MacArthur had hoped to trap the Japanese on this peninsula, but the survivors of Lae and Salamaua escaped overland to the north shore of the Huon Peninsula, while those from Finschhafen withdrew along the coast. American and Australian troops fought in the New Guinea jungles for three more months before the Huon Peninsula was considered secure in February 1944.

At this point, Allied strategy in the Pacific shifted. Rather than capturing Rabaul, the main supply base in the area, MacArthur was directed to continue clearing New Guinea, which he did in a series of amphibious operations that bypassed Japanese defenders rather than fighting up the coast. In April 1944, MacArthur carried out a daring operation that jumped 400 miles up the New Guinea coast to capture the major Japanese supply and naval base at Hollandia on the 26th. From there, he exploited his success and leapfrogged forces along the coast to capture Sarmi on 22 May. On 27 May, American forces landed on Biak Island, where they took until mid-July to finally secure the island. The campaign continued until December 1944, but the last of the Japanese on the island did not surrender until September 1945.

The New Guinea campaign featured two very different kinds of warfare—attrition and maneuver. One was the grinding jungle warfare that lasted from January 1943 until January 1944 and cost the Allies 24,000 battle casualties to advance 300 miles in 20 months. The other began with the Hollandia operation in April 1944, the first of a series of operations that leaped 1,300 miles in just 100 days with 9,500 casualties. At the beginning of the campaign, the Australians did most of the jungle fighting around Wau and on the Huon Peninsula, which gave the Americans time to train and prepare for the amphibious assaults that ended the campaign. The Australians also bought time for American industry to produce the planes, ships, ammunition, and all the other materiel needed to conduct the leapfrog campaign.

NEW ORLEANS (23 September 1814 to 8 January 1815). War of 1812 campaign streamer. On 20 December 1814, a force of about 10,000 British troops landed unopposed at the west end of Lake Borgne, some 15 miles from New Orleans. Their objective was to seize the city and secure control of the lower Mississippi Valley. The British reached Villere's Plantation on the left bank of the Mississippi River, 10 miles below New Orleans, on 23 December. **Andrew Jackson**, the American commander in the South, who had arrived in the city on 1 December, reacted quickly and attacked the British during the night of 23–24 December with some 20,000 men supported by fire from the gunboat *Carolina*. The attack halted the British advance and gave Jackson time to fall back to a dry canal about five miles south of New Orleans, where he built a breastworks about a mile long, with the right flank on the river and the left in a cypress swamp.

A composite force of about 3,500 **regular army** soldiers, militia, sailors, and an assortment of other forces, with another 1,000 in reserve, held the American main line. A smaller American force, perhaps 1,000 militia, defended the right bank of the river. The British commander, Major General Sir Edward Pakenham, brother-in-law of the Duke of Wellington, arrived on 25 December. At dawn on 8 January, Pakenham made a frontal assault on the American breastworks with 5,300 men and simultaneously sent a smaller force across the river to attack the defenses on the right side of the river. The massed fires of Jackson's troops, who were protected by earthworks reinforced with cotton bales, shattered Pakenham's regulars as they advanced across the open ground in front of the American lines.

The British lost 291 killed, including Pakenham, 1,262 wounded, and 48 prisoners; American losses on both sides of the river were 13 killed, 39 wounded, and 19 prisoners. The remaining British withdrew to Lake Borgne and reembarked on 27 January for Mobile, where on 14 February they learned that the Treaty of Ghent, ending the war, had been signed on 24 December 1814.

NEZ PERCE (1877). Indian wars campaign streamer. The southern branch of the Nez Perce Indians, led by **Chief Joseph**, refused to give up their ancestral lands along the Oregon-Idaho border and live on a reservation. In early 1877, negotiations broke down and a group of Nez Perce killed a number of white settlers. When army troops arrived to force them back to the reservation, Chief Joseph undertook an epic retreat of some 1,600 miles through Idaho, Yellowstone National Park, and Montana. During the march, he engaged 11 different army commands in 13 battles and skirmishes in a period of 11 weeks. The Nez Perce chief was a skilled tactician and his warriors demonstrated exceptional discipline in numerous engagements, especially on the Clearwater River on 11 July, in Big Hole Basin during 9–12 August, and in the Bear Paw Mountains, where they eventually surrendered to Colonel **Nelson A. Miles** on 4 October 1877.

NONCOMMISSIONED OFFICER. An **enlisted** soldier holding the rank of corporal or above. Noncommissioned officers, or NCOs, rank below commissioned and warrant officers. The NCO corps is considered the backbone of the army. They are the frontline supervisors for virtually all enlisted soldiers in the army. NCOs lead **infantry** squads, command **tank** crews, and are the chiefs of **artillery** gun sections. **Commissioned officers** at all levels of command have a senior NCO as an adviser for enlisted matters and other duties as assigned. At **company** level, the senior NCO is the **first sergeant**, while at **battalion** and higher levels it is a **command sergeant major**. Headquarters of most large army organizations have a **sergeant major** in each of the primary staff sections. The senior enlisted soldier in the U.S. Army is the **sergeant major of the army**. *See also* Appendix 8, United States Army Rank Insignia; WARRANT OFFICER.

NORMANDY (6 June to 24 July 1944). World War II campaign streamer. June 1944 was a major turning point of World War II in Europe, as the Allies seized the initiative from the Germans, occupying Rome on 4 June and landing at Normandy on 6 June. By mid-1944, the massive mobilization of manpower and materiel in the United States was beginning to bear fruit. Millions of American soldiers had been trained, equipped, and organized into the army's myriad combat and service units. American industrial production reached its wartime peak late in 1943. While there were still some critical shortages—in landing craft, for example—production problems were largely solved and streams of supplies from the United States were reaching Allied fighting forces throughout the world. By the beginning of June 1944, the United States and Great Britain had amassed the largest number of men and the greatest amount of materiel ever assembled, to launch and sustain an amphibious attack in preparation for the long-awaited invasion of the European continent; at the same time, the strategic bombing of Germany was reaching its peak. After studying various options, Allied strategists determined that the best place to make the cross-channel attack was on the beaches of Normandy, east of the Cherbourg Peninsula. Early objectives of the campaign were the deepwater ports at Cherbourg and at Brest in Brittany.

Three months before **D-Day**, the Allies initiated an air campaign to pave the way for the invasion by restricting the Germans' ability to shift reserves in France. The bombing crippled French and Belgian railways, demolished bridges in northwestern France, and attacked German airfields within a 130-mile radius of the landing beaches. The bombing emphasized isolating that part of northwestern France bounded roughly by the Seine and Loire Rivers. An elaborate Allied deception plan carried out in conjunction with the bombing led the Germans to believe that landings would take place farther north, along the Pas de Calais. Opposing the Allies in France was Army Group B of the German Army, which included the Seventh Army in Normandy and Brittany, the Fifteenth Army in the Pas de Calais and Flanders, and the LXXXVIII Corps in Holland, all under the command of Field Marshal **Erwin Rommel**. The commander of all German forces in Western Europe was Field Marshal Karl von Rundstedt, who in addition to Army Group B had at his disposal Army Group G, composed of the First and 19th Armies. In all, the Germans had about 50 infantry and 10 Panzer divisions deployed in France and the Low Countries.

Despite forecasts of unfavorable weather, General **Dwight D. Eisenhower**, the Allied commander in chief, decided to begin the invasion on 6 June 1944. At 0200, one British and two American **airborne** divisions dropped inland to secure exit routes from the beaches for the landing forces. After an intensive air and naval bombardment that began at 0530, assault waves of troops began landing at 0630. More than 5,000 ships, including 9 battleships, 23 cruisers, 104 destroyers, 71 large landing craft of various descriptions, troop transports, mine sweepers, and merchantmen, the largest armada ever assembled, supported the landings that put more than 100,000 fighting men ashore by the evening of 6 June. British forces on the left flank and U.S. forces on the right had comparatively easy going, but the Americans on Omaha Beach, in the center of the landing area, met determined opposition from the German defenders.

During the weeks that followed the landings, the Germans fiercely resisted Allied advances in the hedgerows of Normandy. Cherbourg fell three weeks after the landings, but the port had been destroyed and time-consuming repairs were required before it could be used to relieve the Allied supply problem. Meanwhile, Allied forces deepened the beachhead and by the end of June the most forward positions were about 20 miles inland. Despite the lack of ports, the buildup of Allied forces was swift. There were almost a million men, more than a half-million tons of supplies, and 177,000 vehicles ashore by the first of July. General Omar Bradley's U.S. First Army included four corps with 11 infantry and two armored divisions, while British strength was about the same.

Although eventually successful, the Normandy campaign did not have an auspicious beginning. The airborne assault the night before the landings created a significant diversion to the German defenders, but many of the Allied troops landed far from their intended targets and had a marginal effect on the battle. After the landings, the Germans confounded Allied planners by holding tenaciously to their positions, sustaining considerable casualties, rather than withdrawing behind the Seine River as had been expected. The American landing on Omaha Beach was a near disaster that succeeded only because of the courage and determination of thousands of sailors and soldiers. Once the beaches were secure, the American advance inland bogged down in the hedgerows. It took three weeks for the U.S. VII Corps, commanded by **J. Lawton Collins**, to capture the port city of Cherbourg, while Bradley's First Army suffered 40,000 casualties in moving 20 miles to the town of St. Lo. In spite of the problems, the campaign achieved the objective of securing an Allied foothold on the continent of Europe. In the ensuing months, the flow of manpower and materiel would overwhelm the German defenders and force them out of France, as the Allies finally broke out into open country to begin the **Northern France** campaign. *See also* AIR OFFENSIVE, EUROPE.

NORTHERN APENNINES (10 September 1944 to 4 April 1945). World War II campaign streamer. In August 1944, Allied forces in Italy held the Arno River and were preparing to continue their drive north to destroy the remaining German defenders. Toward the end of the **Rome–Arno** campaign, the Allies had stopped their offensive to give the combat forces a rest in anticipation of a final thrust north. But the halt also gave the Germans time to prepare for their next defensive stand along the so-called Gothic Line in the northern Apennine Mountains. The Allied force, reduced in strength by the necessity to relinquish some divisions for the campaign in Normandy, initiated a drive in September to breech the Gothic Line. On 10 September, General **Mark Clark**, commanding the U.S. Fifth Army, launched his forces into the Gothic Line. Initial resistance was light, but it increased as the advancing American forces approached the mountain.

The Germans gave ground stubbornly and the tactics, terrain, weather, and intensity of combat resembled the fighting the Fifth Army had experienced since it had been in Italy. Battling from mountain to mountain, the campaign continued north for four months, until the Allies ceased large-scale military operations in January 1945. Although there were a few limited attacks, the Allies were content to rest, receive reinforcements, and stockpile munitions and materiel in anticipation of a renewed offensive when the severe Alpine weather lifted. In spite of a constant reduction in men and materiel as the Allies focused greater attention on defeating the German forces in France in 1944, the combat in the northern Apennines demonstrated the fighting capabilities of American soldiers. Their valor and determination as an effective fighting force set the stage for the final rapid advances during the war in Italy that took place in the **Po Valley** in the spring of 1945.

NORTHERN FRANCE (25 July to 14 September 1944). World War II campaign streamer. After the successful landings at **Normandy** in early June 1944,

5. Noncommissioned officers preparing for a patrol during the Northern France campaign of 1944.

the Allied attack bogged down in the hedgerow country of France. The slow progress against determined German defenders raised concerns that the war would become a repeat of **World War I**, when static defensive lines dominated the fighting. On 25 July, a massive air bombardment conducted in coordination with an attack by ground troops penetrated the German lines at St. Lo. General **George S. Patton**'s U.S. Third Army poured through the breach in the direction of Brittany with the object of securing ports needed to continue the Allied buildup on the continent.

The Allied strategic plan was to capture the Breton ports, secure a lodgment area as far east as the Seine River for air and supply bases, and then advance into Germany on a broad front. British general Bernard Montgomery's 21st Army Group was supposed to make the primary thrust east, north of the Ardennes Forest in Belgium. South of the Ardennes, General **Omar Bradley**'s newly formed U.S. 12th Army Group, which included the U.S. First and Third Armies, would make a supporting attack. The northern route was given priority, because it led directly into the Ruhr area, where Germany's industrial power was concentrated. After the breakout at St. Lo, Patton's Third Army turned south and moved rapidly to secure the ports. The Germans, faced with trying to restore their defensive lines or withdrawing east, opted to counterattack into the Allied flank on 7 August and attempt to cut off the American forces headed for the ports. Although initially surprised by the attack, the Allies quickly turned it to their advantage. The German move offered the Allies an opportunity to turn the tables and encircle the attackers.

British forces on the left moved toward the town of Falaise, while U.S. troops to the right executed a wide circling maneuver toward Argentan, roughly halfway between St. Lo and Paris. The Allied intent was for the British and Americans to meet and cut off the German Seventh Army. Caught in a giant pocket, the Germans were able to extricate many troops before the Argentan-Falaise gap was closed on 20 August. The Allied delay in closing the gap has remained a subject of controversy, with Bradley receiving most of the criticism for halting Patton's Third Army on 13 August and waiting for Canadian troops to finally seal the pocket on 19 August. By then, Patton's Third Army was driving eastward toward the Seine and by 25 August it held four footholds on the east side of the river. The Germans lost almost all of two field armies in their unsuccessful defense of Normandy.

The Allies had intended to bypass Paris, to spare the city from heavy fighting, but when Patton crossed the Seine fighting broke between French patriots and Germans in the city. To support the uprising, a column of U.S. and Free French troops were diverted toward Paris and entered the city on 25 August. With the Allies making rapid progress against the Germans in France, General **Dwight D. Eisenhower**, the supreme Allied commander, altered the original plan. He abandoned the idea of stopping at the Seine and instituted a determined pursuit of the enemy toward Germany on a broad front. Because the ports of Cherbourg and Brest now were too far west to support the accelerated movement, the Allies sought to capture ports on the North Sea, including Antwerp, the best port in Europe. Adapting to the new situation, Eisenhower reinforced the British by sending the U.S. First Army alongside the British 21st Army Group toward Aachen in a drive toward Antwerp, while the U.S. Third Army continued east on the subsidiary axis south of the Ardennes. Patton led his army in an enthusiastic pursuit across France, scattering German troops in front of his tanks.

As the Allies moved east, Cherbourg, on the Brittany coast, was the only major port supplying Allied forces in northern France. The movement had been so rapid that the supply services could not keep up with the combat elements. In early September, the Allied drive slowed its pace for lack of supplies, chiefly gasoline. Although the British captured Antwerp intact on 4 September, the port could not be used to relieve the growing logistical crisis, because the Germans controlled the Schelde Estuary, which linked the port to the sea. In late September, the newly activated U.S. Ninth Army took the city of Brest in the Brittany peninsula, but its port had been completely destroyed. In any event, its location so far from the scene of action precluded its usefulness in solving logistical problems. Faced with shortages, rugged terrain, and stiffening German resistance as the Allies neared Germany, the Allies ended the campaign on 14 September with the British and Americans poised to finally cross the border into Germany. The campaign represented one of the most memorable moments in U.S. Army history. **Armored** columns raced across France, taking full advantage of their mobility to prevent a German defensive stand short of their own frontier.

NORTHERN SOLOMONS (22 February 1943 to 21 November 1944). World War II campaign streamer. In the first seven months after Pearl Harbor, the Japanese, at a surprisingly low cost, gained control over a huge area extending from Burma to the Gilbert Islands and from the Aleutians to the Solomons. But the Japanese had overextended themselves. Once the Allies became strong enough to threaten their perimeter from several directions, Japan did not have and could not produce enough planes and ships to defend all points. In view of this danger, the Japanese prepared plans for an attack against the still weak Allied line of communications from the continental United States and Hawaii to Australia, and for further expansion in the South Pacific. In May 1942, they launched a new offensive, moving to Tulagi from the northern Solomons, after which they began building an airstrip at Lunga Point on **Guadalcanal**. From there, they hoped to disrupt the Allied line to Australia by seizing New Caledonia, the Fijis, and

6. *Tanks and infantry fighting on Bougainville Island in the Northern Solomons in March 1944.*

Samoa. At the same time, to protect Rabaul, their main supply base on the island of New Britain, they moved into western New Britain and northeastern **New Guinea**.

The Japanese suffered their first major setback when Allied naval units intercepted an amphibious naval force moving toward Port Moresby in the Coral Sea on 7–8 May 1942. After two days of fighting, the Japanese task force broke off the engagement and withdrew northward. After the Battle of Midway in June 1942, in which the Japanese lost four carriers and hundreds of planes and pilots, the Allies initiated the **Papua** and Guadalcanal campaigns to prevent the Japanese from consolidating their gains. On 2 July 1942, the U.S. Joint Chiefs of Staff issued instructions for the Allied forces in the Southwest Pacific to advance toward Rabaul. In January 1943, the Joint Chiefs ordered **Douglas MacArthur**, the Allied commander in the Southwest Pacific, to prepare detailed plans to carry out the 2 July 1942 directive.

After six months of preparations, the offensive against Rabaul began in late June 1943, when Admiral William F. Halsey's South Pacific forces, operating under MacArthur's strategic direction, landed on the island of New Georgia in the central Solomons. The object of these operations was to secure air bases to support further advances in a two-pronged drive up the Solomons and the New Guinea coast toward Rabaul. Halsey's advance started from Guadalcanal, where air support was based at Henderson Field, and moved toward the Japanese air base at Munda on New Georgia Island, about 200 miles north. Landings on New Georgia began on 20 June 1943, when U.S. Marines, followed by army forces the next day, landed at Segi Point and moved overland to take Viru Harbor on 1 July. The principal effort began on 10 June 1943 with a landing on Rendova Island, just off New Georgia near Munda. From Rendova, marine and army forces invaded New Georgia and closed on the Japanese base at Munda, which fell after nearly six weeks of hard fighting on 5 August 1943. Another Japanese stronghold at Bairoko Harbor, eight miles north of Munda, fell on 25 August. Kolombangara was bypassed with the landing of U.S. Army, U.S. Marine, and New Zealand troops on Vella Lavella and Arundel Islands. There was considerable air and naval action and the Japanese lost heavily in ships and planes, as they first reinforced and then evacuated their island positions. In October, the Allies finally secured the island group.

The next major operation was an invasion of the island of Bougainville, which was approached by landings at Mono and Stirling in the Treasury Islands on 25–27 October 1943. A Marine division landed on the west coast of Bougainville at Empress Augusta Bay on 1 November 1943. Within the month, an army division followed the Marines, who were soon replaced by a second army division. By late November, the beachhead at Empress Augusta Bay was secure, and from there the Allies used their naval and air superiority to contain the Japanese garrison on the island. On 14 February 1944, Allied forces cut the supply line to Rabaul by occupying Green Island in the **Bismarck Archipelago**, just north of Bougainville Island. Despite these measures, the Japanese maintained pressure against the beachhead, mounting a series of heavy but unsuccessful counterattacks in March 1944. After the attacks, Americans began to search for remnants of Japanese units for several months. Although the campaign was declared over on 21 November 1944, for all practical purposes the end came with the defeat of the Japanese counterattacks in March.

— O —

OISE–AISNE (18 August to 11 November 1918). World War I campaign streamer. In mid-August 1918, the French started a series of drives on their front. Five French armies advanced abreast in coordination with the British, conducting the **Somme Offensive** to the north, and the Americans to the east. The U.S. 32d Division was a part of the French 10th Army and was instrumental in the capture of Juvigny on 30 August, which secured tactically important high ground for the Allies. On 9 September, the division moved east to join the U.S. First Army. The U.S. III Corps was a part of the French Sixth Army. As the Germans retired from the Vesle northward to the Aisne Valley in early September, the III Corps took part in the aggressive pursuit operations. Its two divisions carried out successful local attacks, but failed to break through the German line before they were relieved and sent to join the U.S. First Army. A total of about 85,000 Americans took part in the campaign.

OPERATIONAL ART. The employment of military forces within a theater of war to attain strategic objectives through the design, organization, integration, and conduct of **campaigns**. Operational art is the perspective of war that is higher than **tactics**, concerned with battles, and subordinate to **strategy**, which outlines the conduct of a war. Operational art deals with joint forces that employ air, land, and sea power. It became part of army **doctrine** in the 1980s. *See also* CAMPAIGN; STRATEGY; TACTICS.

ORDNANCE CORPS. Branch of the army. During the **Revolutionary War**, ordnance material was under supervision of the Board of War and Ordnance. The branch dates from 1775, when the Continental Congress appointed a commissary general of the artillery stores, essentially the first chief of ordnance. A year later, the Board of War and Ordnance was given responsibility for issuing supplies to troops in the field. In 1812, as part of the preparations for a second war with Great Britain, Congress organized the Ordnance Department, which assumed responsibility for producing arms and ammunition and acquiring, distributing, and storing supplies. The Ordnance Department acquired new responsibilities in 1832, including research, development, and a system of field service. During the **Civil War**, the department effectively provided support for the Union Army, while in the **Spanish–American War** it deployed materiel overseas and provided close combat support for the first time. During **World War I**, the Ordnance Department mobilized the nation's industrial base, developed weapons systems, organized ordnance training, and established overseas supply depots. **World War II** expanded the department's mission of production, procurement, maintenance, and training. The Ordnance Department became the Ordnance Corps in 1950 and has continued to support army forces throughout the world. *See also* BRANCHES OF THE ARMY.

OVERLORD. *See* NORMANDY.

— P —

PACE, FRANK, JR. (1912–1988). Secretary of the army from 1950 to 1953. Born in Arkansas, Pace attended local schools and the Hill School in Pottstown, Pennsylvania, before graduating from Princeton University in 1933. He received a law degree from Harvard University and practiced law in Arkansas from 1936 until 1942, when he entered the army as a second lieutenant in the Army Air Forces. Leaving the army as a major in 1945, he became a special assistant to the U.S. attorney general, executive general to the postmaster general, and then director of the Bureau of the Budget, before becoming secretary of the army in 1950. While in office, Pace managed institution of the changes in organization mandated by the **Army Reorganization Act of 1950** and headed the army during the **Korean War**. After leaving office, he was chairman of the American Council of NATO from 1957 to 1960. *See also* Appendix 4, Secretaries of War and Secretaries of the Army.

PALMER, BRUCE, JR. (1913–1974). Chief of staff of the army from July to October 1972. Born in Texas, Palmer graduated from the **U.S. Military Academy** in 1936. He served in various command and staff positions before participating in **World War II** in the Pacific theater of operations. He commanded the forces that occupied the **Dominican Republic** in 1965 and later was deputy commander of U.S. forces during the **Vietnam War**. In 1972, he served about four months as chief of staff. *See also* Appendix 3, Commanding Generals and Chiefs of Staff of the Army.

PALO ALTO (8 May 1846). Mexican War campaign streamer. Early in 1846, **Zachary Taylor** built a fort on the Rio Grande opposite the Mexican town of Matamoros. On 25 April, the Mexicans sent about 1,600 cavalrymen across the Rio Grande and overwhelmed a force of 60 American horsemen. As the Mexican forces at Matamoros grew stronger, Taylor became concerned about the line of communication with his main base at Point Isabel, near the mouth of the Rio Grande. On 1 May, he moved the bulk of his army to Point Isabel, leaving a small detachment opposite Matamoros. When the Mexicans attacked, Taylor moved to the rescue with about 2,300 men. On the morning of 8 May, little more than halfway to the fort, the Americans encountered an enemy force numbering about 6,000 men, with its right flank resting on an elevation known as Palo Alto. Taylor moved into battle, using **artillery** to cover the **infantry.** The engagement continued until nightfall, when the Mexicans withdrew. Effective use of artillery fire was largely responsible for the American victory. American losses were 9 killed and 47 wounded; the Mexicans suffered more than 700 casualties, including about 320 deaths.

PANAMA (20 December 1989 to 31 January 1990). Armed forces expedition campaign streamer. On 20 December 1989, U.S. forces mounted a joint operation to capture Panama strongman Manuel Antonio Noriega, who was accused of election fraud and drug trafficking. Operation Just Cause included elements from all four services of the U.S. armed forces. About 27,000 army soldiers were involved in the operation, although the actual fighting was limited to a much smaller number. Eighteen army soldiers were killed and 255 were wounded in the operation. Panama City suffered heavy damage in the fighting, as more than 300 Panamanians died before Noriega surrendered to U.S. forces. The invasion forces were withdrawn by early February 1990.

PAPUA (23 July 1942 to 23 January 1943). World War II campaign streamer. For the first five months after attacking Pearl Harbor in Hawaii and invading the **Philippine Islands** in December 1941, the Japanese had the advantage in the Pacific. But by May 1942, the Allies were starting to take the offensive. That month, the Allies repulsed Japanese attempts to take Port Moresby in southeastern **New Guinea** at the Battle of the Coral Sea and the Japanese lost four aircraft carriers and hundreds of planes and pilots at the Battle of Midway. But the two defeats did not stop the Japanese. On 22 July, much to the Allies' surprise, a Japanese landing force came ashore on New Guinea, moved to Buna on the northeast coast of the island, and by mid-August was well established in defensive positions. But when the Japanese attempted to land a force at Milne Bay in late August, some 7,500 Allied troops, including American engineers and antiaircraft artillery, repulsed the threat, forcing a Japanese withdrawal on 4 September. Later that month, a Japanese column moving toward Port Moresby stopped 30 miles short of its objective when its commander received instructions to return to Buna to possibly reinforce Japanese forces on **Guadalcanal.**

General **Douglas MacArthur,** commanding the Allied forces in the Southwest Pacific Area, prepared to take advantage of the Japanese setbacks and sent additional Australian troops to push the invaders back across the mountains. By mid-November, the Japanese had been driven back to their positions on the north coast at Buna, Gona, and Savanna, where they received reinforcements from Rabaul and clung desperately to their beachhead. Two Australian divisions, one U.S. Army **division,** and a separate U.S. Army **regiment** were committed to the fight. In early December, after two weeks of offensive operations resulted in 492 American casualties and no progress, MacArthur sent Major General Robert L. Eichelberger forward with explicit instructions: "Take Buna or don't come back alive!" Eichelberger, a **corps** commander, found the troops exhausted, starved, feverish, and in low spirits. He immediately relieved the division commander and began preparations to renew the offensive. The supply situation improved and the troops' morale rose as they received more food and rest; also, more artillery and air support was made available and five tracked vehicles with machine guns known as Bren carriers arrived to lead the attack.

The Allied attack began again on 5 December and stalled almost immediately, with all five Bren carriers knocked out in the first 20 minutes. But with fresh reserves available, Eichelberger pushed forward, the Australians took Gona Village on 9 December, and five days later the Americans pushed into Buna Village. Although the Japanese managed to resupply and reinforce by sea, by 23 January 1943 the Allies captured the last Japanese position. The campaign cost 8,546 Allied killed and wounded. It made clear that the army was not ready for combat. Its soldiers were insufficiently trained, equipped, and supported in comparison to the Japanese, who had been fighting for five years. But the crucible of combat had produced new leaders, new battle tactics, and new support techniques, all of which would be put to the test in the New Guinea campaign to complete the Allied takeover of the island. *See also* CENTRAL PACIFIC.

PARATROOPERS. *See* AIRBORNE.

PATTERSON, ROBERT PORTER (1891–1952). Secretary of war from 1945 to 1947. Born in New York, Patterson graduated from Union College in 1912, received a law degree from Harvard University three years later, and joined **Elihu Root**'s law firm. Patterson served as a private in the New York National Guard during the campaign in **Mexico** and entered active duty as a second lieutenant at the **Reserve Officers' Training Corps** camp in New York in 1917. While in France during **World War I**, he received the **Distinguished Service Cross** and was promoted to major. After the war, he returned to the practice of law and was appointed a judge in 1930. In 1940, Patterson was appointed undersecretary of war and was responsible for production and procurement during **World War II**. Appointed secretary of war in 1945, he pressed for unification of the armed forces under a single chief of staff. He returned to private practice in 1947 and was killed in a plane crash in 1952. *See also* Appendix 4, Secretaries of War and Secretaries of the Army.

PATTON, GEORGE SMITH (1885–1945). World War II army general. Born in California, Patton attended the Virginia Military Institute before graduating from the **U.S. Military Academy** in 1909. Assigned to the **cavalry**, he quickly established a reputation for his ability as a soldier and his driving energy. He was an aide to **John J. Pershing** during the campaign in **Mexico** and accompanied Pershing to France in 1917, when the United States entered **World War I**. Patton commanded a **tank** brigade during the **St. Mihiel** and **Meuse–Argonne** campaigns. Between the world wars, he served in a variety of assignments and received command of an **armored** division in 1940, as war in Europe appeared imminent. Patton commanded I Corps during the **Algeria–French Morocco** campaign and was reassigned to command II Corps after the American defeat at

Kasserine Pass, where he quickly restored morale and helped the British force the Germans to surrender in **Tunisia**. Given command of the U.S. Seventh Army, he and the British Eighth Army captured the island of **Sicily**. During the campaign, Patton slapped two soldiers in hospitals who he believed were malingering and, amid widespread criticism, was relieved of his command and severely reprimanded by **Dwight D. Eisenhower**.

In the aftermath of the slapping incident, **Omar Bradley**, Patton's subordinate in Sicily, received command of the American forces preparing for the invasion of **Normandy** in 1944, while Patton was relegated to command of a phantom army in England as part of a plan to deceive the Germans as to the location of the invasion. After the breakout at St. Lo, which marked the beginning of the **northern France** campaign, he commanded the U.S. Third Army, which drove rapidly east and then north, moving across France in a series of bold armored sweeps. When the German counterattack in the **Ardennes–Alsace** campaign of December 1944 stopped the Allied drive into Germany, Patton halted his army and, in a dramatic maneuver, turned it 90 degrees and attacked north to relieve the American forces holding the key road intersection at Bastogne. His army crossed the Rhine in March 1945 and, when the war in Europe ended, his troops were in Czechoslovakia. His outspoken criticism of the Soviet Union and U.S. policy toward Germany caused him to be relieved of command of occupation forces in Bavaria. He died of injuries incurred in an automobile accident in December 1945. Patton was the most aggressive senior U.S. military commander in **World War II** and is considered by many to have been the best.

PEARL HARBOR. *See* CENTRAL PACIFIC.

PEKING (14–15 August 1900). China Relief Expedition campaign streamer. In the summer of 1900, the Boxers, a fanatical Chinese nationalist faction, laid siege to the Legation Quarter of Peking (Beijing). In response to the rebellion, the Western powers sent a relief expedition to the city. On 14 August, elements of an army infantry regiment scaled the Tartar Wall around the Outer City of Peking and planted an American flag, the first foreign flag ever to fly on top of that wall. The action opened the way for British units to relieve the legation compound. On the following day, "Reilly's Battery" of the 5th U.S. Artillery blasted open the gates on the American front to start the assault on the Inner City. British troops advanced on the Legation Quarter and broke the 55-day siege.

PENINSULA (17 March to 3 August 1862). Civil War campaign streamer. The army of the Potomac, under Major General **George B. McClellan**, sailed from Alexandria to Fort Monroe on 17 March 1862, marking the beginning of the Peninsula campaign. McClellan began his advance from Fort Monroe in early April, but stopped for a month to besiege a smaller Confederate force under Major General John D. Magruder at Yorktown. During the siege, Major General **Joseph E. Johnston** joined Magruder with his forces. McClellan planned a major assault on 5 May, but on 3 May Johnston began withdrawing up the peninsula.

McClellan pursued, but the Confederate rear guard under Major General **James Longstreet** initiated a delaying action at Williamsburg on 5 May that developed into a major engagement, resulting in 1,866 Federal and 1,570 Confederate casualties. McClellan slowly continued his pursuit and established his main base at White House. Toward the end of May, he sent two corps southwest across the Chickahominy River toward Richmond, while his other three corps stayed north of the river. McClellan was expecting reinforcements from Major General Irwin A. McDowell, whose troops were near Fredericksburg, Virginia. But because of Confederate General **Thomas J. Jackson**'s aggressive offensive operations in the **Valley** campaign, McDowell could afford to send only two divisions to reinforce McClellan.

On 30 May, a heavy rain flooded the Chickahominy, washing out bridges and rendering the stream impossible to cross. Recognizing an opportunity to defeat McClellan, Johnston attacked the Federals south of the stream near Fair Oaks on 31 May. After suffering an initial reverse, the Federals repelled the Confederate attack. Each side committed some 41,000 men during the two-day engagement, with the Federals losing 790 killed and 4,384 wounded, while the Confederates lost 980 killed and 5,729 wounded. Johnston himself was wounded at Fair Oaks and was replaced by Major General **Robert E. Lee**. After the engagement at Fair Oaks, Jackson moved his forces from the Shenandoah Valley to Richmond. In early June, President **Abraham Lincoln** consolidated some 45,000 Union soldiers into the Army of Virginia, commanded by Major General John Pope. When Jackson moved to Richmond, Pope followed with the mission of reinforcing McClellan.

After assuming command of the Confederate Army of Northern Virginia, Lee moved closer to Richmond and erected fortified emplacements to defend the city. In late June, he moved out of his prepared defenses, struck McClellan's right (north) flank, and cut the Federal line of communications to its main base at White House. Fighting across the peninsula, McClellan shifted his base to Harrison's Landing, where he established a strong defensive position to repel the Confederate advance. The operation, known as the Seven Days' Battles, included major engagements at Mechanicsville on 26 June, Gaines' Mill on 27 June, Savage Station on 29 June, Frayser's Farm on 30 June, and Malvern Hill on 1 July. On 3 July, Lee broke contact and returned to his lines near Richmond, ending the fighting during the campaign. Casualties had been heavy on the peninsula. Federal losses in killed, wounded, and missing totaled 15,849; Confederate losses were 20,614. In spite of the higher Confederate casualties, Lee was seen as the victor, because he prevented the larger Federal army from attacking Richmond. For his part, McClellan was viewed as being hesitant. On 3 August, Lincoln directed McClellan to join Pope by way of Aquia Creek on the Potomac, ending the campaign.

PERSHING, JOHN JOSEPH (1860–1948). Chief of staff of the army from 1921 to 1924. Born in Missouri, Pershing attended the State Normal School and graduated from the **U.S. Military Academy** in 1886. Assigned to the cavalry, he participated in the **Pine Ridge** campaign against the Sioux Indians before being assigned as professor of military science and tactics at the University of Nebraska, where he earned a law degree while carrying out his teaching duties. He served with the 10th Cavalry in the **Santiago** campaign during the **Spanish–American War** and afterward was sent to the Philippine Islands, where he participated in the **Mindanao** campaign during the **Philippine Insurrection**. As the military attaché to Japan, he was an observer to the Russo-Japanese War. In 1906, President **Theodore Roosevelt** promoted Pershing to brigadier general, bypassing 862 senior officers. From 1909 to 1913, Pershing was the governor of Moro Province in the Philippines and from 1914 to 1916 he commanded an infantry brigade in San Francisco. In 1915, while assigned to San Francisco, he lost his wife and three daughters in a fire. He led the campaign that pursued the bandit **Pancho Villa** and his band into **Mexico** in 1916.

When the United States entered **World War I** in 1917, President Woodrow Wilson selected Pershing over several other senior officers to lead the American Expeditionary Forces in France. There, Pershing was constantly at odds with Allied leaders who wanted to piecemeal the American soldiers into existing French and British units. Pershing adamantly refused to split American forces and built an American army that eventually held its own sector of the Allied line. In preparing his forces for battle, and in anticipation of moving out of the trenches and conducting mobile warfare, he insisted that they be trained in offensive tactics. The Americans' success in the **St. Mihiel** and **Meuse–Argonne** campaigns eventually justified Pershing's insistence on a separate command. Returning to the United States, Pershing was made a **general of the armies** by Congress. Although he accepted the title, he did not wear the five stars insignia. He became chief of staff of the army in 1921 and served until 1924. He retired from active service in 1924, but remained the senior officer in the army until his death in 1948. *See also* Appendix 3, Commanding Generals and Chiefs of Staff of the Army.

PERSIAN GULF WAR (1990–1995). In response to the Iraqi invasion of Kuwait in August 1990, the army quickly deployed light forces to deter further Iraqi moves into Saudi Arabia. By January 1991, in a move that reflected the changes brought about by the end of the **Cold War**, army forces stationed in Germany to deter a Soviet invasion in Western Europe had moved to Saudi Arabia as part of a United Nations (UN) coalition formed to force Iraq out of Kuwait. The army's forces in the Persian Gulf included seven **divisions** and three armored cavalry **regiments** organized into two **corps** under the control of the U.S. Third Army headquarters. Also fighting as part of Third Army were a British armored division and a French light armored division. By January 1991, the Third Army, armed with more than 11,000 **tanks** and other **armored** vehicles and some 1,000 **helicopters**, was ready to launch a ground offensive against Iraq.

On 24 February 1991, after more than a month of aerial bombardment, the army's forces in Saudi Arabia, in conjunction with the other forces of the UN military coalition, launched the war's ground campaign. In 100 hours of almost constant fighting and moving, the coalition destroyed what had been the fourth largest army in the world. Coalition forces destroyed or captured more than 3,800 tanks, 1,400 armored vehicles, and almost 3,000 artillery pieces of the Iraqi Army. They also captured an estimated 60,000 Iraqi troops and demolished 36 Iraqi divisions. U.S. Army casualties were amazingly light. There were 96 soldiers killed in action, 84 who died from nonbattle causes, and 354 who were wounded in action. The army's equipment losses were comparably small, as only three Abrams tanks and five Bradley fighting vehicles were damaged by enemy fire and a total of five helicopters were destroyed during the ground campaign.

The army forces that deployed to Southwest Asia and performed so successfully during the war were equipped, organized, and trained to dominate the battlefield with a combined arms team that could outmaneuver and outshoot its opponents on any terrain, in any weather, day or night. The army's most visible weapons systems, the Abrams main battle tank and the Apache attack helicopter, were equipped with the latest military technology. The Abrams and the Apache were products of a long military evolution in peace and war, as was the AirLand Battle **doctrine** that guided the army through the war's remarkable 100-hour ground campaign.

The army's experience in the lengthy **Vietnam War** had a profound effect on the conduct of the Persian Gulf War. Most of the army's senior leaders had served as junior officers in Vietnam and they were determined not to repeat the acrimony that existed between the civilian and military leadership. They wanted clear military objectives and widespread political and popular support from the civilian population in the United States. In any event, the war had both and the spectacular results of the ground campaign produced a renewed sense of confidence within the army. *See also* Persian Gulf War campaigns in Appendix 6, Campaigns of the United States Army.

PETERSBURG (15 June 1864 to 2 April 1865). Civil War campaign streamer. After the **Cold Harbor** campaign, the Army of Northern Virginia under **Robert E. Lee** was firmly entrenched in Richmond. Union general **Ulysses S. Grant**, therefore, decided to starve the Confederates into the open by taking Petersburg, through which ran the railways and main roads connecting Richmond with the south. In a move that took Lee by surprise, Grant crossed the James River below Richmond with about 64,000 Union soldiers on 14 June and, the next day, his leading elements reached Petersburg. The city was lightly held, but the final Union assault was delayed, giving Lee time to move into Petersburg in force. A Union assault on 18 June failed to pierce the Confederate defenses and cost Grant 8,150 casualties. At the end of July, Union forces detonated a huge mine they had emplaced under the Confederate fortifications and created a giant crater in the defensive works. However, the succeeding **infantry** assault through the crater failed to exploit the breach in the Confederate line and resulted in another 4,000 Union casualties. Grant settled into siege operations, which lasted until April 1865.

PHILIPPINE INSURRECTION (1899 to 1913). There are 11 campaign streamers for the Philippine Insurrection. Nine of them—**Cavite, Iloilo, Laguna de**

Bay, Malolos, Manila, San Fabian, San Isidro, Tarlac, and Zapote River—cover 1899 and 1900. Two other Philippine Insurrection streamers, **Mindanao** and **Jolo**, cover later campaigns against the Moros that lasted until 1913.

During the **Spanish–American War**, Emilio Aguinaldo, who had led an earlier, unsuccessful insurrection in 1896–1897, organized an army and secured control of several islands, including much of Luzon. The U.S. Army forces that had garrisoned the Philippines undertook a series of operations to subdue the rebel forces. By the end of 1899, only scattered insurrectionist elements remained active in north and south Luzon, and virtually every important town in the Philippines was in American hands by February 1900. During 1900, the war consisted of local pacification programs against the irregular tactics and intimidation used by the forces of insurgent leader Emilio Aguinaldo. On 23 March 1901, Brigadier General Frederick Funston captured Aguinaldo, dealing a severe blow to the insurgent cause and resulting in many surrenders of rebel forces. By April 1902, the last of the rebel leaders had surrendered and on 4 July President **Theodore Roosevelt** announced the official conclusion of the Philippine Insurrection, although it did not mean the end of the shooting. It was 1913 before the last campaign of the insurrection finally came to a close.

PHILIPPINE ISLANDS (7 December 1941 to 10 May 1942). World War II campaign streamer. The Philippine Department had been the outlying U.S. Army command in the Pacific for years. In the summer of 1941, increasing tension between Japan and the United States prompted the **War Department** to set up a new command for the defense of the Philippines. This command, designated the U.S. Armed Forces, Far East, was activated on 26 July 1941 and General **Douglas MacArthur**, who had retired in 1937 to become an adviser to the Philippine government, was returned to active duty and designated commanding general. MacArthur's ground forces consisted of the Philippine Army of 10 divisions and supporting troops, with a total strength of about 100,000, and a U.S. **regular army** contingent of more than 25,000. Of the latter force, the largest unit was the Philippine Division, which consisted of one American **regiment** and two Philippine Scout regiments.

The Japanese attacked the Philippines by air on 8 December 1941, in coordination with their attack on Pearl Harbor, and seriously crippled elements of the American air forces stationed in the islands and damaged naval installations. On 10 December, Japanese forces landed at Aparri and Vigan on the northern coast of Luzon and on 22 December the main body of the invasion force began landing on Luzon at Lingayen Gulf. Other landings were made below Manila and on other islands of the Philippines. Unable to stop the enemy at the shoreline of Luzon, MacArthur withdrew his forces into the Bataan Peninsula, the island of Corregidor, and three other small islands in Manila Bay. This complex retrograde movement was accomplished by 7 January 1942. Meanwhile, on 2 January, the Japanese had occupied Manila, which the United States had declared an open city (of no significant military value and therefore not to be defended) on 24 December. The American and Filipino troops lost most of their supplies during their withdrawal and a Japanese blockade prevented landing supplies and reinforcements.

On 12 March 1942, U.S. president Franklin D. Roosevelt ordered MacArthur to leave the Philippines and move to Australia. MacArthur's successor in command was Lieutenant General **Jonathan M. Wainwright**. On 9 April 1942, with the troops on Bataan reduced by hunger, disease, and casualties to the point of military helplessness, their commander, Major General Edward P. King Jr., surrendered his forces to the Japanese. Wainwright surrendered the remainder of the American forces on Corregidor and elsewhere in the Philippines on 6 May 1942. While the defeat in the Philippines was inevitable once the Japanese crippled the Pacific Fleet at Pearl Harbor, there were some positive consequences for the Allies. The American and Filipino defenders delayed the Japanese timetable for their conquest of South Asia and caused them to commit more manpower and resources than expected. At the same time, the determined resistance against overwhelming odds represented a moral victory for the defenders and provided the American people with some hope in the bleak early days of the war in the Pacific. *See also* CENTRAL PACIFIC.

PICKERING, TIMOTHY (1745–1829). Secretary of war in 1795. Born in Massachusetts, Pickering graduated from Harvard College in 1763 and was commissioned a second lieutenant in the Essex County **militia**. He wrote a guide for militia discipline that was one of several used before **Friedrich Wilhelm von Steuben**'s manual appeared. After participating in the **Long Island** and **Trenton** campaigns of the **Revolutionary War**, Pickering became **adjutant general** of the army in 1777 and was the quartermaster general from 1780 to 1785. After the war, he entered the mercantile business in Philadelphia. After serving as postmaster general from 1791 to 1795, Pickering was secretary of war for 11 months in 1795, before becoming secretary of state for five years. From August to December 1795, he held both offices. *See also* Appendix 4, Secretaries of War and Secretaries of the Army.

PIKE, ZEBULON MONTGOMERY (1779–1813). Army officer and explorer. Born in New Jersey, Pike joined his father's army unit at age 15 and five years later was a second lieutenant. In 1805, **James Wilkinson** sent him with 20 men to find the source of the Mississippi River and assert American claims to the area. He returned after eight months, having mistakenly identified Leech Lake as the source of the river, but he did inform the Indians and British subjects in the area that they were violating American territorial rights. Six years later, Pike was ordered to gain information about Spanish territories in the western part of the continent. In what is now Colorado, he attempted to climb the peak that bears his name, but he failed. He was captured by Spanish troops in Santa Fe and tried by authorities in Chihuahua, but was released in 1807 without his notes and maps. His account of the expedition spurred American expansion into the Southwest. A brigadier general in the **War of 1812**, Pike was killed leading an attack on York during the **Canada** campaign.

PINE RIDGE (November 1890–1891). Indian wars campaign streamer. Better known by the name of the only engagement of the campaign, the Battle of

Wounded Knee, this was the last major campaign between American Indians and the U.S. Army. The confrontation was the result of a movement known as the ghost dance, which spread across western Indian reservations in 1889 and 1890. In North and South Dakota, the Sioux so enthusiastically embraced the new religion that white residents requested additional military protection against possible violence. General **Nelson Miles**, the army commander in the area, encouraged the arrest of Indian leaders. In December 1890, **Sitting Bull** was killed when Indian policemen attempted to arrest him at the Standing Rock Agency. Another Indian leader, Big Foot, escaped arrest and led his band toward the Pine Ridge Agency. Even though the Indian movement was peaceful, army forces located the Indians and escorted them to Wounded Knee Creek, where about 500 soldiers and four small cannon surrounded an Indian village with some 350 people. The intent was to disarm the Indians and neither side anticipated a fight. However, tensions were high and the accidental discharge of a rifle triggered a brief fire fight that scattered the Indians and prompted the army artillery to open fire on the village, killing or wounding 200 Indians, including women and children. The army lost 25 soldiers killed and another 39 wounded. The massacre exacerbated bad feelings on both sides and Wounded Knee continues to symbolize the wrongs inflicted on Native Americans.

PITCHER, MOLLY. *See* MARY LUDWIG HAYS MCCAULEY.

PLATOON. A unit of about 40 or 50 soldiers. The organization of a platoon varies. In **infantry** units a platoon usually has three to five **squads**, while **armor** platoons generally have three to five tanks. Platoons are usually fixed organizations commanded by a lieutenant who is assisted by a senior sergeant. Three or four platoons make up a **company**.

POINSETT, JOEL ROBERTS (1779–1851). Secretary of war from 1837 to 1841. Born in South Carolina, Poinsett was educated by his father and attended the academy of Timothy Dwight at Greenfield Hill, Connecticut. He visited Portugal for health reasons and returned home to study law under H. S. DeSaussure, before touring Europe and Asia. During the **War of 1812**, he was a special agent to the South American states. After serving in the state legislature and the U.S. House of Representatives, he was a special envoy to Mexico and he became the first minister to that country in 1825. Poinsett was secretary of war from 1837 to 1841, when he presided over the continued removal of Indians west of the Mississippi River and concentrated elements of the army at central locations. After leaving office, he retired to his plantation in South Carolina, where he cultivated what came to be known as the poinsettia, a plant he introduced to the United States from Mexico. *See also* Appendix 4, Secretaries of War and Secretaries of the Army.

PORTER, JAMES MADISON (1793–1862). Secretary of war from 1843 to 1844. Born in Pennsylvania, Porter was educated at home and attended Norristown Academy, before joining his brother, a judge, to study law at Reading. He helped raise and served as an officer for a volunteer militia regiment in 1813, became a colonel, was admitted to the bar, and began to practice law. He was instrumental in founding Lafayette College and was president of its board of trustees, as well as professor of jurisprudence and political economy. Nominated to be secretary of war in March 1843, Porter took office and began directing the preparation of a history of American Indian tribes. However, his nomination was rejected by the Senate in January 1844 and he returned to Pennsylvania, where he was elected to the state legislature in 1849. He went into railroading and eventually became president of the Belvedere Delaware Railroad. *See also* Appendix 4, Secretaries of War and Secretaries of the Army.

PORTER, PETER BUELL (1773–1844). Secretary of war from 1828 to 1829. Born in Connecticut, Porter graduated from Yale College in 1791 and studied law in Judge Tapping Reeve's school at Litchfield, before moving to New York to practice law. He served in the New York legislature and in the U.S. House of Representatives, where he chaired the committee that recommended preparing for war with Great Britain leading up to the **War of 1812**. During the war, he led a brigade of New York militia during the **Chippewa** and **Lundy's Lane** campaigns. After the war, Porter served on the U.S.–Canadian boundary commission and was a regent of the State University of New York. He was secretary of war for 11 months and advocated removing the eastern Indians beyond the Mississippi River. *See also* Appendix 4, Secretaries of War and Secretaries of the Army.

PO VALLEY (5 April to 8 May 1945). World War II campaign streamer. In the spring of 1945, the Allied forces in Italy were preparing to continue their advance against the Germans. Having spent the winter resting from the rigors of the **Northern Apennines** campaign, the combat veterans of the U.S. Fifth Army still faced a determined foe. While the Allies prepared to renew the offensive, the Germans took advantage of the respite to prepare a series of three defensive lines in the mountainous terrain. On 5 April, the Americans opened what would be the final campaign in Italy. The fighting was fierce as the Germans initially held their positions, and it appeared that the campaign would be another slow advance over rugged terrain. But by mid-April the defenders were beginning to waver as the Allies maintained constant pressure. On 20 April, both the U.S. Fifth and the British Eighth Armies reached the flat terrain of the Po Valley and for the first time in Italy were able to unleash their **armored** forces along an excellent road network. In the face of the faster pace of operations set by the advancing Allies, resistance began to crumble and, after about 10 days of overwhelming pressure, the German forces in Italy surrendered on 2 May 1945.

By that time, the U.S. Fifth Army had been in combat more than 600 days and 19,475 of its soldiers had been killed in the fighting. From the invasion of **Sicily** in July 1943 to the final German surrender in the Po Valley, the Allied armies had fought their way north through more than 1,000 miles of mountainous terrain against a capable and determined opponent. Although the action in Italy was considered something of a sideshow once the Allies had established themselves in

France after the **Normandy** landings, the soldiers in Italy forced Germany to divert considerable men and materiel from reinforcing the forces in Central Europe.

POWELL, COLIN LUTHER (1937–). Army general and chairman of the U.S. Joint Chiefs of Staff from 1989 to 1993. Born in New York City, Powell was the son of Jamaican immigrants. Upon graduation from the City College of New York, he was commissioned a second lieutenant through the **Reserve Officers' Training Corps** in 1958. He served in various assignments as a junior officer, including the **Vietnam War**, and in 1972 he was selected to be a White House Fellow, in which position he learned how the federal government worked and became acquainted with a number of people who played key roles in his later career. In 1983, he was made the military assistant to the secretary of defense and four years later became the national security adviser.

Powell became the chairman of the Joint Chiefs of Staff in 1989, making him the first **African American** to hold that post. He was chairman during the **Persian Gulf War** and was charged with carrying out President George Bush's orders to the military. He was the most powerful chairman in the history of that office at the time, as a result of legislative changes that made the chairman the senior military officer and primary adviser to the president and secretary of defense, rather than simply the first among equals with other members of the Joint Chiefs of Staff, as had previously been the case. With Bush's detached management style and clear authority, Powell had considerable leeway to formulate the plan and execute the military strategy to accomplish the mission set forth by the president. His performance during the Gulf War received high marks from all participants. He retired from active military service in 1993 and became the U.S. secretary of state in 2001.

PRINCETON (3 January 1777). Revolutionary War campaign streamer. After his successful strike against the British at **Trenton, George Washington** moved back across the Delaware River into Pennsylvania with his Hessian prisoners, but he reoccupied Trenton on 30 and 31 December 1776. Meanwhile, Lord **Charles Cornwallis**, British commander in New Jersey, who had been in New York at the time of the Trenton attack, returned. He entered Trenton with some 6,000 British regulars on 2 January and faced Washington's forces. With their backs to the Delaware, the Americans were in a precarious position. Cornwallis delayed his attack until the following morning, which gave Washington's men an opportunity to quietly retire during the night, their campfires still burning brightly. They moved undetected around the British flank and arrived at Princeton on the morning of 3 January, when they encountered a column of British regulars just leaving the town to join Cornwallis. In a brief engagement, the Americans defeated the British and withdrew before Cornwallis could provide reinforcements from Trenton. Washington moved north, where thickly wooded hills provided protection against a British attack. He established his winter headquarters at Morristown, on the flank of the British line of communications, which compelled William Howe to withdraw his forces in New Jersey back to New Brunswick and points eastward.

PRINCIPLES OF WAR. A set of axioms that guide the conduct of war. The list varies with different armed forces. The U.S. Army first published its principles of war in a 1921 training regulation. They were taken from the work of British major general J. F. C. Fuller, who had developed a set of principles during **World War I** to serve as a guide for his own army. Over the years, the principles have been slightly revised, but U.S. Army **doctrine** still includes nine:

Objective: "Direct every military operation toward a clearly defined, decisive, and attainable objective." The objective is based on the mission of the command.

Offensive: "Seize, retain, and exploit the initiative." This principle suggests that offensive action, or maintenance of the initiative, is the most effective and decisive way to pursue and attain a clearly defined, common objective.

Mass: "Concentrate combat power at the decisive place and time." This principle suggests that superior combat power must be concentrated at the decisive place and time in order to achieve decisive results.

Economy of Force: "Allocate minimum essential combat power to secondary efforts." This principle advocates that minimum means should be employed other than where the main effort is being employed. It is the reciprocal of the principle of mass and requires the acceptance of prudent risk.

Maneuver: "Place the enemy in a position of disadvantage through the flexible application of combat power." Maneuver is the means by which a commander sets the terms of battle, declines battle, or acts to take advantage of tactical actions.

Unity of Command: "For every objective, ensure unity of effort under one responsible commander." This principle ensures that all efforts are focused on a common goal. It is axiomatic that the employment of military forces in a manner that develops their full combat power requires unity of command.

Security: "Never permit the enemy to acquire an unexpected advantage." Security enhances freedom of action by reducing the vulnerability of friendly forces to hostile acts, influence, or surprise. Security can be achieved by establishing and maintaining protective measures or by conducting deception operations to confuse and dissipate the enemy.

Simplicity: "Prepare clear, uncomplicated plans and clear, concise orders to ensure thorough understanding." Direct, simple plans and clear, concise orders are essential to reduce the chances for misunderstanding and confusion in the chaos of battle.

Surprise: "Strike the enemy at a time or place, or in a manner, for which he is unprepared." This principle is to a large degree the reciprocal of the principle of security. Concealing one's own capabilities and intentions creates the opportunity to strike the enemy unaware or unprepared.

PROCTER, REDFIELD (1831–1908). Secretary of war from 1889 to 1891. Born in Vermont, Procter received a bachelor's degree from Dartmouth College in 1851 and an advanced degree three years later. He completed his study of law at Albany Law School and entered practice with a cousin in Boston. In 1861, at the beginning of the **Civil War**, he enlisted in a Vermont **regiment** but was ordered home in 1862, when he contracted tuberculosis. He quickly recovered his health and commanded a Vermont regiment in the **Gettysburg** campaign. After the war, he returned to Vermont to practice law and enter politics. Procter served a term as governor and headed the Vermont delegation to the Republican national convention in 1888, before becoming secretary of war in 1889. In this office, he revised the military justice code and instituted a system of efficiency records and promotion examinations for officers. Elected to the Senate in 1891, he served in that body until his death in 1908. *See also* Appendix 4, Secretaries of War and Secretaries of the Army.

PUERTO RICO (25 July to 13 August 1898). Spanish–American War campaign streamer. After the fall of **Santiago** in July 1898, General **Nelson Miles, commanding general of the army**, took personal charge of an expedition to Puerto Rico. His force of about 3,000 men landed at the towns of Guanica and Guayama on 25 July 1898. Four columns of American troops quickly overran the island. There was some light skirmishing in which a few Americans were wounded, but most of the population received the soldiers with enthusiasm.

PURPLE HEART. A decoration awarded to members of the U.S. armed forces for wounds received in combat. It traces its origins to 1782, when **George Washington** devised the **Badge of Military Merit**. In 1932, the **War Department** revived the decoration as the Purple Heart and, in 1942, President Franklin D. Roosevelt issued an executive order that called for the medal to be awarded to all members of U.S. armed forces wounded in action. The medal is earned only by being wounded as a direct result of enemy action and does not in itself constitute an award for heroic action. *See also* DISTINGUISHED SERVICE CROSS; MEDAL OF HONOR; SILVER STAR.

PYLE, ERNEST TAYLOR (1900–1945). American **World War II** journalist. Born in Indiana, Pyle studied journalism at Indiana University and accepted a position at a local newspaper just before graduation. In 1923, he joined the *Washington Daily News*, where he began covering aviation and became managing editor. In 1935, he began a syndicated column for the Scripps-Howard newspaper chain in which he described his experiences driving across the United States meeting average citizens. In 1940, he covered the London bombings of World War II for the chain and in 1942 covered the U.S. landings in North Africa. Pyle followed American combat forces into **Sicily**, the mainland of Italy, and France, writing about ordinary soldiers in war with understanding, while conveying a special sense of the hardships and fears the combat infantrymen endured. His column appeared in more than 400 daily newspapers, the stories he wrote were compiled in a series of books, and he received the Pulitzer Prize in 1944. At the request of the U.S. Navy, he went to the Pacific in 1945 to cover the war there. He was killed by enemy fire on the island of Ii-Shima near Okinawa in 18 April 1945.

— Q —

QUARTERMASTER CORPS. Branch of the army. The Quartermaster Corps was established on 16 June 1775 as the Quartermaster Department with a quartermaster general as its chief officer. **Nathanael Greene**, the third quartermaster general of the army, reorganized the supply system after **Valley Forge** and established the first depot system. From 1818 to 1860, the quartermaster general was Thomas Sidney Jesup, an able administrator who instituted an improved system of property accountability and experimented with new modes of transportation, including the use of canal boats in the east and camel caravans in the desert Southwest. In 1842, clothing and other items became the responsibility of the department. During the **Civil War**, **Montgomery Meigs**, the quartermaster general, ran the army's first major depot system and oversaw the transportation of unprecedented levels of supplies and personnel throughout the war. The department assumed responsibility for burial of war dead and care of national cemeteries in 1862.

In 1912, Congress consolidated the former subsistence, pay, and quartermaster departments to create the quartermaster corps, which had its own officers, soldiers, and units who were trained to perform supply and service functions on the battlefield. When the army began purchasing motorized vehicles in 1903, the quartermaster corps supplied the petroleum. At the height of **World War II**, the corps was providing over 70,000 different supply items and more than 24 million meals a day. By the end of the war, it had recovered and buried nearly a quarter of a million American service members in temporary cemeteries around the world. The quartermaster corps continues to provide supplies and services to army forces worldwide. *See also* BRANCHES OF THE ARMY; TRANSPORTATION CORPS.

QUEBEC (28 August 1775 to 3 July 1776). Revolutionary War campaign streamer. In June 1775, the Continental Congress, believing the British were preparing to invade New York from **Canada**, authorized seizure of vital points in Canada to guarantee the security of the colonies. Early in the fall of 1775, **Benedict Arnold** left Cambridge, Massachusetts, with about 1,100 men. The column moved by water and land through the Maine wilderness, up the Kennebec River, and down the Chaudiere River, arriving at Quebec on 8 November with only 650 men. A second column of about 2,000 men organized at Fort **Ticonderoga** and led by Brigadier General Richard Montgomery advanced up Lake Champlain and the St. Lawrence River. Starting on 17 September, Montgomery laid siege to the British fort at St. Johns, which fell on 2 November. After occupying Montreal on 13 November, Montgomery joined Arnold near Quebec on 3 December with only 300 men. The rest of his force stayed behind to garrison St. Johns and Montreal. With enlistments of most of the volunteer troops set to expire at the end of the year, the two commanders decided to attack Quebec during the night of 30–31 December 1775. The British garrison repelled the assault, killing or wounding about

100 Americans and taking over 400 prisoners. Montgomery was among those killed. The Americans continued to besiege the city until the spring of 1776, when the reinforced British garrison forced them back to the head of Lake Champlain.

— R —

RAMSEY, ALEXANDER (1815–1903). Secretary of war from 1879 to 1881. Born in Pennsylvania, Ramsey was orphaned at the age of 10 and worked in his granduncle's store. He studied privately, briefly attended Lafayette College, and was admitted to the bar in 1839. He became active in politics, serving two terms in the U.S. House of Representatives before being commissioned governor of Minnesota Territory in 1849. After being investigated for fraud in his negotiations with the Sioux Indians, he was exonerated by the U.S. Senate and settled in St. Paul, where he became mayor in 1853. Ramsey was twice elected governor of Minnesota, served two terms in the U.S. Senate, and became secretary of war in 1879. After leaving office, he headed the Utah commission appointed to deal with the polygamy problem and became president of the Germania Bank of St. Paul. *See also* Appendix 4, Secretaries of War and Secretaries of the Army.

RANGERS. Part of the army's **special operations forces**. Army rangers are highly trained light **infantry** designed to spearhead assaults and conduct raids and scouting missions ahead of conventional forces. They are organized to fight in small units such as **platoons** and **companies**. The history of the U.S. Army's rangers began with units specifically designated ranger units fighting Indian tribes along the American frontier as early as 1670. The rangers of Captain Benjamin Church, for example, brought King Phillip's War to a successful conclusion in 1675. In 1756, Major Robert Rogers, a native of New Hampshire, recruited nine companies of American colonists to fight for the British during the French and Indian War and incorporated ranger tactics into their fighting techniques. Rogers published a list of 28 common-sense rules and a set of standing orders stressing readiness, security, and tactics. Rogers's Rangers carried the war to the French and Indians with scouting parties and raids, using snowshoes, sleds, and even ice skates. After the war, rangers conducted patrols and defended the colonists against sporadic Indian attacks.

In 1777, **Daniel Morgan** organized and led a corps of rangers during the **Saratoga** campaign of the **Revolutionary War**. During the same war, **Francis Marion**, a South Carolina farmer who had learned the Indians' techniques of surprise attack and sudden disappearance while fighting, led a force of guerillas who also used ranger tactics to disrupt British forces after their 1780 victory at **Charleston**. During the **Civil War**, Confederate Colonel John Mosby's rangers operated behind Union lines south of the Potomac River. Equally skillful were the rangers under the command of Colonel Turner Ashby, a Virginian widely known for his daring. The rangers of Ashby and Mosby did great service for the

Confederacy. Specialists in scouting, harassing, and raiding, they were a constant threat and kept large numbers of Union troops occupied. On the Union side, Samuel C. Mean's Loudoun Rangers captured Confederate General **James Longstreet**'s ammunition train and a portion of Mosby's force.

At the beginning of **World War II**, the army organized the 1st Ranger Battalion to conduct missions similar to those performed by British commandos. The designation "rangers" was selected because the British army was already using the term "commandos" and the army wanted a more typically American designation. William O. Darby, a newly promoted army major, organized the battalion, which was activated on 19 June 1942. On 19 August 1942, 44 enlisted men and five officers took part in the ill-fated Dieppe raid conducted by Canadian and British commandos, thus becoming the first American ground soldiers to see action against the Germans in occupied Europe. Under Darby's leadership, the rangers spearheaded the invasion of North Africa during the **Algeria–French Morocco** campaign and conducted behind-the-lines operations in **Tunisia**. The success of the 1st Ranger Battalion led to the activation of more Ranger units that fought in **Sicily** and mainland Italy. During the **Normandy** invasion in June 1944, Rangers assaulted the cliffs of Point du Hoc under intense machine-gun, mortar, and artillery fire and destroyed a German gun battery that would have wreaked havoc on the Allied fleets offshore. Rangers on Omaha Beach led the army's 29th Infantry Division off the beachhead in the face of German machine-gun fire and mortars when Norman D. Cota, the assistant division commander, gave the order that became the ranger motto: "Rangers, Lead the Way!"

During the **Korean War**, rangers saw extensive service, going into battle by air, land, and sea and conducting long-range patrols behind enemy lines to gather intelligence and attack critical headquarters. In the **Vietnam War**, the **helicopter** was the primary means for moving ranger teams into enemy rear areas, where their missions included locating enemy bases and lines of communication. In 1974, the army activated the 75th Infantry (Ranger) Regiment to carry out special missions. In 1983, rangers conducted a daring low-level parachute assault to seize the airfield at Point Salines in **Grenada** and, six years later, they spearheaded the invasion of **Panama**. In 1993, army rangers supporting a United Nations force in Somalia conducted a daylight raid in which several of their helicopters were shot down. In 18 hours of fighting, they killed an estimated 300 Somalis in what many have called the fiercest ground combat since Vietnam. Six rangers died in that action. In October 2001, army rangers were among the first ground combat troops to conduct operations in Afghanistan in the opening phases of the U.S. **war on terrorism**. *See also* SPECIAL FORCES.

RANK. Armies are designed to be hierarchical organizations with individuals at each echelon expected to perform specific functions. **Enlisted** ranks constitute the majority of soldiers in the army; **noncommissioned officers** lead squads and sections; **commissioned officers**, with some exceptions, lead or command at all echelons, platoon and above; and **warrant officers** hold particular, technical positions. The army's chain of command has leaders at each organizational level to issue directives and provide information down to lower ranks as well as receive reports up from them. **George Washington**, commanding the **Continental Army** in the **Revolutionary War**, directed the use of stripes to designate rank for his commissioned and noncommissioned officers. Since then, the army's rank insignia has changed periodically. Today, noncommissioned officers continue to wear stripes to designate rank, while commissioned and warrant officers wear shoulder and collar insignia. *See also* Appendix 8, United States Rank Insignia.

RAWLINS, JOHN AARON (1831–1869). Secretary of war for six months in 1869. Born in Illinois, Rawlins attended local schools and the Rock River Seminary before turning to the study of law in the office of Isaac P. Stevens in Galena, Illinois. Admitted to the bar in 1854, he served as the city attorney, helped organize a regiment of Illinois infantry, and became a major. In 1861, **Ulysses S. Grant**, commanding another Illinois regiment, requested his services. Rawlins remained with Grant throughout the **Civil War**, rose to the rank of major general, and became chief of staff to the **commanding general of the army**, a post created specifically for him. He became Grant's secretary of war in March 1869 and died in office six months later. *See also* Appendix 4, Secretaries of War and Secretaries of the Army.

REED, WALTER (1851–1902). Army doctor whose investigations proved that mosquitoes carried yellow fever. Born in Virginia, Reed was educated at the University of Virginia, where he received his medical degree in 1869. After spending several years in New York, where he worked in the public health field, he joined the **Army Medical Department** in 1875. In 1893, Reed was appointed professor of bacteriology at the Army Medical Center in Washington, D.C., and five years later he headed a board that investigated an outbreak of typhoid fever in army camps where troops were assembled for the **Spanish–American War**. The board's report contributed significantly to understanding the disease and how it could be controlled. In 1900, Reed was sent to Cuba to head a committee doing research on the cause and means of transmission of the yellow fever infecting U.S. troops there. His discovery that a specific mosquito carried the disease led to the eradication of yellow fever in Cuba after **William C. Gorgas**, also a doctor in the Army Medical Department, conducted an extensive eradication program, with spectacular results. In 1900, there were 1,400 reported cases of yellow fever in Havana alone; in 1902 there were none in all of Cuba. Reed returned to teaching in Washington, D.C., in 1901 and died of appendicitis in November 1902.

REGIMENT. The regiment was the tactical and administrative headquarters for the army from its founding in 1775 until 1957. The regiment was composed entirely of a single arm, such as **infantry** or **cavalry**, but with the advent of modern warfare, the army needed a more flexible organization on the battlefield. The battle group concept in the short-lived Pentomic **division** replaced the regiment in 1957, but for a variety of reasons, that idea did not succeed. In 1962, the ROAD

(Reorganized Objective Army Division) made the **battalion** the army's basic tactical headquarters. Today, the regimental designations are mainly used to trace the lineage and honors of army units. Only armored **cavalry** regiments continue to function as tactical and administrative headquarters. But although they carry the designations of their nineteenth-century regimental predecessors, today's armored cavalry regiments are combined arms teams that incorporate infantry, **armor**, and **artillery** units into their organization. The oldest regimental designation in the active army is the 3d Infantry (The Old Guard) stationed in Washington, D.C., which was originally organized in 1784 as the 1st American Regiment. The oldest units in the entire army, dating back to 1636, belong to the Massachusetts **Army National Guard**.

REGULAR ARMY. That portion of the army in the full-time service of the federal government. The regular army traces its beginnings to the **Continental Army**, authorized by Congress on 14 June 1775 with **George Washington** as its commander. The regular army provides forces for rapid worldwide deployment. Members of the regular army are generally considered professional soldiers. *See also* ARMY NATIONAL GUARD; RESERVE COMPONENTS; UNITED STATES ARMY; UNITED STATES ARMY RESERVE.

REIMER, DENNIS JOE (1939–). Chief of staff of the army from 1995 to 1999. Born in Oklahoma, Reimer graduated from the **U.S. Military Academy** in 1962. He served two tours of duty in the **Vietnam War** in the 1960s and graduated from the **Army War College** in 1979. After holding a variety of command and staff positions in the continental United States, Korea, and Germany, he became chief of staff in 1995 and retired from active service in 1999. While in office, he supervised the movement of army forces into the Balkans in support of the NATO peacekeeping operations there. *See also* Appendix 3, Commanding Generals and Chiefs of Staff of the Army.

RESACA DE LA PALMA (9 May 1846). Mexican War campaign streamer. The day after the battle at **Palo Alto**, **Zachary Taylor**, commanding American forces in Mexico, continued advancing toward Matamoros. He encountered the Mexicans in a strong defensive position in a dry riverbed known as the Resaca de la Palma. The **infantry** conducted most of the action, although the **dragoons** (mounted horsemen) played an important part in knocking out the enemy artillery. Eventually, the infantry turned the enemy's left flank, breaking the Mexican line. The rout became a race for the Rio Grande, which the Mexicans won, although many drowned while attempting to cross the river. American losses were 33 killed and 89 wounded. The Mexicans reported 160 killed, 228 wounded, and 159 missing, but Americans estimated that the Mexicans had suffered well over a thousand casualties. When the Americans moved into Matamoros, they found that the Mexican force had disappeared into the interior. Taylor's next objective was the Mexican city of **Monterrey**, but because the route from Matamoros lacked water and forage, he waited until August for the arrival of steamboats to move his army 130 miles upriver to Camargo. Thousands of volunteers poured into Matamoros, but disease and various security and logistic factors limited Taylor to a force of little more than 6,000 men for the Monterrey campaign.

RESERVE COMPONENTS. The reserve components of the U.S. Army consist of the **Army National Guard** and the **U.S. Army Reserve**. Together, they provide trained units and individual soldiers for active duty in time of war and other emergencies that require augmentation of the **regular army**. There are three categories of reserves, the ready reserve, the standby reserve, and the retired reserve:

- The ready reserve consists of members of the Army National Guard and U.S. Army Reserve units that participate in 48 drills and two weeks of active duty training annually; individual mobilization augmentees, who have assignments for wartime duty in units or headquarters and perform two weeks of active duty training each year; and the individual ready reserve, which consists of officers and enlisted soldiers with prior military service who are completing their military obligation.
- The standby reserve includes individual soldiers, officers, and enlisted who have completed their active duty and reserve training requirements or who are unable to maintain membership in units.
- The retired reserve includes individual soldiers, both officers and enlisted, who have completed 20 years of qualifying service for retirement.

RESERVE OFFICERS' TRAINING CORPS. Perhaps better known by its acronym, ROTC, this program trains students in American universities, colleges, high schools, and academies to serve as commissioned officers in the U.S. armed forces. It has provided the majority of **regular army** and **U.S. Army Reserve** officers since **World War II**. Although the program was established by the **National Defense Act of 1916**, the concept has its roots in the eighteenth century with the colonial citizen soldiers. The federal government established the **U.S. Military Academy** in 1802 to produce officers for the army, but most officers in militia and volunteer units in the nineteenth century were civilians temporarily in uniform. The need to rapidly expand the army for the **Civil War** led to the Morrill Act of 1862, which granted public lands to establish colleges and required that military tactics be offered as part of the curriculum to the land-grant institutions. The federal government provided some funding, while the **War Department** assigned regular or retired officers as professors of military science and tactics. Although by 1893 there were some 79 colleges and universities providing some level of military instruction to male students, between 1865 and 1919 the Military Academy produced most of the officers for the regular army.

Early in the nineteenth century, a number of military planners and business people suggested that the army needed a systematic program to provide commissioned officers that could cope with the larger forces they envisioned that the United States, as an emerging world power, would soon need. In 1913, General **Leonard Wood**, then **chief of staff of the army**, conducted several summer military training camps for college students. These camps formed the model for camps established for businessmen after **World War I** started in Europe. In 1915 and 1916, some 13,000 business and professional men received training in the camps. The National Defense Act of 1916 authorized the ROTC. Established too late to provide a significant number of officers for World War I, the program was expanded in 1920. By 1928, there were 85,000 ROTC students in 225 colleges and universities and 100 high schools and academies, and the program commissioned about 6,000 officers each year. In World War II, most officers were commissioned from the **enlisted** ranks through Officer Candidate Schools, although the ROTC program produced 120,000 officers. Since World War II, the ROTC has been the army's primary source of officers, although the number of schools offering the program has fluctuated according to the nation's political climate and requirements of the military.

RESOR, STANLEY ROGERS (1917–). Secretary of the army from 1965 to 1971. Born in New York, Resor attended the Groton School, graduated from Yale University in 1939, and entered law school at Yale. In 1942, he was commissioned a second lieutenant from the Yale **Reserve Officers' Training Corps** program. During **World War II**, he served in the European theater and was awarded a **Silver Star** and a **Purple Heart**. He returned to Yale Law School after the war, received his degree in 1946, and entered private practice in New York City, specializing in corporate law. After a brief time as undersecretary of the army, Resor became secretary in 1965 and was in office during most of the **Vietnam War**. During his tenure, the army provided support to civil authorities during civil disturbances and instituted the **All-Volunteer Force**. After leaving office, Resor served as an ambassador and was an undersecretary of defense before returning to private practice of law in 1979. *See also* Appendix 4, Secretaries of War and Secretaries of the Army.

REVOLUTIONARY WAR (1775–1783). American colonists had been chaffing at the British government's attempts to maintain control over its empire in the New World for some time prior to 1775. On September 1774, representatives from each of the colonies met to form a Continental Congress to present a unified front for voicing their protests to the British government. Officers in the British army who had served in the colonies believed that the rebels would be easily cowed by a display of force. When open warfare erupted in the spring of 1775 between the colonists and British troops, the New England militia bore the brunt of the initial clashes at **Lexington** and Concord. Within a week of the war's first encounters, 20,000 militiamen laid siege to **Boston**. In June, at the Battle of Bunker Hill, which was actually fought on Breed's Hill, British officers marched their regiments up the hill in a frontal assault against the American's fortified defensive position, rather than conduct a flanking movement. British officers perhaps hoped the frontal assault would demonstrate to the part-time soldiers the power of professional **infantry**. The British won the battle, but by fighting from defensive positions, the militia had been successful in preserving the lives of Americans who could fight another day.

But Americans recognized there were shortcomings to the militia and decided that a regular military force would be required to stand up to the British army. On

14 June, Congress named the New England militia assembled at Boston the **Continental Army** and authorized 10 companies of riflemen, six from Pennsylvania and two each from Maryland and Virginia, to be raised as national forces and, with the New Englanders, to provide the nucleus of a permanent force that would be supplemented by militia units as required. A year later, Congress established an executive department for military affairs, the Board of War and Ordnance. This office eventually evolved into the **War Department** in 1789, headed by the **secretary of war**, the civilian head of the army.

As commander in chief of the new army, the Continental Congress named **George Washington**, whose strength of character, resourcefulness, and military experience served the new nation well as it struggled through its difficult formative years. Under Washington's leadership, the Continental Army developed a modified version of European linear tactics for its infantry. Combined with the traditional irregular colonial practices, it produced a looser sort of fighting formation than was used in European warfare. American **infantry**, although schooled and disciplined to a degree, took advantage of available cover and used aimed fire rather than the massed fire common to the British.

After the Declaration of Independence on 4 July 1776, the Continental Army's mission changed from defense of American rights to national survival. With few other national institutions in existence in America, the army was essentially the new nation. Realizing that loss of the army could lead to the collapse of the American cause, Washington tried to avoid battles that would put his forces at risk. But at the same time, he needed to win battles to maintain morale at home and obtain support from countries abroad. In late 1776, Washington managed to keep the army intact after the fall of New York City during the **Long Island** campaign and then led his soldiers across the Delaware River on Christmas night to surprise the British garrison at **Trenton**. Eight days later, he defeated another British force at **Princeton**. The war continued to have its ups and downs. In September 1777, the young republic survived the loss of its capital at Philadelphia, but in October, Major General **John Burgoyne** surrendered the British forces at Saratoga, prompting France to become an American ally.

With the British engaged in a worldwide struggle against France while it was trying to keep its American colonies in line, Washington needed only to maintain the army in the field long enough for Great Britain to tire of the struggle. Although his soldiers suffered at **Valley Forge** during the winter of 1777–1778, through the efforts of **Friedrich Wilhelm von Steuben**, the first **inspector general** of the army, the Continentals emerged from the ordeal with enough training and confidence to stand up to British regulars. The army distinguished itself at **Monmouth** in the summer of 1778, but by 1781 American fortunes were at a low point. The British were sweeping through the South and one of the Continental Army's most distinguished commanders, **Benedict Arnold**, had deserted. But in October 1781 a Franco-American force under Washington and the **Marquis de Lafayette** compelled the British forces commanded by **Lord Charles Cornwallis** to surrender at **Yorktown**. Disheartened by the defeat and exhausted by over six years of war, Great Britain finally recognized American independence. The Treaty of Versailles formally concluded the American Revolution and brought an end to English, French, and Spanish conflicts in the Americas on 20 January 1783. Spain received Florida and Great Britain got the Bahamas. *See also* Revolutionary War campaigns in Appendix 6, Campaigns of the United States Army.

RHINELAND (15 September 1944 to 21 March 1945). World War II campaign streamer. By the autumn of 1944, the Allied forces in Europe had moved to Germany's western border after successful landings in both **Northern France** and **Southern France**. But logistical problems had become acute. Although the U.S. First Army, under Lieutenant General Courtney H. Hodges, had penetrated the so-called West Wall, the German border defensive line, in several places lack of supplies prevented exploitation of the breaks, while bad weather, restrictive terrain, and the dense fortifications along the German border combined to create obstacles of major proportions. For two of General **Dwight D. Eisenhower**'s subordinate commanders, British General Bernard Montgomery and **George S. Patton,** Eisenhower's decision to advance into Germany on a broad front was a

U.S. Army Military History Institute.

7. Soldiers from the 39th Infantry supported by tanks pass through the Siegfried Line at the beginning of the Rhineland campaign.

mistake in light of the logistical limitations. Each of the two commanders wanted all resources put behind his part of the front to support a single major drive into Germany, with the goal of disorganizing the defense and gaining an early capitulation. The debate continued through the late summer and much of the fall of 1944, but Eisenhower, backed by the advice of his logisticians, stuck to the plan of advancing with all armies abreast, though with greater emphasis in the north.

Because of the logistical crisis, Eisenhower assigned first priority to clearing the seaward approaches to Antwerp. The Allies had captured the port in September, but the Germans controlled access to the sea. But before logistical problems forced the Allied offensive to halt, Eisenhower decided to make a bold move in an effort to exploit the German disorganization that had resulted from the rapid Allied drive across France. He authorized using the First Allied Airborne Army, which had one British and two U.S. **airborne** divisions under Lieutenant General Lewis H. Brereton, to support the British Second Army. The plan was to get across the three major water obstacles in the Netherlands—the Maas, Waal, and Lower Rhine Rivers—to outflank the West Wall and put the British in position for a subsequent drive into Germany along the relatively open north German plain. The parachute drop on 17 September achieved complete surprise, but the Germans were more organized than expected. Strong resistance limited the gains to a 50-mile salient into Holland, leaving the Allied forces well short of a bridge across the Rhine.

With the failure of the airborne operation, British forces concentrated on opening the approaches to Antwerp, but it was November before the way was cleared for the first Allied ship to enter the port. Meanwhile, a supreme effort by the supply services had improved the overall logistical situation and, in early November, U.S. forces launched a major offensive toward the Rhine. But bad weather, natural and artificial defenses along the German border, and a resourceful defense on the part of German troops limited gains. By mid-December, the U.S. First and Ninth Armies had reached the Roer River east of Aachen, some 22 miles inside Germany, and the U.S. Third and Seventh Armies had reached the West Wall along the Saar River northeast of Metz, but except in the Seventh Army sector Allied forces were still a long way from the Rhine. As the Allies prepared for the winter, they were surprised to find that the Germans were not quite ready to give up the defense of their homeland. An unexpected German counteroffensive in the Ardennes Forest delayed the final campaign of the war in Europe until March 1945. *See also* ARDENNES–ALSACE; NORMANDY.

RIDGWAY, MATTHEW BUNKER (1895–1993). Chief of staff of the army from 1953 to 1955. Born in Virginia, Ridgway graduated from the **U.S. Military Academy** in 1917. He served in a variety of diplomatic and military assignments and was on the army's **general staff** in 1941, when he received command of the 82d Airborne Division during **World War II**. Ridgway led the division in **Sicily** and **Normandy** and assumed command of an **airborne** corps in 1944. After the war, he held a number of command and staff positions. He was on the army staff in 1950 when he was called upon to replace Walton H. Walker as commander of the U.S. Eighth Army in the **Korean War**, after Walker was killed in an auto accident during the **Chinese Communist Forces Intervention**. Ridgway moved quickly to restore the Eighth Army's morale and stop the Chinese attack. In April 1951, he replaced **Douglas MacArthur** as the United Nations commander when MacArthur was relieved of the post by President **Harry Truman**. Ridgway became supreme allied commander of the North Atlantic Treaty Organization forces in Europe in 1952 and was appointed chief of staff of the army in 1954. While in office, he advocated a strong ground army, warning against too much reliance on air power and nuclear weapons, and he opposed U.S. involvement in the **Vietnam War**. *See also* Appendix 3, Commanding Generals and Chiefs of Staff of the Army.

ROGERS, BERNARD WILLIAM (1921–). Chief of staff of the army from 1976 to 1979. Born in Kansas, Rogers graduated from the **U.S. Military Academy** and was commissioned a second lieutenant in 1943. After teaching at the Military Academy, he attended Oxford as a Rhodes scholar. He commanded a **battalion** in the **Korean War** and a **division** during the **Vietnam War**. He became chief of staff in 1976 and, while in office, he supervised the army's move to 24 divisions, established readiness priorities, and suggested a limited draft. He was appointed supreme allied commander of NATO forces in Europe in 1979 and he retired from active service in 1987. *See also* Appendix 3, Commanding Generals and Chiefs of Staff of the Army.

ROME–ARNO (22 January to 9 September 1944). World War II campaign streamer. Allied forces landing in Italy in September 1943 quickly liberated the port of Naples and captured the airfields at Foggia, but by the end of the year, a German army of some 23 divisions had slowed the advance. In mid-January 1944, the Allies were facing the formidable Gustav Line, the German defensive positions that stretched across the Italian peninsula just south of Rome. On 22 January, the Allies attempted to outflank the German line with an amphibious landing at **Anzio**, some 35 miles south of Rome, while launching an offensive against the Gustav line. The objective of the Anzio operation was to reach Rome by 1 February, but that plan failed when the beachhead came under heavy attack by German forces. As a consequence, General **Mark Clark**, commanding the U.S. Fifth Army, was faced with the necessity of making a breakthrough to reach the forces at Anzio. After almost four months of tough infantry combat along the Gustav Line, the Allies finally broke through the German defenses on 16 May and made contact with the forces at Anzio on 25 May.

After the linkup, the combined forces focused on Rome and, on 4 June, the first Fifth Army units entered the city, marking the liberation of the Italian capital. But the stay in Rome was short for the combat troops, who within days were on the move again, heading north to complete the destruction of the German forces holding Italy. With the invasion of **Normandy** receiving the priority for units and equipment, the Allied forces in Italy were reduced to a total of 14 divisions facing some 17 German divisions. It took another month for the Allied drive to reach the Arno River, where they halted offensive operations and gave the combat units a rest. The campaign ended with both sides taking a breather while they prepared for what would be the final battles of the war in Italy.

The campaign was essentially an infantryman's war, with the outcome decided by countless, hard-fought small-unit actions over rough, mountainous terrain. The constant shortages of troops and available materiel in Italy as the Allies prepared for the invasion of France further exacerbated the difficulties facing commanders in Italy. Although hundreds of miles of territory had been liberated in the campaign, the Allied armies in Italy faced another nine months of fighting before the war would be over. *See also* NAPLES–FOGGIA.

ROMMEL, ERWIN JOHANNES EUGEN (1891–1944). German World War II general. Born in Heidenheim, Germany, Rommel served with distinction in **World War I**. After the war, he stayed in the army, wrote a widely read book on **infantry tactics**, and taught at Dresden Military Academy. A Nazi sympathizer, he commanded Adolf Hitler's headquarters during the 1939 German invasion of Poland and led an **armored** division when Germany attacked France in 1940. From 1941 to 1943, he commanded the Afrika Korps in North Africa, where he dealt a severe defeat to U.S. Army forces at Kasserine Pass during the **Tunisia** campaign. He was recalled to Germany before the Axis forces were forced out of North Africa and, in December 1943, he was transferred to France to inspect the German seacoast defenses and assume command of the forces there. Rommel advocated a mobile defense rather than relying on fixed defenses at the shore to stop an invasion force, but his superiors disagreed. After the Allies came ashore at **Normandy** in June 1944, he was severely wounded in an air attack in July. Implicated in a plot to kill Hitler, Rommel committed suicide in October 1944 to avoid a trial and retaliation against his family. He was a talented tactical commander whose exploits with the Afrika Korps gained him something of a cult status after World War II.

ROOSEVELT, THEODORE (1858–1919). Army officer and 26th president of the United States. Born in New York City, Roosevelt graduated from Harvard University in 1880 and became a dynamic political leader. He enthusiastically supported the military and in 1897 became assistant secretary of the navy. As an advocate of the **Spanish–American War**, he used his political influence to gain an appointment as lieutenant colonel in the 1st **U.S. Volunteer** Cavalry. When the regimental commander, **Leonard Wood**, left for a higher assignment, Roosevelt took command and led the Rough Riders, as the unit was known, in its famous charge during the **Santiago** campaign. Although they were a **cavalry** regiment, the Rough Riders were dismounted during the charge; also, they charged up Kettle Hill, not San Juan Hill. The well-publicized action helped Roosevelt get elected as governor of New York and put him on the 1900 presidential ticket as vice presidential running mate to William McKinley, who won the election. When McKinley was assassinated in 1901, Roosevelt became president. He remained in office until 1909. While president, he supported **Elihu Root**'s efforts for an army **general staff** and approved legislation to make the **Army National Guard** a viable federal reserve.

ROOT, ELIHU (1845–1937). Secretary of war from 1899 to 1904. Born in New York, Root graduated from Hamilton College in 1864 and New York University Law School in 1867. He practiced law in New York City, until President William McKinley named him secretary of war in 1899. In the aftermath of the **Spanish–American War**, Root sought to reform the army and make it a more capable organization that could support the United States' growing international role. He proposed a plan to reduce the power of the bureau chiefs and establish a **general staff** headed by a **chief of staff of the army**, who would replace the **commanding general of the army** and act as chief adviser and executive agent for the president on military policy. Despite the opposition of commanding general of the army **Nelson A. Miles**, the **adjutant general**, and the bureau chiefs, Congress adopted Root's proposal in 1903. His reforms include expanding the army's school system and establishing the **Army War College**, increasing the size of the army, helping modernize the **Army National Guard**, rotating officers out of long-term assignments in the bureaus to bring fresh ideas into the **War Department**, and establishing a general staff that could provide central direction and long-range planning for the army. The success of his efforts make him one of the most important secretaries in the army's history. After leaving office, Root was secretary of state from 1905 to 1909 and represented New York in the U.S. Senate for two terms. In 1912 he was awarded the Noble Peace Prize for promoting international arbitration. *See also* Appendix 4, Secretaries of War and Secretaries of the Army.

ROUGH RIDERS. *See* ROOSEVELT, THEODORE.

ROYALL, KENNETH CLAIBORNE (1894–1971). Secretary of war from July to September 1947 and **secretary of the army** from September 1947 to April 1949. Born in North Carolina, Royall graduated from the University of North Carolina in 1914 and received a law degree from Harvard in 1917. He served in France in **World War I** and later organized a **field artillery** battery in the North Carolina **Army National Guard**. During **World War II**, he was the deputy fiscal director for the Army Service Forces. He became undersecretary of war in 1945 and secretary in 1947. Under the provisions of the **National Security Act of 1947**, he became the last secretary of war, the first secretary of the army, and the last army secretary to hold cabinet status. While in office, he supervised the separation of the U.S. Air Force from the army. After leaving office, he returned to practicing law in New York City. *See also* Appendix 4, Secretaries of War and Secretaries of the Army.

RYUKYUS (26 March to 2 July 1945). World War II campaign streamer. Early in the war, U.S. strategists planned to bypass the Philippine Islands and conduct the B-29 strategic bombing program from bases in China. But the Japanese closed the Burma Road in 1942, cutting off the land route to support China and, as a result, Allied bombers were never based there. The Allies then planned to capture Taiwan as a base for strategic bombers. With the capture of the Mariana

Islands in 1945 during the **Western Pacific** campaign, bases there were used for strategic bombing operations, so Taiwan was bypassed and the troops scheduled for that operation invaded Okinawa and other islands in the Ryukyus in March 1945. The campaign began on the 26th with the capture of small islands near Okinawa, where U.S. forces established forward naval bases. An amphibious assault on Okinawa took place on 1 April and the fighting lasted until June. For the first time, Americans invaded what the Japanese considered their home soil, and the defense was fanatic. The Americans suffered heavy casualties. The U.S. Navy lost some 25 American ships and had damage to 165 others, as Japanese suicide flyers, the *kamikazes*, desperately attempted to save the Ryukyus from U.S. occupation. Among the nearly 35,000 American casualties was Lieutenant General Simon B. Buckner Jr., commander of the U.S. Tenth Army, who was killed on 18 June. Four days later, General **Joseph W. Stilwell**, who had served much of the war in China, arrived to assume command of the Tenth Army.

Capturing the Ryukyus gave Allied naval and air forces excellent bases within 700 miles of the Japanese home islands. Throughout June and July, Japan was subjected to increasingly intensive air attack and naval bombardment from Allied forces based in the islands, putting the Allies in position for a final assault on the Japanese homeland. In preparation for the invasion of Japan, General **Douglas MacArthur** was given command of all army forces and Admiral Chester Nimitz headed all naval forces, but the war ended without the invasion.

— S —

ST. CLAIR, ARTHUR (1736–1818). Commanding general of the army from 1791 to 1792. Born in Scotland and educated at the University of Edinburgh, St. Clair purchased a commission as ensign in the British army and served in Canada. He resigned from the British army in 1762 and purchased an estate in Pennsylvania. He served in various civil and military positions and was eventually promoted to major general in 1777. During the **Revolutionary War**, St. Clair commanded Fort Ticonderoga and after abandoning it to the British during the **Saratoga** campaign was court-martialed, but was exonerated of blame for losing the post. While serving as commanding general, he led an expedition into Indian country, where his force was defeated at the Wabash River during the **Miami** campaign. He resigned in 1792 and a congressional inquiry exonerated him of blame for the expedition's failure. See also Appendix 3, Commanding Generals and Chiefs of Staff of the Army.

ST. MIHIEL (12–16 September 1918). World War I campaign streamer. By September 1918, the Allies faced only one major threat to lateral rail communications behind their front, the St. Mihiel salient, near the Paris–Nancy line. Preparations for this salient's reduction began with the transfer of the U.S. First Army headquarters from La Ferté-sous-Jouarre in the Marne region to Neufchateau on the Meuse, immediately south of St. Mihiel in mid-August. The 14 American and four French divisions assigned to the U.S. First Army for the operation contained adequate **infantry** and machine-gun units, but were short of **artillery**, **tank**, air, and other support units. The French provided over half the artillery and nearly half the airplanes and tanks for the St. Mihiel operation.

Shortly before the offensive was to begin, jeopardizing the long-standing desire of U.S. First Army commander **John J. Pershing** to conduct an independent American operation, the Allied commander in chief proposed to reduce the size of the St. Mihiel attack and divide the American forces into three groups: one for the salient offensive and two for fronts to the east and west of the Argonne Forest. Pershing remained adamant in his insistence that the First Army should not be broken up. A compromise was reached by which the St. Mihiel attack was subordinated to the much larger offensive to be launched on the **Meuse–Argonne** front in late September, while the First Army would remain intact. Pershing agreed to limit operations by employing only the minimum force needed to reduce the salient in three or four days, while at the same time preparing for a major role in the Meuse–Argonne drive.

The St. Mihiel offensive began on 12 September. Two U.S. **corps** made the main attack against the south face of the salient. Another U.S. corps carried out a secondary thrust against the west face along the heights of the Meuse, while the French II Colonial Corps conducted a holding attack against the apex to keep the Germans in the salient. The First Army held three U.S. divisions in reserve. Total Allied forces in the offensive included some 550,000 American and 100,000 other Allied (mostly French) troops. The First Army had more than 3,000 guns, 400 French tanks, and 1,500 airplanes. U.S. Army Colonel **William Mitchell** directed the heterogeneous air force, composed of British, French, Italian, Portuguese, and American units, in what proved to be the largest single air operation of the war. American squadrons flew 609 of the airplanes, most of which had been manufactured by the French or British. The attack went so well on the first day that Pershing accelerated the offensive. By the morning of 13 September, the U.S. 1st Division, advancing from the east, joined with the U.S. 26th Division, moving in from the west, and before evening all objectives in the salient had been captured. Pershing halted further advances so the American units could be withdrawn for the coming offensive in the Meuse–Argonne sector.

In its first major independent operation, the U.S. First Army captured 16,000 prisoners at a cost of 7,000 casualties, eliminated the threat of an attack on the rear of Allied fortifications at Nancy and Verdun, greatly improved Allied lateral rail communications, and opened the way for a possible future offensive to seize Metz and the Briey iron fields.

SANCTUARY COUNTEROFFENSIVE (1 May to 30 June 1970). Vietnam **War** campaign streamer. During the American withdrawal from South Vietnam in 1970, there was increased concern over the enemy's strength in its Cambodian sanctuaries. The emergence of an anti-Communist government in Cambodia prompted the North Vietnamese and Viet Cong (VC) to move on the Cambodian capital of Phnom Penh. Lon Nol, the new pro-Western leader of Cambodia, appealed to the United States for assistance and U.S. president Richard M. Nixon relaxed the restrictions on moving against the North Vietnamese and VC bases inside Cambodia. American and South Vietnamese forces began large-scale offensives in Cambodia on 1 May 1970. Eight major U.S. Army and South Vietnamese operations took place in Cambodia in May and June with the object of cutting enemy communication lines, seizing the sanctuary areas, and capturing the Central Office for South Vietnam, the shadowy control center for enemy military operations in central South Vietnam.

SAN FABIAN (6–19 November 1899). **Philippine Insurrection** campaign streamer. Brigadier General Lloyd Wheaton and his command sailed from Manila on 6 November and landed at San Fabian the next day. Five days later, the U.S. troops routed insurgents at San Jacinto and on 20 November linked up with Major General Arthur MacArthur's column at Dagupan, where McArthur's soldiers had recently captured **Tarlac**.

SAN ISIDRO (12 April to 30 May 1899; 15 October to 19 November 1899). **Philippine Insurrection** campaign streamer. This streamer represents two campaigns. After capturing Santa Cruz during the **Laguna de Bay** campaign, Major General Henry W. Lawton assembled his troops at La Loma Church and advanced on San Isidro. Army forces dispersed the insurgent troops in the area and returned to Manila on 30 May. In October, Lawton took up where he left off in June at the end of the **Zapote River** campaign and led his column up the Rio Grande de la Pampagna toward San Isidro, an insurgent stronghold Major General Arthur MacArthur had held briefly in May. Lawton captured San Isidro on 19 October and neared **San Fabian** on Lingayen Gulf on 18 November.

SAN JUAN HILL. *See* ROOSEVELT, THEODORE; SANTIAGO.

SANTA ANNA, ANTONIO LOPEZ DE (1794–1876). Mexican general and politician. Born in Jalapa, Santa Anna was dictator of Mexico while commanding an army of 6,000 soldiers that defeated and killed the defenders of the Alamo in Texas. He was defeated at the San Jacinto River and imprisoned for eight months before going into exile. Returning from exile in 1846, he was president of Mexico during the **Mexican War** and commanded the Mexican Army in the field. He failed to defeat the Americans at **Buena Vista** and was defeated at **Cerro Gordo**. Driven out of Mexico City by **Winfield Scott**'s army, Santa Anna was once again exiled, but he returned to power in 1853 as perpetual dictator, only to be driven from the country by revolutionaries two years later. In 1867, with the death of the emperor Maximillian, Santa Anna tried to return but was captured, sentenced to death, and then allowed to retire to New York. He returned to Mexico for good in 1872.

SANTIAGO (22 June to 11 July 1898). **Spanish–American War** campaign streamer. When the Spanish fleet took refuge in Santiago Bay on 29 May 1898, the U.S. Navy asked the army to reduce the defenses guarding the entrance. The

War Department directed General William Rufus Shafter to embark his corps, which had been assembled around Tampa, and sail for Cuba. After many delays, and in an atmosphere of the utmost confusion, the embarkation of some 17,000 men began on 11 June 1898 and lasted four days. On 20 June, the convoy reached a point off Santiago, but it was two days before the troops landed. Rear Admiral William T. Sampson wanted them to land near the entrance of the bay, where a powerful fort dominated the area, and to storm the positions guarding the sea approaches. Shafter considered this plan too dangerous and followed the advice of General Calixto Garcia, a Cuban insurgent leader, who recommended Daiquiri, 18 miles east of Santiago Bay, as a landing site. The campaign got under way on 22 June with a confused landing operation that, fortunately for the Americans, was unopposed. About 6,000 troops were landed on the first day and started to march to Santiago. The Spaniards had not planned to make a determined stand until the Americans reached Santiago's outer defenses, so the advance to Santiago was virtually unopposed. The exception was a brief fight with the rear guard of a retiring Spanish force at Las Guasima, where the Americans suffered a loss of 16 killed and 52 wounded and the Spaniards lost 12 killed and 14 wounded.

Santiago's most important defenses were along a series of ridges known as San Juan and at the village of El Caney to the north. Shafter decided to first attack El Caney, which had about 500 Spanish defenders, and to follow with a frontal assault on the San Juan positions held by about 1,200 Spaniards. The American attacking forces totaled some 8,000 men. Shafter launched the attack on 1 July 1898. The attack on El Caney initially made little headway against the determined Spanish resistance, but the Americans met with success when **artillery** moved forward and fired directly on the defenders. After considerable confusion, and some temporary reverses along the San Juan ridges, the Spanish positions finally fell to the American assault, which included an assault on Kettle Hill on the northern end, where **Theodore Roosevelt** and his Rough Riders distinguished themselves in what became known as the charge up San Juan Hill. The Spanish forces moved back to a second line of defense, but except for a heavy exchange of artillery fire on 2 July there was no more fighting. The Santiago fighting resulted in 1,475 American and more than 550 Spanish casualties. On 3 July 1898, the Spanish fleet attempted to escape from Santiago Bay, triggering a dramatic running fight with the American fleet blockading the harbor. All the Spanish ships were destroyed, with a loss of about 600 men, while the Americans lost only one man killed and one seriously wounded. Following the fleet's disaster, General Jose Toral, the Spanish commander in Santiago, surrendered the 11,500 troops in the city and some 12,000 troops stationed elsewhere in the province of Santiago.

SARATOGA (2 July to 17 October 1777). Revolutionary War campaign streamer. British strategy in 1777 had two major objectives. The first was to split New England from the rest of the American states by a drive from Canada and the second was to seize Philadelphia, seat of the revolutionary government. The Saratoga campaign covers the first objective and the **Brandywine** campaign covers the second. The British campaign in upper New York began in June 1777 with a two-pronged drive from Canada. **John Burgoyne** led a force of about 7,500 British soldiers, accompanied by some 400 Indians, down Lake Champlain and compelled 2,500 **Continental Army** soldiers and militia under **Arthur St. Clair** to evacuate **Ticonderoga** on 27 June. Other American forces in the area moved southward, slowing the heavy British force in the rugged terrain. Another British force consisting of some 700 regulars and Tories and a band of 1,000 Indians moved east from Fort Oswego on Lake Ontario into the Mohawk Valley to join Burgoyne at Albany. This force surrounded Fort Stanwix, which guarded the head of the Mohawk Valley, on 2 August, but quit the siege in mid-August when a relief force of 950 Continentals under **Benedict Arnold** scattered Britain's Indian allies.

On 13 and 14 September, Burgoyne crossed the Hudson River at Saratoga and faced an American force of about 7,000 under **Horatio Gates**. On 19 September, Burgoyne attacked Bemis Heights, where Gates's force held strongly entrenched positions. At Freeman's Farm, just forward of the main positions, the Americans yielded the field but inflicted twice as many casualties (600) as they suffered and held the heights. For more than two weeks, Burgoyne remained inactive, while **Henry Clinton**, commanding the British troops in New York City, made an ineffectual effort to send relief forces up the Hudson. On 7 October, Burgoyne moved toward the American left with 1,650 troops, but was repulsed in a sharp fight known as the Battle of Bemis Heights. Two days later, he retired to a position near Saratoga where, virtually surrounded by an American force now grown to nearly 10,000 men, he surrendered his army of about 5,000 men and large military stores. The British defeat forced them to restrict further operations to the southern coast, while the American success encouraged France to provide forces that would contribute to American victory in the Revolutionary War.

SAVANNAH (29 December 1778; 16 September to 10 October 1779). Revolutionary War campaign streamer. The two battles at Savannah, Georgia, are represented by a single **campaign streamer**. On 29 December 1778, a British expeditionary force of 3,500 men overwhelmed and outmaneuvered the American defending force. The city was garrisoned with loyalist irregulars as the British regulars moved on to capture Augusta in January 1779. Later in the year, a combined force of 1,500 Americans under **Benjamin Lincoln** and more than 5,000 Frenchmen who were landed by Charles H. T. D'Estang's French fleet, which lay off the mouth of the Savannah River, laid siege to the city, which was defended by about 3,200 British. After a poorly coordinated assault on the British defenses was repulsed with heavy losses, Lincoln and D'Estang could not agree on what to do next, so the French fleet boarded their ships and sailed away, while Lincoln led his men north of the Savannah River, leaving Georgia under British control

SCHOFIELD, JOHN McALLISTER (1831–1906). Secretary of war from 1868 to 1869 and **commanding general of the army** from 1888 to 1895. Born in New York, Schofield graduated from the **U.S. Military Academy** in 1853 and was commissioned into the **artillery**. He served briefly in the field and returned to the academy to teach philosophy. In 1861, at the beginning of the **Civil War**, he joined the Missouri militia and in 1864 he was a corps commander and received a commission as brigadier general in the **regular army**. After the war, Schofield commanded a number of military departments and served a brief term as secretary of war. He became the commanding general of the army in 1888 and served in that capacity until his retirement from active service in 1895. While serving as commanding general, he was instrumental in clarifying lines of authority within the army. He also initiated efficiency reports on the performance of officers and recommended denying promotions to incompetent officers. *See also* Appendix 3, Commanding Generals and Chiefs of the Army; Appendix 4, Secretaries of War and Secretaries of the Army.

SCHWARZKOPF, H. NORMAN, Jr. (1934–). U.S. Army general who commanded the United Nations (UN) coalition forces in the **Persian Gulf War**. Born in New Jersey, Schwarzkopf spent time as a child in Iran with his father, a U.S. Army officer, and in 1956 graduated from the **U.S. Military Academy**. He was an adviser to the South Vietnamese army and commanded a U.S. Army infantry **battalion** during the **Vietnam War**. After a variety of command and staff assignments, he was deputy commander of the U.S. forces that invaded **Grenada** in 1983 and was critical of that operation, which made him eager to improve joint operations. In 1988, he assumed leadership of the U.S. Central Command, which was responsible for planning and conducting U.S. military efforts in the Middle East. When Iraq invaded Kuwait in 1990, he was given overall command of the UN forces that assembled in and around Saudi Arabia to force the Iraqi Army out of Kuwait. He planned and commanded the successful coalition war effort. Schwarzkopf was regarded as essential to maintaining the multinational coalition and was highly regarded as one of America's great field commanders. Since his retirement in 1991, he has written his memoirs and defended the controversial decision that ended the ground war after only 100 hours and allowed elements of **Saddam Hussein**'s Republican Guard to escape into Iraq.

SCOTT, HUGH LENOX (1853–1934). Chief of staff of the army from 1914 to 1917. Born in Kentucky, Scott graduated from the **U.S. Military Academy** in 1876. He participated in the **Nez Perce** campaign and became an authority on the language, customs, and history of the Plains Indians. He was at **Wounded Knee** and was in charge of **Geronimo**'s incarceration for three years. Scott was wounded while serving in the **Philippine Insurrection**. He served four years as superintendent of the U.S. Military Academy and became army chief of staff in 1914. During his tenure, he supervised the concentration of troops on the border in preparation for the expedition in **Mexico** and laid the foundation for mobilizing, training, and equipping the army for **World War I**. He retired from active service in 1917, but was recalled shortly thereafter to inspect the battlefield in Europe. After permanently retiring in 1919, he was a member of the Board of Indian Commissioners. See also Appendix 3, Commanding Generals and Chiefs of Staff of the Army.

SCOTT, WINFIELD (1786–1866). Commanding general of the army from 1841 to 1861. Born in Virginia, Scott briefly attended the College of William and Mary before taking up the study of law. He enlisted in a local **cavalry** troop in 1807 and was commissioned a captain in the **regular army** the next year. During the **War of 1812**, he was a brigadier general and fought at **Chippewa** and **Lundy's Lane**, where he was wounded, and his success in those campaigns made him a national hero. Scott served in the **Black Hawk, Creek,** and **Seminole** campaigns and supervised moving the Cherokee Indians to reservations west of the Mississippi River. In 1841, he became commanding general of the army. During the **Mexican War**, he led the expedition that landed in March at **Vera Cruz**, marched overland to Mexico City, and on the way to capturing the capital in September 1847, accomplished one of the army's most spectacular successes when they routed the Mexican Army at **Cerro Gordo**. Although a professional soldier, Scott had political ambitions. Receiving the Whig nomination for president in 1852, he was defeated by Franklin Pierce. In 1855, he was promoted to lieutenant general, making him the first man since **George Washington** to hold that rank. When the **Civil War** started in 1861, he remained loyal to the Union, in spite of his Virginia birth. After the Union defeat at **Bull Run** in July 1861, he retired and was replaced by **George B. McClellan**. Scott died in 1866 at West Point. *See also* Appendix 3, Commanding Generals and Chiefs of Staff of the Army.

SECOND KOREAN WINTER (28 November 1951 to 30 April 1952). Korean War campaign streamer. As 1951 drew to a close, a lull settled over the battlefields of Korea. Fighting tapered off to a routine of patrol clashes, raids, and small-unit struggles for key positions. The lull resulted from the decision by General **Matthew Ridgway**, commander of the United Nations (UN) forces in Korea, to halt offensive operations. The cost of major assaults on the enemy's defenses would be more than the results could justify. Furthermore, the possibility of an armistice agreement emerging from the recently reopened talks ruled out the mounting of any large-scale offensive by either side. On 21 November, Ridgway ordered the U.S. Eighth Army to cease offensive operations and begin an active defense of its front. Attacks were limited to those necessary to strengthen the main line of resistance and to establish an adequate outpost line. *See also* UN SUMMER–FALL OFFENSIVE.

SECOND MANASSAS. *See* MANASSAS.

SECRETARY AT WAR. In 1781, the Continental Congress established the office of secretary at war to replace the board of war, the ancestor of the **War Department**, which had proved unwieldy in managing the **Continental Army**. The first secretary was **Benjamin Lincoln**, who held the office from 1781 to 1783, when he resigned at the end of the **Revolutionary War**. The office remained vacant until **Henry Knox** was appointed to the post in 1785. When Congress created the War Department in 1789, the title of the civilian head was changed to **secretary of war** and Knox remained in office under that title. A major difference in the two offices was that the secretary at war reported to Congress, while the secretary of war reported to the president, who was designated "commander in chief."

SECRETARY OF THE ARMY. The civilian who heads the Department of the Army. The secretary is appointed by the president and approved by Congress. The position of secretary of the army replaced **secretary of war** under the provisions of the **National Security Act of 1947**. This legislation created the Department of Defense and made the army, navy, and air force separate military departments, each with a civilian secretary. The secretary of defense was designated a cabinet-level position, while the service secretaries lost that status. At the same time, the **War Department** became the Department of the Army, a less bellicose and more precise designation that more accurately describes the institution's peacetime and wartime roles. On 17 September 1947, **Kenneth C. Royall**, the last secretary of war, became the first secretary of the army. *See also* Appendix 4, Secretaries of War and Secretaries of the Army.

SECRETARY OF WAR. The concept of civilian control over the military took root early in colonial America, as legislators were determined to prevent any footholds for a potential military dictatorship. Shortly after **George Washington** became the first president in 1789, Congress established a **War Department** that was headed by the secretary of war. The new secretary was a member of the cabinet and was directly responsible to the president rather than Congress. **Henry Knox** was the first secretary. As the civilian head of the army, the secretary had a clear role within the national government, but the relationships with the commanding general and senior army commanders in the field were sometimes stormy as the nation's military establishment developed and matured. Secretaries in the late nineteenth century saw the commanding general as a rival for power and generally exercised their statutory control of the War Department's fiscal affairs by allying themselves with the department's bureau chiefs. After the **Spanish–American War**, **Elihu Root**, who became secretary of war in 1899, instituted a number of reforms that began to shape the army and the War Department into a more effective force. Under the provisions of the **National Security Act of 1947**, when the War Department became the Department of the Army, the title of the department head was changed to "secretary of the army." *See also* Appendix 4, Secretaries of War and Secretaries of the Army.

SEMINOLES (20 November 1817 to 31 October 1818; 28 December 1835 to 14 August 1842; 15 December 1855 to May 1858). Indian wars campaign streamer. The three periods represented by this campaign streamer are generally referred to as the Seminole Wars, the first of which began in November 1817, when Seminole Indians massacred about 50 Americans near an army post in Georgia. The attack was the climax of a series of Indian raids against American settlements in Spanish Florida. Brigadier General Edmund P. Gaines, Indian commissioner of the area, attempted to retaliate, but the Seminoles confined his force of 600 regulars to Fort Scott. Major General **Andrew Jackson** was ordered to take over the operation and he organized a force of about 4,000 volunteers, militia, Creek Indians, and regulars to invade Florida in the spring of 1818. Jackson destroyed Seminole camps; captured Pensacola, the capital of Spanish Florida, and other Spanish strongholds; and executed two British subjects accused of inciting and arming the Indians. Jackson's activities threatened American relations with Great Britain, but facilitated Spain's cession of Florida to the United States in 1819. The Seminole problem was temporarily allayed, but not solved.

A Seminole massacre of 108 **regular army** soldiers on 28 December 1835 initiated the Second Seminole War. As more American settlers moved into Florida, the Seminoles, loosely organized under the part-white warrior Osceola, prepared to fight. Osceola had no ancestral standing in the tribe, but inspired his followers with courage and determination. Brigadier General Duncan L. Clinch took the offensive with 200 men, but was defeated by Osceola's forces on 31 December on the Withlacoochee River. At about the same time, Major General **Winfield Scott** was dispatched to Florida to direct operations against the Seminoles. Meanwhile, Gaines, the Indian commissioner, on his own authority raised about 1,000 men in New Orleans and headed for Florida in February 1836. At Fort Drane, he took supplies intended for Scott's use and pressed forward until attacked by Seminoles. Scott helped extricate the beleaguered force and Gaines returned to New Orleans. Scott's proposed three-pronged offensive was delayed by Gaines's use of Scott's supplies, the expiration of volunteer enlistments, and the temporary diversion of troops to deal with the **Creeks** in Georgia and Alabama. Before the campaign got underway, Scott was recalled to Washington to face charges of dilatoriness and of casting slurs on the fighting qualities of volunteers.

After Scott's departure, Major General Thomas S. Jesup conducted a series of small actions against the Seminoles and captured Osceola in October 1837. **Zachary Taylor** defeated a sizeable Indian force near Lake Okeechobee on Christmas Day 1837, his force suffering 138 casualties in the battle. After Taylor's expedition, regular army troops conducted a number of small operations, while Colonel William J. Worth developed a plan to destroy the Indian's crops during the summer. The plan succeeded in driving a number of Seminoles from their swampy retreats in 1842. About 5,000 regulars participated in the campaign and almost 1,500 were killed. About 20,000 volunteers also participated. The effort cost $35 million and ended with the removal of 3,500 Seminoles to Indian Territory, although about 350 Indians remained in Florida.

The remaining Seminoles kept the peace for a number of years, but in December 1855 increasing inroads by white settlers drove the Indians to attack an army camp. The attack triggered the Third Seminole War, fought mainly by **U.S. Volunteers**, rather than regulars. On 5 March 1857, the final fight took place, after which 165 of the Seminoles agreed to leave for Indian Territory, although about 120 remained in Florida. The United States finally declared the wars against the Seminoles officially over on 8 May 1858.

SERGEANT. *See* NONCOMMISSIONED OFFICER.

SERGEANT MAJOR. The term is both a position and the highest rank an **enlisted** soldier can hold in the U.S. Army. The army first established the position during the **Revolutionary War**, when **Friedrich Wilhelm von Steuben** designated the sergeant major head of all **noncommissioned officers** and made him responsible for their conduct. Duties of the sergeant major included maintaining discipline, preparing duty rosters, and conducting parades. Since the first appearance of sergeants major in 1799, their number and placement in the Army has varied, but they have generally been authorized at **battalion** level and above. In June 1920, however, the position disappeared for 38 years, when Congress grouped all enlisted soldiers into seven pay grades (E-1 through E-7) with no regard for job or specialty, making master sergeant the highest rank and eliminating the position of sergeant major. The rank returned in June 1958, when Congress authorized two additional pay grades, **first sergeant** (E-8) and sergeant major (E-9). The rank of E-9 includes all sergeants major, **command sergeants major**, and the **sergeant major of the army**. *See also* Appendix 8, United States Army Rank Insignia.

SERGEANT MAJOR OF THE ARMY. The senior **enlisted** soldier in the army. The position was created on 4 July 1966 and the first sergeant major of the army, **William O. Woolridge**, was sworn into office seven days later. The position was established to promote confidence in the enlisted ranks and increase the prestige, operating effectiveness, and career incentives for senior enlisted soldiers. Appointed by the **chief of staff of the army** and serving at the pleasure of the **secretary of the army**, the sergeant major of the army provides advice and counsel on the needs and interests of the army's enlisted soldiers. Since 1966, the sergeants major of the army have helped make the **noncommissioned officer** corps more professional, represented the interests of the enlisted force in the highest councils of the army, and raised the morale of soldiers during their visits to duty stations around the world. *See Also* Appendix 5, Sergeants Major of the Army; Appendix 8, United States Army Rank Insignia.

SERGEANTS MAJOR ACADEMY. Established in January 1973, the Sergeants Major Academy is the army's executive agent for **noncommissioned officer** education. Located at Fort Bliss, Texas, the academy develops and conducts resident and nonresident courses for senior noncommissioned officers to prepare them for future assignments. *See also* SERGEANT MAJOR.

SEVEN DAYS BATTLE (1862). *See* PENINSULA.

SHARPSBURG. *See* ANTIETAM.

SHENANDOAH (7 August to 28 November 1864). Civil War campaign streamer. After Confederate general **Robert E. Lee** had firmly established his defensive positions at **Petersburg**, he sent Major General Jubal A. Early with one corps on a raiding expedition up the Shenandoah Valley in western Virginia to ease pressure that Union forces had been exerting from that direction. Skillfully eluding Union opposition in the valley, Early made a rapid drive north and then east that carried him to the northern outskirts of Washington, D.C., by 11 July.

Here he skirmished briskly in the vicinity of Fort Stevens. On that same day, a body of troops hastily dispatched by **Ulysses S. Grant**, commanding general of the Union armies, arrived on the scene and Early discreetly retreated. To remedy defects in the command structure that had permitted Early to elude superior forces, Grant combined four separate commands into one that included Washington, D.C., western Maryland, and the Shenandoah Valley. General **Philip Sheridan** was assigned to the new command, with orders to destroy Early. Sheridan spent the next four months in the Shenandoah Valley, where he defeated Early at Winchester and Fisher's Hill in September and finally shattered Early's Confederate forces at Cedar Creek on 19 October. Sheridan then laid waste to the Shenandoah Valley to stop further Confederate raids and destroy sources of food for Lee's army.

SHERIDAN, PHILIP HENRY (1831–1888). Commanding general of the army from 1883 to 1888. Born in New York, Sheridan received a basic education in public schools after his family moved to Ohio. He graduated from the **U.S. Military Academy** in 1853. When the **Civil War** started in 1861, he was still an infantry lieutenant serving in Oregon. He was a staff officer for the first few months of the war, but by 1862 he was commanding a division as a brigadier general. At **Chattanooga**, Sheridan came to **Ulysses S. Grant**'s attention when Sheridan's division broke the Confederate defensive line on Missionary Ridge. When Grant became commanding general of the army, he named Sheridan to head the cavalry corps in the Army of the Potomac, which subsequently supported the **Wilderness**, **Spotsylvania**, and **Cold Harbor** campaigns during the 1864 Union advance toward Richmond. In late 1864, Grant sent him to the **Shenandoah** Valley, where he defeated the Confederate forces under Jubal Early and destroyed the crops, as part of the economic warfare being used to defeat the South. After the war, Sheridan remained in the army, directed campaigns against the Indians in a vast area from Montana to Texas, and staunchly supported Grant for president. Just before Sheridan's death in 1888, Congress voted to promote him to the rank of four-star general as a measure of their respect for his service. *See also* Appendix 3, Commanding Generals and Chiefs of Staff of the Army.

SHERMAN, WILLIAM TECUMSEH (1820–1891). Commanding general of the army from 1869 to 1883. Born in Ohio, Sherman attended a local academy before graduating from the **U.S. Military Academy** in 1840. He was named for the Shawnee Indian leader **Tecumseh** and "William" was not added to his name until he was baptized into the Catholic Church in 1830. He served in the **Seminole** campaign after graduation and was in California policing gold-mining areas during the **Mexican War**. He left the army in 1853 and, after trying a variety of jobs, he was heading a military academy in Louisiana when the **Civil War** started in 1861. Sherman rejoined the army and commanded a brigade at **Bull Run**. After a series of positions in the west in which he met with mixed success, he eventually followed **Ulysses S. Grant** in command of the western theater of war in 1864. After successfully occupying **Atlanta** in September 1863, he conducted his famous "march to the sea," destroying property to reduce the Confederacy's ability to continue the war. After the war, he followed Grant as commanding general of the army and, in this position, he established a school for **infantry** and **cavalry** and supervised the army's continuing campaigns against the Indians. His Atlanta campaign had a profound effect on American military history as he moved warfare away from mass attacks by infantry toward the concept of total war, in which the entire population of the enemy was targeted. *See also* Appendix 3, Commanding Generals and Chiefs of Staff of the Army.

SHILOH (6–7 April 1862). Civil War campaign streamer. After capturing Forts **Henry and Donelson**, Union forces in the west under General **Henry W. Halleck** moved to occupy positions on the Tennessee River. On 6 April 1862, Confederate general Albert Sydney Johnston surprised **Ulysses S. Grant**'s army of some 40,000 men upriver, near Shiloh Church in Tennessee. Johnston was killed during the fighting and General Pierre G. T. Beauregard assumed command. In spite of Johnston's death, the first day went well for the Confederates, but on the second day Grant, with help from General Don Carlos Buell's Army of the Ohio, counterattacked and regained the lost ground. The Confederates then withdrew to Corinth, Mississippi, and there was no Federal pursuit. At Shiloh, of nearly 63,000 Federals engaged, 1,754 were killed, 8,408 were wounded, and 2,885 were missing. Confederate losses were 1,723 killed, 8,012 wounded, and 959 missing. The lengthy casualty lists came as a shock to both sides and put aside any notions that the war would be over any time soon. Because he had not fortified his positions at Shiloh, Grant's reputation suffered, until his success at **Vicksburg** a year later.

SHINSEKI, ERIC K. (1942–). Chief of staff of the army from 1999. Born in Hawaii, Shinseki graduated from the **U.S. Military Academy** in 1965. He served two combat tours in the **Vietnam War** and held a variety of command and staff positions in Germany and the United States. He commanded the North Atlantic Treaty Organization peacekeeping forces in the Balkans in 1997, before becoming the chief of staff of the army in 1999. While in office, he initiated the army's transformation program in an effort to make the army a readily deployable force. *See also* Appendix 3, Commanding Generals and Chiefs of Staff of the Army.

SICILY (9 July to 17 August 1943). World War II campaign streamer. The Allied decision to invade Sicily was made at a conference held in Casablanca from 14 to 23 January 1943, when it had become apparent that an invasion of the European continent across the English Channel would not be possible in 1943. In the meantime, the Allied military resources assembled in North Africa during the **Algeria–French Morocco** and **Tunisia** campaigns were used to force Italy out of the war, divert German strength from the Russian front, and open the Mediterranean Sea as a route to the East.

British general Sir Harold R. L. Alexander commanded the 15th Army Group, which included the British Eighth Army under General Bernard Montgomery and the newly established U.S. Seventh Army under **George S. Patton**. In addition, the U.S. Army's 82d **Airborne** Division dropped behind the invasion beaches to forestall enemy reaction to the landings. The total invasion force numbered some 160,000 men. Before the invasion, Allied planes raided western Sicily to deceive the defenders about the planned landings on the southern and eastern coasts of the island. The raids also caused the German armor to disperse, making it difficult for the defenders to mount quick, concentrated counterattacks. On 10 July 1943, the invasion began in winds of near gale proportions, making the landings difficult, but giving the Allies the advantage of surprise against defenders who were not expecting a landing in such conditions. The Allied plan was to capture the dominating ground in the east-central part of the island and then take Messina, a port city on the strait between Sicily and mainland Italy. But recovering from their initial surprise, the German forces quickly blocked the most direct route to Messina by concentrating against the British Eighth Army in the vicinity of Catania.

With the British stalled in the eastern portion of the island, Patton sent a mobile provisional corps under Major General Geoffrey Keyes to the northwest, cut the island in two, and captured Palermo by 22 July. The move destroyed the morale of the 275,000 Italian troops on the island and put the Americans into position to attack from the west and remove the blocking forces in front of the British. As the U.S. Seventh Army drove east across Sicily, the Germans withdrew across the Strait of Messina to the mainland. Despite attacks by Allied aircraft, some 60,000 Germans reached the mainland safely. On 17 August 1943, American patrols pushed into Messina, ending the campaign. In 38 days, the Allied forces on Sicily killed or wounded about 29,000 German and Italian soldiers and captured 140,000 more. American losses totaled 2,237 killed and 6,544 wounded and captured, while the British suffered 12,843 casualties, including 2,721 killed. *See also* AIR OFFENSIVE, EUROPE, NAPLES–FOGGIA.

SIGNAL CORPS. Branch of the army. In 1856, Albert James Myer, an army doctor in Texas, conceived the idea of a military signal service. When the army adopted his visual system of flags on 21 June 1860, the Signal Corps was born, with Myer as its chief. Myer first used the system on active service in New Mexico later that year. Using flags for daytime signaling and a torch at night, the system was used in **Civil War** combat in June 1861 to direct the fire of a harbor battery at Fort Calhoun against the Confederate positions opposite Fort Monroe, Virginia. Until March 1863, when Congress authorized a Signal Corps for the duration of the war, Myer relied on detailed personnel. Civil War innovations included an unsuccessful balloon experiment during the **Bull Run** campaign and the successful employment of the electric telegraph on the battlefield. During the war, the wigwag system of flags, which required line of sight between signaling stations, waned in the face of the telegraph. After the war, in 1867, the telegraph became a Signal Corps responsibility and by 1880 the corps had constructed, and was maintaining, some 4,000 miles of telegraph lines along the nation's western frontier. In 1870, the corps established a congressionally mandated national weather service. The weather bureau became part of the Department of Agriculture in 1891, but the signal corps retained responsibility for military meteorology.

During the **Spanish–American War** and the **Philippine Insurrection**, the signal corps supplied telephone and telegraph wire lines and cable communications, fostered the use of telephones in combat, employed combat photography, and renewed the use of balloons. Shortly after the Spanish–American War, the corps constructed the Washington-Alaska Military Cable and Telegraph System, introducing the first wireless telegraph in the Western Hemisphere. An Aeronautical Division was established in the office of the army's chief signal officer in 1907 and, a year later, the Wright brothers tested the first airplane built to army specifications. Army aviation was part of the Signal Corps until 1918, when it became the Army Air Service.

In **World War I**, the signal corps worked with private industry to perfect radio tubes and in 1918 introduced radiotelephones to the European theater. While the new American voice radios were superior to the radiotelegraph sets, telephone and telegraph remained the major communications technology of World War I. The signal corps demonstrated the first army radar in the 1930s and, even before the United States entered **World War II**, had started mass production of radar sets. Along with tactical FM (frequency modulation) radio, which the corps also developed in the 1930s, radar was the most important communications development of World War II.

In the **Korean War**, terrain and distance limited the use of wire communications, so the signal corps' VHF (very high frequency) radio provided tactical communications. During the **Vietnam War**, the demand for high-quality telephone and message circuits led to the deployment of tropospheric-scatter radio links that could provide many circuits between locations more than 200 miles apart. Increased communications requirements in the Vietnam War led to the development of a satellite service and a commercial fixed-station system known as the Integrated Wideband Communications System, which provided the Southeast Asia link in the Defense Communications System. In 1988, the army began fielding mobile-subscriber equipment, a tactical cellular telephone system. With the growing number of computer systems in the army, the signal corps is developing digital communications systems that will enable rapid exchange of information. See also ARMY AIR CORPS; BRANCHES OF THE ARMY.

SILVER STAR. Third highest award for valor awarded to members of the army. Established by Congress on 9 July 1918, it is awarded for gallantry in action not sufficient to warrant the **Medal of Honor** or the **Distinguished Service Cross**. *See also* PURPLE HEART.

SITTING BULL (TATANKA IYOTAKA) (ca. 1831–1890). Hunkpapa Lakota Sioux chief. With an impressive war record against enemy tribes and a reputation as a political chief and spiritual leader, Sitting Bull was one of the most important Indian leaders the U.S. Army encountered. He played key roles in battles in Montana and the Dakotas in 1863–1865 and became the principal leader of the bands that refused to stay on reservations. Although present at the **Little Big Horn**, he was by then an old chief and did not play a significant role in the fighting. After the Little Big Horn, Sitting Bull and a small band of followers sought refuge in Canada, but the decrease in the size of the buffalo herds forced him to surrender and return to the United States in July 1888. During the ghost dance troubles in 1889–1890, Sitting Bull feuded with the Indian agent at the Standing Rock Reservation and was killed on 15 December 1890 when Indian policemen attempted to arrest him. *See also* PINE RIDGE.

SOMME DEFENSIVE (21 March to 6 April 1918). World War I campaign streamer. On 21 March 1918, three German armies began an offensive that rapidly broke through British defense lines. With the objective of splitting the Allied lines, the German attack had created a gap between the French and British armies by 27 March. But the Germans lacked reserves to exploit their initial success, so the Allies were able to halt the offensive by 6 April. On 25 March 1918, at the height at the German drive, General **John J. Pershing**, commander of the American Expeditionary Force, made four U.S. Army divisions available to the French, but only a few American units, totaling about 2,200 soldiers, participated in the campaign.

SOMME OFFENSIVE (8 August to 11 November 1918). World War I campaign streamer. On 8 August, the British began the Somme Offensive with an attack on the Amiens salient. The British Fourth Army, which included two American divisions, struck the northwestern edge of the salient in coordination with the French First Army's attack from the southwest. No artillery barrage forewarning the enemy preceded the attack, as the British spearheaded their assault with some 600 **tanks**. The surprised Germans gave up 16,000 prisoners as their positions were overrun and, by the end of the month, they had evacuated the entire Amiens salient. The drive to breach the main Hindenburg Line began at the end of September, with the U.S. II Corps forming part of the British Fourth Army. About 54,000 Americans participated in the campaign and, when the corps was relieved on 21 October, it had served 26 days in the line and suffered 11,500 casualties.

SOUTHERN FRANCE (15 August to 14 September 1944). World War II campaign streamer. Once the Allies had successfully secured the beachheads in **Normandy** in June 1944, shipping and landing craft were available to stage the long-planned invasion of southern France. With fighting in the **Northern France** campaign still raging at Argentan-Falaise, the U.S. Seventh Army landed on the Mediterranean shores of France southwest of Cannes on 15 August 1944. The landing force consisted of the leading elements of three U.S. infantry divisions, an **airborne** task force, and French commandos. Once ashore the Seventh Army received assistance from Free French forces. The initial objectives of the campaign were to keep the Germans from reinforcing their forces in Normandy with troops from southern France and to provide the Allies a supplementary line of communications through Mediterranean ports. Resistance during the landings was comparatively light. After the force landed, the advance north was rapid, so that by 11 September patrols from the southern and northern Allied forces met near Dijon, France. The campaign ended on 14 September and the next day the U.S. Sixth Army Group, composed of the U.S. Seventh Army and the First French Army, became operational under the command of Lieutenant General Jacob L. Devers. The newly formed army group became part of the Allied Expeditionary Force, commanded by **Dwight D. Eisenhower**. It moved north toward Germany while maintaining contact with the U.S. Third Army.

SOUTHERN PHILIPPINES (27 February to 4 July 1945). World War II campaign streamer. In January 1945, General **Douglas MacArthur** landed American forces on **Luzon**, in what the Allies believed would be the penultimate step to defeating Japan. The Japanese had expended most of their remaining air and naval resources in an unsuccessful defense of **Leyte** and the ground forces on Luzon, although numerous, were not well equipped. But with the Leyte campaign in its final stages and the forces on Luzon making progress against a determined Japanese attrition defense, MacArthur, with no direction from higher authority, decided to mount a major campaign in February 1945 to liberate the remaining Philippine Islands. Several factors entered into MacArthur's decision. He believed his promise, made in 1942, to return to the Philippines meant all the islands, not just Leyte and Luzon. He also saw the potential need for the islands, with their cities, airfields, and ports, as staging areas for the massive invasion of Japan that in February 1945 still loomed large in Allied planning. There was also a desire to liberate all Filipinos from their Japanese captors as soon as possible.

On 28 February 1945, American forces landed on the island of Palawan. The landings were largely unopposed, but on the third day savage combat erupted. The fighting lasted for about five days, after which the remaining Japanese simply withdrew into the mountains and jungles, a scenario that would repeat itself throughout the campaign. U.S. Army forces lost 12 killed and 56 wounded; the Japanese suffered almost 900 dead, approximately half the island's garrison. In the next few months, American forces landed on the smaller islands around Palawan, with little or no opposition. On 10 March, American forces landed on Mindanao, with little opposition on the beaches, and soon captured Zamboanga City. Fighting was heavy as the Americans moved off the coastal plain, but the Japanese defensive line broke on 23 March. The Eighth Army continued operations in the southern Philippines through June, conducting more than 50 landings and clearing Japanese from the area.

Eichelberger told MacArthur that organized Japanese resistance ended on 30 June, but since not all the Japanese received that message, American soldiers encountered isolated pockets of resistance until the end of the war on 15 August 1945, when some 22,000 Japanese emerged from the jungles of Mindanao to surrender. Overall, the campaign attained its primary objective of eliminating Japanese military power in the area at a small cost in comparison to other Pacific campaigns. It cost the U.S. Army approximately 2,100 dead and 6,990 wounded, while more than 10,000 Japanese died in combat and another 8,000 or more died from starvation or disease.

SPANISH–AMERICAN WAR (1898). Reacting to war fever after the U.S. Navy battleship *Maine* exploded in Havana harbor on 15 February 1898, Congress authorized thousands of **Army National Guard** troops to be called to active duty. But the army was not immediately up to the challenge of organizing, equipping, training, and caring for the raw recruits flooding into its training camps. There were plenty of men available, but there were very few officers capable of planning and coordinating the operations necessary to make good use of the available forces. The real failures in the war centered on the joint operations that moved the army's forces from the United States to Cuba. Transportation, or more accurately, the lack of transportation, was a significant problem during the **Santiago** campaign. Many of the problems could have been resolved had there been an organized planning staff to examine the deficiencies of port facilities in Tampa and Cuba. Fortunately, the comic opera performance of joint operations in the Spanish–American War were conducted against an essentially ineffective enemy.

In June 1898, after a confused amphibious operation that began in Tampa, Florida, an army expeditionary force landed in Cuba, drove the Spanish from the San Juan Heights overlooking the port of **Santiago**, and prompted the Spanish fleet that had taken refuge in the port to flee into the waiting guns of the U.S. Navy. Other Army expeditionary forces landed in **Puerto Rico** and the Philippines, the

U.S.–Army Military History Institute.

8. Army forces landing in Cuba during the Santiago campaign in 1898.

latter landing following Commodore George Dewey's victory over a Spanish fleet in Manila Bay. The victory in the Philippines left the islands under U.S. control and the army's relatively easy occupation of **Manila** proved to be the beginning of a long relationship with the Philippines.

The Treaty of Paris ended the war on 10 December 1898. Spain left Cuba and the United States took Puerto Rico and Guam and paid Spain $20 million for the Philippine Islands. With the end of the war, the army's task of establishing American authority over the islands began in earnest. For the next four years, army troops conducted a series of brutal, arduous counterguerrilla campaigns during the **Philippine Insurrection**. *See also* Spanish–American War campaigns in Appendix 6, Campaigns of the United States Army.

SPECIAL FORCES. Branch of the army. Special Forces are organized in small teams to conduct raids and reconnaissance missions behind enemy lines. They can also train, advise, and assist military and paramilitary organizations in other countries to conduct counterinsurgency operations. The first Special Forces unit in the army was formed on 11 June 1952, when the 10th Special Forces Group was activated at Fort Bragg, North Carolina, with 10 soldiers—one **commissioned officer**, one **warrant officer**, and eight **enlisted** soldiers, mostly **noncommissioned officers**. Within months, volunteers reported by the hundreds and completed the initial phase of training. Their primary function was to infiltrate by land, sea, or air, deep into enemy-occupied territory, and organize the potential to conduct Special Forces operations, with emphasis on guerrilla warfare. Secondary missions included deep-penetration raids, intelligence missions, and counterinsurgency operations. Special Forces were designed to spend months, even years, deep within hostile territory, be self-sustaining, and speak the language of their target area.

During the 1950s, the army's Special Forces grew into a formidable organization. In 1956, the 14th Special Forces Operational Detachment, with 16 soldiers, went into Thailand, Taiwan, and Vietnam. More detachments soon followed, as the U.S. increased its commitment to the **Vietnam War**. In 1961, President John F. Kennedy visited Fort Bragg, where he became interested in the Special Forces. His interest led to a major expansion of Special Forces during the 1960s, as a total of 18 groups were organized in the **regular army** and the **reserve components**. Kennedy's visit to Fort Bragg also led to the adoption of the Special Forces' distinctive green beret. Kennedy commented on the berets, which were worn by soldiers in the field but were not official gear, and his favorable comments led their official adoption. Since then, army's Special Forces have been known popularly as the Green Berets. Special Forces saw extensive service in Vietnam and gained widespread recognition among the American public as elite soldiers.

The years immediately following Vietnam were lean ones for the Special Forces. A number of the groups were inactivated and there was a general deemphasis of special operations, as the army concentrated on conventional warfare. But during the Ronald Reagan presidency the need for Special Forces capabilities rose with an increase in Communist insurgencies in Africa, Asia, and Central America. As a result of renewed emphasis on special operations in the 1980s, Special Forces became a branch of the army on 9 April 1987. During the 1980s, Special Forces teams were deployed to dozens of countries around the world and served alongside conventional army units in the invasion of **Panama** in December 1989.

In October 2001, Special Forces teams were among the first U.S. military elements to enter Afghanistan in support of the United States' **war on terrorism**. They initiated contact with Northern Alliance forces fighting against the Taliban regime and assisted with the American bombing campaign by identifying targets on the ground. In December, three Special Forces soldiers were killed and a number of others injured when an errant U.S. bomb hit very close to their positions. The three noncommissioned officers were the first American military personnel to be killed in the war. *See also* BRANCHES OF THE ARMY; RANGERS; SPECIAL OPERATIONS FORCES.

SPECIAL OPERATIONS FORCES. Those elements of the army trained in unconventional warfare. Special operations forces have long been part of the U.S. Army. During the French and Indian War, in the colonial period, Rogers' **Rangers**, stalking the enemy in woods and swamps, were America's first unconventional forces. The tradition continued during the **Revolutionary War** with **Francis Marion**, the "Swamp Fox," whose troops harassed the British with a success out of all proportion to their small numbers. In the **Civil War**, the Confederate colonel John Singleton Mosby led a band of raiders that became the terror of Union generals. But it was not until **World War II** that special operations troops came into their own. Known formally as the First Special Service Force, the Devil's Brigade was a joint Canadian-American venture that began in July 1942 at Fort William Henry Harrison in Montana.

Airborne-trained and well led, the brigade saw most of its action in Italy, but also fought in France, where it was inactivated in 1944. Darby's Rangers, named for their commander, Major William O. Darby, were activated in Ireland in June 1942 as the 1st Ranger Battalion. The battalion fought throughout Western Europe, but achieved its greatest fame when it scaled the cliffs of Pointe du Hoc during the **Normandy** invasion.

In the Pacific, the Alamo Scouts led U.S. Rangers and Filipino guerrillas in an attack on a Japanese prison camp at Cabantuan, freeing all 511 Allied prisoners held there. Colonel Frank D. Merrill's 5307th Composite Unit (Provisional), a 3,000-man force known as Merrill's Marauders, was organized with the idea of destroying Japanese communications and supply lines while the Allies opened the Burma Road. During the **India–Burma** campaign, the troops, with no **tanks** or artillery to support them, walked over 1,000 miles throughout dense, almost impenetrable jungles to defeat the veteran soldiers of the Japanese 18th Division and capture Myitkina airfield, the only all-weather airfield in Burma, in May 1944.

In addition to the larger units that conducted special operations in World War II, there were many small units operating behind enemy lines to develop information networks, provide instructions to local fighters, and conduct guerrilla warfare. It was a new kind of special operations, taking a bit of the Swamp Fox and a bit of Mosby and combining it with new techniques of airborne and guerrilla fighting. These teams laid the foundation for the army's **Special Forces**. In late 2001, elements of the army's special operations forces were among the first U.S. military units to see action in America's **war on terrorism**.

SPENCER, JOHN CANFIELD (1788–1855). Secretary of war from 1841 to 1843. Born in New York, Spencer entered college at Williamstown, Massachusetts, and transferred to Union College in New York, where he graduated with honors in 1806. He later became secretary to the governor of New York and opened a law practice. After holding a number of state government positions, he served a term in the U.S. House of Representatives. Spencer was defeated in a bid for the U.S. Senate, but served for a number of years in the state legislature and became secretary of state for New York in 1839. Appointed secretary of war in 1841, he served until 1843. Nominated to the U.S. Supreme Court in 1842, he was rejected by the Senate. *See also* Appendix 4, Secretaries of War and Secretaries of the Army.

SPOTSYLVANIA (8–21 May 1864). Civil War campaign streamer. After failing to outflank the Confederates in the **Wilderness** campaign, General **Ulysses S. Grant** persisted in his attempt to get around General **Robert E. Lee's** flank. On 7 May, Grant moved south toward Spotsylvania, Virginia, only to find that Lee had already fortified the area. General **George G. Meade's** Army of the Potomac struck repeatedly at the Confederate positions, but was repulsed with heavy losses. On 20 May, Grant slipped south in another effort to envelop his opponent. Lee once again avoided the trap and retired to the North Anna River, where he established a defensive position that Grant considered too strong to attack. In the two major attacks at Spotsylvania on 10 and 12 May, during which about 66,000 men were committed, Union losses were 10,119 killed and wounded and about 800 missing. Confederate losses were estimated at between 9,000 and 10,000, including about 4,000 taken prisoner. During the Wilderness campaign, General J. E. B. Stuart's cavalry had effectively harassed and slowed Union movements. To reduce this threat, Major General **Philip H. Sheridan** moved his cavalry corps toward Richmond in mid-May on a 16-day raid that drew Stuart after him. Sheridan fought several running engagements, culminating in a victory at Yellow Tavern, where Stuart was killed. The raid and Stuart's death effectively ended the offensive power of Lee's cavalry.

SQUAD. The smallest unit in the U.S. Army. It is composed of four to 10 **enlisted** soldiers and led by a **noncommissioned** officer. Three or four squads make up a **platoon**. The comparable sized unit in **artillery** and **armor** units is a section.

STAHR, ELVIS JACOB, JR. (1916–1998). Secretary of the army from 1961 to 1962. born in Kentucky, Stahr graduated in 1936 from the University of Kentucky, where he was a member of the **Reserve Officers' Training Corps**. He studied law at Oxford University on a Rhodes Scholarship and received three degrees. In 1939, he entered the practice of law in New York City. He was called to active military duty two years later. As an officer–student, Stahr studied Chinese at Yale University and he later served in the China–Burma–India theater during **World War II**, until he left the army in 1945. He then returned to law and in 1948 became the dean of the College of Law at the University of Kentucky, where he stayed until 1956. After holding a number of academic positions, Stahr became secretary of the army in 1961. During his tenure, the army reorganized the **division** structure and was increased in size as a result of the Berlin crisis. Stahr left office in 1962 and became the president of Indiana University. Since 1982, he has practiced law in Washington, D.C., been a member of several international delegations, and served on several presidential commissions. *See also* Appendix 4, Secretaries of War and Secretaries of the Army.

STANTON, EDWIN McMASTERS (1814–1869). Secretary of war from 1862 to 1868. Born in Ohio, Stanton left school as a teenager but continued to study on his own. He attended Kenyon College, but withdrew for financial reasons and then studied law, before being admitted to the bar in 1836. In 1957, his law career took him to Washington, D.C., where he became the U.S. attorney general for the last few months of President James Buchanan's administration. He returned to private life when **Abraham Lincoln** became president. Stanton was openly critical of Lincoln's policies and became a friend of **George B. McClellan** when the latter was appointed **commanding general of the army**. Nevertheless, he accepted Lincoln's appointment as secretary of war, replacing **Simon Cameron**.

An abrupt and rigid man, Stanton made few friends in the **War Department**, but he soon brought order out of the chaos of Cameron's brief tenure. In spite of his friendship with McClellan, Stanton pushed to have the general removed when his performance faltered and the secretary was an early supporter of **Ulysses S. Grant**. When Lincoln was assassinated in 1865, Stanton stayed in office and worked against reconstruction policies, seeking harsher treatment of the defeated states. When President Andrew Johnson asked for Stanton's resignation in 1867, the secretary initially refused, but he finally left office in 1868 and resumed his legal practice. After becoming president, Grant appointed Stanton to the Supreme Court, but Stanton died four days after he was confirmed. See also Appendix 4, Secretaries of War and Secretaries of the Army.

STEUBEN, FRIEDRICH WILHELM RUDOLF GERHARD AUGUSTIN VON (1730–1794). *See* VON STEUBEN, FRIEDRICH WILHELM RUDOLF GERHARD AUGUSTIN.

STEVENS, ROBERT TEN BROECK (1899–1983). Secretary of the army from 1953 to 1955. Born in New Jersey, Stevens graduated from Phillips Andover Academy in 1917, interrupted his studies to serve as a second lieutenant in

World War I, and graduated from Yale University in 1921. He joined a textile firm, the J. P. Stevens Company, after graduation and became its president in 1929. He attended a special civilian course at the **Command and General Staff College** in 1941 and then entered active duty with the army as a lieutenant colonel. During **World War II**, Stevens served in the quartermaster general's procurement section and after the war he returned to the J. P. Stevens Company as chairman of the board. He became secretary of the army in 1953. While in office, he defended the army against charges advanced by Senator Joseph McCarthy and supervised the army's reductions after the **Korean War**. In 1955, he once again returned to the J. P. Stevens Company as president and he served as chairman of the executive committee until 1974. *See also* Appendix 4, Secretaries of War and Secretaries of the Army.

STILWELL, JOSEPH (1883–1946). World War II army general. Born in Florida, Stilwell graduated from the **U.S. Military Academy** in 1904 and was assigned to the Philippines, thus beginning a career closely associated with Asia. Fluent in Chinese, he was an intelligence officer in China during **World War I** and was the U.S. military attaché there in the late 1930s. In 1942, he became the U.S. commander of the China–Burma–India theater, where he attempted to persuade the Nationalist Chinese leader, Chiang Kai-shek, to build an effective force to counter the Japanese. Frustrated with Chiang Kai-shek's refusal to reform the Chinese Army, Stilwell was unable to prevent the Japanese from capturing northern Burma and cutting the link between China and India in 1942. Two years later, with Chinese forces trained by his staff, he finally succeeded in regaining a large portion of the area lost to the Japanese. Stilwell was recalled to the United States in 1944 at the request of Chiang Kai-shek and given command of the Tenth Army. The Tenth was involved in the planning for the invasion of Japan, which proved unnecessary when Tokyo surrendered in August 1945. *See also* BURMA 1942; CHINA DEFENSIVE; INDIA–BURMA.

STIMSON, HENRY LEWIS (1867–1950). Secretary of war from 1911 to 1913 and from 1940 to 1945. Born in New York, Stimson was educated at Phillips Andover Academy, graduated from Yale University in 1888, and received a degree from Harvard Law School in 1890. He joined **Elihu Root's** law firm and in 1906 became U.S. attorney for the southern district of New York. After an unsuccessful bid for governor, Stimson became secretary of war in 1911 and carried on the reforms initiated by Root. He supported the authority of the **chief of staff of the army** over the **adjutant general** and ordered troops to the Mexican border before leaving office in 1913. In 1917, Stimson entered active service in the army as an officer in the **judge advocate general's** department and he served in the **field artillery** in France during **World War I**. He returned to his legal career at the end of the war. After spending two years as governor general of the Philippines, he became secretary of state in 1929 and returned to private life in 1933. Stimson was called upon again to be secretary of war in 1940 and he served in that capacity through **World War II**, supervising the expansion of the army and working in close cooperation with **George C. Marshall**, the chief of staff of the army. Stimson was closely involved with the decision to use the atomic bomb against Japan to end the war in 1945. *See also* Appendix 4, Secretaries of War and Secretaries of the Army.

STONE, MICHAEL PATRICK WILLIAM (1925–). Secretary of the army from 1989 to 1993. Born in London, England, Stone has resided in the United States since 1929. During **World War II**, he served with the British Royal Navy and received pilot training in the United States. After the war, he graduated from Yale University in 1948 and studied law at New York University Law School, before entering the business world. He was the director of the U.S. mission for the Agency for International Development in Cairo, Egypt, and was involved in implementing the Kissinger Commission recommendations in the Caribbean Basin Initiative countries, before becoming the assistant secretary of the army for financial management in 1986. For the next several years, he held a number of positions in the Department of Defense and the **Department of the Army** and he became secretary of the army in 1989. While he was in office, the army participated in the invasion of **Panama** and the **Persian Gulf War**. *See also* Appendix 4, Secretaries of War and Secretaries of the Army.

STRATEGY. The use of political, economic, psychological, and military power of a state to attain specific goals. Strategy involves the employment of military forces to secure objectives designated by political authority through the application or threat of force. It is the art and science of employing the armed forces and other elements of national power during peace and war to secure national security objectives. Activities at the strategic level of war include establishing national or multinational objectives, determining a sequence for initiatives, defining limits and assessing risks for the use of military and other elements of power, and developing plans and providing military forces and other capabilities necessary to achieve those objectives. *See also* OPERATIONAL ART; TACTICS; WAR.

SULLIVAN, GORDON RUSSELL (1937–). Chief of staff of the army from 1991 to 1995. Born in Massachusetts, Sullivan graduated from Norwich University in 1959 and was commissioned a second lieutenant through the **Reserve Officers' Training Corps**. He served in a variety of command and staff positions and saw service in the **Vietnam War**. He became chief of staff in 1991 and led the army through a significant reduction in force structure after the **Persian Gulf War** that included numerous base closures and doctrinal changes that moved the army into the information age. He retired from active service in 1991. *See also* Appendix 3, Commanding Generals and Chiefs of Staff of the Army.

SUMMERALL, CHARLES PELOT (1867–1955). Chief of staff of the army from 1926 to 1930. Born in Florida, Summerall graduated from the **U.S. Military Academy** in 1892. After various assignments in the United States, he participated in the **Philippine Insurrection** and the **China Relief Expedition**. He held a number of command staff positions prior to **World War I**, when he commanded **artillery** units in France. After the war, he commanded various army organizations, until 1926, when he became chief of staff. While in office, Summerall directed the formation of a mechanized force. He retired from active service in 1931 and was president of the Citadel, a military school in South Carolina. *See also* Appendix 3, Commanding Generals and Chiefs of Staff of the Army.

SUMMER–FALL 1969 (9 June to 31 October 1969). **Vietnam War** campaign streamer. In January 1969, President Richard M. Nixon announced the reduction of the U.S. military presence in South Vietnam by the withdrawal of 25,000 troops by 31 August. American troop strength peaked at 543,400 in April 1969 and dropped to 505,500 by mid-October. During the summer and fall of 1969, responsibility for planning and conducting operations were increasingly turned over to the South Vietnamese, as U.S. troops withdrew amid American reaffirmations of support for the Republic of South Vietnam. Enemy attacks concentrated on South Vietnamese positions and U.S. combat deaths were down in the early fall, as American forces switched to small-unit actions. *See also* COUNTEROFFENSIVE, PHASE VI.

SUMTER (12–13 April 1861). **Civil War** campaign streamer for the first battle of the war. In late December 1860, Confederates besieged Fort Sumter, located on an island in the harbor at Charleston, South Carolina, and garrisoned with 90 Federal troops under the command of Major Robert Anderson. Anticipating a Union attempt to reinforce the garrison, Brigadier General Pierre G. T. Beauregard, commander of Confederate forces in the Charleston area, demanded the surrender of the fort on 11 April 1861. Anderson rejected the demand and the next morning Confederate batteries began a 34-hour bombardment of the fort. The Federal garrison returned fire, but on April 13 Anderson was compelled to surrender. He was allowed to evacuate his command by sea on the following day. The action at Sumter outraged the North and President **Abraham Lincoln** called for 75,000 volunteers. The South's reaction to Sumter was for Virginia, Arkansas, North Carolina, and Tennessee to join the Confederate States of America, which had been formed shortly after Lincoln's election in 1960. Both sides began preparing armies for the coming war and the first major encounter took place at **Bull Run** in April.

— T —

TACTICS. The methods and techniques used to conduct combat operations on the battlefield. Commonly understood, tactics provide the framework for conducting combat operations quickly and effectively. Tactics provide an ordered arrangement and maneuver of units in relation to each other and the enemy in order to realize the units' full combat potential. It is the means by which **corps** and smaller unit commanders use their available combat power to attain the tactical objectives assigned them. The results of combat actions at the tactical level can determine victory or defeat at the strategic or operational levels of war. *See also* OPERATIONAL ART; STRATEGY.

TAFT, ALPHONSO (1810–1891). Secretary of war from 1876 to 1877. Born in Vermont, Taft attended local schools and then taught school to earn enough money so he could attend Amherst Academy. He graduated from Yale College in 1833 and taught there while studying law. After being admitted to the Connecticut bar in 1838, he moved to Ohio and started a law practice in Cincinnati. He served as superior court judge before becoming secretary of war in 1876. After serving just over a year, he became attorney general of the United States and then was minister to Austria-Hungary and Russia. His son, **William Howard Taft**, was also secretary of war, in the early twentieth century, as well as president of the United States. *See also* Appendix 4, Secretaries of War and Secretaries of the Army.

TAFT, WILLIAM HOWARD (1857–1930). Secretary of war from 1904 to 1908 and 27th president of the United States. Born in Ohio, Taft was the son of **Alphonso Taft** and attended Woodward High School in Cincinnati. He graduated from Yale University in 1878 and received a law degree from Cincinnati Law School in 1880. Admitted to the bar in 1880, he held a series of judicial government positions until 1900. He became president of the Philippines Commission in that year and was the first civil governor of the Philippine Islands from 1901 to 1904. He declined an appointment to the U.S. Supreme Court and became the secretary of war in 1904. As a close adviser to the president, **Theodore Roosevelt**, Taft settled a potential rebellion in Cuba and organized the U.S. effort to build the Panama Canal. He was elected president of the United States in 1908 and was defeated in a 1912 reelection bid. After eight years as a law professor at Yale University, he was appointed chief justice of the Supreme Court. He resigned for health reasons in February 1930 and died a month later. *See also* Appendix 4, Secretaries of War and Secretaries of the Army.

TANK. A fully tracked, heavily **armored** vehicle primarily used as a high-velocity, direct-fire cannon. Tanks were introduced to the battlefield in **World War I**, when the U.S. Army relied largely on the French to supply them with the new weapons. After the war, the army was slow to develop its own tanks, but **World War II** prompted development of the M4-A Sherman tank. Although inferior on an individual basis to German tanks, the Sherman eventually prevailed on the battlefield because of its numbers and reliability. More than 45,000 were produced for the U.S. Army, Great Britain, and the Soviet Union during the war. The army continued to use various models of improved Sherman tanks during the **Korean War**. The A-3 version of the Sherman tank mounted a 76.2-mm gun, weighed 35 tons, and reached the speed of 29 miles an hour.

In the 1950s, the army developed a new main battle tank, the M-60 tank, with a 105-mm gun. First fielded in 1960, the M-60 was continually improved; the A-3 model weighed 57 tons and traveled up to 30 miles an hour. The M-1 Abrams tank made its appearance in the 1970s and was initially armed with the army's reliable 105-mm gun, but it was soon upgraded to a 120-mm smoothbore cannon. The Abrams's turbine engine makes it capable of moving the 67-ton tank at speeds up to 50 miles an hour. With its laser range finder, ballistic computer, and stabilized gun, the Abrams was arguably the best tank in the world at the end of the twentieth century. Although it has the capacity to carry almost 500 gallons of fuel, its high rate of consumption limits its cruising range to about 280 miles and its operational range to about 130 miles. During the ground campaign of the **Persian Gulf War**, the Army's Abrams tanks dominated the battlefield.

TARLAC (5–20 November 1899). Philippine Insurrection campaign streamer. After their success during the **Malolos** campaign, Major General Arthur MacArthur's forces advanced through the central Luzon plain, seized Tarlac on 12 November, and reached Dagupan eight days later. There MacArthur met Brigadier General Lloyd Wheaton and his command, which had just finished the **San Fabian** campaign. The Tarlac campaign brought an apparent end to the rebellion and President **Theodore Roosevelt** announced the official conclusion of the insurrection on 4 July 1902. However, guerrilla fighting continued in the Philippines until 1913, when the last phase of the **Jolo** campaign finally ended.

TASK FORCE SMITH (1950). The first U.S. Army ground unit to enter combat in the **Korean War**. The task force was named for Lieutenant Colonel Charles B. Smith, commander of the 1st Battalion, 21st **Infantry** Regiment. The battalion consisted of 406 officers and men. In addition to its rifles, the task force was armed with two 75-mm recoilless rifles, two 4.2-inch mortars, six 2.36-inch rocket launchers known as bazookas, and four 60-mm mortars. Each man was issued 120 rounds of ammunition and C-rations for two days. Most of the men were 20 or fewer years old; only one in six had combat experience. Smith's mission was to block the main road to Pusan as far north as possible in an effort to stop the North Korean invasion force that was sweeping south through Korea. The task force flew to an airfield near Pusan and moved north to Taejon by train, arriving there on 2 July 1950. On 4 July, elements of the 52d **Field Artillery** Battalion with six 105-mm howitzers joined the task force. While the troops rested, Smith and his officers drove north to reconnoiter. About three miles north of Osan, Smith found an ideal blocking position, a line of low rolling hills about 300 feet above the level ground. The position also commanded the main railroad line to the east and afforded a clear view to Suwon, about eight miles north. The task force moved north to occupy the position Smith had selected and at about 0300 on 5 July the soldiers began to dig foxholes in cold, rainy weather to await the North Korean advance.

Shortly after 0700, movement was detected to the north and a column of eight North Korean T-34 tanks soon approached across the open plain from Suwon. At 0816, the artillery opened the first American ground fire of the Korean War. The high-explosive rounds had no effect on the tanks and the battery had only six antitank rounds, all of which were with a single howitzer. As they approached the forward howitzer, the two lead North Korean tanks were hit and damaged. One caught fire and two of its crew members came out of the turret with their hands up; a third came out with a burp gun and fired it against an American machine-gun position beside the road, killing an assistant gunner, the first American ground fatality of the Korean War. A third tank knocked out the howitzer, allowing the rest of the tanks to move south with no effective resistance.

By 1015, 33 North Korean tanks had driven through the American position, having killed or wounded some 20 Americans, and most of the American vehicles had been destroyed. Smith held his position as long as he dared, but casualties mounted rapidly and his men eventually were down to fewer than 20 rounds of ammunition each. Enemy tanks were to the rear of the American position, so Smith consolidated his force in a circular perimeter on the highest ground east of the road. At about 1630, Smith ordered a withdrawal. Under heavy enemy fire, the poorly trained American troops abandoned weapons and equipment in sometimes precipitous flight. There was no enemy pursuit, but at Chonan only 185 men of the task force could be accounted for. Subsequently, C Company came in with 65 soldiers, bringing the total to 250, and more trickled back to American positions during the following week. Approximately 150 American infantrymen were killed, wounded, or missing after the battle. North Korean casualties were approximately 42 dead and 85 wounded, with four tanks destroyed or immobilized.

Task Force Smith is noteworthy because it conducted the first ground combat between North Korean and U.S. forces. It was not a major battle and it only briefly delayed the enemy, but it is a vivid reminder to the U.S. Army that it must always keep its soldiers prepared to engage in combat with little or no warning. "No more Task Force Smiths" has become a watchword for army readiness. *See also* UN DEFENSIVE.

TAYLOR, MAXWELL DAVENPORT (1901–1987). Chief of staff of the army from 1955 to 1959 and chairman of the Joint Chiefs of Staff from 1962 to 1964. Born in Missouri, Taylor graduated from the **U.S. Military Academy** in 1922. After service in Hawaii, he studied French in Paris and until 1932 taught French and Spanish at the Military Academy. He attended the **Command and General Staff College** and studied Japanese at the American embassy in Tokyo from 1935 to 1939. After graduating from the **Army War College** in 1940, Taylor served on a Hemispheric defense mission to Latin America. Early in **World War II**, he was chief of staff of the 82d **Airborne** Division. He commanded the 101st Airborne Division at **Normandy** and led it across Western Europe until the defeat of Germany. After the war, Taylor commanded U.S. forces in Berlin and in 1953 assumed command of the Eighth Army for the final operations of the **Korean War**. While chief of staff of the army, he opposed U.S. dependence on the doctrine of massive retaliation against the Soviet bloc, urged increases in conventional forces and flexible response, and guided army operations in Little Rock, Arkansas, and in Lebanon, Berlin, and Taiwan. He retired from active duty in 1959. From 1962 to 1964, he returned to active duty to serve as chairman of the Joint Chiefs of Staff and he then served as ambassador to South Vietnam until 1965. He was chairman of the Foreign Intelligence Advisory Board from 1965 to 1969. Taylor died in Washington, D.C., on 19 April 1987. *See also* Appendix 3, Commanding Generals and Chiefs of Staff of the Army.

TAYLOR, ZACHARY (1784–1850). **Mexican War** general and 12th president of the United States. Born in Virginia, Taylor received little formal education and saw his first military service in 1806 as a short-term volunteer. He procured a commission in 1808, served in the **War of 1812** under **William Henry Harrison**, and resigned when the army was reduced in strength after the war. He rejoined the army as a major in 1816, served the next two decades along the western frontier, and participated in the **Black Hawk** campaign. In 1837, he was ordered to Florida, where he participated in the war against the **Seminoles**. During the **Mexican War**, he commanded the northern invasion forces and in this capacity won victories at **Palo Alto** and **Resaca de la Palma** in May 1846, captured **Monterrey** in October, and held off the army of the Mexican commander, General **Santa Anna**, at **Buena Vista** in February 1947, even though many of his troops had been sent to **Vera Cruz** for the southern invasion under **Winfield Scott**. Taylor emerged from the war a national hero, became the Whig candidate for president, and was elected in 1848. He died in 1850, 16 months after taking office.

TECUMSEH (ca. 1768–1813). Shawnee Indian chief. Tecumseh was born in present-day Ohio. His father and two brothers were killed fighting to defend their lands against encroaching white settlers. Tecumseh sought to establish an Indian nation capable of stopping the settlement of the Ohio Valley. In 1811, **William Henry Harrison**, governor of Indiana Territory, attacked the village of Tecumseh's brother, Tenskwatawa, who was known as the Prophet. Tenskwatawa died in the battle at **Tippecanoe**, along with Tecumseh's hopes of an Indian confederation. Tecumseh went into service for the British and commanded the Indian allies in the **War of 1812** as a brigadier general. He was killed in fighting at the Thames in Upper Canada in 1813. With his death, most Indian resistance north of the Ohio River ended.

TET COUNTEROFFENSIVE (30 January to 1 April 1968). Vietnam War campaign streamer. In late January 1968, American and South Vietnamese forces began the lunar new year Tet holiday expecting the usual 36-hour holiday truce. However, during the night of 29 January, Communist forces launched assaults in the northern and central provinces. Some 84,000 Viet Cong (VC) and North Vietnamese Army (NVA) troops attacked or fired upon 36 of 44 provincial capitals, five of six autonomous cities, 64 of 242 district capitals, and 50 hamlets. In addition, the enemy raided a number of military installations, including almost every airfield. Although most of the fighting died out after about three days, the cities of Saigon and Hue experienced intense and sustained attacks. The attack in Saigon began with a sapper attack against the American embassy, while other assaults were directed against the presidential palace, the Vietnamese joint general staff compound, and nearby Ton San Nhut air base. At Hue, eight enemy battalions infiltrated the city and the fight to expel them lasted almost a month. American and South Vietnamese units lost over 500 killed, while VC and NVA battle deaths may have been somewhere between 4,000 and 5,000.

The Tet offensive was seen as a major military defeat for the Communists, because it failed to either spawn an uprising or gain appreciable support among the South Vietnamese. U.S. strength in South Vietnam totaled more than 500,000 and General **William Westmoreland**, commander of the U.S. forces in Vietnam, believing he had an opportunity to quickly end the war, requested more than 200,000 troops. But the American public was discouraged by the offensive, as it became apparent that the United States could not control the scope or duration of the war. The Communist offensive dealt a setback to the pacification program. The intense fighting needed to root out VC elements that clung to fortified positions inside the towns increased the numbers of refugees in Vietnam. In the densely populated Mekong Delta, for example, there were approximately 14,000 refugees in January 1968 and some 170,000 after Tet.

TET 69 COUNTEROFFENSIVE (23 February to 8 June 1969). Vietnam War campaign streamer. On 23 February, the 1969 Tet lunar holiday, U.S. Navy units and installations at Da Nang, Tan An, Ben Luc, Go Dan Ha, and Tra Cu came under numerous and widespread attacks associated with a new enemy offensive, but units in these areas were poised to meet these attacks and they caused only minimal damage. From the beginning of Tet through the month of June, Communist forces tried to sustain an offensive. Their inability to do so was largely because of aggressive ground operations by American and South Vietnamese forces. Between 23 February and 8 June 1969, some 70 ground operations resulted in heavy enemy loss of life and materiel. In May, elements of the U.S. Army's 101st Airborne Division and South Vietnamese forces attacked North Vietnamese Army (NVA) units on Dong Ap Bia Mountain in the A Shau Valley, which closely paralleled the border with Laos. Intense fighting resulted in heavy casualties on both sides and the mountain became known as **Hamburger Hill**. After the battle, both sides abandoned their positions and the NVA retreated to sanctuaries in Laos. The battle was widely criticized for wasting lives after U.S. president Richard Nixon earlier in the year had announced a policy of turning the war over to the South Vietnamese. The controversy seemed to strengthen Nixon's resolve to get U.S. forces out of Vietnam.

THAYER, SYLVANUS (1785–1872). Army engineer and superintendent of the **U.S. Military Academy.** Born in Massachusetts, Thayer attended Dartmouth for three years before entering the Military Academy and graduating in 1808. He saw service in the **War of 1812** and studied military institutions in Europe before returning to the academy in 1817 as superintendent. He remained in this position until 1833. During his tenure, he organized the cadets into a battalion, established an academic board, divided classes into sections based on merit, and instituted semiannual examinations. Having established these changes, he fought to keep them in place and many elements of his system remain in place today. For his efforts, Thayer is known as the "Father of the Military Academy." He also recruited **Dennis Hart Mahan** as a member of the faculty. Upon leaving the academy, he returned to work as an army coastal engineer. In recognition of his long service, he received a brevet promotion to brigadier general before his retirement in May 1863. He later founded the Thayer School of Engineering at Dartmouth University.

THIRD KOREAN WINTER (1 December 1952 to 30 April 1953). Korean War campaign streamer. Other than a few patrol clashes, there was little activity anywhere along the front in Korea as 1953 began. On 11 February, Lieutenant General **Maxwell D. Taylor** took command of the Eighth Army to replace the retiring Lieutenant General James A. Van Fleet. Armistice negotiations, which had stalled in late 1952, resumed in April. The prisoner-of-war question was settled when each side was provided with an opportunity to persuade those captives who refused repatriation to their homeland to change their minds. Meanwhile, Chinese Communist forces (CCF) had renewed attacks against the U.S. Eighth Army's outpost line as spring approached. By the time the war ended with the cease-fire in July, these attacks had increased in frequency and intensity and had become nearly as heavy as those of May 1951, during the **CCF Spring Offensive**. *See also* KOREA, SUMMER–FALL 1952.

TICONDEROGA (10 May 1775). Revolutionary War campaign streamer. On 10 May 1775, an American force of some 80 men led by Colonels Ethan Allen of Vermont and **Benedict Arnold** of Connecticut surprised the British garrison of about 40 men at Fort Ticonderoga, New York, which surrendered without a fight. Allen then seized nearby Crown Point, at the southern end of Lake Champlain, on 12 May and Arnold temporarily occupied St. John's, a fort across the Canadian border, on 16 May. Under the direction of **Henry Knox**, the Americans moved most of the 100 cannon and the military stores captured at Ticonderoga to **Boston** to supply the American army besieging the city.

TIENTSIN (13 July 1900). China Relief Expedition campaign streamer. In June 1900, in response to the Boxer Rebellion in **Peking** (Beijing), an international column of sailors and marines from a number of European nations, organized under British command and including 112 Americans, attempted to go to the relief of hostages held by the Boxers. The column met with severe resistance after it left Tientsin (Tianjin) and failed to get through. The United States dispatched a **regiment** of army **infantry** and a battalion of U.S. Marines from Manila. The force landed at Taku on 7 July 1900 and joined contingents of other powers in an attack on Tientsin, which fell on 13 July. The Americans suffered 95 casualties.

TILLEY, JACK L. (1948–). Sergeant major of the army as of 24 June 2000. Born in Washington, Tilley entered the army in November 1966. After serving in the **Vietnam War** and at Fort Benning, Georgia, he left the army for two years, then enlisted again in September 1971. He graduated from the **Sergeants Major Academy** and was the **command sergeant major** in a variety of units, including the U.S. Central Command and the U.S. Army Space and Missile Command, before becoming sergeant major of the army. See also Appendix 4, Sergeants Major of the Army.

TIPPECANOE (21 September to 18 November 1811). Indian wars campaign streamer. In 1804 Shawnee Indian chief **Tecumseh** and his medicine man brother, the Prophet, encouraged by the British, attempted to form an Indian confederacy in the Northwest. **William Henry Harrison**, governor of Indiana Territory, determined to break up the confederacy before it could organize a major attack. In September 1811, Harrison led a well-trained force of 320 **regular army** soldiers and 650 militia from Vincennes up the Wabash River. After building Fort Harrison at Terre Haute, Harrison marched with 800 men toward the main Indian village on Tippecanoe Creek and on 6 November encamped in battle order on the north bank of the Wabash. In the absence of Tecumseh, Harrison met with the Prophet, who implied he would not attack while a peace proposal was under consideration. But just before dawn on 7 November, the Indians attacked Harrison's forces. In a wild hand-to-hand encounter, the Indians were routed and their village was destroyed. Harrison lost 39 killed and missing, 151 wounded; the Indians suffered similar losses. The battle did not solve the Indian problems in the Northwest and the tribes of the area allied themselves with the British during the **War of 1812**.

TRANSPORTATION CORPS. Branch of the army. Prior to the **War of 1812**, military transportation took a back seat in the national military strategy, but it became apparent after the war that some form of organized transportation support was needed to guarantee the new nation's ability to successfully engage and defeat an enemy. In 1818, Thomas S. Jesup was appointed quartermaster general and he initiated a number of programs that improved the army's transportation capability and encouraged American westward expansion. During the **Civil War**, transportation was an integral part of military **logistics**. Railroads became an efficient means of moving military forces and equipment and by 1864 five of the nine divisions in the quartermaster department dealt with transportation issues. The **Spanish–American War** highlighted the need for a separate transportation service within the quartermaster department. In **World War I**, W. W. Attebury, a former railroad executive, was appointed director general of transportation. A Transportation Corps was established in 1918, but it was abolished after the war. In March 1942, as the army mobilized for **World War II**, the transportation functions were consolidated into the Transportation Division of the newly created Services of Supply; three months later, the army created the Transportation Corps. By the end of the war, the corps had moved more than 30 million soldiers within the continental United States and 7 million soldiers plus 126 million tons of supplies overseas. It continues to provide transportation services to the army worldwide. See also BRANCHES OF THE ARMY; QUARTERMASTER CORPS.

TRENTON (26 December 1776). Revolutionary War campaign streamer. When the British captured Forts Washington and Lee on the Hudson above Manhattan in mid-November 1776, **George Washington** and his army retreated across New Jersey with British commander William Howe in close pursuit. After Washington crossed the Delaware River into Pennsylvania with about 3,000 men, Howe went into winter quarters in New York City, leaving garrisons in several New Jersey towns, including Trenton. In December 1776, with severe shortages of food, clothing, and ammunition gnawing at American morale and enlistments in the **Continental Army** close to expiring, Washington decided to conduct a surprise attack on the British garrison in Trenton, a 1,400-man Hessian force. On Christmas night, he led about 2,400 men in boats across the icy Delaware River. Moving in two columns, they moved into Trenton and completely surprised the British garrison. After a short fight, the Hessians surrendered, although some 400 of the garrison escaped southward to Bordentown, New Jersey, when two other American columns failed to cross the Delaware in time to intercept them. About 30 were killed and 918 were captured on the British side. American losses were four dead and four wounded. With a victory in hand to raise the morale of his troops and demonstrate that the American cause was alive and well, Washington recrossed the Delaware before the British could launch a pursuit.

TRUMAN, HARRY S. (1884–1972). Army **artillery** officer and 33d president of the United States. Born in Missouri, Truman applied to the **U.S. Military Academy** after graduating from high school, but was rejected because of poor eyesight. On 14 June 1905, he became a charter member of the newly formed Battery B of the Missouri National Guard. Truman served as battery clerk until discharged in 1911. When the United States entered **World War I** in April 1917, Truman reenlisted and was elected first lieutenant of Battery F, 2d Missouri **Field Artillery**. On 5 August 1917, the 2d Missouri was federalized, redesignated the 129th Field Artillery Regiment, and assigned to the 60th Field Artillery Brigade, 35th Division. On 29 March 1918, Truman and the 129th boarded the *George Washington* for the voyage to France, where he was promoted to captain and given command of Battery D. He led the battery during the **St. Mihiel** and **Meuse–Argonne** campaigns. At the end of the war, his regimental commander recommended him for the rank of major in the **regular army**, but Truman declined the commission and was mustered out on 6 May 1919.

Truman tried his hand unsuccessfully in business, before a friend from his army days introduced him to the boss of the local Democratic machine in Kansas City, who appointed Truman overseer of highways. After serving a number of terms on the Jackson County court, Truman was elected to the U.S. Senate from Missouri. As chairman of a special committee to investigate national defense spending during World War II, he gained recognition for his impartial uncovering waste and of collusion between some corporations and army agents and he saved the government hundreds of millions of dollars.

Truman became Franklin Roosevelt's vice president in 1945 and, upon Roosevelt's death later that year, Truman became president. In one of his first major decisions as president, Truman approved using the newly developed atomic bomb against Japan, which ended **World War II** before the army had to invade the Japanese home islands. In the summer of 1948, Truman signed legislation that reinstated Selective Service and issued Executive Order 9981, ordering the desegregation of the armed forces. In June 1950, he ordered U.S. troops into Korea after North Korea invaded South Korea. During the **Korean War**, when **Douglas MacArthur**, commanding the United Nations forces, exceeded his authority, Truman, with the support of the U.S. Joint Chiefs of Staff, relieved MacArthur of command in April 1951. *See also* AFRICAN AMERICANS.

TUNISIA (17 November 1942 to 13 May 1943). World War II campaign streamer. When the Allies landed in North Africa during the **Algeria–French Morocco** campaign in late 1942, the Germans moved reinforcements into Tunisia from Sicily, eventually bringing in more than 150,000 additional troops, and stopped the Allied drive short of the Tunisian capital of Tunis. German Field Marshal **Erwin Rommel**'s Afrika Korps, falling back in front of the British Eighth Army's drive from Egypt, established positions behind the so-called Mareth Line in southeastern Tunisia and maintained contact with the German reinforcements. Having consolidated a beachhead in Tunisia, Rommel assumed the offensive on 14 February 1943. German armored units moved south into central Tunisia, as Rommel attempted to maneuver around the southern flank of the British First Army, commanded by Lieutenant General Kenneth N. A. Anderson, and capture the Allied base of operations around Tebessa. The Germans defeated the Allies in a series of sharp armored actions, forced a withdrawal of American troops through the Kasserine Pass, and advanced almost one hundred miles before the Allies finally stopped them on 22 February. With the failure of his counteroffensive, Rommel withdrew. During early March, the Germans attempted two lesser offensives, one against the British First Army and the other against the British Eighth Army, both of which failed, allowing the Allies to resume their offensive.

The U.S. II Corps, now commanded by **George S. Patton**, attacked toward the flank and rear of the Mareth Line, while elements of the British Eighth Army outflanked the Axis position and broke through into the eastern coastal region of central Tunisia. Within a month, all Axis troops had been compressed into a small bridgehead covering the Cape Bon Peninsula. In the final phase of the operation, Major General **Omar N. Bradley** assumed command of the U.S. II Corps so Patton could begin preparations for the invasion of **Sicily**. A massive Allied attack pushed through Bizerte and Tunis, forcing the surrender of the last of some 275,000 Germans and Italians on the Cape Bon Peninsula on 12 May 1943.

— U —

UN DEFENSIVE (27 June to 15 September 1950). Korean War campaign streamer. At 0400, Sunday, 25 June 1950, North Korean forces attacked across the 38th parallel into the Republic of Korea. On 27 June, U.S. president **Harry**

S. Truman ordered American air and naval forces to support the South Korean troops and the next day he authorized the use of U.S. ground units in Korea. The United Nations (UN) condemned the attacks and recommended establishing a unified command to defend South Korea. When the UN asked the United States to provide a commander, Truman appointed General **Douglas MacArthur** to the post.

The initial strategy was to trade space in Korea for time. On 2 July, **Task Force Smith**, made up of two rifle companies and supporting units from the 24th **Division** in Japan, was flown to Pusan and moved by train and truck to defensive positions near Osan, 30 miles south of Seoul, where it was supposed to fight a delaying action while the rest of the division moved to Korea. A North Korean division, supported by 30 tanks, hit the small task force on 5 July and forced it to withdraw with heavy losses of men and equipment. In early July, the rest of the division reached Korea and occupied defensive positions along the Kum River, 60 miles south of Osan, and by 15 July the 25th Division had also arrived in Korea.

The rest of July passed with a series of hard-fought battles along the quickly established defensive perimeter. By the beginning of August, the UN forces had withdrawn behind the Naktong River, where Lieutenant General Walton H. Walker, commander of the U.S. Eighth Army, ordered a final stand on a 140-mile perimeter around the port of Pusan. During the next month and a half, 14 North Korean divisions dissipated their strength against the Pusan perimeter, while Walker shuttled forces to prevent any serious penetrations. By mid-August, the offensive capability of the Eighth Army had been augmented by the arrival of another U.S. Army division, U.S. Marines, and British and Republic of Korea forces. With these reinforcements, MacArthur was ready to begin an offensive. *See also* UN OFFENSIVE.

UN OFFENSIVE (16 September to 2 November 1950). Korean War campaign streamer. After stopping the North Korean advance in September 1950, General **Douglas MacArthur**, commander of the United Nations (UN) forces in Korea, planned an amphibious landing at Inchon, a port on the Yellow Sea 25 miles west of Seoul, to recapture the city and block North Korean troop movements and supply routes. Concurrently, the U.S. Eighth Army, holding the Pusan perimeter, moved north, driving the North Koreans toward the U.S. X Corps that landed at Inchon. On 15 September, a U.S. Marine battalion, covered by air strikes and naval gunfire, captured Wolmi Island, just offshore from Inchon. By that afternoon, Marine assault troops were in the port and the First Marine Division pressed toward Kimpo Airfield, the Han River, and Seoul. The airfield was soon captured and used by U.S. Air Force cargo planes to augment the stream of supplies landed by the U.S. Navy at Inchon. On 26 September, after heavy fighting between UN forces and the determined North Koreans, MacArthur announced that Seoul was in friendly hands.

As planned, the Eighth Army began its offensive to the north on 16 September. Progress was limited at first, but when the North Koreans realized that MacArthur's intent was to trap them in the south, they fled north with heavy losses of men and materiel. Elements of the U.S. X Corps and the Eighth Army made contact late on 26 September, linking the UN forces. Organized enemy resistance continued in the Eighth Army sector until the last days of September, but in late October the advance quickened as enemy resistance weakened and thousands of enemy troops surrendered. The X Corps, which had been withdrawn from combat after the Inchon invasion to prepare for an amphibious landing on the east coast of Korea, landed the First Marine Division at Wonsan on 26 October; three days later, the U.S. Army's 7th Division landed unopposed at Iwon, 80 miles to the north. The UN forces then began moving north to destroy enemy forces and occupy major North Korean cities. *See also* UN DEFENSIVE.

UN SUMMER–FALL OFFENSIVE (9 July to 27 November 1951). Korean War campaign streamer. On 10 July 1951, North Korea and the United Nations (UN) command in Korea opened peace negotiations at Kaesong. At the first meeting, both sides agreed that military operations would continue until an armistice agreement was signed, although neither side was particularly interested in starting any large-scale offensives while the peace talks were in progress. UN military activity was limited to combat patrolling, **artillery** and air bombardment, and the occasional repulsing of enemy attacks. On 22 August, North Korea stopped negotiations and the Eighth Army launched a series of limited-objective attacks to improve its defensive positions. September was characterized by local attacks, counterattacks, and combat patrols. On 25 October, armistice negotiations resumed at the new site of Panmunjom. *See also* CCF (CHINESE COMMUNIST FORCES) SPRING OFFENSIVE.

UNIFORMS. The army's uniforms have changed almost constantly over its long history, reflecting changes in mission, logistics, and style. During the **Revolutionary War**, blue differentiated American soldiers from the British red and French white uniforms. The influence of the Napoleonic wars saw the three-cornered hat replaced by a cap, on which metal branch insignia appeared in 1832. By 1851, the white trousers had been replaced by sky blue in deference to the stains caused by winter mud, while branch colors had appeared on the frock coat. During the **Civil War**, Union forces continued to wear blue, while the Confederates wore gray, a traditional, economical color for state militia forces. After the war, the forage cap became the standard head gear, with officers adding the national symbol of the eagle to the cap in 1895. In 1902, in deference to the need for concealment on a smokeless battlefield, cotton khaki and wool olive drab became the duty uniforms, while army blue was limited to dress uniforms.

World War I saw the addition of distinctive shoulder sleeve insignia, British-style helmets, and French overseas caps that could be folded and placed in a pocket. **World War II** saw the introduction of the steel helmet and liner, fatigues with large cargo pockets, combat boots, and the layered field jacket. In 1946, the Army ended the use of distinctive officer and enlisted uniforms; in 1949, the Uniform Board established separate garrison and field uniforms; and in 1956, army green replaced olive drab as the color of duty uniforms. During the **Cold War**, starched olive green fatigues made their appearance along with name tapes and the distinctive gold "U.S. ARMY" tape. The **Vietnam War** brought a change to tropical clothing and subdued insignia, which eliminated bright colors from distinctive unit patches. Jungle boots with canvas inserts and camouflage fatigues were also introduced in Vietnam. The **Persian Gulf War** saw the introduction of battle dress uniforms with desert markings.

In 1961, the army started using berets to distinguish particular groups of soldiers, as **Special Forces** began wearing their green berets. That was followed by the **rangers** wearing black berets in 1975 and the **airborne** soldiers, or paratroopers, wearing maroon berets in 1980. In 2001, when the army adopted a black beret for all soldiers, the rangers changed to tan. Special Forces and paratroopers continued to wear their distinctive colors.

UNITED STATES ARMY. The U.S. Army consists of the **regular army** and the **reserve components** (the **Army National Guard** and the **U.S. Army Reserve**). The army is the oldest U.S. armed force. It dates its founding to 14 June 1775, when the Second Continental Congress established the **Continental Army**, but the army's heritage has its roots in the colonial period, when militia forces protected the first American settlers. The militia tradition is carried on by the reserve components. *See also* Appendix 1, Resolution of the Continental Congress Adopting the Continental Army.

UNITED STATES ARMY RESERVE (USAR). The Army Reserve traces its origins to the creation of the Medical Reserve Corps in 1908. In 1916, Congress passed the **National Defense Act**, which created the Officers' Reserve Corps, Enlisted Reserve Corps, and **Reserve Officers' Training Corps**. In **World War I**, 89,500 officers from the Officers' Reserve Corps participated, of which one-third were medical doctors. More than 80,000 soldiers of the Enlisted Reserve Corps served, with 15,000 assigned to medical units. After the war, the Officers' Corps and the Enlisted Reserve Corps were combined into the Organized Reserve Corps, a name that lasted into the 1950s. During the Great Depression, the **Civilian Conservation Corps** (CCC) placed young men in barracks and military-style organizations to work in national forests and other outdoor projects. Between 1933 and 1939, more than 30,000 officers from the Organized Reserve Corps served as commanders or staff officers at 2,700 CCC camps.

In June 1940, the army began calling members of the Organized Reserve Corps to active duty as war in Europe portended a U.S. role. More than 200,000 members of the Organized Reserve served in the army during **World War II**, providing 29 percent of the officers. During the **Korean War**, more than 240,000 soldiers of the Organized Reserve were called to active duty and more than 400 reserve units served in the war. While the war was still being fought, Congress changed the Organized Reserve Corps to the U.S. Army Reserve.

In 1961, more than 69,000 army reservists were called to active duty during the Berlin Crisis in the **Cold War**. The call-up, lasting from September 1961 to August 1962, was hampered by a number of problems, including old equipment, lack of equipment, shortage of unit soldiers, and difficulty locating individual soldiers. In the late 1960s, the Army Reserve was reorganized to consist primarily of combat support and combat service support units, with combat arms units concentrated in the **Army National Guard**. At the same time, a federal statute established a chief of the Army Reserve. The position was to be filled by a USAR general officer appointed by the president for a four-year term, with advice and consent of the U.S. Senate.

There was no large-scale reserve call-up for the **Vietnam War**, although some 5,900 USAR soldiers constituting 42 units were ordered to active duty and 3,500 soldiers in 35 units went overseas during the war. In 1973, the United States adopted a policy of maintaining an active duty force capable of maintaining peace and deterring aggression, supported by well-trained, well-equipped reserves. Since then, the army's reserve components have been closely integrated with the **regular army**. The 1991 **Persian Gulf War** required the largest call-up of the reserve components since the Korean War. More than 84,000 army reservists supported the war effort and more than 40,000 served in Southwest Asia. In December 1995, the president authorized a reserve call-up as part of America's support to the NATO peacekeeping forces in the Balkans. The Army Reserve provided civil affairs, postal, medical, engineer, transportation, psychological operations, and firefighting units, beginning in January 1996. The initial call-up was of 3,888 soldiers activated for up to 270 days. In May 1996, the number increased to 7,000 to allow overlap of deploying and redeploying units and individual soldiers. The majority of army reservists ordered to active duty served in Germany, but substantial numbers saw duty in Bosnia and Hungary.

UNITED STATES MILITARY ACADEMY. After the **Revolutionary War**, several soldiers and legislators, including **George Washington**, **Henry Knox**, **Alexander Hamilton**, and John Adams, urged the creation of an institution devoted to the art and science of warfare. As a result of their efforts, President Thomas Jefferson signed legislation on 16 March 1802 to establish the U.S. Military Academy at West Point, New York, a Revolutionary War fortress. The academy foundered after the **War of 1812**, until **Sylvanus Thayer**, credited with being the "father of the Military Academy," was appointed superintendent in 1817. Thayer established a board to determine academic policy, instilled military discipline, and emphasized honorable conduct. Although he expanded the curriculum to make the academy an institution that educated men in the profession of arms, civil engineering became an important aspect of a cadet's studies and, for the first half of the nineteenth century, academy graduates constructed many of the nation's railway lines, bridges, harbors, and roads. After the experience of the **Mexican War**, academy graduates commanded forces on both sides during the **Civil War**. In the 60 major battles fought in the war, 55 had academy graduates commanding both sides, while the remaining five had a graduate commanding on at least one side. Academy graduates, including **Ulysses S. Grant**, **Joseph J. Johnston**,

Robert E. Lee, George B. McClellan, Philip Sheridan, William Sherman, and **Thomas J. Jackson,** set high standards of military leadership during the war. In the latter half of the nineteenth century, the U.S. Military Academy broadened its curriculum. With the creation of army postgraduate command and staff schools, the academy was considered the first step in an officer's education that would continue throughout an army career. In **World War I,** academy graduates such as **John J. Pershing** and **Peyton C. March** distinguished themselves as the size of the army rapidly increased. After the war, **Douglas MacArthur,** as superintendent, sought to diversify the academic curriculum and pushed for major changes in the physical fitness and intramural athletic programs. During **World War II, Dwight D. Eisenhower,** MacArthur, **Omar Bradley, Henry H. Arnold, Mark Clark, George S. Patton, Joseph Stilwell,** and **Jonathan Wainwright** were among the many academy graduates who rose to senior leadership positions. After the war, there were significant revisions to the curriculum to keep up with developments in science and technology, the increasing need to understand other cultures, and the rising level of general education in the army.

The **Korean War** and the **Vietnam War** saw another generation of academy graduates rise to the top of the army's leadership. In Korea, MacArthur initially commanded the United Nations forces. He was replaced by **Matthew B. Ridgway,** who was in turn followed by **Maxwell Taylor. William C. Westmoreland** and **Creighton Abrams** faced the difficult challenges of Vietnam and, more recently, **H. Norman Schwarzkopf** commanded the UN coalition in the **Persian Gulf War.** In recognition of the increasing role of minorities and women, minority recruiting increased significantly in the 1960s and, after considerable controversy, the first female cadets entered the academy in 1976. Toward the end of the twentieth century, the curriculum changed, permitting cadets to major in a wide range of subjects from the sciences to the humanities. After almost two hundred years of educating army officers and undergoing significant changes in response to the demands of warfare and society, the academy's mission has remained essentially unchanged since 1802: to provide leaders of character who are committed to the academy's motto of "Duty, Honor, Country."

UNITED STATES VOLUNTEERS. Raised locally, funded by the federal government, and generally under the overall command of U.S. Army officers, these forces augmented the **regular army,** National Guard, and organized militia during the nineteenth century. When authorized by Congress, state governors nominated local leaders to be commissioned as officers who recruited temporary units up to the size of **regiments.** The units, in keeping with U.S. tradition, elected company officers. The volunteers did not exist in peacetime. They were raised only as necessary and, unlike the militia, which could not stay in federal service longer than nine months or serve outside the country, the U.S. Volunteers were enlisted for terms of one to three years and, during the **Mexican War,** the **Spanish–American War,** and the **Philippine Insurrection,** did fight outside the United States. They were also used during the **War of 1812,** the **Civil War,** and many campaigns of the **Indian wars.** In the twentieth century, when draftees and volunteers made the army a truly national force, the U.S. Volunteers were no longer needed. *See also* ARMY NATIONAL GUARD.

UPTON, EMORY (1838–1881). Military educator and reformer. Born in New York, Upton graduated from the **U.S. Military Academy** in 1861. During the **Civil War**, he rose from second lieutenant to brevet major general. During the **Spotsylvania** campaign in 1864, he was promoted to brigadier general after he led 12 regiments in an assaulting column that penetrated the Confederate defenses. The column deployment, an alternative to the traditional linear tactics that cost heavily in lives throughout the war, was a precursor to his future as a military reformer. After the war, he became a vocal advocate of making the army more efficient and effective. A protégé of General **William T. Sherman**, Upton traveled as part of a multinational tour of foreign military establishments that resulted in an 1878 report, *The Armies of Asia and Europe*, that contained his observations and recommendations. While superintendent of the **Artillery School of Practice** at Fort Monroe, Virginia, Upton introduced combined arms training and case studies to add intellectual vigor to the largely practical curriculum. The school became the model for the army's officer education system. In 1881, for reasons not completely clear, Upton committed suicide while serving in San Francisco. Years after his death, **Elihu Root**, a reformist **secretary of war**, published Upton's *The Military Policy of the United States*, which argued that a professional army, supported and guided by a **general staff**, should be the foundation for the nation's defense establishment.

UTES (September 1879 to November 1880). **Indian wars** campaign streamer. In September 1879, the Indian agent at White River Agency in Colorado had a dispute with Northern Utes and requested army assistance. In response, a column of 200 men deployed from Fort Steele, Wyoming. On 29 September, 300 to 400 warriors attacked the column and surrounded it in Red Canyon. The command was relieved by cavalry forces on 2 October and reinforced with the arrival of more troops on 5 October. In the meantime, the Indian agent and most of his staff at the White River Agency had been massacred. Before the Utes were finally pacified in November 1880, several thousand troops had taken the field.

— V —

VALLEY (15 May to 17 June 1862). **Civil War** campaign streamer. During the **Peninsula** campaign, Union forces in the Shenandoah Valley of Virginia presented a potential threat to Richmond. When Major General **Joseph E. Johnston** moved his army to the peninsula to stop the Federal invasion by General **George B. McClellan, Thomas J. Jackson**, with about 10,000 Confederates, started operations in the valley to create a diversion that would keep Federal forces from moving toward Richmond to support McClellan. On 23 March, Jackson attacked a Federal division at Kernstown and suffered defeat, but he won a strategic victory by presenting a threat to Harpers Ferry and Washington, D.C., that diverted forces from McClellan. The Union forces of Major General Nathaniel P. Banks in the Shenandoah Valley, with the dual missions of protecting Washington and destroying Jackson, eventually reached a total strength about three times that of the Confederates. But Jackson maneuvered Banks's forces with great skill, made two and a half trips up and down the valley in about six weeks, and defeated larger Union forces at McDowell, Front Royal, Winchester, Cross Keys, and Port Republic.

VALLEY FORGE (1777–1778). Site of the **Continental Army** encampment for the winter of 1777–1778. Although there were probably worse winters for the army during the **Revolutionary War**, the ordeal of Valley Forge, Pennsylvania, is most remembered because **George Washington**, in an effort to encourage greater support for the army, wrote letters to Congress emphasizing the soldiers' sufferings there. The encampment was also significant because, during the winter, **Friedrich Wilhelm von Steuben** greatly improved the army's discipline and **Nathanael Greene** overhauled the **logistics** system. In popular memory, Valley Forge has become symbolic of endurance in adversity.

VAN AUTREVE, LEON L. (1920–2002). Sergeant major of the army from 1973 to 1975. Born in Belgium, Van Autreve moved to the United States with his family when he was very young. The family settled in Ohio, where he attended elementary and high school and joined the Ohio National Guard in 1938. He left the **Army National Guard** in 1940 to take a railroad job, but was drafted and inducted into the **regular army** in October. He fought in **World War II** in Europe and left the army in 1945 to attend Ohio Northern University. Van Autreve later returned to the army, by 1962 was a battalion **sergeant major**, and spent the next 11 years in that capacity, including service in the **Vietnam War**. He became the sergeant major of the army in 1973 and while in office presided over a rejuvenation of the **noncommissioned officer** corps after the Vietnam War. He retired on 30 June 1975 with more than 31 years of active service. *See also* Appendix 6, Sergeants Major of the Army.

VANCE, CYRUS (1917–2002). Secretary of the army from 1962 to 1964. Born in West Virginia, Vance attended the Kent School in Connecticut, graduated from Yale University in 1939, and received a law degree there in 1942. He enlisted in the navy and became an ensign in the Naval Reserve. He served on destroyers in the Atlantic and Pacific Oceans in **World War II** and after the war went into law and business. After serving in a number of public service positions, Vance became secretary of the army in 1962. During his tenure, the army underwent a significant reorganization and provided troops in support of the integration of universities in Mississippi and Alabama. Leaving office in 1964, Vance became the deputy secretary of defense for three years and continued in public service as a special representative of the president to Cyprus and Korea. He was the chief U.S. negotiator at the Paris peace talks that ended the **Vietnam War** and served as secretary of state from 1977 to 1980. *See also* Appendix 4, Secretaries of War and Secretaries of the Army.

VERA CRUZ (9–29 March 1847). Mexican War campaign streamer. While Zachary Taylor was fighting in northern Mexico, **Winfield Scott, commanding general of the army**, was preparing to launch another invasion. His army, numbering about 13,000 men, which included many soldiers transferred from Taylor's command, sailed for the coastal town of Vera Cruz on 2 March 1847. Landing operations near Vera Cruz began on 9 March. This first major amphibious landing by the U.S. Army was unopposed, since the Mexican commander, General Juan Morales, decided to keep his force of only 4,300 men behind the city's walls. In order to save lives, Scott chose to take Vera Cruz by siege rather than by assault. The city capitulated on 27 March, after undergoing a demoralizing bombardment. The Americans lost 19 killed and 63 wounded. The Mexican military suffered only about 80 casualties.

VESSEY, JOHN WILLIAM, JR. (1922–). Army general officer who was chairman of the Joint Chiefs of Staff from 1982 to 1985. Born in Minnesota, Vessey joined the Minnesota National Guard while he was in high school. In 1940, his unit was called to active duty and he fought with distinction in **World War II**, for which he received a battlefield commission at **Anzio**. After the war, he attended the **command and general staff college**, the Armed Forces Staff College, and the Industrial College of the Armed Forces and saw service in the **Vietnam War**. In 1976 Vessey became commander of the Eighth Army in Korea, where he also served as the commander in chief of the U.S.–Republic of Korea Combined Forces Command and the United Nations Command, and in 1979 he became the vice chief of staff of the army under General **Edward C. Meyer**, chief of staff. While chairman of the Joint Chiefs of Staff, Vessey improved global war planning, enhanced the quality of the advice given to the president, and worked toward developing greater cooperation among the armed forces in joint operations. He retired from duty on 30 September 1985.

VICKSBURG (29 March to 4 July 1863). Civil War campaign streamer. In 1863, the Union's principal objective in the western theater of operations was to gain strategic control of the Mississippi River and split the Confederacy. Vicksburg, a port city on the Mississippi, was a key link between Confederate forces to the east and west of the river. The city was defended by some 30,000 Confederates under Major General John G. Pemberton, while other Confederate forces under General **Joseph E. Johnston** were concentrated in the vicinity of Jackson, Mississippi, some 40 miles east of Vicksburg. Union General **Ulysses S. Grant** had the mission to capture Vicksburg and Port Hudson. He started the campaign with 45,000 men organized into three **corps**. Grant's plan was to interpose his army between Pemberton and Johnston and then prevent them from joining forces, while the Federals captured Vicksburg.

In late March, Major General **William Tecumseh Sherman** conducted a demonstration north of Vicksburg to distract the attention of the city's defenders while two corps, under Major Generals John A. McClernand and James B. McPherson, made a wide swing to the south on the west side of the Mississippi and prepared to cross the river at Bruinsburg, about 30 miles below Vicksburg. On the night of 16–17 April, David D. Porter sailed his Union fleet down the river, enduring a heavy bombardment as he passed Vicksburg, but losing only one transport during the passage. On 30 April, the transports began ferrying 23,000 Federal troops across the river. Sherman's corps then followed the same route and joined Grant early in May. Grant then moved toward Jackson, capturing the city of Raymond on 12 May. When Pemberton attempted to join Johnston, Grant sent two corps on to Jackson while the third deployed to stop Pemberton's. The Confederate forces were driven out of Jackson on 14 May and Grant defeated Pemberton at Champion's Hill on 16 May and Black River Bridge on 17 May, driving him back into Vicksburg. Federal assaults on 18 and 22 May failed to breach the Confederate defenses and Grant laid siege to the city. By 1 June, he had 50,000 men surrounding 30,000 defenders; another 27,000 arrived later in the month. On 4 July, Pemberton surrendered. Federal losses during the campaign were about 3,500; Confederate losses were more than 8,000 killed, wounded, and missing.

While Grant was laying siege to Vicksburg, a 15,000-man force under Union General Nathaniel Banks moved north from New Orleans and attacked Port Hudson, which fell on 8 July 1863, giving control of the entire Mississippi River to the Union and splitting the Confederacy. The Union successes marked the end of the Mississippi River campaign. The surrender of Vicksburg came the same week as the Union victory at **Gettysburg**, marking the turning point of the Civil War in the Union's favor.

VIETNAM WAR (1960–1973). There is no precise start date for this war. The army dates the beginning of the first campaign of the war, **Advisory,** as 15 March 1962, but army Special Forces teams were in Vietnam well before then. The U.S. political involvement goes back to President **Harry S. Truman**'s 1950 decision to provide aid to the French, who were fighting to retain their colonies. After the French were defeated at Dien Bien Phu in 1954, they agreed to the creation of a Communist North Vietnam north of the 17th parallel. The United States attempted to create a nation out of South Vietnam and provided military advisers and other assistance. In 1961, President John F. Kennedy sent army **Special Forces** to train and organize paramilitary forces and establish camps along South Vietnam's borders to reduce the flow of men and materiel into the country. U.S. Army advisers trained the South Vietnamese Army in conventional tactics and provided advice during field operations. Repeated coup attempts and continued Communist infiltration and subversion brought the South Vietnamese government to the point of collapse by 1964. The deteriorating situation prompted Lyndon B. Johnson, who became president upon Kennedy's death in 1963, to begin escalating the American military presence in 1965. By the end of that year, 184,000 American troops were in South Vietnam.

Over the next four years, American troop strength in Vietnam eventually rose to 550,000. But the troops had no clear military objective. The Johnson administration wanted to force the North Vietnamese and their Viet Cong allies in the South to either negotiate or abandon their attempts to reunify Vietnam by force.

9. A flight of UH-1 "Huey" helicopters prepares to pick up infantry troops in Vietnam.

Prohibited from invading North Vietnam, **William C. Westmoreland**, the commander of U.S. forces in Vietnam, adopted a strategy of attrition, in which they sought to inflict enough casualties on the enemy in the South to make him more amenable to American objectives, vague though they were. In the mountains of the central highlands, the jungles of the coastal lowlands, and the plains around the South Vietnamese capital of Saigon, American forces attempted to locate and destroy the elusive enemy. Although search-and-destroy operations inflicted significant losses, the Communists never wavered from their goal of dominating South Vietnam. In February 1968, during the Vietnamese lunar new year celebrations, the North Vietnamese and Viet Cong launched the countrywide **Tet Counteroffensive**. Although repulsed with crippling losses to the Viet Cong, the offensive confirmed the feelings of a growing number of Americans that the Saigon regime was not worth spilling more American blood over.

During the next five years, the army withdrew its forces from Vietnam, turning the war over to the South Vietnamese, while Richard M. Nixon, the third U.S. president to preside over the war, sought to balance troop withdrawals with efforts to preserve American honor and ensure the survival of South Vietnam. By 1972, the American military presence in Vietnam was down to 24,000. In the end, the army's efforts to preserve South Vietnam proved fruitless. The Paris Peace

Accords on Vietnam, signed on 27 January 1973, ended American involvement in the war. The accords provided for a truce between North and South Vietnam, the withdrawal of American forces, and the return of American prisoners of war. After the last American forces left Vietnam on 29 March 1973, North and South Vietnamese forces engaged in a civil war in which the North eventually prevailed. In April 1975, after North Vietnamese forces overran South Vietnam, some 7,000 Americans and Vietnamese were hastily evacuated from Saigon by air, thus finally ending U.S. involvement with Vietnam.

During the Vietnam War, the army concentrated on training its forces to conduct tactical operations without much consideration for the activities of the other services or the type of war they were fighting. The wartime experience of the senior U.S. military leadership had been at the tactical level in **World War II** and in the **Korean War**, and the senior civilian leadership had little or no experience setting realistic strategic objectives. Because the army had no clearly defined strategic objective on which to base **campaign** planning, as they had in World War II and to a lesser degree Korea, senior leaders focused on tactical operations. While operations were generally well planned and executed, battles simply became ends unto themselves. A lack of clearly defined and tangible strategic objectives also deprived the national leadership of the ability to demonstrate progress in the war. In World War II and Korea, military progress was relatively easy to measure by following operations on a map as ground forces moved forward. In Vietnam, however, it was virtually impossible to define progress clearly, a fact that led to the unfortunate body-count system for measuring success.

After the war, the army went through a considerable period of adjustment to determine what had gone wrong with its conduct of the war. The officer corps undertook a close self-examination and developed a renewed interest in the fundamentals of warfare, resulting in a major change in military education and training. **Operational art** and tactical maneuver received increased interest and new technologies were tapped to develop smart weapons. The **Cold War** received renewed attention and the army developed the AirLand Battle **doctrine**, designed to defeat the Soviets in Europe. The army's junior leaders who went on to hold high leadership positions in the **Persian Gulf War** remembered the lack of clear objectives in Vietnam and insisted that the purpose of the Gulf War be made clear to both the armed forces and the American public. *See also* Vietnam War campaigns in Appendix 6, Campaigns of the United States Army.

VILLA, FRANCISCO PANCHO (1878–1923). Mexican revolutionary general. Born in Hacienda Rio Grande, Durango, Mexico, Villa was a fugitive during most of his early life. He joined the successful uprising against Mexican dictator Porfirio Diaz in 1909. After a falling out with Francisco Madero, the leader of the revolt, Villa fled to the United States. When Madero was killed the next year, Villa formed the Division del Norte and joined with Venustiano Carranza to lead a successful revolt in 1914 against Victoriano Huerta, the man who replaced Madero. But Villa and Carranza soon became rivals and Villa retreated to the mountains with his supporters. In March 1916, Villa conducted a raid across the

U.S. border on Columbus, New Mexico, to provoke an American reaction that would cause a nationalist backlash and weaken Carranza's popular support. U.S. president Woodrow Wilson reacted by sending a punitive expedition of 12,000 troops under **John J. Pershing** to pursue Villa into **Mexico**. Unable to capture Villa, the expedition antagonized the Mexicans. As U.S. attention was drawn to the war in Europe, Wilson withdrew the American troops in 1917. Villa was pardoned by the Mexican government in 1920 and assassinated in 1923.

VITTORIA VENETO (24 October to 4 November 1918). World War I campaign streamer. Toward the end of World War I, Americans participated in campaigns in Italy. The American Expeditionary Force sent a **regiment** with hospital troops attached to the Italian front in July 1918 to boost the morale of the Italians. This force of about 1,200 men took part in the last great Italian offensive against the Austrians, at the Battle of Vittorio Veneto.

VON STEUBEN, FRIEDRICH WILHELM LUDOLF GERHARD AUGUSTIN (1730–1794). Revolutionary War general. Born in Magdeburg, Germany, von Steuben served as an **infantry** officer in the Prussian Army and as an aide under Frederick the Great. In 1777, he went to the United States and, claiming to be a lieutenant general and nobleman (he was neither), applied for a commission in the **Continental Army**. Congress accepted his offer to serve without pay and he reported to **George Washington** at **Valley Forge**. Von Steuben developed **tactics** for the army that adapted European methods to the American situation and he demonstrated them using a model company. He was appointed **inspector-general** of the Continental Army in 1778, received a command in 1780, and took part in the siege of **Yorktown**. In 1783, he became a naturalized citizen of the United States.

VUONO, CARL EDWARD (1934–). Chief of staff of the army from 1987 to 1991. Born in Pennsylvania, Vuono graduated from the **U.S. Military Academy** in 1957. He served in Korea and saw service in the **Vietnam War**. In 1973, he graduated from the **Army War College** and from 1976 to 1977 was an executive officer to the chief of staff of the army. Vuono commanded a **division** in Europe, served as deputy commanding general of the Training and Doctrine Command, and commanded the U.S. Army Combined Arms Center, before becoming chief of staff in 1987. During his tenure, he saw increasingly friendly relations with the Soviet Union and an end to the **Cold War**. He also oversaw operations in **Panama** and the **Persian Gulf War**. He retired from active duty in 1991. *See also* Appendix 3, Commanding Generals and Chiefs of Staff of the Army.

— W —

WAINWRIGHT, JONATHAN MAYHEW (1883–1953). World War II army general. Born in the state of Washington, Wainright graduated from the **U.S. Military Academy** in 1906 and served in **World War I** as a captain. In 1940, he received command of the U.S. Army forces on the island of Luzon in the Philippines.

During the Japanese invasion in 1941, he moved his forces to defensive positions on the Bataan Peninsula. When General **Douglas MacArthur** left the **Philippine Islands**, Wainwright assumed command of Bataan and the island fortress of Corregidor. Given command of all U.S. forces in the Philippines, he was forced to surrender to the Japanese in May 1942. He spent the rest of **World War II** as a prisoner of war. In 1945, he was liberated in Manchuria and took part in the formal Japanese surrender ceremony in Tokyo Bay. After receiving a hero's welcome when he returned to the United States, he continued on active duty until his retirement in 1947.

WAR. There is a wide variety of definitions for war, but there are several critical elements that must be included. War is a violent activity carried out by organized groups; war is a mutual activity in which two or more groups are trying to defeat one another while attempting to avoid their own defeat; and war is waged with the goal of victory. In the modern view, there are three broad levels or divisions of war: **tactics, operational art,** and **strategy**. Over the years, the U.S. Army has developed what can be termed an American way of war. The United States justifies its wars as defending American lives, property, or values and frequently mobilizes its military forces for idealistic crusades. The nation long relied on citizen–soldiers rather than a large, standing army to wage its wars. Until the **Cold War**, the United States did not maintain large, peacetime forces. The military forces of the United States rely on massive firepower to overwhelm its foes, as a way of saving as many American lives as possible. Although most Americans see themselves as peace loving, the United States has exhibited the capability of waging devastating warfare that frequently demands unconditional surrender of its opponents and takes advantage of the most sophisticated weaponry that technology can provide.

WAR DEPARTMENT. Executive department for military affairs prior to 1947. The **Continental Army** was initially administered by the Continental Congress. The War Department evolved after a lengthy process of trial and error in military administration. In June 1776, three weeks before the Declaration of Independence, Congress established a Board of War and Ordnance composed of five legislators to oversee raising and outfitting land forces. A year later, in July 1777, the name was changed to the Board of War, which had first three and then five individuals who were not members of Congress; in late 1778, Congress revised the composition of the board to include two members of Congress and three nonmembers; and in 1781 Congress set up a War Office headed by a **secretary at war**, although Congress often continued to act directly on military matters. In August 1789, three months after **George Washington** became the first president, Congress created the War Department as the executive office for military matters. The department was headed by the newly designated **secretary of war**, who replaced the earlier secretary at war and who was responsible to the president, commander in chief of the military forces of the United States, rather than to Congress. Over time, the organization of the department added and modified a series of bureaus intended to handle specific functions. In the absence of any retirement system, the bureau chiefs enjoyed virtual lifetime appointments, thereby greatly limiting the actual influence of secretaries who came and went every few years. Real power lay in a congressional–bureau alliance that produced a geographical pattern of army expenditures that bore little relation to a national conception of military policy. Lacking an effective internal mechanism for coordination, the War Department suffered from overlapping and conflicting functions among the largely autonomous bureaus.

During the **Spanish–American War**, the bureaus encountered significant problems in transportation, supply, and medical affairs. After the war, a presidential commission recommended changes to War Department operations, particularly consolidation of supply bureau functions. When Secretary of War **Elihu Root** took office in August 1899, he heeded the commission's recommendations and argued that a modern army must be able both to plan efficiently for future operations and to exert executive control over current ones. His efforts resulted in the creation of a **general staff** to replace the bureaus and of a **chief of staff of the army** to replace the **commanding general of the army**. The War Department became the **Department of the Army** in 1947, under the **National Security Act** of that year.

WAR OF 1812 (1812–1815). Significant causes of the War of 1812 included the continuing conflict between British and U.S. interests in the Northwest Territory and the desire of American expansionists to seize Canada while the Great Britain was preoccupied with the Napoleonic Wars in Europe. In the first year of the war, the army struggled with mismanagement in the **War Department**, incompetent generals, and militia forces that refused to serve outside U.S. boundaries. By 1814, the army had largely redeemed itself. In July of that year, near the Canadian village of **Chippewa**, American troops under **Winfield Scott** stood their ground against British regulars, supposedly causing the surprised and impressed enemy commander to shout, "Those are regulars, by God!" Two months later, the army's spirited defense of **Fort McHenry** near Baltimore inspired Francis Scott Key to write the words to the "Star Spangled Banner," which became the American national anthem.

The Treaty of Ghent ended the war on 24 December 1914 and restored the prewar status quo between the United States and Great Britain. In January 1815, **Andrew Jackson** secured the Mississippi Valley for the United States with his defeat of the British at **New Orleans**, even though the war had been formally ended a month earlier. Although the United States failed in its bid to conquer Canada or obtain concessions from Great Britain on neutral rights, the army's performance during the war gained it respect abroad and inspired a sense of national pride and confidence at home. *See also* War of 1812 campaigns in Appendix 6, Campaigns of the United States Army.

WAR ON TERRORISM (2001–). On 11 September 2001, Muslim terrorists attacked the United States homeland by flying airliners into buildings in New York

City and Washington, D.C., killing more than 3,000 people. Four airliners were hijacked and then used as weapons of war in closely coordinated suicide attacks that came as a complete surprise. Two planes were flown into the two World Trade Center towers in New York City, destroying both buildings. Another airliner was flown into the Pentagon, just outside Washington, D.C. A fourth plane, believed to be heading for a second target in Washington, D.C., crashed into the Pennsylvania countryside when passengers attempted to overpower the hijackers. The plane that hit the Pentagon killed a number of soldiers, including the army's deputy chief of staff for personnel, a lieutenant general.

The events of 11 September prompted the president of the United States, George W. Bush, to declare a war on terrorism, to be conducted against the perpetrators of the attacks and any governments that supported them. He also instituted a homeland defense program to increase security and awareness among the American public of the possibility of further terrorist attacks. Army forces were quickly called upon to support both the homeland defense efforts and the war on terrorism.

Nearly 300 military policemen from three Maryland **Army National Guard** units helped secure the Pentagon crash site. Among the first rescue workers at the Pentagon were dozens of soldiers from **Walter Reed** Army Medical Center. Search-and-rescue teams spent the night digging through rubble at the Pentagon to uncover casualties, while army medics set up a treatment station in the center courtyard of the Pentagon and treated at least three firemen for smoke inhalation. Within days of the attack, the **U.S. Army Reserve**'s 311th Quartermaster Mortuary Affairs Company, based in Puerto Rico, arrived to begin identifying remains of people killed in the attack. In New York City, the Army **Corps of Engineers** supported the extensive recovery operations that began immediately after the attacks on the World Trade Center. Army engineers provided emergency electrical power for the recovery operation and the opening of the financial district. Corps employees completed a debris operations plan for New York City and the Federal Emergency Management Agency. Structural experts and surveyors from the corps were sent to New York to help the city evaluate some of the more complicated building situations.

In October, the United States began an extensive bombing campaign in Afghanistan, a country long suspected of harboring terrorists. The military action included the army's **special operations forces** and other units. Very early in the campaign, **Special Forces** teams were on the ground in Afghanistan providing assistance to the Northern Alliance, an opposition force to the ruling Taliban regime, which was protecting Osama bin Laden, the mastermind behind the 11 September attacks. On 19 October, army **rangers** and Special Forces soldiers conducted raids on an airfield in southern Afghanistan. In November, elements of the army's 10th Mountain Division deployed in Afghanistan to provide force protection for U.S. troops at an old Soviet air base outside of Kabul, the capital of the country. December saw the first U.S. military casualties in Afghanistan. Three Special Forces **noncommissioned officers** were killed and 19 other soldiers were wounded north of Kandahar, Afghanistan, when a 2,000-pound U.S. bomb missed its intended target. A U.S. Air Force B-52 bomber supporting the ground forces apparently dropped the bomb about 100 meters from two Special Forces teams and Afghan opposition fighters.

As part of the campaign against terrorism, the army's **reserve components** prepared to help provide security for America's air travelers. About 10,000 National Guard and U.S. Army Reserve troops were to be activated to support America's homeland defense and civil-support operations. Within months of the attacks, 5,000 National Guard soldiers deployed to 422 commercial airports nationwide to provide an immediate improvement in security. More reserve component soldiers were called to active duty to support the war in Afghanistan.

WARRANT OFFICER. An officer appointed by a warrant from the **secretary of the army**. Warrant officers are technical experts who manage and maintain increasingly complex battlefield systems. They can command detachments, units, activities, or vessels. As leaders and technical experts, they provide valuable skills, guidance, and expertise to commanders and organizations in their particular field. The Army Warrant Officer Corps includes more than 25,000 men and women in the **regular army** and **reserve components**. There are five grades of warrant officer. The initial appointment is as a warrant officer (WO1), with promotion to chief warrant officer two (CW2) coming after two years. Competitive promotions to chief warrant officer three (CW3), four (CW4), and five (CW5) occur about every six years for aviation warrant officers and five years for warrant officers in other technical fields. *See also* Appendix 8, United States Army Rank Insignia; COMMISSIONED OFFICER; ENLISTED; NONCOMMISSIONED OFFICER.

WASHINGTON, GEORGE (1732–1799). Commanding general of the army from 1775 to 1783 and from 1798 to 1799. Born in Virginia, Washington was a district adjutant general in the Virginia militia at the age of 20. In 1754, as a lieutenant colonel, he led an unsuccessful campaign against the French at Fort Duquesne in the upper Ohio Valley. He became the commander of the Virginia militia in 1755 and was a Virginia delegate to the First and Second Continental Congresses in 1774 and 1775. On 15 June 1775, Congress elected him general and commander-in-chief of the Continental Army, a position he held until 23 December 1783.

Washington led the Continental Army through the **Boston, Trenton, Princeton, Brandywine, Germantown, Monmouth**, and **Yorktown** campaigns. His drive and determination motivated the soldiers of the army during the **Revolutionary War** and he communicated regularly with the Congress and the state governors to ensure that the coalition of thirteen sovereign states held together. Although the army suffered a series of defeats in the first years of fighting the British, Washington learned from early mistakes and led the nation to victory at Yorktown in 1781, the deciding battle of the war. He resigned as commander-in-chief in December 1783 and returned to his plantation at Mount Vernon in Virginia.

He served as the president of the Constitutional Convention in 1787 and was the first president of the United States, from 1789 to 1797. From 13 July 1798 until his death on 14 December 1799, he served a second term as the senior officer of the army. In 1976, Congress posthumously appointed Washington **general of the armies** of the United States, making him the highest-ranking officer to have served in the U.S. Army. *See also* Appendix 2, Resolution of the Continental Congress Appointing George Washington as Commander in Chief of the Continental Army; Appendix 3, Commanding Generals and Chiefs of Staff of the Army.

WAYNE, ANTHONY (1745–1796). Commanding general of the army from 1792 to 1796. Born in Pennsylvania, Wayne was educated at his uncle's private academy, where he studied surveying, and later supervised a land settlement project in Nova Scotia. In January 1776, Congress made him a colonel of the Fourth Pennsylvania Battalion, and a year later he was appointed a brigadier general in the **Continental Army**. He was wounded at Three Rivers, served with distinction at **Brandywine**, and fought at **Germantown, Monmouth,** and **Yorktown**. He blocked the British occupation of West Point when **Benedict Arnold** defected in 1780. Wayne left the army in 1783 and from 1791 to 1792 represented the state of Georgia in Congress. President **George Washington** appointed him commanding general of the army in 1792 to rebuild the army, and he served as the senior officer in the army from 13 April that year until his death on 15 December 1796. In 1794, During the **Miami** Indian campaign, Wayne routed the northwestern Indians at the battle of Fallen Timbers. He later died near Erie, Pennsylvania, while traveling home from the frontier. *See also* Appendix 3, Commanding Generals and Chiefs of Staff of the Army.

WEDEMEYER, ALBERT COADY (1896–1990). World War II army general. Born in Nebraska, Wedemeyer graduated from the **U.S. Military Academy** in 1919. He saw service in China and the Philippines and was an exchange student at the German *Kriegsakademie*. He was the primary author of the "Victory Plan," which laid out the broad strategy for mobilizing American resources for World War II. During the war, he participated in the councils that managed the war from Washington, D.C. In 1944, he replaced General **Joseph Stilwell** in China as commander and the chief of staff to Chiang Kai-shek. After the war, Wedemeyer recommended continued U.S. support for the Nationalist Chinese. He retired from active service in 1951. His memoirs are particularly critical of U.S. and British World War II policies that allowed the rise of communism after the war. He believed that had China remained friendly to the West, neither the **Korean War** nor the **Vietnam War** would have occurred.

WEEKS, JOHN WINGATE (1860–1926). Secretary of war from 1921 to 1925. Born in New Hampshire, Weeks attended local schools and taught school for a year while still a teenager. He graduated from the U.S. Naval Academy in 1881 and served in the navy until 1883. He served with the Massachusetts naval militia on coastal patrol during the **Spanish–American War** and retired from the naval reserve in 1900 as a rear admiral. Weeks served in a variety of elected positions, including U.S. representative and U.S. senator, and was a Republican candidate for president in 1916, before being appointed secretary of war in 1921. While secretary, he supervised the final transition of the army to a peacetime footing after **World War I**, established the Army Industrial College, and appeared before Congress to defend the adequacy of U.S. air defenses against charges made by General **William Mitchell**. He resigned in 1925 and died at Lancaster, New Hampshire, on 12 July 1926. *See also* Appendix 4, Secretaries of War and Secretaries of the Army.

WESTERN PACIFIC (15 June 1944 to 2 September 1945). World War II campaign streamer. After capturing the Marshall Islands during the **Eastern Mandates** campaign in the first half of 1944, Admiral Chester Nimitz, commanding the U.S. forces moving along the **Central Pacific** route of advance toward Japan, turned his attention to the Mariana Islands. From bases in the Marianas, the Allies could support further naval operations and conduct air strikes against Japanese industrial and military installations. In anticipation of operations in the Western Pacific, on 16 February Nimitz launched a massive carrier raid on Truk Island in the Caroline Islands and, in two-and-a-half days of bombing, rendered it untenable for the Japanese. The Allies had long considered Truk to be Japan's key bastion in the Central Pacific and, with the success of the February raid, Nimitz prepared for an invasion of the Marianas in June, to be followed in September by an advance into the western Carolines.

Nimitz invaded the Marianas with amphibious assaults by U.S. Army and Marine forces on Saipan on 15 June 1944, on Guam on 20 July, and on Tinian on 23 July. All three islands were strongly garrisoned by Japanese troops who contested every yard of ground. The fall of Saipan on 9 July, at a cost of 10,437 U.S. Marine and 3,674 U.S. Army casualties, precipitated a political crisis in Japan that resulted in the fall of the cabinet of Hideki Tojo. Resistance on Guam ended on 10 August with 7,800 U.S. casualties. Tinian fell on 1 August and gave the Allies one of the best bomber bases in the Pacific, paid for by 328 dead and 1,571 wounded U.S. soldiers and marines. With the Marianas secured, the next step in the island-hopping campaign was the Palau Islands, the last Japanese-held islands between the Americans and the Philippines. Capturing the Marianas brought Japan within reach of the army air forces' huge new bomber, the B-29 Superfortress, which was able to make a nonstop flight of the 1,400 miles to Tokyo and back. Construction of airfields to accommodate B-29s began in the Marianas before the shooting had stopped and, in late November 1944, strategic bombing of Japan began. Destruction wrought on the cities of Japan was enormous. Thousands of Japanese civilians were killed and millions were made homeless by the bombing, but only a relatively small percentage of Japan's industrial facilities were destroyed, not enough to seriously affect the Japanese capacity to resist.

On 15 September, a marine division landed on Peleliu Island, met strong resistance, and by 20 September held only a small beachhead. Two days later, an army division landed on the smaller, less heavily defended Angaur Island, and by

20 September had most of the island under its control, although it took another ten days for the island to be declared secure. With the situation well in hand on Angaur, an army **regiment** moved to Peleliu on 23 September, followed by a second army regiment on 15 October, and the island was finally declared secure on 27 November. With the two islands secure, fighting effectively ended, although the official end of the campaign did not come until the end of the war.

WESTMORELAND, WILLIAM CHILDS (1914–). Chief of staff of the army from 1968 to 1972. Born in South Carolina, Westmoreland graduated from the **U.S. Military Academy** in 1936. He participated in **World War II** in Africa and Europe. After the war, he taught at the **Command and General Staff College** and the **Army War College**. During the **Korean War**, he commanded an **airborne** regimental combat team. In 1964, Westmoreland became the commander of the U.S. Military Assistance Command in the **Vietnam War**. He served in this post during the buildup of U.S. forces and escalation of hostilities and was selected to be chief of staff in 1968. While in office, he supervised the disengagement from Vietnam and the end of the draft and he focused his efforts on improving service life, officer professionalism, job attractiveness, and public understanding of the army. He retired from active duty in 1972 and ran unsuccessfully for governor of South Carolina in 1974. In 1982, Westmoreland sued the CBS television network for libel after it broadcast a program charging him with keeping intelligence estimates of enemy strength low. The controversial case was settled out of court in 1985. *See also* Appendix 3, Commanding Generals and Chiefs of Staff of the Army.

WEST POINT. Revolutionary War fort and site of the **U.S. Military Academy**. During the Revolutionary War, the commanding plateau on the west bank of the Hudson River was strategically important to both sides because it controlled traffic on the river. **George Washington** considered West Point to be the most important strategic position in America. He selected Thaddeus Kosciuszko to design the fortifications for West Point in 1778 and a year later Washington transferred his headquarters there. During the war, **Continental Army** soldiers built forts, batteries, and redoubts and extended a 150-ton iron chain across the Hudson to control river traffic. The position was never captured by the British, despite **Benedict Arnold**'s treason, and West Point remains the oldest continuously occupied military post in America.

WEST, TOGO DENNIS, JR. (1942–). Secretary of the army from 1993 to 1998. Born in North Carolina, West was valedictorian at Atkins High School and graduated from Howard University with degrees in electrical engineering in 1965 and law in 1968. He was law clerk for Judge Harold R. Tyler Jr. in New York until 1969, when he received a commission in the **Judge Advocate General Corps**, where he served until 1973. From then until 1993, he alternated between the private practice of law and government service in the Department of Defense. On 22 November 1993, West became secretary of the army and he served until 1998, when he became the secretary of veterans affairs. *See also* Appendix 4, Secretaries of War and Secretaries of the Army.

WEYAND, FREDERICK CARLTON (1916–). Chief of staff of the army from 1974 to 1976. Born in California, Weyand attended the University of California at Berkeley and was commissioned a second lieutenant through the **Reserve Officers' Training Corps** in 1938. He served in the China–Burma–India theater during **World War II** and commanded an infantry battalion in the **Korean War**. After the war, he was a military assistant to the **secretary of the army** and in 1958 he graduated from the **Army War College**. He commanded a **division** and a **field force** during the **Vietnam War** and was a military adviser to the Paris Peace talks in 1969, before taking command of the U.S. Military Assistance Command in Vietnam. Weyand became the chief of staff in 1974 and retired in 1976. While chief of staff, he oversaw the army's moves to improve its combat-to-support troop ratio, achieve a 16-division force, and improve personnel and logistical readiness. *See also* Appendix 3, Commanding Generals and Chiefs of Staff of the Army.

WHEELER, EARLE GILMORE (1908–1975). Chief of staff of the army from 1962 to 1964. Born in Washington, D.C., Wheeler graduated from the **U.S. Military Academy** in 1932. He served in China for three years before attending the **Command and General Staff College** in 1942. He served in **World War II** and graduated from the **Army War College** on his way to becoming chief of staff in 1962. While in office, he undertook a substantial reorganization of the army and responded to the Cuban missile crisis, the school integration conflict, and the increased troop deployment during the **Vietnam War**. Wheeler served as chairman of the Joint Chiefs of Staff from 1964 to 1970. While he was chairman, the United States increased its troop strength in Vietnam. After shifts in public opinion resulted in deescalation of the war, he oversaw the Vietnamization program, whereby South Vietnamese forces assumed increased responsibility for the conduct of the war. He retired in 1970 and died in Frederick, Maryland, in 1975. *See also* Appendix 3, Commanding Generals and Chiefs of Staff of the Army.

WHITE, THOMAS E. (1944–). Secretary of the army from 31 May 2001. Born in Michigan, White graduated from the **U.S. Military Academy** in 1967. He served two tours of duty in Vietnam, held several command and staff positions, and graduated from the **Army War College**, before retiring as a brigadier general in 1990. Before becoming secretary of the army, he had been an executive with Enron Energy Services. Since the terrorist attacks on 11 September 2001, he has overseen the army's role in the U.S. **war on terrorism**. *See also* Appendix 4, Secretaries of War and Secretaries of the Army.

WICKHAM, JOHN ADAMS, JR. (1928–). Chief of staff of the army from 1983 to 1987. Born in New York, Wickham graduated from the **U.S. Military Academy** in 1950. After troop duty in Europe, he attended Harvard University and held a number of positions, including aide to the chief of staff of the army. He saw service in the **Vietnam War** and was an aide to the secretary of defense for three years, before becoming chief of staff in 1983. While in office, Wickham increased the size of the army to 18 regular divisions and 10 reserve divisions and urged measures to care for army families. He retired from active service in 1987. *See also* Appendix 3, Commanding Generals and Chiefs of Staff of the Army.

WILDERNESS (4–7 May 1864). Civil War campaign streamer. In early May 1864, the Army of the Potomac, under General **George G. Meade**, consisted of three infantry corps of about 25,000 men each and a cavalry corps. General **Ambrose Burnside**'s **corps** of 20,000 men, which **Ulysses S. Grant**, commanding general of the Union Armies, kept directly under his command for a time before assigning it to Meade, brought the striking force to a total strength of more than 100,000 effectives. General Benjamin Franklin Butler's Army of the James, operating on the peninsula between Richmond and Hampton, Virginia, numbered about 25,000. On the Confederate side, General **Robert E. Lee**'s Army of Northern Virginia, about 70,000 strong, was organized into three infantry corps, under Generals **James Longstreet**, Richard S. Ewell, and A. P. Hill, and a cavalry corps under Major General J. E. B. Stuart. Meade's forces were located generally north of the Rapidan River, east of Culpepper, while Lee's were west and south of **Chancellorsville** in an area known as the Wilderness. Meade's forces, including Burnside's corps, moved south across the Rapidan on 4 May, attempting to slip past Lee's right (east) flank and envelop the Confederate Army. When the Union forces halted briefly near Chancellorsville, Lee struck hard at Meade's right (west) flank. Grant and Meade swung the troops into line and fought back. The battle continued during 5 and 6 May without a decision, but the Union attempt to envelop Lee had failed. Of 101,895 Federals engaged, 2,246 were killed, 12,037 wounded, and 3,383 were missing. Confederate losses were estimated at about 7,750 killed and wounded.

WILKINS, WILLIAM (1779–1865). Secretary of war from 1844 to 1845. Born in Pennsylvania, Wilkins moved to Pittsburgh with his family in 1783 and graduated from Dickinson College in Carlisle in 1802. He studied law and returned to Pittsburgh to become a member of the Allegheny County bar. After election to the state legislature in 1819, he resigned in 1820 to become the presiding judge of the Fifth Judicial District. He was elected to the U.S. House of Representatives in 1828, but resigned before taking office. Elected to the U.S. Senate in 1831, Wilkins resigned to become minister to Russia and then in 1844 became secretary of war. While in office, he favored territorial expansion and the annexation of Texas. Leaving office in 1845, he returned to Pittsburgh, where he served in the Pennsylvania Senate and became a major general in the home guard. He died in Pittsburgh on 23 June 1865. *See also* Appendix 4, Secretaries of War and Secretaries of the Army.

WILKINSON, JAMES (1757–1825). Commanding general of the army from 1796 to 1798 and from 1800 to 1812. Born in Maryland, Wilkinson studied medicine in Philadelphia before becoming a captain in the **Continental Army** in 1775. Promoted to brigadier general, he was also secretary of the Board of War, the predecessor to the **War Department**, until he was forced to resign both positions in 1778 because of his role in a cabal against the commander in chief, **George Washington**. He became clothier general of the army in 1779, but resigned in 1781 because of irregularities in accounts. He participated in civil and militia activities in Pennsylvania and Kentucky, until returning to federal service as a lieutenant colonel in 1791. Wilkinson became the senior officer in the army in 1796 and served in that capacity until 1798, when he was transferred to the southern frontier to deal with regional Indian tribes. In 1800, he was once again the senior officer in the army and he served until 1812, when he was the subject of a congressional inquiry into his private ventures and intrigues. A court-martial cleared him in 1811. He served as a major general in the **War of 1812** and was relieved from active service in 1813, after a failed invasion of Montreal during the **Canada campaign**. He was later cleared of any wrongdoing by a military inquiry board. *See also* Appendix 3, Commanding Generals and Chiefs of Staff of the Army.

WINTER–SPRING 1970 (1 November 1969 to 30 April 1970). Vietnam War campaign streamer. In November 1969, an increase in enemy attacks marked the start of a Communist winter offensive. The offensive was highlighted by increased harassment incidents and attacks throughout South Vietnam. The attacks were heaviest around Saigon and were directed primarily against South Vietnamese military installations to disrupt the pacification program. By February 1970, the focus of enemy activity shifted north and it reached a peak in April 1970. Communist forces staged their heaviest attacks in the central highlands, near Civilian Irregular Defense Group camps at Dak Seang, Dak Pek, and Ben Het. They also conducted numerous attacks by fire and several sapper attacks against U.S. fire support bases. U.S. and South Vietnamese forces concentrated on operations to destroy enemy forces, penetrate base camps and installations, and seize enemy supplies and materiel. These operations sought to deny the enemy the initiative and to inflict heavy losses in men and materiel. During this period, three brigades of the U.S. Army's 1st Infantry Division were withdrawn from Vietnam.

WOMEN'S ARMY CORPS. In May 1942, as part of the mobilization effort for **World War II**, Congress established a Women's Army Auxiliary Corps (WAAC). The WAACs were noncombatants served under separate regulations. By 1943, there were more than 60,000 on active duty, with almost 1,000 in England and Africa. Congress eliminated "Auxiliary" from the name in September 1943 and "WACs" were given the same grade titles, pay, benefits, and privileges as men, but could not command male units, serve in combat, or be promoted higher than lieutenant colonel, with one exception. **Oveta Culp Hobby**, the first director of the WAAC and the WAC, held the rank of colonel.

WAACs had held jobs only as clerks, cooks, drivers, and telephone operators, but with the change to "WAC" they were eligible for a wider variety of positions.

By the end of World War II, WACs were serving in all theaters of war in virtually all noncombat jobs. After the war, the **chief of staff of the army, Dwight D. Eisenhower**, recognized the valuable wartime service of WACs and wanted the WAC to become part of the **regular army** and the Organized Reserve Corps. In 1948, therefore, Congress made the WAC a branch of the army. For the next 30 years, WACs served in the army in separate units commanded by women. During that time, directors of the corps worked to remove restrictions placed on WACs and, in 1967, their efforts were rewarded with a bill that gave them equal status for retirement and promotion.

In 1971 a WAC officer was promoted to brigadier general for the first time. Women continued to see improvements after 1967, as further statutory changes allowed them to command men, fly noncombat aircraft, remain on active duty while pregnant, and attend senior service schools. In 1978, with women serving throughout the army, Congress eliminated the WAC as a separate branch. Not all women in uniform were happy with the change. Some missed the camaraderie of women serving together and the cohesiveness of their units. By the 1990s, women were serving in most **branches of the army**. *See also* UNITED STATES ARMY RESERVE; WOMEN IN THE ARMY.

WOMEN IN THE ARMY. Women have played a role in the army since its creation in 1775, but until early in the twentieth century their status was generally informal and limited to such positions as nurse or laundress, although there a few women who disguised themselves and fought as men. The **Army Nurse Corps** was created in 1901, but its members were not initially accorded proper military rank or status. The Women's Army Auxiliary Corps was created in 1942 and a year later it became the **Women's Army Corps**. In 1948, Congress passed the Women's Armed Services Integration Act, which allowed women to hold rank and accorded them military privileges, but excluded them from combat, set limits on the percentage of the army that women could constitute, and prohibited them from holding rank higher than lieutenant colonel.

The restrictions on rank and the numbers of women in the army were lifted in 1967 as the army faced a recruiting shortage as a result of the unpopular **Vietnam War**. The number of women in the army rose over the next few years and the first women were promoted to general officer in 1970. The elimination of the draft and adoption of the **All-Volunteer Force** in 1973 led to changes in personnel policies that allowed women to command units with both men and women, ended separate training for male and female recruits, and stopped the mandatory discharge of pregnant women. In 1976, women were admitted to the **U.S. Military Academy** for the first time. Women served in all major military deployments in the 1990s. Some 800 female soldiers served in the **Panama** campaign and thousands more deployed during the **Persian Gulf War**.

WOOD, LEONARD (1860–1927). Chief of staff of the army from 1910 to 1914. Born in New Hampshire, Wood was educated at Pierce Academy in Middleboro, Massachusetts, before attending Harvard Medical School, where he became a doctor of medicine in 1884. The next year, he became a contract surgeon with the army. In 1889, he became a line officer, but was considered something of an outsider by many career officers. He fought in the final **Indian wars** and earned a **Medal of Honor** for his conduct in the campaign that captured **Geronimo**. In 1898, during the **Spanish–American War**, he was a colonel in the Rough Riders, before turning the command over to **Theodore Roosevelt**. Wood was governor of the Moro Province in the Philippine Islands from 1903 to 1906 and became chief of staff of the army on 22 April 1910. While chief of staff, he was a leading proponent of national preparedness, streamlined army administrative procedures, and increased officer strength. He strengthened the reorganization begun by his predecessor, **James Franklin Bell**, and joined with **Henry Lewis Stimson**, the **secretary of war**, to shift the considerable power of the **adjutant general** to the chief of staff and the **general staff**.

After leaving office in 1914, Wood spent **World War I** training recruits in Kansas and resenting not having received a combat command in France. An ambitious man, he ignored the traditional restrictions on military officers being involved in politics and attempted to gain a presidential nomination in 1920 while still on active duty. He served on a special mission to the Philippines before retiring in 1921 to become the governor general of the Philippines, where he served until he died of a brain tumor in 1927. *See also* Appendix 3, Commanding Generals and Chiefs of Staff of the Army.

WOODRING, HARRY HINES. (1890–1967). Secretary of war from 1936 to 1940. Born in Kansas, Woodring was educated in public schools and at the age of 16 started working as a janitor at a bank where he eventually became owner. He enlisted in the army as a private and was commissioned a second lieutenant during **World War I**. After the war, he sold his bank and was elected governor of Kansas before becoming the assistant secretary of war, in which capacity he supervised procurement matters. Becoming secretary in 1936, he continued the recommendation of his predecessor to increase the strength of the **regular army, Army National Guard**, and Reserve Corps. He also directed revision of mobilization plans and stressed the need to perfect the peacetime protective force. Woodring returned temporarily to private life in 1940, ran unsuccessfully for governor of Kansas in 1946, and ran for the Democratic nomination for that post in 1956. He died at Topeka, Kansas, on 9 September 1967. *See also* Appendix 4, Secretaries of War and Secretaries of the Army; UNITED STATES ARMY RESERVE.

WOOLDRIDGE, WILLIAM (1922–). Sergeant major of the army from 1966 to 1968. Born in Oklahoma, Wooldridge moved with his family to Texas in 1925. He enlisted in the army in 1940 and served on detached duty with British forces in Iceland for the first three years of **World War II**. In 1944, he received two **Silver Stars** in Europe. He served in a variety of units in the United States and Europe and in the **Vietnam War** before being selected to be the first sergeant major of the army in 1966. While in that post, he spent almost half of his time on the road to attain a sense of what the **enlisted** ranks were thinking so he could communicate this to the **chief of staff of the army**. Wooldridge became the **sergeant major** of the Military Assistance Command in Vietnam in 1968 and he retired in 1972. His reputation was later tarnished by his part in a scandal involving the army's **noncommissioned officers'** clubs in Vietnam. *See also* Appendix 5, Sergeants Major of the Army.

WORLD WAR I (1917–1918). Within three months of America's entry into World War I, the U.S. Army's 1st Infantry Division was marching through Paris in a Fourth of July parade that raised French spirits and offered tangible evidence of the U.S. commitment. After a number of gloomy predictions that an unprepared America would be unable to provide timely help to the Allies, the presence of U.S. troops elated the British and French and dashed German morale.

When the United States entered the war, Allied leaders believed they now had a renewed supply of bodies to once again throw against the German trenches. They wanted to take whatever troops and units the U.S. Army could provide and integrate them into their operations. American officers, however, were not at all receptive to the French and British plan. The **Civil War** had taught Americans that entrenched defensive positions exacted a deadly toll from an attacking force, but Europeans had not yet learned that lesson and repeatedly launched strategic offensive operations involving millions of men, only to see them dissolve in the

10. *A gun crew from the 6th Field Artillery provides support in September 1918.*

U.S. Army Military History Institute.

smoke and mud of the Western Front. General **John J. Pershing**, commander of the American Expeditionary Force, insisted that U.S. forces would fight only under American commanders using American **doctrine** to conduct operations. His insistence on an independent American command in World War I has come to be an enduring characteristic of U.S. Army operations.

U.S. Army forces saw their first combat at **Cambrai** in late 1917. During the first half of 1918, American soldiers and their officers gained experience by participating in a number of Allied campaigns. When the German offensive of 1918 penetrated to the outskirts of the French capital, American soldiers played a key role in turning back the enemy tide at Chateau-Thierry in June during the **Aisne** campaign. Two months later, the First U.S. Army launched its initial offensive at **St. Mihiel**. In the **Meuse–Argonne** campaign, the American Expeditionary Force made a significant contribution to the final Allied drive before the armistice in November 1918. World War I ended on 11 November 1918 at 1100. The Treaty of Versailles, negotiated at the Paris Peace Conference in 1919, set territorial losses, divided the colonial possessions of the losers, and set German reparations.

World War I was fought primarily on the ground by armies of **infantry** whose primary method of mobility was walking, but by the end of the war the machines that would dominate the future of warfare made their debut. On land, the internal combustion engine powered **tanks** and trucks, revolutionizing tactical mobility much as railroads had changed strategic mobility in the nineteenth century, and the new engines expanded warfare into a new dimension in heavier-than-air machines that carried men into the sky. The army initially saw the airplane as the eyes of the ground forces, seeking out and reporting the locations of enemy formations. The fragile nature of early aircraft argued that realistically there could be no combat role for them, and in the U.S. Army they were assigned to the **Signal Corps**. In World War I, however, European armies routinely used airplanes in combat. When America entered the war, air operations were already a part of warfare. During the war, the U.S. Army relied on Europeans for airplanes, but the experience laid the foundations for American air power. Air power advocates such as **William Mitchell** began to push for a separate air service, independent of the army. *See also* World War I campaigns in Appendix 6, Campaigns of the United States Army.

WORLD WAR II (1941–1945). In World War II, the U.S. Army faced a variety of opponents in several different theaters of operations in Africa, Asia, Europe, and the Pacific. After the Japanese attack on Pearl Harbor in December 1941, the army's major tasks were to stave off further disaster, preserve American morale, and prepare to go on the offensive. The first few months of the war brought mostly bad news. In the **Philippine Islands**, cut off from relief, American forces under **Douglas MacArthur** held out for over four months against overwhelming Japanese air, naval, and ground power before finally surrendering in May 1942. When MacArthur, complying with Roosevelt's orders to remove himself to Australia prior to the surrender, vowed to return, it gave the nation a symbol of defiance.

But when the army began offensive operations later in 1942, its soldiers received a rude introduction to modern combat. At the beginning of the **Papua** campaign in the Pacific, they found themselves bogged down in the jungle against strong Japanese positions. In North Africa, they initially faced little opposition in the **Algeria–French Morocco** campaign, but suffered heavy losses at the hands of German Field Marshal **Erwin Rommel**'s *Afrika Korps* near Kasserine Pass in **Tunisia**.

The army learned from its early mistakes. American troops recovered from the defeat at Kasserine Pass and helped force the surrender of Axis forces in North Africa. Under the leadership of **Dwight D. Eisenhower** and **George S. Patton Jr.**, they joined other Allied forces to drive the Germans and Italians from **Sicily** in late 1943. Facing stiff opposition, American and Allied troops landed on the Italian mainland at **Anzio** in January 1944 and then advanced slowly up the peninsula to Rome. On 6 June 1944, Eisenhower's Allied armies landed in **Normandy** and, after two months of near stalemate in the hedgerows of France, American troops under **Omar N. Bradley** broke through the German defenders and raced across **Northern France** to the German border. In a last-ditch counteroffensive in the **Ardennes–Alsace** campaign in December 1944, the German Army briefly delayed the final Allied push into the German heartland in the spring of 1945. But Germany's unconditional surrender came on 7 May. The surrender document was signed at Reims, France, by Admiral Hans von Friedeburg and General Alfred Jodl for the Germans and Lieutenant Walter Bedell Smith, Eisenhower's chief of staff, for the Allies.

On the other side of the world, MacArthur, commanding Allied forces in the Southwest Pacific theater, began leapfrogging his forces along the northern **New Guinea** coastline. Army troops joined their U.S. Navy and Marine Corps counterparts to advance through the **Northern Solomons** as the Allies moved across the Pacific, approaching ever closer to the Japanese homeland. In northern Burma, **Joseph W. Stilwell**'s Chinese army, aided by a special infiltration force of Americans commanded by Frank Merrill, pushed the Japanese defenders back, laid siege to the key crossroads city of Myitkyina, and eventually opened the Burma Road. In October 1944, MacArthur's forces landed at **Leyte** in the Philippine Islands, making good on his 1942 promise to return. By February 1945, American forces had retaken Manila and were reestablishing American authority over the main Philippine island of **Luzon**. A planned invasion of the Japanese home islands proved unnecessary after President **Harry S. Truman** directed dropping the world's first atomic bomb on Hiroshima on 6 August. This was followed by the dropping of a second atomic bomb on Nagasaki on 9 August. Japan surrendered unconditionally on 14 August and a cease-fire went into effect the next day. The formal surrender was signed aboard the U.S. Navy battleship *Missouri* in Tokyo harbor on 2 September.

The army's World War II military operations would not have been possible without the industrial capacity of the United States. With the American homeland untouched by the war, and producing a seemingly endless stream of everything from airplanes that dominated the skies to infantry boots that occupied the ground, it was the epitome of industrial warfare. In Europe, America's arsenal provided the soldiers on the ground with virtually anything they needed to defeat Germany. In the Pacific, the blow that finally forced the Japanese surrender came not from ground combat units but from the American scientific research and development community, as the army supervised the development of the atomic bomb that forced Japan to surrender and finally brought to an end history's greatest armed conflict. *See also* World War II campaigns in Appendix 6, Campaigns of the United States Army.

WOTHERSPOON, WILLIAM WALLACE (1850–1921). Chief of staff of the army for about six months in 1914. Born in Washington, D.C., Wotherspoon served aboard U.S. Navy ships for three years before being commissioned a second lieutenant in the army in 1873. He served in various positions as a company grade officer and participated in the **Philippine Insurrection.** As head of the **Army War College,** he was largely responsible for making it an autonomous institution rather than part of the **general staff.** After a brief period as chief of staff, he retired in 1914 and was the superintendent of public works for the state of New York for a number of years. *See also* Appendix 3, Commanding Generals and Chiefs of Staff of the Army.

WOUNDED KNEE. *See* PINE RIDGE.

WRIGHT, LUKE EDWARD (1846–1922). Secretary of war from 1908 to 1909. Born in Tennessee, Wright attended public schools in Memphis and enlisted in the Confederate Army at the age of 15. He was promoted to second lieutenant in 1863 for bravery under fire. After the **Civil War,** he entered the University of Mississippi in 1867. He did not graduate, but read law in his father's office and entered into practice in Memphis. He was the attorney general for Tennessee before becoming governor of the Philippines in 1904. Wright was appointed ambassador to Japan in 1906 and became secretary of war in 1908. While secretary, he stressed actions to eliminate unfit officers and promoted the army's use of aviation technology. He returned to private life in 1909 and died in Memphis in 1922. *See also* Appendix 4, Secretaries of War and Secretaries of the Army.

— Y —

YANG-TSUN (6 August 1900). China Relief Expedition campaign streamer. On 4 August 1900, an allied force of 18,000 men began moving toward **Peking** (Beijing) to rescue hostages held by the Boxers, a group of fanatic Chinese nationalists. The American contingent, some 2,500 men under **Adna Romanza Chaffee,** included **infantry, cavalry,** and **artillery** units from the army and a battalion of U.S. Marines. On the way to the city, the allied forces fought engagements at Peitsang, which fell on 5 August, and Yang-tsun, which they captured the next day.

YORK, ALVIN CULLUM (1887–1964). Army soldier and **World War I** hero. Born in Tennessee, York was a fundamentalist Christian who disapproved of war. He sought an exemption from military service as a conscientious objector, but his draft board rejected his request. Convinced that God wanted him to fight for his country, he resolved his doubts about fighting. During the **Meuse–Argonne** campaign, he was a corporal serving in the army's 82d Infantry Division. On 8 October 1918, he was one of three section leaders in a 17-man patrol ordered to silence German machine guns that were holding up his battalion's advance near Chatel-Chehery. When the patrol leader and the other two section leaders were killed or wounded during a series of fire fights with German defenders, York took charge and continued the mission. Under his leadership, the patrol eliminated two major obstacles to the battalion's advance, captured 132 prisoners, and evacuated all wounded soldiers, both American and German. York has been credited with capturing 35 machine guns and killing as many as 28 Germans during the action. Although those numbers cannot be verified, there is no doubt that he did capture several guns and kill most of the Germans the patrol encountered. For his heroism, York received the **Distinguished Service Cross**, the French Croix de Guerre, and the **Medal of Honor**. After the war, York rejected offers of commercial ventures and returned home to Tennessee to farm and founded a school for undereducated children. In the years before **World War II**, he approved a film about his life, *Sergeant York*, starring Gary Cooper and supported U.S. defense measures and aid to the Allies.

YORKTOWN (18 September to 19 October 1781). Revolutionary War campaign streamer. After 1778, the main theater of the war shifted to the South as the British tried to reestablish control of that area. By 1781, they were convinced that this could not be accomplished as long as Virginia was a base for American military operations. Therefore, in January 1781 **Henry Clinton**, the British commander in America, sent American turncoat **Benedict Arnold** with 1,600 British troops on a raid up the James River. By late May, the British had accumulated about 7,200 men in Virginia, including the remnants of **Charles Cornwallis**'s force, which had come up from North Carolina after being defeated at the battle at **Guilford Court House**. Cornwallis was given command of the British forces in Virginia and in late May and early June led them on raids deep into the state. Initially, he was opposed only by a smaller force commanded by the **Marquis de Lafayette**, but in mid-June Lafayette was reinforced by troops under **Anthony Wayne** and Baron **Friedrich von Steuben**. Cornwallis turned back to the coast to establish a base at Yorktown from which he could maintain sea communications with Clinton in New York.

In the north, **George Washington** was preparing his army, recently reinforced with about 4,000 French troops under Lieutenant General Jean B. de Rochambeau, for an attack on New York. When he received confirmation that the French fleet had departed the French West Indies with troops that would be available for operations in the Chesapeake Bay area until mid-October, he decided to go to Virginia with a substantial part of his army, including the French regulars under

Rochambeau. Leaving half the American army to keep Clinton in New York, Washington crossed the Hudson River between 20 and 26 August and moved south across New Jersey and Pennsylvania to Maryland. The French fleet arrived off Yorktown on 30 August and debarked 4,800 French regulars to reinforce Lafayette. On 5 September, the fleet fought an indecisive naval engagement off the Virginia capes with a British fleet that Clinton had dispatched to evacuate Cornwallis from Yorktown. After several days of maneuvering at sea, the British fleet retired to New York for repairs, leaving the French fleet in control of Chesapeake Bay and Cornwallis trapped in Yorktown.

With the British fleet in New York, Washington and Rochambeau embarked their forces in Maryland and sailed down the Chesapeake and up the James River to a point near Williamsburg, Virginia. From there, the allied army, numbering about 8,600 Americans and 7,800 French, moved forward on 28 September and began siege operations against Yorktown on 6 October, taking advantage of the heavy French artillery. By 14 October, the British positions were sufficiently weakened to allow the allies to capture key outposts. After a night counterattack on 16 October failed to recapture key defense points, Cornwallis requested an armistice on 17 October and surrendered his command of about 8,000 men on 19 October. The British lost 156 killed and 326 wounded; the Americans lost 20 killed and 56 wounded; and the French lost 52 killed and 134 wounded. Although they still had substantial forces in America, British hopes for victory collapsed with Cornwallis's defeat. The most significant result of the defeat in Yorktown was that British political leaders lost the will to carry on with the war. In March 1782, the new cabinet opened the direct negotiations with the American peace commissioners in Europe that ultimately ended the Revolutionary War.

YOUNG, SAMUEL BALDWIN MARKS (1840–1924). Chief of staff of the army from 1903 to 1904. Born in Pittsburgh, Young attended Jefferson College before enlisting in 1861 as a private in the Pennsylvania infantry, where he was commissioned a captain. He served with the Army of the Potomac during the **Civil War** and after the war entered the **regular army** as a second lieutenant and served on the western frontier. He was on the organizing faculty of the School of Application for Infantry and Cavalry at Fort Leavenworth, Kansas, and he commanded a brigade in both the **Spanish–American War** and the **Philippine Insurrection**. In 1902, Young became the first president of the **Army War College** and was the **commanding general of the army** for one week in 1903, before becoming the first chief of staff of the army. While chief of staff, he supervised the formation of the **general staff**. He retired from active service in 1904. *See also* Appendix 3, Commanding Generals and Chiefs of Staff of the Army.

YPRES–LYS (19 August to 11 November 1918). World War I campaign streamer. In late August and early September 1911, the British Second and Fifth Armies, assisted by the U.S. II Corps, eliminated the Lys salient in Belgium. When the Germans began retiring in the sector south of the Lys in October to shorten their lines, the Belgian army group, which consisted of Belgian, British, and French troops, moved forward. By 20 October, Ostend and Bruges had been captured and the Allied left was at the Dutch frontier. In mid-October, General **John J. Pershing** dispatched two American divisions to the French Army of Belgium to give impetus to the drive to cross the Scheldt River, southwest of Ghent. A general attack began on 31 October and continued intermittently until hostilities ended on 11 November. During the attack, U.S. forces forced a crossing of the Scheldt southeast of Heurne on 2 November and they made a second crossing of the river at the site of the destroyed Hermelgem-Syngem bridge on 10 November. Casualties of the two American divisions in these operations totaled about 2,600. Between 19 August and 11 November, about 108,000 Americans participated in the campaign.

— Z —

ZAPOTE RIVER (13 June 1899). Philippine Insurrection campaign streamer. After the success of Major General Henry W. Lawton's column at Laguna de Bay and San Isidro in April and May 1899, they overran strong insurgent entrenchments on the Zapote River in June. The rainy season in mid-1899 called a halt to further operations in Luzon. During this pause, the first Philippine scout units were organized and large numbers of additional American troops arrived, bringing the strength of the American forces in the Philippines to some 47,500 men by the end of the year. *See also* LAGUNA DE BAY; SAN ISIDRO.

Appendix 1
Resolution of the Continental Congress Adopting the Continental Army, 14 June 1775

The resolutions being read, were adopted as follows:

Resolved, That six companies of expert rifflemen, be immediately raised in Pennsylvania, two in Maryland, and two in Virginia; that each company consist of a captain, three lieutenants, four serjeants, four corporals, a drummer or trumpeter, and sixty-eight privates.

That each company, as soon as compleated, shall march and join the army near Boston, to be there employed as light infantry, under the command of the chief Officer in that army.

That the pay of the Officers and privates be as follows, viz. A captain @ 20 dollars per month; a lieutenant @ 13⅓ dollars; a serjeant @ 8 dollars; a corporal @ 7⅓ dollars; a drummer (or trumpeter) @ 7⅓ doll.; privates @ 6⅔ dollars; to find their own arms and cloaths.

That the form of the enlistment be in the following words:

I have, this day, voluntarily enlisted myself, as a soldier, in the American continental army, for one year, unless sooner discharged: And I do bind myself to conform, in all instances, to such rules and regulations, as are, or shall be, established for the government of the said Army.

Upon motion, *Resolved*, that Mr. [George] Washington, Mr. [Philip] Schuyler, Mr. [Silas] Dean, Mr. [Thomas] Cushing, and Mr. [Joseph] Hewes be a committee to bring in a draft of Rules and Regulations for the government of the army.

Source: Robert K. Wright Jr. and Morris J. MacGregor Jr., *Soldier–Statesmen of the Constitution* (Washington, D.C.: U.S. Army Center of Military History, 1987), 175.

Appendix 2

Resolution of the Continental Congress Appointing George Washington as Commander in Chief of the Continental Army, 15 June 1775

The report of the committee being read and debated,

Resolved, That a General be appointed to command all the continental forces, raised, or to be raised, for the defence of American liberty.

That five hundred dollars, per month, be allowed for his pay and expenses.

The Congress then proceeded to the choice of a general, by ballot, when George Washington, Esq. Was unanimously elected.

Source: Robert K. Wright Jr. and Morris J. MacGregor Jr., *Soldier–Statesmen of the Constitution* (Washington, D.C.: U.S. Army Center of Military History, 1987), 176.

Appendix 3
Commanding Generals
and Chiefs of Staff of the Army

COMMANDING GENERALS, 1775–1903

George Washington	15 June 1775 to 23 December 1783
Henry Knox	23 December 1783 to 20 June 1784
John Doughty	20 June 1784 to 12 August 1784
Josiah Harmar	12 August 1784 to 4 March 1791
Arthur St. Clair	4 March 1791 to 5 March 1792
Anthony Wayne	13 April 1792 to 15 December 1796
James Wilkinson	15 December 1796 to 13 July 1798
George Washington	13 July 1798 to 14 December 1799
Alexander Hamilton	14 December 1799 to 15 June 1800
James Wilkinson	15 June 1800 to 27 January 1812
Henry Dearborn	27 January 1812 to 15 June 1815
Jacob J. Brown	15 June 1815 to 24 February 1828
Alexander Macomb	19 May 1828 to 25 June 1841
Winfield Scott	25 June 1841 to 1 November 1861
George B. McClellan	1 November 1861 to 11 March 1862
Henry W. Halleck	23 July 1862 to 9 March 1864
Ulysses S. Grant	9 March 1864 to 4 March 1869
William T. Sherman	4 March 1869 to 1 November 1883
Philip H. Sheridan	1 November 1883 to 5 August 1888
John M. Schofield	14 August 1888 to 29 September 1895
Nelson A. Miles	5 October 1895 to 8 August 1903

CHIEFS OF STAFF, 1903–

Samuel B. M. Young	15 August 1903 to 8 January 1904
Adna R. Chaffee	9 January 1904 to 14 January 1906
John C. Bates	15 January 1906 to 13 April 1906
J. Franklin Bell	14 April 1906 to 21 April 1910
Leonard Wood	22 April 1910 to 20 April 1914
William W. Wotherspoon	21 April 1914 to 15 November 1914
Hugh L. Scott	16 November 1914 to 21 September 1917
Tasker H. Bliss	22 September 1917 to 18 May 1918
Peyton C. March	19 May 1918 to 30 June 1921

John J. Pershing	1 July 1921 to 13 September 1924
John L. Hines	14 September 1924 to 20 November 1926
Charles P. Summerall	21 November 1926 to 20 November 1930
Douglas MacArthur	21 November 1930 to 1 October 1935
Malin Craig	2 October 1935 to 31 August 1939
George C. Marshall	1 September 1939 to 18 November 1945
Dwight D. Eisenhower	19 November 1945 to 7 February 1948
Omar N. Bradley	7 February 1948 to 16 August 1949
J. Lawton Collins	16 August 1949 to 5 August 1953
Matthew B. Ridgway	5 August 1953 to 30 June 1955
Maxwell D. Taylor	30 June 1955 to 30 June 1959
Lyman L. Lemnitzer	1 July 1959 to 30 September 1960
George H. Decker	1 October 1960 to 30 September 1962
Earle G. Wheeler	1 October 1962 to 2 July 1964
Harold K. Johnson	3 July 1964 to 2 July 1968
William C. Westmoreland	3 July 1968 to 30 June 1972
Bruce Palmer Jr.	1 July 1972 to 11 October 1972
Creighton W. Abrams Jr.	12 October 1972 to 4 September 1974
Frederick C. Weyand	3 October 1974 to 30 September 1976
Bernard W. Rogers	1 October 1976 to 21 June 1979
Edward C. Meyer	22 June 1979 to 21 June 1983
John A. Wickham Jr.	23 June 1983 to 23 June 1987
Carl E. Vuono	23 June 1987 to 21 June 1991
Gordon R. Sullivan	21 June 1991 to 20 June 1995
Dennis J. Reimer	20 June 1995 to 20 June 1999
Eric K. Shinseki	21 June 1999–

Appendix 4
Secretaries of War and Secretaries of the Army

SECRETARIES AT WAR

Benjamin Lincoln	30 October 1781 to 12 November 1783
Henry Knox	8 March 1785 to 11 September 1789

SECRETARIES OF WAR

Henry Knox	12 September 1789 to 31 December 1794
Timothy Pickering	2 January 1795 to 10 December 1795
James McHenry	27 January 1796 to 13 May 1800
Samuel Dexter	13 May 1800 to 31 January 1801
Henry Dearborn	5 March 1801 to 7 March 1809
William Eustis	7 March 1809 to 13 January 1813
John Armstrong	13 January 1813 to 27 September 1814
James Monroe	27 September 1814 to 2 March 1815
William H. Crawford	1 August 1815 to 22 October 1816*
John C. Calhoun	8 October 1817 to 7 March 1825
James Barbour	7 March 1825 to 23 May 1828
Peter B. Porter	26 May 1828 to 9 March 1829
John H. Eaton	9 March 1829 to 18 June 1831*
Lewis Cass	1 August 1831 to 5 October 1836*
Joel R. Poinsett	7 March 1837 to 5 March 1841
John Bell	5 March 1841 to 13 September 1841*
John C. Spencer	12 October 1841 to 3 March 1843
James M. Porter	8 March 1843 to 30 January 1844
William Wilkins	15 February 1844 to 4 March 1845
William L. Marcy	6 March 1845 to 5 March 1849
George W. Crawford	8 March 1849 to 23 July 1850*
Charles M. Conrad	15 August 1850 to 7 March 1853
Jefferson Davis	7 March 1853 to 6 March 1857
John B. Floyd	6 March 1857 to 29 December 1860*
Joseph Holt	18 January 1861 to 5 March 1861
Simon Cameron	5 March 1861 to 15 January 1862
Edwin M. Stanton	20 January 1862 to 28 May 1868*
John M. Schofield	1 June 1868 to 13 March 1869

John A. Rawlins	13 March 1869 to 6 September 1869*
William W. Belknap	25 October 1869 to 2 March 1876
Alphonso Taft	8 March 1876 to 22 May 1876
James D. Cameron	22 May 1876 to 3 March 1877
George W. McCrary	12 March 1877 to 10 December 1879
Alexander Ramsey	10 December 1879 to 5 March 1881
Robert T. Lincoln	5 March 1881 to 5 March 1885
William C. Endicott	5 March 1885 to 5 March 1889
Redfield Procter	5 March 1889 to 5 November 1893*
Stephen B. Elkins	17 December 1891 to 5 March 1893
Daniel S. Lamont	5 March 1893 to 5 March 1897
Russell A. Alger	5 March 1897 to 1 August 1899
Elihu Root	1 August 1899 to 31 January 1904
William H. Taft	1 February 1904 to 30 June 1908
Luke E. Wright	1 July 1908 to 11 March 1909
Jacob M. Dickinson	12 March 1909 to 21 May 1911
Henry L. Stimson	22 May 1911 to 4 March 1913
Lindley M. Garrison	5 March 1913 to 10 February 1916*
Newton D. Baker	9 March 1916 to 4 March 1921
John W. Weeks	5 March 1921 to 13 October 1925
Dwight F. Davis	14 October 1925 to 5 March 1929
James W. Good	6 March 1929 to 18 November 1929
Patrick J. Hurley	9 December 1929 to 3 March 1933
George H. Dern	4 March 1933 to 27 August 1936*
Harry H. Woodring	25 September 1936 to 20 June 1940*
Henry L. Stimson	10 July 1940 to 21 September 1945
Robert P. Patterson	27 September 1945 to 18 July 1947
Kenneth C. Royall	19 July 1947 to 17 September 1947

* Denotes a period when there was a secretary of war ad interim.

SECRETARIES OF WAR AD INTERIM

Alexander J. Dallas	2 March 1815 to 1 August 1815
George Graham	22 October 1816 to 8 October 1817
Levi Woodbury	18 June 1831 to 1 August 1831
Benjamin F. Butler	5 October 1836 to 7 March 1837
Albert Miller Lea	13 September 1841 to 12 October 1841
Winfield Scott	23 July 1850 to 15 August 1850
Joseph Holt	29 December 1860 to 18 January 1861
Ulysses S. Grant	12 August 1867 to 13 January 1868
William T. Sherman	6 September 1869 to 25 October 1869
Lewis A. Grant	5 November 1891 to 17 December 1891
Hugh L. Scott	10 February 1916 to 9 March 1916
Patrick J. Hurley	18 November 1929 to 9 December 1929
Harry H. Woodring	27 August 1936 to 25 September 1936
Louis A. Johnson	20 June 1940 to 10 July 1940

SECRETARIES OF THE ARMY

Kenneth C. Royall	17 September 1947 to 27 April 1949*
Gordon Gray	20 June 1949 to 12 April 1950
Frank Pace Jr.	12 April 1950 to 20 January 1953*
Robert T. Stevens	4 February 1953 to 21 July 1955
Wilber M. Brucker	21 July 1955 to 19 January 1961
Elvis J. Stahr Jr.	25 January 1961 to 30 June 1962
Cyrus Vance	5 July 1962 to 21 January 1964
Stephen Ailes	28 January 1964 to 1 July 1965
Stanley R. Resor	2 July 1965 to 20 June 1971
Robert F. Froehlke	1 July 1971 to 14 May 1973
Howard H. Callaway	15 May 1973 to 3 July 1975*
Martin R. Hoffman	5 August 1975 to 13 February 1977
Clifford L. Alexander Jr.	14 February 1977 to 20 January 1981*
John O. Marsh Jr.	29 January 1981 to 14 August 1989
Michael P. W. Stone	15 August 1989 to 19 January 1993*
Togo Dennis West Jr.	22 November 1993 to 1 January 1998*
Louis E. Caldera	2 July 1998 to 19 January 2001*
Thomas E. White	31 May 2001–

* Denotes a period when there was an acting secretary of the army.

ACTING SECRETARIES OF THE ARMY

Gordon Gray	28 April 1949 to 19 June 1949
Earl D. Johnson	20 January 1953 to 4 February 1953
Norman R. Augustine	3 July 1975 to 5 August 1975
Percy A. Pierre	21 January 1981 to 29 January 1981
John W. Shannon	20 January 1993 to 26 August 1993
Gordon R. Sullivan	27 August 1993 to 21 November 1993
Robert M. Walker	2 January 1998 to 1 July 1998
Gregory R. Dahlberg	20 January 2001 to 4 March 2001
Joseph W. Westphal	5 March 2001 to 30 May 2001

Appendix 5
Sergeants Major of the Army

William O. Wooldridge	11 July 1966 to 31 August 1968
George W. Dunaway	1 September 1968 to 30 September 1970
Silas L. Copeland	1 October 1970 to 30 June 1973
Leon L. Van Autreve	1 July 1973 to 30 June 1975
William G. Bainbridge	1 July 1975 to 30 June 1979
William A. Connelly	1 July 1979 to 30 June 1983
Glen E. Morrell	1 July 1983 to 30 June 1987
Julius W. Gates	1 July 1987 to 30 June 1991
Richard A. Kidd	1 July 1991 to 30 June 1995
Gene C. McKinney	1 July 1995 to October 1997
Robert E. Hall	21 October 1997 to 22 June 2000
Jack L. Tilley	23 June 2000–

Appendix 6
Campaigns of the United States Army

This appendix lists the 174 streamers currently authorized to be carried on the staff of the army flag. Each streamer is 2¾ inches wide by four feet long and carries the embroidered designation and the date(s) of the campaign or battle. The colors are the same as the ribbon awarded to soldiers for service during that war. Each campaign has an entry in this dictionary.

REVOLUTIONARY WAR (1775–1781)
Colors: scarlet with a white stripe

Lexington	19 April 1775
Ticonderoga	10 May 1775
Boston	17 June 1775 to 17 March 1776
Quebec	28 August 1775 to 3 July 1776
Charleston	28–29 June 1776; 29 March to 12 May 1780
Long Island	26–29 August 1776
Trenton	26 December 1776
Princeton	3 January 1777
Saratoga	2 July to 17 October 1777
Brandywine	11 September 1777
Germantown	4 October 1777
Monmouth	28 June 1778
Savannah	29 December 1778; 16 September to 10 October 1779
Cowpens	17 January 1781
Guilford Court House	15 March 1781
Yorktown	28 September to 19 October 1781

WAR OF 1812 (1812–1815)
Colors: scarlet with two white stripes

Canada	18 June 1812 to 17 February 1815
Chippewa	5 July 1814
Lundy's Lane	25 July 1814
Bladensburg	17–29 August 1814
Fort McHenry	13 September 1814
New Orleans	23 September 1814 to 8 January 1815

MEXICAN WAR (1846–1847)
Colors: green with one white stripe

Palo Alto	8 May 1846
Resaca de la Palma	9 May 1846
Monterrey	21 September 1846
Buena Vista	22–23 February 1847
Vera Cruz	9–29 March 1847
Cerro Gordo	17 April 1847
Contreras	18–20 August 1847
Churubusco	20 August 1847
Molino del Rey	8 September 1847
Chapultepec	13 September 1847

CIVIL WAR (1861–1865)
Colors: blue and gray equally divided

Streamers displayed on the Army flag are blue on top and gray on the bottom. Units with service in the Confederate States Army display streamers with gray on top and blue on the bottom. The Bull Run, Manassas, and Antietam campaigns are displayed by such units with streamers embroidered "First Manassas," "Second Manassas," and "Sharpsburg," respectively.

Sumter	12–13 April 1861
Bull Run	16–22 July 1861
Henry and Donelson	6–16 February 1862
Mississippi River	6 February 1862 to 9 July 1863
Peninsula	17 March to 3 August 1862
Shiloh	6–7 April 1862
Valley	15 May to 17 June 1862
Manassas	7 August to 2 September 1862
Antietam	3–17 September 1862
Fredericksburg	9 November to 15 December 1862
Murfreesborough	26 December 1862 to 4 January 1863
Vicksburg	29 March to 4 July 1863
Chancellorsville	27 April to 6 May 1863
Gettysburg	29 June to 3 July 1863
Chickamauga	16 August to 22 September 1863
Chattanooga	23–27 November 1863
Wilderness	4–7 May 1864
Atlanta	7 May to 2 September 1864
Spotsylvania	8–21 May 1864
Cold Harbor	22 May to 3 June 1864
Petersburg	4 June 1864 to 2 April 1865
Shenandoah	7 August to 28 November 1864
Franklin	17–30 November 1864
Nashville	1–16 December 1864
Appomattox	3–9 April 1865

INDIAN WARS (1790–1891)
Colors: scarlet with two black stripes

Miami	January 1790 to August 1795
Tippecanoe	21 September to 18 November 1811
Creeks	27 July 1813 to August 1814; February 1836 to July 1837
Seminoles	20 November 1817 to 31 October 1818; 28 December 1835 to 14 August 1842; 15 December 1855 to May 1858
Black Hawk	26 April to 20 September 1832
Comanches	1867–1875
Modocs	1872–1873
Apaches	1873; 1885–1886
Little Big Horn	1876–1877
Nez Perce	1877
Bannocks	1878
Cheyennes	1878–1879
Utes	September 1879 to November 1880
Pine Ridge	November 1890 to January 1891

SPANISH–AMERICAN WAR (1898)
Colors: yellow with two blue stripes

Santiago	22 June to 11 July 1898
Puerto Rico	25 July to 13 August 1898
Manila	31 July to 13 August 1898

CHINA RELIEF EXPEDITION (1900)
Colors: yellow with blue edges

Tientsin	13 July 1900
Yang-tsun	6 August 1900
Peking	14–15 August 1900

PHILIPPINE INSURRECTION (1899–1913)
Colors: blue with two red stripes

Manila	4 February to 17 March 1899
Iloilo	8–12 February 1899
Malolos	24 March to 16 August 1899
Laguna de Bay	8–17 April 1899
San Isidro	12 April to 30 May 1899; 15 October to 19 November 1899
Zapote River	13 June 1899
Cavite	7–13 October 1899; 4 January to 9 February 1900
Tarlac	5–20 November 1899
San Fabian	6–19 November 1899
Mindanao	4 July 1902 to 31 December 1904; 22 October 1905

Jolo   1–24 May 1905; 6–8 March 1906; 6 August 1906;
                        11–15 June 1913

MEXICAN EXPEDITION (1916–1917)
Colors: yellow with one blue stripe and green borders

Mexico   14 March 1916 to 7 February 1917

WORLD WAR I (1917–1918)
Colors: double rainbow

Cambrai   20 November to 4 December 1917
Somme Defensive   21 March to 6 April 1918
Lys   9–27 April 1918
Aisne   27 May to 5 June 1918
Montdidier–Noyon   9–13 June 1918
Champagne–Marne   15–18 July 1918
Aisne–Marne   18 July to 6 August 1918
Somme Offensive   8 August to 11 November 1918
Oise–Aisne   18 August to 11 November 1918
Ypres–Lys   19 August to 11 November 1918
St. Mihiel   12–16 September 1918
Meuse–Argonne   26 September to 11 November 1918
Vittoria Veneto   24 October to 4 November 1918

WORLD WAR II (1941–1945)

American Theater
Colors: blue with two groupings of white, black, red, and white stripes; blue, white, and red in the center

Antisubmarine   7 December 1941 to 2 September 1945

Asiatic–Pacific Theater
Colors: orange with two white, red, and white stripe groupings; blue, white, and red stripes in the center

Philippine Islands   7 December 1941 to 10 May 1942
Burma, 1942   7 December 1941 to 26 May 1942
Central Pacific   7 December 1941 to 6 December 1943
East Indies   1 January to 22 July 1942
India–Burma   2 April 1942 to 28 January 1945
Air Offensive, Japan   17 April 1942 to 2 September 1945
Aleutian Islands   3 June 1942 to 24 August 1943
China Defensive   4 July 1942 to 4 May 1945
Papua   23 July 1942 to 23 January 1943

Guadalcanal	7 August 1942 to 21 February 1943
New Guinea	24 January 1943 to 31 December 1944
Northern Solomons	22 February 1943 to 21 November 1944
Eastern Mandates	31 January to 14 June 1944
Bismarck Archipelago	15 December 1943 to 27 November 1944
Western Pacific	15 June 1944 to 2 September 1945
Leyte	17 October 1944 to 1 July 1945
Luzon	15 December 1944 to 4 July 1945
Central Burma	29 January to 15 July 1945
Southern Philippines	27 February to 4 July 1945
Ryukyus	26 March to 2 July 1945
China Offensive	5 May to 2 September 1945

European–African–Middle Eastern Theater
Colors: green and brown with two stripe groupings, one of green, white, red and the other of white, black, and white stripes; blue, white, and red stripes in center

Egypt–Libya	11 June 1942 to 12 February 1943
Air Offensive, Europe	4 July 1942 to 5 June 1944
Algeria–French Morocco	8–11 November 1942
Tunisia	17 November 1942 to 13 May 1943
Sicily	9 July to 17 August 1943
Naples–Foggia	18 August 1943 to 21 January 1944 (Air); 9 September 1943 to 21 January 1944 (Ground)
Anzio	22 January to 24 May 1944
Rome–Arno	22 January to 9 September 1944
Normandy	6 June to 24 July 1944
Northern France	25 July to 14 September 1944
Southern France	15 August to 14 September 1944
Northern Apennines	10 September 1944 to 4 April 1945
Rhineland	15 September 1944 to 21 March 1945
Ardennes–Alsace	16 December 1944 to 25 January 1945
Central Europe	22 March to 11 May 1945
Po Valley	5 April to 8 May 1945

KOREAN WAR (1950–1953)
Colors: light blue bordered on each side with white; with a white center stripe

UN Defensive	27 June to 15 September 1950
UN Offensive	16 September to 2 November 1950
CCF Intervention	3 November 1950 to 24 January 1951
First UN Counteroffensive	25 January to 21 April 1951
CCF Spring Offensive	22 April to 8 July 1951
UN Summer–Fall Offensive	9 July to 27 November 1951
Second Korean Winter	28 November 1951 to 30 April 1952
Korea, Summer–Fall 1952	1 May to 30 November 1952

Third Korean Winter   1 December 1952 to 30 April 1953
Korea, Summer 1953   1 May to 27 July 1953

VIETNAM (1962–1973)
Colors: yellow with green borders and three red stripes centered

Advisory	15 March 1962 to 7 March 1965
Defense	8 March to 24 December 1965
Counteroffensive	25 December 1965 to 30 June 1966
Counteroffensive, Phase II	1 July 1966 to 31 May 1967
Counteroffensive, Phase III	1 June 1967 to 29 January 1968
Tet Counteroffensive	30 January to 1 April 1968
Counteroffensive, Phase IV	2 April to 30 June 1968
Counteroffensive, Phase V	1 July to 1 November 1968
Counteroffensive, Phase VI	2 November 1968 to 22 February 1969
Tet 69 Counteroffensive	23 February to 8 June 1969
Summer–Fall 1969	9 June to 31 October 1969
Winter–Spring 1970	1 November 1969 to 30 April 1970
Sanctuary Counteroffensive	1 May to 30 June 1970
Counteroffensive, Phase VII	1 July 1970 to 30 June 1971
Consolidation I	1 July to 30 November 1971
Consolidation II	1 December 1971 to 29 March 1972
Cease–Fire	30 March 1972 to 28 January 1973

ARMED FORCES EXPEDITIONS
Colors: blue with a narrow blue, white, and red stripe in the center and a narrow green, yellow, red, and black stripe on each edge

Dominican Republic	28 April 1965 to 21 September 1966
Grenada	23 October to 21 November 1983
Panama	20 December 1989 to 31 January 1990

SOUTHWEST ASIA, PERSIAN GULF WAR (1990–1995)
Colors: tan with a black border and center stripe; a green stripe on each side of the black center stripe and red, white, and blue stripes centered on each side of the center stripe

Defense of Saudi Arabia	2 August 1990 to 16 January 1991
Liberation and Defense of Kuwait	17 January to 11 April 1991
Cease-Fire	12 April 1991 to 30 November 1995

KOSOVO (1999)
Colors: blue stripe on top and a red stripe on the bottom with a grouping of red, white, and blue stripes centered

Kosovo Air Campaign	24 March to 10 June 1999

Appendix 7

United States Army Casualties by War[a]

War or Conflict	Battle Total Serving	Other Deaths	Deaths	Wounds Not Mortal[b]
Revolutionary War 1775–1783	— [c]	4,044	—	6,004
War of 1812 1812–1815	286,730[d]	1,950	—	4,000
Mexican War 1846–1848	78,718[d]	1,721	11,550	4,152
Civil War Union Forces 1861–1865[e]	2,128,948	138,154	221,374	280,040
Spanish–American War 1898[f]	280,564	369	2,061	1,594
World War I 1917–1918[g]	4,057,101	50,510	55,868	193,663
World War II 1941–1945[h, i]	11,260,000	234,874	83,400	565,861
Korean War 1950–1953[j]	2,834,000	27,709	2,452[k]	77,596
Vietnam War 1964–1973[l]	4,368,000	30,922	7,272	96,802
Persian Gulf War 1990–1991[m]	306,730	96	84	354

[a] Data prior to World War I are based on incomplete records in many cases. Casualty data are confined to dead and wounded and, therefore, exclude personnel captured or missing in action who were subsequently returned to military control.

[b] Data in this column represent the total number (incidence) of wounds.

[c] Not known, but estimates range from 184,000 to 250,000 for all services (army, navy, marines).

[d] Total for all services (army, navy, marines) as reported by the commissioner of pensions in his annual report for fiscal year 1903.

[e] Authoritative statistics for the Confederate forces are not available. Estimates of the number who served range from 600,000 to 1,500,000. The final report of the provost marshal general, 1863–1866, indicates 133,821 Confederate deaths (74,524 battle and 59,297 other), based upon incomplete returns. In addition, an estimated 26,000 to 31,000 Confederate personnel died in Union prisons.

[f] Number serving covers the period 21 April to 13 August 1898, while dead and wounded data are for the period 1 May to 31 August 1898. Active hostilities ceased on 13 August 1898, but ratifications of the Treaty of Peace were not exchanged between the United States and Spain until 11 April 1899.

[g] Includes air service. Battle deaths and wounds not mortal include casualties suffered by American forces in northern Russia up until 25 August 1919, and in Siberia to 1 April 1920. Other deaths cover the period 1 April 1917, to 31 December 1918.

[h] Data are for the period 1 December 1941 through 31 December 1946, when hostilities were officially terminated by presidential proclamation, but few battle deaths or wounds not mortal were incurred after the Japanese acceptance of the Allied peace terms on 14 August 1945. Number serving in the army from 1 December 1941 through 31 August 1945 were 10,420,000.

[i] Includes army air forces.
[j] Tentative final data based on information available as of 30 September 1954, at which time 24 persons were still carried as missing in action.
[k] As reported in Frank Reister, "Battle Casualties and Medical Statistics: U.S. Army Experience in the Korean War" (Washington, D.C.: Surgeon General of the Department of the Army, 1973). This figure represents nonbattle admissions in Korea and includes deaths resulting from injuries, suicides, homicides, and disease.
[l] Number serving covers the period 4 August 1964, through 27 January 1973 (date of cease-fire). Wounds not mortal exclude 150,332 persons not requiring hospital care. Known status of casualties is as of 30 September 1995.
[m] Data taken from Harry G. Summers Jr., *Persian Gulf War Almanac* (New York: Facts on File, 1995).

Appendix 8
United States Army Rank Insignia

Over the army's history there have been many variations in the ranks, titles, and insignia for members of the army. Military rank is a badge of leadership. Responsibility for personnel, equipment, and mission grows with each increase in rank. Pay grades, by comparison, are administrative classifications used primarily to standardize compensation across the military services. The "E" in E-1 stands for "enlisted," while the "1" indicates the pay grade for that position. The other pay categories are "W" for warrant officers and "O" for commissioned officers. Some enlisted pay grades have two ranks. For example, the ranks of corporal and specialist have the same pay grade of E-4, but because a corporal is expected to fill a leadership role, it is a higher rank than a specialist, even though both receive the same amount of pay. This appendix shows the current title, the three-character alphanumeric abbreviation, pay grade, and insignia for the army today. Entries are in order of rank, from highest to lowest.

GENERAL OFFICERS

General of the Army

General GEN (O-10)

Lieutenant General LTG (O-9)

Major General MG (O-8)

Brigadier General BG (O-7)

FIELD GRADE OFFICERS

Colonel COL (O-6)

Lieutenant Colonel LTC (O-5)

Major MAJ (O-4)

COMPANY GRADE OFFICERS

Captain CPT (O-3)

First Lieutenant 1LT (O-2)

Second Lieutenant 2LT (O-1)

WARRANT OFFICERS

Chief Warrant Officer CW5 (W-5)

Chief Warrant Officer CW4 (W-4)

Chief Warrant Officer CW3 (W-3)

Chief Warrant Officer CW2 (W-2)

Chief Warrant Officer CWO (W-1)

ENLISTED

Sergeant Major of the Army SMA (E-9)

Command Sergeant Major CSM (E-9)

Sergeant Major SGM (E-9)

First Sergeant 1SG (E-8)

Master Sergeant MSG (E-8)

Sergeant First Class SFC (E-7)

Staff Sergeant SSG (E-6)

Sergeant SGT (E-5)

Corporal CPL (E-4)

Specialist SP4 (E-4)

Private First Class PFC (E-3)

Private PVT (E-1, E-2)

Bibliography

CONTENTS

INTRODUCTION

There are thousands of books that deal with historical aspects of the U.S. Army and countless more in which the army receives significant attention. This bibliography, therefore, can only hope to be a guide to sources for more detailed information on the army's history rather than a definitive list of every source of information. Even so, it is a significant list. To make it somewhat manageable, it is divided into four sections, each with subcategories. Because the literature covers more than two centuries of history, it is rather uneven in its coverage. Not all of the army's senior leaders were prominent figures during their tenures, nor did the army have a role in every aspect of America's history. The ebb and flow of historical events in America, nationally and internationally, have greatly influenced the attention accorded the army's past. Information on a particular subject may be found in more than one section of this bibliography. For example, in addition to the references listed for a prominent general officer in the biographical section, more information on the officer may also be found under the wars in which he participated.

The first section of the bibliography is the reading list that the chief of staff of the army compiled in 2000. This professional reading list was designed to provide the army's present and future leaders a solid foundation for understanding the army's role in the development of the American nation and provoke critical thinking about the profession of arms and the role of land power. The selected works examine the past and consider the future. The chief of staff's list is divided into four categories oriented to soldiers and leaders as they move up through the ranks to positions of greater responsibility in the army. As a group, these books examine the history of the U.S. Army and the key role it has played in the development of the United States. The bibliographic entry for each book in this category includes a brief overview of its contents.

The second section of this bibliography includes a wide range of material on the history of the U.S. Army. Because the army's past is inextricably linked to that of America, the first subsection in this part contains works that put the army's role in the context of the rest of U.S. military history. The works in this category supplement Allan Millett and Peter Maslowski's *For the Common Defense: A Military History of the United States of America* (New York: Free Press, 1984) and Russell F. Weigley's *The American Way of War: A History of United States Military Strategy and Policy* (Bloomington: Indiana University Press, 1977), both of which are on the chief of staff's reading list. The next subsection includes both official references and narrative works on the general history of the army. The annual reports of the secretaries of war and secretaries of the army were submitted to Congress from 1822 to 1968 and the annual historical summaries prepared by historians at the army's Center of Military History since 1969 provide an overview of the army's activities each year. *A Guide to the Study and Use of Mili-*

tary History, edited by John E. Jessup and Robert W. Coakley (Washington, D.C.: Government Printing Office, 1980), provides a good starting point for studying the history of the army and Russell F. Weigley's *History of the United States Army* (Bloomington: Indiana University Press, 1984) also offers an excellent introduction to the subject.

The campaign streamers attached to the army flag represent the battles and wars fought for the nation. Each of the army's wars is covered in a single subsection and these subsections are arranged chronologically and follow the section on the general history of the army. Taken together, these subsections constitute the second largest part of the bibliography. The selections in the bibliography in most cases focus on the army's role in each war. Although the Continental Army did not come into existence until 1775, most of the men who organized and led it during the Revolutionary War were experienced soldiers who learned their craft during the colonial period of American history. The section entitled "Colonial Foundations" includes works that focus on events and factors that shaped the beginnings of the army. Each of the sections on major wars contains general references on the conflict as well as selected works on major events. While there is a category for each war, because the Civil War and World War II have both had a tremendous influence on the army and the American nation, they constitute the two largest categories in this section.

The Civil War was a significant event for both the United States and its army. It was the nation's most important nineteenth-century war and continues to influence the army. The war has generated a large and rich literature and a select bibliography barely scratches the surface of the body of works widely available. The single most important reference work for students of the Civil War is the multivolume *War of the Rebellion: A Compilation of the Official Records of the Union and Confederate Armies* (Washington, D.C.: Government Printing Office, 1870–1888). Generally referred to as the *Official Records*, the 128 volumes contain plans, orders, and correspondence from both the Union and Confederate armies. In addition to the *Official Records*, the U.S. government also published the *Medical and Surgical History of the War of the Rebellion* (1870–1922) and the *Official Army Register of the Volunteer Force of the United States* (1865–67). These sources are not exhaustive, but they provide an excellent starting point for any scholarly research on the war.

As with the Civil War, World War II was a profound experience for the army and it has produced an extensive literature. While the U.S. government did not produce anything on World War II that was comparable to the Civil War's *Official Records*, army historians at the Center of Military History did extensive research and wrote *The U.S. Army in World War II*. Popularly known as the *Green Books*, this multivolume series is based on the army's records of the war and describes the organization, plans, and operations of the War Department and the army in all theaters between 1939 and 1945. It includes a massive amount of information about the activities of the U.S. Army in World War II. In an effort to provide an aid to finding information in the series, the Center of Military History published the *Readers Guide to the U.S. Army in World War II* (Washington, D.C.: Government Printing Office, 1992) to the series. Compiled and edited by Richard D. Adamczyk and Morris J. MacGregor, the guide provides a synopsis and a list of key topics for each volume in the series. It also provides an index to the topics in the volume descriptions. During the commemoration of the 50th anniversary of World War II, the U.S. Army Center of Military History published a series of 40 illustrated brochures that describe the campaigns in which U.S. Army troops participated during the war. Each brochure describes the strategic setting, traces the operations of the major American units involved, and analyzes the impact of the campaign on future operations.

Because the actions of leaders have greatly influenced the course of America's wars and battles, supplementary information can be found in the third section of this bibliography, which includes biographies of the people who played prominent roles in the army's history.

Much of the history of the U.S. Army has been shaped by its leaders and soldiers. Their lives and deeds breathe life into all the army's endeavors, in both peace and war. Consequently, the section on biographies is by far the largest in the bibliography. It has three subsections: collections of biographies and other references about army personalities; soldiers' personal memoirs; and biographies and other works pertaining to the individuals covered by entries in the dictionary. In the collections portion, William Gardner Bell's *Secretaries of War and Secretaries of the Army and Commanding Generals and Chiefs of Staff, 1775–1995* and Mark F. Gillespie, Glen R. Hawkins, Michel B. Kelly, and Preston Pierce's *The Sergeants Major of the Army* contain biographical information and illustrations of the army's senior officials. All three volumes are published by the Government Printing Office in Washington, D.C., and are periodically updated by the U.S. Army Center of Military History. A wider range of officers during the early history of the army is covered in Francis B. Heitman's *Historical Register of Officers of the Continental Army, 1775–1783* and *Historical Register and Dictionary of the United States Army, 1789–1903*; Thomas H. S. Hamersly's *Complete Army and Navy Register of the United States of America, 1776–1887*; George W. Cullum's *Biographical Register of the Officers and Graduates of the United States Military Academy*, which covers 1802 to 1950 with occasional updates; and the official *Army Register*, published regularly from 1815 to 1985. Other sources for recent army leaders include official biographical sketches provided by various public affairs offices. Many of the army's senior officials receive brief mention in one or more widely available biographical references. These works include the *Dictionary of American Biography* with supplements; Webster's *American Military Biographies*; various editions of *Who's Who in America*, *Who Was Who in America*, and *Who Was Who in American History—The Military*; the *Encyclopedia Americana* and *Encyclopedia Britannica*; and *Current Biography*.

The selections in the memoirs category reflect the views of soldiers of all ranks from all periods of the army's history who have published their stories but for whom there is no entry in this dictionary. The periods covered range from the Revolutionary War to the Persian Gulf War and the soldiers include virtually all ranks from private to general. These selections are only a small fraction of personal memoirs by soldiers. Many others have been privately published and still others have been compiled by historical groups seeking to preserve the memory of local veterans. Of particular note are *Company Commander* (New York: Ballantine Books, 1966), by Charles MacDonald, who was a World War II veteran and prominent historian, and *"Bayonet! Forward": My Civil War Reminiscences* (Gettysburg, Pa.: Stan Clark Military Books), by Joshua Lawrence Chamberlain, the officer widely credited with saving the battle of Gettysburg for Union forces during the Civil War.

The individuals category of the biography section includes references on those individuals with dictionary entries. Not surprisingly, the more prominent of these individuals have received wide attention and in these cases, in a select bibliography, the problem is what to leave out rather than what to include. Individuals with dictionary listings who do not appear in this category may have served in quieter times, may have been too modest about their accomplishments to have left a published memoir, or may not have been the subject of a biography. Some individuals have published books that, although not necessarily autobiographical, will offer insight into their lives and the contributions they made to the army. Those books have also been included in this section.

Following the biographical references is the fourth section, which covers a wide variety of select topics. These topics generally cover a period of two or more wars and, in many cases, further information on them can be found in the history and biography sections. The last few subsections in this section include specialized types of references, such as chronologies, encyclopedias, and bibliographies.

For information in addition to the references listed in this bibliography, two army organizations, the Center of Military History in Washington, D.C., and the Institute of Military History at Carlisle Barracks, Pennsylvania, are essential resources for researching army history. The center's historians write the army's official histories and maintain the status of lineage and honors for all army units, while the institute houses an extensive archive of historical material on the army. The Internet also offers considerable material on the history of the U.S. Army and both these organizations have excellent Web sites that make available a considerable amount of historical information.

In spite of the length of this bibliography, it only includes a small portion of the body of literature on the history of the U.S. Army. The total number of works on the subject is virtually incalculable. More than 50,000 books and pamphlets have been published on the Civil War alone and the majority of those will make some reference to the history of the army. Not included in the bibliography are thousands of articles and essays in professional journals and other periodicals on various elements of the army's history. With the advent of the Internet, there is a growing body of material available on line that relates to army history. This bibliography does provide an extensive list of sources for the general reader who wants to learn more about how the U.S. Army evolved into the most powerful land force in the world at the beginning of the twenty-first century.

I. CHIEF OF STAFF OF THE ARMY READING LIST

A. Cadets, Soldiers, and Junior Noncommissioned Officers

Ambrose, Stephen E. *Band of Brothers: E Company, 506th Regiment, 101st Airborne from Normandy to Hitler's Eagle's Nest*. New York: Simon & Schuster, 1992.
This book gives an idea of the sacrifices American soldiers endured during World War II. Even through all their dangers and hardships, they enjoyed a brotherhood of comrades they could find nowhere else and would never know again.

Atkinson, Rick. *The Long Gray Line*. New York: Owl Books, 1999.
The author examines the experiences of the West Point class of 1966 and shows how their individual careers epitomized the problems faced by their generation and by the army officer corps.

Brokaw, Tom. *The Greatest Generation*. New York: Random House, 1998.
In a series of narratives, the reader is exposed to the stories of a cross section of American citizens, soldiers, sailors, airmen, and marines who fought and won World War II.

Fehrenbach, T. R. *This Kind of War: A Study in Unpreparedness*. Washington, D.C.: Brassey's, 1994.
This is the ultimate story of a nation's lack of military preparedness. It has two intertwining themes: a bluntly told narrative history of the Korean War and the historical social–political–military context of the war.

Heller, Charles E., and William A. Stofft, eds. *America's First Battles: 1776–1965*. Lawrence: University Press of Kansas, 1986.
The first battle in a war can reveal the strengths and weaknesses of armies—both winners and losers. This book examines the first major engagement of nine American wars from the Revolutionary War through Vietnam, with an emphasis on the army's weaknesses.

Hogan, David W., Jr. *225 Years of Service: The U.S. Army 1775–2000*. Washington, D.C.: U.S. Army Center of Military History, 2000.
This pamphlet gives a brief overview of how the army has served the nation since the formation of the Continental Army. It covers the army's performance in major conflicts and numerous other missions throughout American history.

Keegan, John. *The Face of Battle*. New York: Vintage, 1977.
This book recounts warfare from the soldier's perspective in three very different battles. It brings to life the sights, sounds, and smells of the battlefields at Agincourt, Waterloo, and the Somme, while debunking several long-held myths and romantic visions of warfare.

Moore, Harold G., and Joseph L. Galloway. *We Were Soldiers Once, and Young*. New York: Random House,1992.
This is a straightforward combat narrative portraying the personal side of men in battle. It provides a detailed view of combat in Vietnam and explains why the battle of the Ia Drang Valley was an important learning experience for both sides.

Myrer, Anton. *Once an Eagle*. New York: Holt, Rinehart, and Winston, 1968.
This is one of the most important military novels ever written. Its stark and realistic descriptions of men in combat are classic and it provides a penetrating analysis of the challenges of leadership and the moral dilemmas of command.

Shaara, Michael. *The Killer Angels*. New York: Ballantine Books, 1974.
This Pulitzer Prize–winning fictional account of the battle at Gettysburg, a pivotal three-day fight during the American Civil War, is based on solid historical research. It takes a close, personal look at the battle and tells the story of how great and ordinary men reacted when faced with extraordinary circumstances.

B. Company Grade Officers, Warrant Officers, and Noncommissioned Officers

Ambrose, Steven. *Citizen Soldiers*. New York: Simon & Schuster, 1997.
This broad look at the U.S. Army on the Western Front in World War II considers strategy discussions of generals, the tactics employed by junior officers, and the life of the combat soldier. It centers on the American citizen soldiers who were called from civilian life to defeat Germany's Third Reich.

Coffman, Edward M. *The War to End All Wars: The American Military Experience in World War I*. New York: Oxford University Press, 1968.
This is a classic account of the American military experience in World War I as the U.S. Army converted itself from a small imperial constabulary to a modern mass army. This is the best single-volume account of that remarkable transformation.

Huntington, Samuel P. *The Soldier and the State*. Cambridge, Mass.: Belknap Press, 1957.
The author traces the concept of military professionalism through the two world wars and provides an analysis of the nature and scope of professional officers. It describes the basic tenets of the professional soldier in American society.

Linderman, Gerald F. *Embattled Courage: The Experience of Combat in the American Civil War*. New York: Free Press, 1987.
This work examines the beliefs and behavior of volunteers from the Union and Confederate armies during the Civil War. Volunteers initially believed in the nobility of war, fighting fair, and the justness of their cause, but the brutal experience of combat eventually eroded these beliefs, but not their beliefs in their comrades or their determination to survive.

MacDonald, Charles B. *Company Commander*. 1947. Reprint ed.; Springfield, N.J.: Burford, 1999.
This personal account gives a vivid sense of the responsibilities of an infantry company commander in World War II. It provides a sense of what it was like for an inexperienced officer to be thrust into a leadership role in combat, the personal skills it took to survive, and the intangibles that held small units together in combat.

Marshall, S. L. A. *Men against Fire: The Problem of Battle Command in Future War.* 1947. Reprint ed., Gloucester, Mass.: Peter Smith, 1978.

An analysis of the difficulties infantry commanders face in motivating soldiers in combat. The author presents his explanation of why soldiers fail to fire their weapons in battle and how the lack of moral leadership can destroy the effectiveness of fighting organizations.

Millett, Alan R., and Peter Maslowski. *For the Common Defense: A Military History of the United States of America.* New York: Free Press, 1984.

This volume is a leading textbook of American military history. It examines the American experience from colonial times to the fall of Saigon in 1975 as it traces the evolution of American military policy.

Scales, Robert H., Jr. *Certain Victory.* Reprint. Fort Leavenworth, Kans.: U.S. Army Command and General Staff College Press, 1994.

This is a history of the U.S. Army in the Persian Gulf War. It provides an excellent summary of how the professional American soldier of the 1980s differed from the drug-riddled and racially divided army of the 1970s.

Stoler, Mark A. *George C. Marshall: Soldier–Statesman of the American Century.* Boston: Twayne, 1989.

George Marshall was trained as a nineteenth-century citizen–soldier but was commissioned into a twentieth-century army of empire. This account of the life of one of America's foremost soldier–diplomats explains how he lived in multiple worlds and harmonized the conflicts between them.

Willard, Tom. *Buffalo Soldiers.* New York: Tom Doherty, 1996.

Told through the eyes of a young man saved from slavery who becomes a sergeant major in the army, this novel tells the story of the black units the Indians referred to as "Buffalo Soldiers."

C. Field Grade Officers, Chief Warrant Officers, and Senior Noncommissioned Officers

Appleman, Roy E. *East of Chosin: Entrapment and Breakout in Korea, 1950.* College Station: Texas A. & M. University Press, 1987.

This is the story of the 3,000 American soldiers who fought the battle of the Changjin (Chosin) Reservoir during the initial Communist Chinese intervention in the Korean War. Although this story is not as well known as other tactical disasters in Korea, it says a great deal about the overall poor condition of the U.S. Army during the early days of the war.

Cosmas, Graham A. *An Army for Empire: The United States Army and the Spanish American War.* 2d ed. Shippensburg, Pa.: White Mane, 1994.

In 1898, the U.S. Army was an institution in transition. In size, organization, and general attitudes, it had changed little from its Indian fighting days. This is a study of the organization, administration, and strategic direction of the army awakening to its new responsibilities in a new century.

Doughty, Robert A. *The Evolution of U.S. Army Tactical Doctrine, 1946–1976.* Fort Leavenworth, Kans.: Combat Studies Institute, 1979.

This study of doctrine in the Cold War army explains the major developments of the period and puts them in a political and technological context. It reveals the difficulties the army faced in developing a doctrine responsive to a variety of contingencies while remaining focused on a possible Warsaw Pact invasion of Western Europe.

Jomini, Antoine-Henri. *Jomini and His Summary of the Art of War.* Reprint ed. Harrisburg, Pa.: Stackpole, 1965.

Jomini was a major influence on interpreting Napoleon's style of warfare and some scholars consider him the father of strategic thinking. Jomini was a student of history and a prolific writer and this is his classic study of warfare from Fredrick the Great to Napoleon.

MacDonald, Charles B., and Sidney T. Mathews. *Three Battles: Arnaville, Altuzzo, and Schmidt.* Washington, D.C.: U.S. Army Center of Military History, 1952.
This volume examines small-unit combat during three battles in Europe in World War II. Based on interviews and recollections of the participants, it is one of the best books ever written about war from the soldier's perspective.

McPherson, James M. *Battle Cry of Freedom: The Civil War Era.* New York: Oxford University Press, 1988.
The Civil War transformed America from a loose collection of semi-independent states into a single nation. This one-volume history integrates the political, social, and military events of two decades of turmoil from the start of the Mexican War to the end of the Civil War.

Nye, Roger H. *The Challenge of Command.* Wayne, N.J.: Avery, 1986.
This bibliographical essay provides a guide that emphasizes attaining military excellence through reading and experience.

Palmer, Dave R. *Summons of the Trumpet: U.S.–Vietnam in Perspective.* San Rafael, Calif.: Presidio, 1978.
This is a straightforward account of America's military and political involvement in Vietnam from 1954 to 1973, as the United States took charge of the war from the South Vietnamese and deployed American ground forces aggressively against the Viet Cong and North Vietnamese Army.

Van Creveld, Martin. *Supplying War: Logistics from Wallenstein to Patton.* New York: Cambridge University Press, 1977.
Although victory in war is generally considered the result of brilliant strategy and tactical genius, this classic study highlights the impact of logistics on warfare. It shows that what is possible on the battlefield depends on what takes place behind the front and often determines victory or defeat.

Weigley, Russell F. *The American Way of War: A History of United States Military Strategy and Policy.* 1973. Reprint ed., Bloomington: Indiana University Press, 1977.
Tracing the evolution of military strategy and policy, this survey presents a unifying view of American military history. It is a good starting point for studying the army's participation in America's past wars and thinking about its role in future conflicts.

D. Senior Leaders

Clausewitz, Carl von. *On War.* Ed. and trans., Peter Paret and Michael Howard. Princeton, N.J.: Princeton University Press, 1984.
Written in the early days of the Industrial Revolution, this classic study of the art of war remains the most significant attempt in Western history to understand the internal dynamics of war and its role as an instrument of policy. First published in 1832, it has stimulated generations of soldiers, statesmen, and intellectuals.

Greenfield, Kent Roberts, ed. *Command Decisions.* Washington, D.C.: Office of the Chief of Military History, 1960.
By analyzing key decisions of Allied, German, and Japanese commanders in World War II, this book examines the concerns and considerations of military leaders and policy makers.

The decisions covered include matters of strategic importance and issues of civil–military relations with significant postwar future consequences.

Howard, Michael. *War in European History*. Oxford: Oxford University Press, 1976.
This volume deals with military forces in the context of the societies that produced them and that they serve. It traces the development of warfare and its relationship to technical, social, and economic change.

Kennedy, Paul. *The Rise and Fall of the Great Powers*. New York: Random House, 1987.
This classic work examines the dangers of failing to link a vibrant economy with military power. It uses historical examples to support the thesis that over the past five centuries great empires flourished and won wars because a superior economic force backed their military power.

Kissinger, Henry. *Diplomacy*. New York: Simon & Schuster, 1994.
Drawing on his vast reservoir of historical knowledge and experience with statecraft and foreign policy, the author explains the tools of diplomacy. He emphasizes the importance of geopolitics, ideology, *realpolitik*, the balance of power, the search for equilibrium, and the nation-state.

Murray, Williamson, and Alan R. Millett, eds. *Military Innovation in the Interwar Period*. New York: Cambridge University Press, 1996.
In their examination of seven areas of innovation—armored warfare, amphibious warfare, strategic bombing, tactical bombing, submarine warfare, carrier aviation, and radar—this collection compares and contrasts the experiences of various national military institutions during the period between World Wars I and II.

Neustadt, Richard E., and Ernest R. May. *Thinking in Time*. New York: Free Press, 1986.
This book is a primer on how to use historical experience to determine what might be done today to improve prospects for tomorrow and proposes techniques for the proper employment of history in decision making.

Paret, Peter. ed. *Makers of Modern Strategy from Machiavelli to the Nuclear Age*. Princeton, N.J.: Princeton University Press, 1986.
This volume offers a historical guide to strategic theory and the use of organized violence from the Renaissance to the atomic era. Its 28 essays focus on American and European military history and provide an introduction to a wide range of topics in military history.

Skelton, William B. *An American Profession of Arms: The Army Officer Corps, 1784–1861*. Lawrence: University Press of Kansas, 1992.
In tracing the development of the professional officer corps in the U.S. Army between the founding of the republic and the onset of the Civil War, this study examines the roots of the American profession of arms as an institution and a system of ideas and values.

Summers, Harry. *On Strategy*. Novato, Calif.: Presidio, 1982.
This critical examination of the U.S. military in Vietnam suggests that American strategists might have fared better had they adhered more closely to the theories of Clausewitz. It contrasts Clausewitz's strategic theory with the American practice of selecting war goals, employing the principles of war, and allocating resources during the war.

Thucydides, *The Peloponnesian War*. Translated by Rex Warner. Baltimore: Penguin, 1972.
This classic account of the power struggle in the Mediterranean before the Roman empire was written by the man widely considered the first modern historian. The story has many lessons; the danger of an all-powerful democratic state, the arrogance of great-power politics, the lure of conquest, the cult of personality in war, and the delicate balance between the military and the political structures of a state.

II. HISTORIES

A. U.S. Military History

Bernardo, C. Joseph, and Eugene H. Bacon. *American Military Policy: Its Development Since 1775*. Harrisburg, Pa.: Stackpole, 1955.

Dupuy, R. Ernest, and Trevor N. Dupuy. *Military Heritage of America*. New York: McGraw-Hill, 1956.

Esposito, Vincent, ed. *The West Point Atlas of American Wars*. 2 vols. New York: Praeger, 1959.

Hagen, Kenneth J., and William R. Roberts, eds. *Against All Enemies: Interpretations of American Military History from Colonial Times to the Present*. New York: Greenwood, 1986.

Hammond, Paul. *Organizing for Defense: The American Military Establishment in the Twentieth Century*. Princeton, N.J.: Princeton University Press, 1961.

Jessup, John E., and Robert W. Coakley, eds. *A Guide to the Study and Use of Military History*. Washington, D.C.: Government Printing Office, 1980.

Kauffman, William W., ed. *Military Policy and National Security*. Princeton, N.J.: Princeton University Press, 1956.

Leckie, Robert. *The Wars of America*. 2 vols. New York: HarperPerennial, 1993.

Matloff, Maurice, ed. *American Military History*. Revised ed. Washington, D.C.: Government Printing Office, 1973.

Millett, Allan R., and Peter Maslowski. *For the Common Defense: A Military History of the United States of America*. New York: Free Press, 1984.

Millis, Walter. *Arms and Men: A Study in American Military History*. New York: Putnam, 1956.

Nelson, Otto L., Jr. *National Security and the General Staff*. Washington, D.C.: Combat Forces Press, 1946.

Smith, Louis. *American Democracy and Military Power: A Study of Civil Control of the Military Powers in the United States*. Chicago: University of Chicago Press, 1951.

Upton, Emory. *The Military Policy of the United States*. Washington, D.C.: Government Printing Office, 1904.

Weigley, Russell F. *The American Way of War: A History of United States Military Strategy and Policy*. Bloomington: Indiana University Press, 1977.

Williams, T. Harry. *Americans at War: The Development of the American Military System*. Baton Rouge: Louisiana State University Press, 1960.

Yoshpe, Harry B., and Stanley L. Falk. *Organization for National Security*. Washington, D.C.: Industrial College of the Armed Forces, 1963.

B. History of the U.S. Army

Carter, William Harding. *The American Army*. Indianapolis: Bobbs-Merrill, 1915.

Dupuy, Ernest. *The Compact History of the United States Army*. New York: Hawthorne Books, 1956.

Ganoe, William Addleman. *History of the United States Army*. New York: Appleton–Century, 1924.

Heller, Charles, and William A. Stofft, eds. *America's First Battles, 1776–1965*. Lawrence: University Press of Kansas, 1986.

Kleinman, Forrest K., and Robert S. Horowitz. *The Modern United States Army*. Princeton, N.J.: D. Van Nostrand, 1964.

Kreidberg, Marvin A., and Merton G. Henry. *History of Military Mobilization in the United States Army, 1775–1945*. Washington, D.C.: Government Printing Office, 1984.

Spaulding, Oliver Lyman. *The United States Army in War and Peace*. New York: Putnam, 1937.

U.S. War Department. *Annual Reports. Report of the Secretary of War*. Washington, D.C.: Government Printing Office, 1823–1947.

Weigley, Russell F. *Towards an American Army: Military Thought from Washington to Marshall*. New York: Columbia University Press, 1962.

——. *History of the United States Army*. 2d ed. Bloomington: Indiana University Press, 1984.

C. Colonial Foundations

Ferling, John E. *A Wilderness of Miseries: War and Warriors in Early America*. Westport, Conn.: Greenwood, 1980.

Hunt, George T. *The Wars of the Iroquois*. Madison: University of Wisconsin Press, 1940.

Kohn, Richard H. *Eagle and Sword: The Beginnings of the Military Establishment in America*. New York: Free Press, 1975.

Leach, Douglas E. *The Northern Colonial Frontier, 1607–1763*. New York: Holt, Rinehart, and Winston, 1966.

——. *Arms for Empire: A Military History of the British Colonies in North America*. New York: Macmillan, 1973.

Peckham, Howard H. *The Colonial Wars, 1698–1763*. Chicago: University of Chicago Press, 1964.

Vaughn, Alden T. *New England Frontier: Puritans and Indians, 1620–1675*. Boston: Little, Brown, 1965.

D. Revolutionary War

Babits, Lawrence E. *A Devil of a Whipping: The Battle of Cowpens*. Chapel Hill: University of North Carolina Press, 1998.

Bill, Alfred H. *Valley Forge: The Making of an Army*. New York: Harper, 1952.

Blanco, Richard L., ed. *The American Revolution, 1775–1783: An Encyclopedia*. 2 vols. New York: Garland, 1998.

Boatner, Mark M. *Encyclopedia of the American Revolution*. ed. New York: David McKay, 1974.

Brooks, Victor. *The Boston Campaign: April 19, 1775–March 17, 1776*. Conshohocken, Pa.: Combined, 1999.

Carp, Lawrence D. *To Starve the Army at Pleasure: Continental Army Administration and American Political Culture*. Chapel Hill: University of North Carolina Press, 1982.

Coakley, Robert W., and Stetson Conn. *The War of the American Revolution*. Washington, D.C.: Government Printing Office, 1975.

Cress, Lawrence D. *Citizens in Arms: The Army and Militia in American Society to the War of 1812*. Chapel Hill: University of North Carolina Press, 1983.

Dann, John C. ed. *The Revolution Remembered. Eyewitness Accounts of the War for Independence*. Chicago: University of Chicago Press, 1983.

Elsberg, John W., ed. *Papers on the Constitution*. Washington, D.C.: Government Printing Office, 1990.

French, Allen. *The First Year of the Revolution*. Boston: Houghton Mifflin, 1934.

Gross, Robert A. *The Minutemen and Their World*. New York: Hill & Wang, 1976.

Guthman, William H. *March to Massacre: A History of the First Seven Years of the United States Army, 1784–1791*. New York: McGraw-Hill, 1970.

Higginbotham, Don. *The War of American Independence: Military Attitudes, Policies, and Practices*. New York: Macmillan, 1971.

Hoffman, Ronald, and Peter J. Albert, eds. *Arms and Independence: The Military Character of the American Revolution*. Charlottesville: University Press of Virginia, 1984.

Jacobs, James Ripley. *The Beginnings of the U.S. Army, 1783–1812*. Philadelphia: University of Pennsylvania Press, 1962.

Ketchum, Richard M. *Saratoga: Turning Point of America's Revolutionary War*. New York: Henry Holt, 1997.

Kohn, Richard H. *Eagle and Sword: Beginnings of the Military Establishment in America, 1783–1802*. New York: Free Press, 1975.

Macksey, Piers. *The War for America, 1771–1783*. Cambridge, Mass.: Harvard University Press, 1964.

Mags, Terry M. *Historical Dictionary of the American Revolution*. Lanham, Md.: Scarecrow Press, 1999.

Middlekauff, Robert. *The Glorious Cause: The American Revolution, 1763–1789*. New York: Oxford University Press, 1982.

Montross, Lyn. *Rag, Tag and Bobtail: The Story of the Continental Army, 1775–1783*. New York: Harper, 1952.

Palmer, Dave R. *The Way of the Fox: American Strategy in the War for America, 1775–1783*. Westport, Conn.: Greenwood, 1975.

Peckham, Howard H. *The War for Independence: A Military History*. 2 vols. New York: Macmillan, 1958.

Prucha, Francis P. *The Sword of the Republic: The United States Army on the Frontier, 1783–1840*. New York: Macmillan, 1969.

Risch, Erna. *Supplying Washington's Army*. Washington, D.C.: Government Printing Office, 1983.

Royster, Charles. *A Revolutionary People at War: The Continental Army and American Character, 1775–1783*. Chapel Hill: University of North Carolina Press, 1979.

Shy, John. *A People Numerous and Armed*. New York: Oxford University Press, 1976.

Tourtellet, Arthur B. *William Diamond's Dream: The Beginnings of the War of the American Revolution*. Garden City, N.Y.: Doubleday, 1959.

U.S. Air Force Academy. *Military History of the American Revolution: Proceedings of the Sixth Military History Symposium, USAF Academy, 1974*. Washington, D.C.: Government Printing Office, 1976.

Wallace, Willard. *Appeal to Arms: A Military History of the American Revolution*. New York: Harper, 1951.

Ward, Christopher. *The War of the Revolution*. 2 vols. New York: Macmillan, 1952.

Ward, Harry M. *The Department of War, 1781–1795*. Pittsburgh: University of Pittsburgh Press, 1962.

Wood, W. J. *Battles of the Revolutionary War, 1775–1781*. New York: Da Capo, 1995.

Wright, Robert K., Jr. *The Continental Army*. Washington, D.C.: Government Printing Office, 1983.

Wright, Robert K., Jr., and Morris J. Macgregor Jr. *Soldier Statesman of the Constitution*. Washington, D.C.: Government Printing Office, 1987.

E. War of 1812

Adams, Henry. *The War of 1812*. Edited by H. S. DeWeed. Harrisburg, Pa.: Infantry Journal Press, 1944.

Beirne, Francis F. *The War of 1812*. New York: Dutton, 1949.

Brooks, Charles B. *The Siege of New Orleans*. Seattle: University of Washington Press, 1961.

Coles, Harry L. *The War of 1812*. Chicago: University of Chicago Press, 1965.

Crackel, Theodore J. *Mr. Jefferson's Army: Political and Social Reform of the Military Establishment, 1801–1809*. New York: New York University Press, 1987.

Elting, John R. *Amateurs to Arms! A Military History of the War of 1812*. New York: Da Capo, 1995.

Gilpin, Alex R. *The War of 1812 in the Old Northwest*. East Lansing: Michigan State University Press, 1958.

Hitsman, J. MacKay. *The Incredible War of 1812*. Toronto: University of Toronto Press, 1961.

Mahon, John K. *The War of 1812*. Gainesville: University of Florida Press, 1972.

Mason, Philip, ed. *After Tippecanoe: Some Aspects of the War of 1812*. East Lansing: Michigan State University Press, 1963.

Muller, Charles. *The Darkest Day, 1812: The Washington–Baltimore Campaign*. Philadelphia: Lippincott, 1963.

Remini, Robert V. *The Battle of New Orleans: Andrew Jackson and America's First Military Victory*. New York: Viking, 1999.

Skeen, C. Edward. *Citizen Soldiers in the War of 1812*. Lexington: University Press of Kentucky, 1998.

F. Mexican War

Bauer, K. Jack. *The Mexican War, 1846–1848*. New York: Macmillan, 1974.

Bill, Alfred Hoyt. *Rehearsal for Conflict: The War With Mexico, 1846–1848*. New York: Knopf, 1947.

Connor, Seymour V., and Odie B. Faulk. *North America Divided: The Mexican War, 1846–1848*. New York: Oxford University Press, 1971.

Dawson, Joseph G., III. *Doniphan's Epic March: The 1st Missouri Volunteers in the Mexican War*. Lawrence: University Press of Kansas, 1999.

Dufour, Charles L. *The Mexican War: A Compact History, 1846–1848*. New York: Hawthorne Books, 1968.

Henry, Robert Selph. *The Story of the Mexican War*. Indianapolis: Bobbs-Merrill, 1959.

Johannsen, Robert W. *To the Halls of the Montezumas: The Mexican War in the American Imagination*. New York: Oxford University Press, 1985.

Lavender, David. *Climax at Buena Vista*. Philadelphia: Lippincott, 1966.

Moseley, Edward R., and Paul C. Clark. *Historical Dictionary of the United States–Mexican War*. Lanham, Md.: Scarecrow Press, 1997.

Nichols, Edward J. *Zach Taylor's Little Army*. Garden City, N.Y.: Doubleday, 1963.

Singletary, Otis A. *The Mexican War*. Chicago: University of Chicago Press, 1960.

Smith, George Winston, and Charles Judah. *Chronicles of the Gringos: The U.S. Army in the Mexican War, 1846–1848: Accounts of Eyewitnesses and Combatants*. Albuquerque. University of New Mexico Press, 1968.

Winders, Richard Bruce. *Mr. Polk's Army: The American Military Experience in the Mexican War*. Texas A. & M. University Military History Series, no. 51. College Station: Texas A. & M. Press, 1997.

G. Civil War

Alan, William. *History of the Campaign of Gen. T. J. (Stonewall) Jackson in the Shenandoah Valley of Virginia from November 4, 1861, to June 17, 1862*. Philadelphia: J. B. Lippincott, 1880.

Barrett, John G. *Sherman's March through the Carolinas*. Chapel Hill: University of North Carolina Press, 1956.

Bearss, Edwin Cole. *The Campaign for Vicksburg*. 3 vols. Dayton, Ohio: Morningside, 1985–1986.

Boatner, Mark M., III. *The Civil War Dictionary*. New York: David McKay, 1959.

Carter, Samuel. *The Siege of Atlanta*. New York: St. Martin's, 1973.

Carter, Samuel, III. *The Final Fortress: The Campaign for Vicksburg, 1862–1863*. New York: St. Martin's, 1980.

Castel, Albert. *Decision in the West. The Atlanta Campaign of 1864*. Lawrence: University Press of Kansas, 1992.

Catton, Bruce. *Mr. Lincoln's Army*. Garden City, N.Y.: Doubleday, 1951.

——. *Glory Road*. Garden City, N.Y.: Doubleday, 1954.

——. *The Centennial History of the Civil War*. 3 vols. Garden City, N.Y.: Doubleday, 1961–1965.

——. *A Stillness at Appomattox*. New York: Simon & Schuster, Washington Square Press, 1970.

Chamberlain, Joshua Lawrence. *The Passing of the Armies: An Account of the Final Campaign of the Army of the Potomac, Based on Personal Reminiscences of the Fifth Army Corps*. New York: Putnam, 1915.

Coddington, Edwin B. *The Gettysburg Campaign: A Study in Command*. New York: Random House, 1984.

Cooling, Benjamin F. *Forts Henry and Donelson: Key to the Confederate Heartland*. Knoxville: University of Tennessee Press, 1988.

Cox, Jacob D. *Atlanta*. New York: Scribner, 1882.

——. *The March to the Sea: Franklin and Nashville*. New York: Scribner, 1882.

Cozzens, Peter. *This Terrible Sound: The Battle of Chickamauga*. Urbana: University of Illinois Press, 1992.

——. *The Shipwreck of Their Hopes: The Battles for Chattanooga*. Urbana: University of Illinois Press, 1994.

Crawford, Samuel Wylie. *The Genesis of the Civil War: The Story of Sumter, 1860–1861*. New York: C. L. Webster, 1887.

Cullen, Joseph P. *The Peninsular Campaign: McClellan and Lee Struggle for Richmond*. Harrisburg, Pa.: Stackpole, 1973.

Davis, Burke. *Sherman's March*. New York: Random House, 1980.

Davis, William D. *Battle at Bull Run: A History of the First Major Campaign of the Civil War*. Garden City, N.Y.: Doubleday, 1977.

Doubleday, Abner. *Chancellorsville and Gettysburg*. New York: Scribner, 1882.

Dowdey, Clifford. *Lee's Last Campaign: The Story of Lee and His Men against Grant, 1864*. Boston: Little, Brown, 1960.

Esposito, Vincent J., ed. *The West Point Atlas of the Civil War*. New York: Frederick A. Praeger, 1962.

Foote, Shelby. *The Civil War: A Narrative*. 3 vols. New York: Random House, 1958–1974.

Furguson, Ernest B. *Chancellorsville 1863: The Souls of the Brave*. New York: Knopf, 1992.

Gallagher, Gary W. ed. *Antietam: Essays on the 1862 Maryland Campaign*. Kent, Ohio: Kent State University Press, 1989.

——, ed. *Struggle for the Shendandoah: Essays on the 1864 Valley Campaign*. Kent, Ohio: Kent State University Press, 1991.

——. *The Fredericksburg Campaign: Decision on the Rappahannock*. Chapel Hill: University of North Carolina Press, 1995.

Glatthaar, Joseph T. *The March to the Sea and Beyond: Sherman's Troops in the Savannah and Carolinas Campaigns*. New York: New York University Press, 1985.

Greene, Francis V. *The Mississippi*. New York: Scribner, 1882.

Henderson, G. F. R. *The Civil War, a Soldier's View: A Collection of Civil War Writings*. Edited by Jay Luvaas. Chicago: University of Chicago Press, 1950.

Hennessy, John J. *Return to Bull Run: The Campaign and Battle of Second Manassas*. New York: Simon & Schuster, 1993.

Humphreys, Andrew A. *From Gettysburg to the Rapidan: The Army of the Potomac, July, 1863, to April, 1864*. New York: Scribner, 1883.

——. *The Virginia Campaign of 1864 and 1865*. New York: Scribner, 1883.

Long, E. B., and Barbara Long. *Civil War Day by Day: An Almanac, 1861–1865*. Garden City, N.Y.: Doubleday, 1971.

Luvaas, Jay, and Harold W. Nelson. *The U.S. Army War College Guide to the Battle of Gettysburg*. Carlisle, Pa.: South Mountain Press, 1986.

——. *The U.S. Army War College Guide to the Battle of Antietam: The Maryland Campaign in 1862*. Carlisle, Pa.: South Mountain Press, 1987.

——. *The U.S. Army War College Guide to the Battle of Chancellorsville*. Carlisle, Pa.: South Mountain Press, 1988.

Matter, William D. *If It Takes All Summer: The Battle of Spotsylvania*. Chapel Hill: University of North Carolina Press, 1988.

Montgomery, James. *The Shaping of a Battle: Gettysburg*. Philadelphia: Chilton, 1959.

Nevins, Allan. *Ordeal of the Union*. 8 vols. New York: Scribner, 1947–1971.

Palfrey, Francis W. *Antietam and Fredericksburg*. New York: Scribner, 1882.

Patterson, Robert A. *A Narrative of the Campaign in the Valley of the Shenandoah, in 1861*. Philadelphia: Campbell, 1865.

Pleasants, Henry, Jr. *The Tragedy of the Crater*. Boston: Christopher, 1938.

Pond, George E. *The Shenandoah Valley in 1864*. New York: Scribner, 1883.

Rhea, Gordon C. *The Battle of the Wilderness, May 5–6, 1864*. Baton Rouge: Louisiana State University Press, 1994.

Ropes, John Codman. *The Army under Pope*. New York: Scribner, 1881.

Scott, Robert Garth. *Into the Wilderness with the Army of the Potomac*. Bloomington: Indiana University Press, 1985.

Sears, Stephen. *Landscape Turned Red: The Battle of Antietam*. New Haven, Conn.: Ticknor and Fields, 1983.

——. *To the Gates of Richmond: The Peninsula Campaign*. New York: Ticknor and Fields, 1992.

Sefton, James E. *The United States Army and Reconstruction, 1865–1877*. Baton Rouge: Louisiana State University Press, 1967.

Sommers, Richard J. *Richmond Redeemed: The Siege of Petersburg*. Garden City, N.Y.: Doubleday, 1981.

Spruill, Matt. ed. *The U.S. Army War College Guide to the Battle of Chickamauga*. Lawrence: University Press of Kansas, 1993.

Swinton, William. *Twelve Decisive Battles of the War: A History of the Eastern and Western Campaigns, in Relation to the Actions That Decided Their Issue*. New York: Dick and Fitzgerald, 1867.

Sword, Wiley. *Shiloh: Bloody April*. New York: Morrow, 1974.

——. *Mountains Touched with Fire: Chattanooga Besieged, 1863*. New York: St. Martin's, 1995.

Tanner, Robert G. *Stonewall in the Valley: Thomas J. "Stonewall" Jackson's Shenandoah Valley Campaign, Spring 1862*. Garden City, N.Y.: Doubleday, 1976.

Trudeau, Noah Andre. *Bloody Roads South: The Wilderness to Cold Harbor, May–June, 1864*. Boston: Little, Brown, 1989.

——. *The Last Citadel: Petersburg, Virginia, June 1864–April 1865*. Boston: Little, Brown, 1991.

——. *Out of the Storm: The End of the Civil War, April–June 1865*. Boston: Little, Brown, 1994.

Tucker, Glenn. *Chickamauga: Bloody Battle in the West*. Dayton, Ohio: Morningside, 1975.

U.S. War Department. *The War of the Rebellion: A Compilation of the Official Records of the Union and Confederate Armies*. 128 vols. Washington, D.C.: Government Printing Office, 1880–1901.

Webb, Alexander S. *The Peninsula: McClellan's Campaign of 1862*. New York: Scribner, 1881.

Wert, Jeffry D. *From Winchester to Cedar Creek: The Shenandoah Campaign of 1864*. Carlisle, Pa.: South Mountain Press, 1987.

Williams, Kenneth P. *Lincoln Finds a General: A Military Study of the Civil War*. 5 vols. New York: Macmillan, 1949–1959.

Williams, T. Harry. *Lincoln and His Generals*. New York: Knopf, 1952.

H. Indian Wars

Andrist, Ralph. *The Long Death: The Last Days of the Plains Indians*. New York: Macmillan, 1962.

Armstrong, Perry A. *The Sauks and the Black Hawk War*. Springfield, Ill.: H. W. Rokker, 1887.

Chalmers, Harvey. *The Last Stand of the Nez Perce*. New York: Twayne, 1962.

Connell, Evan S. *Son of the Morning Star*. San Francisco: North Point, 1984.

Downey, Fairfax. *Indian Wars of the U.S. Army, 1776–1865*. Garden City, N.Y.: Doubleday, 1963.

Faulk, Odie B. *The Geronimo Campaign*. New York: Oxford University Press, 1969.

——. *Crimson Desert: Indian Wars of the American Southwest*. New York: Oxford University Press, 1974.

Foreman, Grant. *Indian Removal: The Emigration of the Five Civilized Tribes of Indians*. Norman: University of Oklahoma Press, 1932.

Jensen, Richard E., R. Eli Paul, and John E. Carter. *Eyewitness at Wounded Knee*. 1991.

Josephy, Alvin M., Jr. *The Nez Perce Indians and the Opening of the Northwest*. New Haven, Conn.: Yale University Press, 1965.

——. *The Patriot Chiefs: A Chronicle of American Indian Resistance*. New York: Penguin, 1994.

Mahon, John K. *History of the Second Seminole War, 1835–1842*. Gainesville: University Press of Florida, 1967.

Murray, Keith S. *The Modocs and Their War*. Norman: University of Oklahoma Press, 1959.

National Park Service. *Soldier and Brave: Military and Indian Affairs in the Trans-Mississippi West, Including a Guide to Historic Sites and Landmarks*. New York: Harper and Row, 1963.

King, Charles. *Campaigning with Crook*. Norman: University of Oklahoma Press, 1964.

Murray, Keith A. *The Modocs and Their War*. Norman: University of Oklahoma Press, 1959.

Prucha, Francis P. *The Sword of the Republic: The United States Army on the Frontier*. Lincoln: University of Nebraska Press, 1964.

———. *The Great Father: The United States Government and the American Indians*. Lincoln: University of Nebraska Press, 1984.

Rickey, Don. *Forty Miles a Day on Beans and Hay: The Enlisted Soldier Fighting the Indian Wars*. Norman: University of Oklahoma Press, 1963.

Stevens, Frank D. *The Black Hawk War*. Chicago: Frank E. Stevens, 1903.

Tebbel, John. *The Compact History of the Indian Wars*. New York: Hawthorne Books, 1966.

Thrape, Dan L. *The Conquest of Apacheria*. Norman: University of Oklahoma Press, 1967.

Thwaites, Reuben Gold. *The Story of the Black Hawk War*. Madison: Wisconsin State Historical Society, 1892.

Utley, Robert M. *The Last Days of the Sioux Nation*. New Haven, Conn.: Yale University Press, 1963.

———. *Frontiersmen in Blue: The United States Army and the Indian, 1848–1865*. New York, Macmillan, 1967.

———. *Frontier Regulars: The United States Army and the Indian, 1866–1890*. New York, Macmillan, 1973.

Viola, Herman J. *Little Bighorn Remembered: The Untold Story of Custer's Last Stand*. Times Books, 1999.

Welch, James, with Paul Stekler. *Killing Custer: The Battle of the Little Bighorn and the Fate of the Plains Indians*. New York: Penguin, 1995.

Wellman, Paul I. *The Indian Wars of the West*. Garden City, N.Y.: Doubleday, 1954.

Wooster, Robert. *The Military and United States Indian Policy*. New Haven, Conn.: Yale University Press, 1988.

I. Spanish–American War

Alger, Russell A. *The Spanish–American War*. New York: Harper, 1901.

Berner, Brad K. *The Spanish–American War: A Historical Dictionary*. Lanham, Md.: Scarecrow Press, 1998.

Correspondence Relating to the War with Spain Including the Insurrection in the Philippine Islands and the China Relief Expedition: April 15, 1898 to July 30, 1902. 2 vols. Washington, D.C.: Government Printing Office, 1993.

Cosmos, Graham A. *An Army for Empire: The United States Army in the Spanish–American War*. Columbia: University of Missouri Press, 1971.

De Quesada, Alejandro M. *The Spanish–American War in Tampa Bay*. Charleston, S.C.: Arcadia, 1999.

Freidel, Frank. *The Splendid Little War*. Boston: Little, Brown, 1958.

Rosenfield, Harvey. *Diary of a Dirty Little War: The Spanish–American War of 1898*. Westport, Conn.: Praeger, 2000.

Trask, David E. *The War with Spain in 1898*. New York: McMillan, 1981.

Ziel, Ron. *Birth of the American Century: Centennial History of the Spanish American War*. Mattituck, N.Y.: Amereon, 1997.

J. Philippine Insurrection

Gates, John M. *Schoolbooks and Krags: The U.S. Army in the Philippines, 1898–1902*. Westport, Conn.: Greenwood, 1973.

LeRoy, James A. *The Americans in the Philippines: A History of the Conquest and First Years of Occupation*. 2 vols. Best Books, 1914.

Linn, Brian M. *The U.S. Army and Counterinsurgency in the Philippine War, 1899–1902*. Chapel Hill, University of North Carolina Press, 1989.

——. *The Philippine War*. Lawrence: University Press of Kansas, 1999.

Sexton, William T. *Soldiers in the Sun*. Harrisburg, Pa.: Military Service, 1939. 2d ed. 1944, retitled *Soldiers in the Philippines: A History of the Insurrection*.

Welch, Richard E. *Response to Imperialism: The United States and the Philippine-American War, 1899–1902*. Chapel Hill: University of North Carolina Press, 1979.

K. World War I

American Battle Monuments Commission. *American Armies and Battlefields in Europe: A History, Guide, and Reference Book*. Washington, D.C.: Government Printing Office, 1938.

Braim, Paul F. *The Test of Battle: The American Expeditionary Forces in the Meuse–Argonne Campaign*. 1987. Rev. ed. Shippensburg, Pa.: White Mane, 1997.

Evans, Martin Marix. *Retreat, Hell! We Just Got Here! The American Expeditionary Force in France, 1917–1918*. New York: Osprey, 1998.

Farwell, Byron. *Over There: The United States in the Great War, 1917–1918*. New York: Norton, 2000.

Hallas, James H., ed. *Doughboy War: The American Expeditionary Force in World War I*. Boulder, Colo.: Rienner, 1999.

Hogg, Ian. *Historical Dictionary of World War I*. Lanham, Md.: Scarecrow Press, 1997.

Johnson, Douglas V., and Rolfe L. Hillman Jr., eds. *Soissons 1918*. College Station: Texas A. & M. University Press, 1999.

Mead, Gary. *The Doughboys: America and the First World War*. New York: Overlook, 2001.

Venzon, Anne C., ed. *The United States in the First World War: An Encyclopedia*. New York: Garland, 1995.

L. World War II: General

Cline, Ray S. *Washington Command Post: The Operations Division*. Washington, D.C.: Government Printing Office, 1951.

Coles, Harry L., and Albert K. Weinberg. *Civil Affairs: Soldiers Become Governors*. Washington, D.C.: Government Printing Office,1964.

Greenfield, Kenneth Roberts, ed. *Command Decisions*. Washington, D.C.: Government Printing Office, 1960.

Greenfield, Kent Roberts, Robert R. Palmer, and Bell I. Wiley. *The Organization of Ground Combat Troops*. Washington, D.C.: Government Printing Office, 1947.

Hogan, David W. *U.S. Army Special Operations in World War II*. Washington, D.C.: Government Printing Office, 1992.

Kirkpatrick, Charles E. *An Unknown Future and a Doubtful Present: Writing the Victory Plan of 1941*. Washington, D.C.: Government Printing Office, 1990.

McManus, John C. *The Deadly Brotherhood: The American Combat Soldier in World War II*. Novato, Calif.: Presidio, 1998.

Morton, Louis. *Strategy and Command: The First Two Years*. Washington, D.C.: Government Printing Office, 1962.
Pogue, Forrest C. *The Supreme Command*. Washington, D.C.: Government Printing Office, 1954.
Polmar, Norman, and Thomas B. Allen, eds. *World War II. America at War, 1941–1945*. New York: Random House, 1994.
Smith, R. Elberton. *The Army and Economic Mobilization*. Washington, D.C.: Government Printing Office, 1959.
Treadwell, Mattie E. *The Women's Army Corps*. Washington, D.C.: Government Printing Office,1954.
Watson, Mark S. *Chief of Staff: Prewar Plans and Preparations*. Washington, D.C.: Government Printing Office, 1950.
Williams, Mary H. *U.S. Army in World War II: Chronology, 1941–1945*. Washington, D.C.: Government Printing Office, 1960.
Ziemke, Earl F. *Stalingrad to Berlin: The German Defeat in the East*. Washington, D.C.: Government Printing Office, 1968.
Ziemke, Earl F., and Magna E. Bauer. *Moscow to Stalingrad: Decision in the East*. Washington, D.C.: Government Printing Office, 1987.

M. World War II: Europe and the Mediterranean

Ambrose, Stephen E. *Citizen Soldiers: The U.S. Army from the Normandy Beaches to the Bulge to the Surrender of Germany, June 7, 1944–May 7, 1945*. New York: Simon & Schuster, 1997.
Blumenson, Martin. *Breakout and Pursuit*. Washington, D.C.: Government Printing Office, 1961.
——. *Anzio: The Gamble That Failed*. Washington, D.C.: Government Printing Office, 1963.
——. *Salerno to Cassino*. Washington, D.C.: Government Printing Office, 1969.
Clarke, Jeffrey J., and Robert Ross Smith. *Riviera to the Rhine*. Washington, D.C.: Government Printing Office, 1993.
Cole, Hugh M. *The Lorraine Campaign*. Washington, D.C.: Government Printing Office, 1950.
——. *The Ardennes: Battle of the Bulge*. Washington, D.C.: Government Printing Office, 1965.
Fisher, Ernest F., Jr. *Cassino to the Alps*. Washington, D.C.: Government Printing Office, 1977.
Garland, Albert N., and Howard McGraw Smith. *Sicily and the Surrender of Italy*. Washington, D.C.: Government Printing Office, 1965.
Harris, Gordon A. *Cross Channel Attack*. Washington, D.C.: Government Printing Office, 1951.
Howe, George F. *Northwest Africa: Seizing the Initiative in the West*. Washington, D.C.: Government Printing Office, 1957.
MacDonald, Charles B. *The Last Offensive*. Washington, D.C.: Government Printing Office, 1973.
—— *A Time for Trumpets: The Untold Story of the Battle of the Bulge*. 1985.
Mansoor, Peter R. *The GI Offensive in Europe: The Triumph of American Infantry Divisions, 1941–1945*. Lawrence: University Press of Kansas, 1999.
Marshall, S. L. A. *Bastogne: The First Eight Days*. Washington, D.C.: Government Printing Office, 1988.

Prefer, Nathan N. *Patton's Ghost Corps: Cracking the Siegfried Line*. Novato, Calif.: Presidio, 1998.

U.S. Army Center of Military History. *Salerno: American Operations from the Beaches to the Volturno, 9 September–6 October 1943*. Washington, D.C.: Government Printing Office, 1943.

———. *From the Volturno to the Winter Line, 6 October–15 October 1943*. Washington, D.C.: Government Printing Office, 1944.

———. *Utah Beach to Cherbourg, 6–27 June 1944*. Washington, D.C.: Government Printing Office, 1944.

———. *Fifth Army at the Winter Line, 15 November 1943–15 January 1944*. Washington, D.C.: Government Printing Office, 1945.

———. *Omaha Beachhead*. Washington, D.C.: Government Printing Office, 1945.

———. *Small Unit Actions*. Washington, D.C.: Government Printing Office, 1946.

———. *St-Lo*. Washington, D.C.: Government Printing Office, 1946.

———. *Anzio Beachhead, 22 January–25 May 1944*. Washington, D.C.: Government Printing Office, 1947.

———. *The War against Germany: Europe and Adjacent Areas*. Washington, D.C.: Government Printing Office, 1951.

———. *The War against Germany and Italy: Mediterranean and Adjacent Areas*. Washington, D.C.: Government Printing Office, 1951.

Weigley, Russell F. *Eisenhower's Lieutenants: The Campaigns of France and Germany, 1941–1945*. Bloomington: Indiana University Press, 1981.

N. World War II: Pacific

Appleman, Roy E., James M. Burns, Russel A. Gugeler, and John Stevens. *Okinawa: The Last Battle*. Washington, D.C.: Government Printing Office, 1948.

Cannon, M. Hamlin. *Leyte: The Return to the Philippines*. Washington, D.C.: Government Printing Office, 1954.

Crowl, Philip A. *Campaign in the Marianas*. Washington, D.C.: Government Printing Office, 1960.

Crowl, Philip A., and Edmond G. Love. *Seizure of the Gilberts and Marshalls*. Washington, D.C.: Government Printing Office, 1955.

Miller, John, Jr. *Guadalcanal: The First Offensive*. Washington, D.C.: Government Printing Office, 1949.

———. *Cartwheel: The Reduction of Rabaul*. Washington, D.C.: Government Printing Office, 1959.

Milner, Samuel. *Victor in Papua*. Washington, D.C.: Government Printing Office, 1957.

Morton, Louis. *The Fall of the Philippines*. Washington, D.C.: Government Printing Office, 1953.

Prefer, Nathan N. *Vinegar Joe's War: Stilwell's Campaign in Burma*. Novato, Calif.: Presidio, 2000.

Romanus, Charles F., and Riley Sutherland. *Stilwell's Command Problems*. Washington, D.C.: Government Printing Office, 1956.

———. *Stilwell's Mission to China*. Washington, D.C.: Government Printing Office, 1956.

———. *Time Runs Out in CBI*. Washington, D.C.: Government Printing Office, 1959.

Smith, Robert Ross. *The Approach to the Philippines*. Washington, D.C.: Government Printing Office, 1953.

———. *Triumph in the Philippines*. Washington, D.C.: Government Printing Office,1963.
U.S. Army Center of Military History. *To Bizerte with the II Corps, 23 April–13 May 1943*. Washington, D.C.: Government Printing Office, 1943.
———. *Papuan Campaign: The Buna–Sananandan Operation, 16 November 1942–23 January 1943*. Washington, D.C.: Government Printing Office, 1944.
———. *The Admiralties: Operations of the 1st Cavalry Division, 29 February–18 May 1944*. Washington, D.C.: Government Printing Office, 1945.
———. *Merrill's Marauders, February–May 1944*. Washington, D.C.: Government Printing Office, 1945.
———. *The Capture of Makin, 20–24 November 1943*. Washington D.C.: Government Printing Office, 1946.
———. *Guam: Operations of the 77th Division, 21 July–10 August 1944*. Washington, D.C.: Government Printing Office, 1946.
Well, Anne Sharp. *Historical Dictionary of World War II: The War against Japan*. Lanham, Md.: Scarecrow Press, 1999.

O. Korean War

Appleman, Roy E. *South to the Naktong, North to the Yalu*. Washington, D.C.: Government Printing Office, 1961.
Gugeler, Russel A. *Combat Actions in Korea*. Washington, D.C.: Government Printing Office, 1970.
Hermes, William G. *Truce Tent and Fighting Front*. Washington, D.C.: Government Printing Office, 1966.
Marshall, S. L. A. *Pork Chop Hill: The American Fighting Man in Action*. Nashville, Tenn.: Battery Press, 1953.
Miller, John, Jr., Owen J. Carroll, and Margaret Tackley. *Korea, 1950*. Washington, D.C.: Government Printing Office, 1952.
Mossman, Billy C. *Ebb and Flow*. Washington, D.C.: Government Printing Office, 1990.
Ridgway, Matthew B. *The Korean War*. Garden City, N.Y.: Doubleday, 1967.
Sawyer, Robert K. *Military Advisors in Korea: KMAG in Peace and War*. Washington, D.C.: Government Printing Office, 1963.
Schnabel, James. F. *Policy and Direction: The First Year*. Washington, D.C.: Government Printing Office, 1972.
Weintraub, Stanley. *MacArthur's War: Korea and the Undoing of an American Hero*. New York: Free Press, 2000.

P. Vietnam War

Bergen, John D. *Military Communications: A Test for Technology*. Washington, D.C.: Government Printing Office, 1986.
Bergerud, Eric M. *Red Thunder, Tropic Lightning: The World of a Combat Division in Vietnam*. New York: Penguin, 1994.
Cash, John A., John N. Albright and Allan Sandstrum. *Seven Firefights in Vietnam*. Washington, D.C.: Government Printing Office, 1970.
Clarke, Jeffrey J. *Advice and Support: The Final Years, 1965–1973*. Washington, D.C.: Government Printing Office, 1988.

Karnow, Stanley. *Vietnam: A History*. New York: Viking, 1983.

Kinnard, Douglas. *The War Managers: American Generals Reflect on Vietnam*. New York: Da Capo, 1991.

LeGro, William E. *Vietnam from Cease Fire to Capitulation*. Washington, D.C.: Government Printing Office, 1981.

Moise, Edwin E. *Historical Dictionary of the Vietnam War*. Lanham, Md.: Scarecrow Press, 2001.

Nolan, Keith William. *Ripcord: Screaming Eagles under Siege, Vietnam 1970*. Novato, Calif.: Presidio, 2000.

MacGarrigle, George L. *Combat Operations: Taking the Offensive, October 1996 to October 1997*. Washington, D.C.: Government Printing Office, 1998.

Meyerson, Joel D. *Images of a Lengthy War*. Washington, D.C.: Government Printing Office, 1986.

Palmer, Bruce, Jr. *The 25-Year War: America's Military Role in Vietnam*. Lexington: University Press of Kentucky, 1984.

Palmer, Dave R. *Summons of the Trumpet: U.S.–Vietnam in Perspective*. Novato, Calif.: Presidio, 1978.

Scoville, Thomas W. *Reorganizing for Pacification Support*. Washington, D.C.: Government Printing Office, 1982.

Spector, Ronald H. *Advice and Support: The Early Years, 1941–1960*. Washington, D.C.: Government Printing Office, 1983.

Summers, Harry G., Jr. *On Strategy: A Critical Analysis of the Vietnam War*. Carlisle Barracks, Pa.: Army War College Strategic Studies Institute, 1982.

Zaffiri, Samuel. *Hamburger Hill: The Brutal Battle for Dong Ap Bia, May 11–20, 1969*. Novato, Calif.: Presidio, 2000.

Q. Cold War

Epley, William W., ed. *International Cold War Military Records and History: Proceedings of the International Conference*. Washington, D.C.: Government Printing Office, 1996.

Halle, Louis J. *The Cold War as History*. New York: Harper and Row, 1967.

Smith, Joseph, and Simon Davis. *Historical Dictionary of the Cold War*. Lanham, Md.: Scarecrow Press, 2000.

Ziemke, Earl F. *The U.S. Army in the Occupation of Germany, 1944–1946*. Washington, D.C.: Government Printing Office, 1975.

R. Persian Gulf War

Atkinson, Rick. *Crusade: The Untold Story of the Persian Gulf War*. Boston: Houghton Mifflin, 1993.

Clancy, Tom, with Fred Franks Jr. *Into the Storm: A Study in Command*. New York: Putnam, 1997.

Gehring, Stephen P. *From the Fulda Gap to Kuwait: U.S. Army, Europe, and the Gulf War*. Washington, D.C.: Government Printing Office, 1998.

Houlahan, Thomas. *Gulf War: The Complete History*. New London, Conn.: Schrenker Military Publishing, 1999.

Newell, Clayton R. *Historical Dictionary of the Persian Gulf War, 1990–1991*. Lanham, Md.: Scarecrow Press, 1998.

Scales, Robert H. *Certain Victory: The United States Army in the Gulf War*. Washington, D.C.: Office of the Chief of Staff, U.S. Army, 1993.

Schubert, Frank N., and Theresa L. Kraus, eds. *The Whirlwind War: The United States Army in Operations Desert Shield and Desert Storm*. Washington, D.C.: Government Printing Office, 1995.

Summers, Harry G. *Persian Gulf War Almanac*. New York: Facts on File, 1995.

Swain, Richard M. *"Lucky War": Third Army in Desert Storm*. Fort Leavenworth, Kans.: U.S. Army Command and General Staff College Press, 1994.

Taylor, Thomas. *Lightning in the Storm: The 101st Air Assault Division in the Gulf War*. New York: Hippocrene Books, 1994.

III. BIOGRAPHIES

A. Collections

Bell, William Gardner. *Secretaries of War and Secretaries of the Army*. 1981. Revised ed., Washington, D.C.: Government Printing Office, 1992.

——. *Commanding Generals and Chiefs of Staff, 1775–1995*. 1983. Revised ed., Washington, D.C.: Government Printing Office, 1999.

Billias, George Athan, ed. *George Washington's Generals*. New York: Morrow, 1964.

Boritt, Gabor S., ed. *Lincoln's Generals*. New York: Oxford University Press, 1994.

Cullum, George W. *Biographical Register of the Officers and Graduates of the United States Military Academy*. 3 vols. 3d ed., revised and enlarged. Boston: Houghton Mifflin, 1891. Vols. 4–9. West Point, N.Y.: Aegis of Association of Graduates, U.S. Military Academy, 1901–1950.

Fuller, John F. C. *Grant and Lee: A Study in Personality and Generalship*. London: Eyre and Spottiswoode, 1933.

Gillespie, Mark F., Glen R. Hawkins, Michel B Kelly, and Preston E. Pierce. *The Sergeants Major of the Army*. Washington, D.C.: Government Printing Office, 1995.

Hamersly, Thomas H. S. *Complete Army and Navy Register of the United States of America, 1776–1887*.

Heitman, Francis B. *Historical Register of Officers of the Continental Army during the War of the Revolution, April 1775 to December 1783*. Reprint ed. Baltimore: Clearfield, 2000.

Ingersoll, Lurton D. *A History of the War Department of the United States with Biographical Sketches of the Secretaries*. Washington, D.C.: Francis B. Mohun, 1880.

Pratt, Fletcher. *Eleven Generals: Studies in American Command*. New York: William Sloan's Associates, 1949.

Rodenbough, Theophilus R., and William L. Haskin, eds. *The Army of the United States: Historical Sketches of Staff and Line with Portraits of Generals-in-Chief*. New York: Maynard, Merrill, 1896.

Sifakis, Stewart. *Who Was Who in the Civil War*. New York: Facts on File, 1988.

Spiller, Roger J., et al., eds. *Dictionary of American Military Biography*. 3 vols. Westport, Conn.: Greenwood, 1984.

Williams, T. Harry. *Lincoln and His Generals*. New York: Knopf, 1952.

——. *McClellan, Sherman, and Grant*. The 1962 Brown and Haley Lectures. New Brunswick, N.J.: Rutgers University Press, 1962.

B. Memoirs

Avery, James Henry. *Under Custer's Command: The Civil War Journal of James Henry Avery.* Compiled by Karla Jean Husby. Edited by Eric J. Wittenburg. Washington, D.C.: Brassey's, 2000.

Birdwell, Dwight W. *A Hundred Miles of Bad Road: An Armored Cavalryman in Vietnam, 1967–1968.* Novato, Calif.: Presidio, 2000.

Bond, Otto F., ed. *Under the Flag of the Nation: Diaries and Letters of Owen Johnston Hopkins, A Yankee Volunteer in the Civil War.* Columbus: Ohio State University Press, 1998.

Brady, James. *The Coldest War: A Memoir of Korea.* New York: St. Martin's, 2000.

Bray, Robert, and Paul Bushnell, eds. *Diary of a Common Soldier in the American Revolution, 1775–1783: An Annotated Edition of the Military Journal of Jeremiah Greenman.* Dekalb: Northern Illinois University Press, 1978.

Burriss, T. Moffatt. *Strike and Hold: A Memoir of the 82d Airborne in World War II.* Washington, D.C.: Brassey's, 2000.

Castel, Albert. *Tom Taylor's Civil War.* Lawrence: University Press of Kansas, 2000.

Cooper, Belton Y. *Death Traps: The Survival of an American Armored Division in World War II.* Novato, Calif.: Presidio, 1998.

Cornet, Alan G. *Gone Native: An NCO's Story.* New York: Ballantine, 2000.

Courtney, Richard D. *Normandy to the Bulge: An American Infantry GI in Europe during World War II.* Carbondale: Southern Illinois University Press, 2000.

Gause, Damon. *The War Journal of Major Damon "Rocky" Gause.* Boston: Little, Brown, 1999.

Hayes, Roger. *On Point: A Rifleman's Year in the Boonies: Vietnam, 1967–1968.* Novato, Calif.: Presidio, 2000.

Hildebrand, James E. *Cannon Fodder: From Basic to Purple Heart, Letters to Home.* Las Cruces, N. Mex.: Yucca Tree, 1999.

Hines, Walter. *Aggies of the Pacific War: New Mexico A & M and the War with Japan.* Las Cruces, N. Mex.: Yucca Tree, 1999.

Hogan, Eva B. *The Last Buffalo: Walter E. Potts and the 92nd "Buffalo" Division in World War I.* Austin, Tex.: Eakin, 2000.

Humphries, James F. *Through the Valley: Vietnam, 1967–1968.* Boulder, Colo.: Rienner, 1999.

Kotlowitz, Robert. *Before Their Time: A Memoir.* New York: Delta, 1999.

Lawrence, Joseph Douglas. *Fighting Soldier: The AEF in 1918.* Edited by Robert H. Ferrell. Boulder, Colo.: Colorado Associated University Press, 1985.

MacDonald, Charles B. *Company Commander.* New York: Ballantine, 1966.

Mack, Richard E. *Memoir of a Cold War Soldier.* Kent, Ohio: Kent State University Press, 2000.

Major, James Russell. *The Memoirs of an Artillery Forward Observer, 1944–1945.* Manhattan, Kans.: Sunflower University Press, 1999.

McDonough, James R. *Platoon Leader.* Novato, Calif.: Presidio, 1985.

McKenzie, John. *On Time, on Target: The World War II Memoir of a Paratrooper in the 82d Airborne.* Novato, Calif.: Presidio, 2000.

Post, John Michael., ed. *John T. McMahon's Diary of the 136th New York, 1861–1864.* Shippensburg, Pa.: White Mane, 1993.

Sneden, Robert Knox. *Eye of the Storm: A Civil War Odyssey.* Edited by Charles F. Bryan and Nelson D. Lankford. New York: Free Press, 2000.

Stroup, Russell Cartwright. *Letters from the Pacific: A Combat Chaplain in World War II.* Edited by Richard Cartwright Austin. Columbia: University of Missouri Press, 2000.

TeCube, Leroy. *Year in Nam: A Native American Soldier's Story*. Lincoln: University of Nebraska Press, 1999.
Terry, Addison. *The Battle for Pusan: The Korean War Memoir of a Field Artilleryman*. Novato, Calif.: Presidio, 2000.
Triplet, William S. *A Youth in the Meuse–Argonne: A Memoir, 1917–1918*. Edited by Robert H. Ferrell. Columbia: University of Missouri Press, 2000.
Vernon, Alex. *The Eyes of Orion: Five Lieutenants in the Persian Gulf War*. Kent, Ohio: Kent State University Press, 1999.

C. Individuals

Abrams, Creighton Williams, Jr.

Sorley, Lewis. *Thunderbolt: General Creighton Abrams and the Army of His Times*. New York: Simon & Schuster, 1992.

Alger, Russell Alexander

Russell Alexander Alger: Late Senator in the Congress of the United States from Michigan. Lansing: n.p., 1907.

Armstrong, John

Armstrong, John. *Notices on the War of 1812*. 2 vols. New York: Wiley and Putnam, 1840.
Skeen, C. Edward. *John Armstrong, 1758–1843: A Biography*. Syracuse, N.Y.: Syracuse University Press, 1981.

Arnold, Benedict

Fritz, Jean. *Traitor: The Case of Benedict Arnold*. New York: Putnam, 1997.
Flexner, James Thomas. *The Traitor and the Spy: Benedict Arnold and John Andre*. New York: Harcourt, Brace, 1953.
Martin, James Kirby. *Benedict Arnold, Revolutionary Hero: An American Warrior Reconsidered*. New York: New York University Press, 1997.
Wallace, Willard M. *Traitorous Hero: The Life and Fortunes of Benedict Arnold*. New York: Harper, 1954.

Arnold, Henry Harold

Arnold, H. H. *Global Mission*. New York: McGraw-Hill, 1989.

Baker, Newton Diehl

Beaver, Daniel R. *Newton D. Baker and the American War Effort, 1917–1919*. Lincoln: University of Nebraska Press, 1966.
Cramer, C. H. *Newton D. Baker: A Biography*. Cleveland, Ohio: World, 1961.
Palmer, Frederick. *Newton D. Baker: America at War*. 2 vols. New York: Dodd, Mead, 1931.

Barbour, James

Long, William S. *James Barbour*. N.p., 1913.
Lowery, Charles D. *James Barbour: A Jeffersonian Republican*. Birmingham: University of Alabama Press, 1984.

Barton, Clara

Barton, William E. *Life of Clara Barton*. 2 vols. New York: AMS Press, 1922.
Oates, Stephen. *A Woman of Valor: Clara Barton and the Civil War*. New York: Free Press, 1994.

Bell, J. Franklin

Raines, Edgar F., Jr. "Major General J. Franklin Bell and Military Reform: The Chief of Staff Years, 1906–1910." 2 vols. Ph.D. dissertation, University of Wisconsin-Madison, 1976.

Belknap, William Worth

Impeachment of William W. Belknap, Late Secretary of War. Washington, D.C.: Government Printing Office, 1876.

Bell, John

The Life, Speeches, and Public Service of John Bell. New York: Rudd and Carleton, 1860.
Parks, Joseph H. *John Bell of Tennessee*. Baton Rouge: Louisiana State University Press, 1950.

Black Hawk

Black Hawk. *Black Hawk: An Autobiography*. Edited by Donald Jackson. Urbana: University of Illinois Press, 1964.
Nichols, Roger L. *Black Hawk and the Warrior's Path*. Arlington Heights, Ill.: Harlan Davidson, 1992.

Bliss, Tasker H.

Palmer, Frederick. *Bliss, Peacemaker: The Life and Letters of General Tasker Howard Bliss*. New York: Dodd, Mead, 1934.
Trask, David F. *General Tasker Howard Bliss and the "Sessions of the World," 1919*. Philadelphia: American Philosophical Society, 1966.

Bradley, Omar N.

Bradley, Omar N. *A Soldier's Story*. New York: Henry Holt, 1951.
Bradley, Omar N., and Clay Blair. *A General's Life: An Autobiography*. New York: Simon & Schuster, 1983.
Whiting, Charles. *Bradley*. Illustrated History of the Violent Century series. New York: Ballantine, 1971.

Brown, Jacob J.

Latham, Frank B. *Jacob Brown and the War of 1812*. New York: Cowles, 1971.

Brucker, Wilber Marion

Brucker, Clara H. *To Have Your Cake and Eat It*. New York: Vantage, 1968.

Burgoyne, John

Hargrove, Richard J., Jr. *General John Burgoyne*. Wilmington: University of Delaware Press, 1983.
Howson, Gerald. *Burgoyne of Saratoga*. New York: Crown, 1979.
Mintz, Max M. *The Generals of Saratoga: John Burgoyne and Horatio Gates*. New Haven, Conn.: Yale University Press, 1992.

Burnside, Ambrose

Marvel, William. *Burnside*. Chapel Hill: University of North Carolina Press, 1991.

Calhoun, John Caldwell

Calhoun, John C. *The Papers of John C. Calhoun*. 20 vols. Columbia: University of South Carolina Press, 1959–1991.
Coit, Margaret L. *John C. Calhoun, American Patriot*. Boston: Houghton Mifflin, 1950.
Current, Richard N. *John C. Calhoun*. New York: Washington Square, 1963.
Niven, John. *John C. Calhoun and the Price of Union: A Biography*. Baton Rouge: Louisiana State University Press, 1988.
Wiltse, Charles M. *John C. Calhoun, 1782–1828*. 3 vols. Indianapolis: Bobbs-Merrill, 1944–1951.

Cameron, Simon

Bradley, Erwin S. *Simon Cameron, Lincoln's Secretary of War: A Political Biography*. Philadelphia: University of Pennsylvania Press, 1966.

Cass, Lewis

Hickman, George H. *The Life of General Lewis Cass*. Baltimore: N. Hickman, 1848.
McLaughlin, Andrew C. *Lewis Cass*. 1879. Reprint ed. Boston: Houghton Mifflin, 1972.
Smith, William L. *Fifty Years of Public Life: The Life and Times of Lewis Cass*. New York: Derby and Jackson, 1856.
Woodford, Frank B. *Lewis Cass: The Last Jeffersonian*. New Brunswick, N.J.: Rutgers University Press, 1950.

Chaffee, Adna R.

Carter, William Harding. *The Life of Lieutenant General Chaffee*. Chicago: University of Chicago Press, 1917.

Chamberlain, Joshua Lawrence

Trulock, Alice Rains. *In the Hands of Providence: Joshua L. Chamberlain and the American Civil War*. Chapel Hill: University of North Carolina Press, 1992.

Chief Joseph

Beal, Merrill D. *"I Will Fight No More Forever": Chief Joseph and the Nez Perce War*. Seattle: University of Washington Press, 1963.

Clark, Mark Wayne

Blumenson, Martin. *Mark Clark: Last of the Great World War II Commanders*. New York: Congdon and Weed, 1984.
Clark, Mark W. *From the Danube to the Yalu*. New York: Harper, 1954.

Clark, William

See Lewis, Meriwether.

Clay, Lucius DuBignon

Backer, John H. *Winds of History: The German Years of Lucius DuBignon Clay*. New York: Van Nostrand Reinhold, 1983.
Clay, Lucius D. *Decision in Germany*. New York: Doubleday, 1950.

Clinton, Henry

Willcox, William B. *Portrait of a General: Sir Henry Clinton in the War of Independence*. New York: Knopf, 1964.

Collins, J. Lawton

Collins, J. Lawton. *War in Peacetime: The History and Lessons of Korea*. Boston: Houghton Mifflin, 1969.
——. *Lightning Joe: An Autobiography*. Baton Rouge: Louisiana State University Press, 1979.

Cornwallis, Charles

Wickwire, Franklin, and Mary Wickwire. *Cornwallis: The American Adventure*. New York: Harcourt Brace, 1970.

Crawford, William Harris

Butler, Benjamin F. *Sketches of the Life and Character of William H. Crawford*. Albany, N.Y.: Packard and Van Benthuysen, 1824.

Cutler, Everette W. *William Harris Crawford*. Charlotte: University of North Carolina Press, 1965.
Mooney, Chase C. *William H. Crawford, 1772–1834*. Lexington: University Press of Kentucky, 1974.

Crazy Horse

McMurtry, Larry. *Crazy Horse*. New York: Viking Penguin, 2001.
Sandoz, Mari. *Crazy Horse, Strange Man of the Oglalas*. Lincoln: University Press of Nebraska, 1942.

Crook, George

Aleshire, Peter. *The Fox and the Whirlwind: General George Crook and Geronimo: A Paired Biography*. New York: Wiley, 2000.
Crook, George. *General George Crook: His Autobiography*. Edited by Martin F. Schmitt. Norman: University of Oklahoma Press, 1946.

Custer, George Armstrong

Custer, George A., and Elizabeth Custer. *The Custer Story: The Life and Intimate Letters of General George A. Custer and His Wife Elizabeth*. Edited by Marguerite Merington. New York: Devin-Adair, 1950.
Monaghan, Jay. *Custer: The Life of General George Armstrong Custer*. Boston: Little, Brown, 1959.
Utley, Robert M. *Cavalier in Buckskin: George Armstrong Custer and the Western Military Frontier*. Norman: University of Oklahoma Press, 1988.

Davis, Benjamin O., Jr.

Davis, Benjamin O., Jr. *An Autobiography*. Washington, D.C.: Smithsonian Institution Press, 1991.

Davis, Benjamin O., Sr.

Fletcher, Marvin E. *America's First Black General: Benjamin O. Davis, Sr., 1880–1970*. Lawrence: University Press of Kansas, 1989.

Davis, Jefferson

Chance, Joseph E. *Jefferson Davis's Mexican War Regiment*. Jackson: University of Mississippi, 1991.
Cutting, Elizabeth B. *Jefferson Davis, Political Soldier*. New York: Dodd, Mead, 1930.
Davis, Jefferson. *The Papers of Jefferson Davis*. 9 vols. Edited by Lynda L. Curtis et al. Baton Rouge: Louisiana State University Press, 1971– .
Davis, William C. *Jefferson Davis: The Man and His Hour*. New York: HarperCollins, 1991.
Dodd, William E. *Jefferson Davis*. New York: Russell and Russell, 1966.

Eaton, Clement. *Jefferson Davis*. New York: Macmillan, 1977.
Langhein, Eric. *Jefferson Davis, Patriot.* New York: Vantage, 1962.

Dearborn, Henry

Brown, Lloyd A., and Howard H. Peckham. *Revolutionary War Journal of Henry Dearborn.* Chicago: Caxton Club, 1939. Reprint ed., New York: Da Capo, 1971.
Coffin, Charles, comp. *The Lives and Services of Major General John Thomas, Colonel Thomas Knowlton, Colonel Alexander Scammell, Major General Henry Dearborn.* New York: Egbert, Hovery & King, 1845.
Erney, Richard Alton. *The Public Life of Henry Dearborn.* New York: Arno, 1979.

Dickinson, Jacob McGavock

The Jacob McGavock Dickinson Papers. Nashville: Tennessee State Library and Archives, 1959.

Doniphan, Alexander

Robinson, Jacob S. *A Journal of the Santa Fe Expedition under Colonel Doniphan.* Princeton: Princeton University Press, 1932.

Eisenhower, Dwight D.

Ambrose, Stephen E. *Ike, Abilene to Berlin: The Life of Dwight D. Eisenhower.* New York: Harper and Row, 1973.
——. *Eisenhower: Soldier, General of the Army, President-Elect.* New York: Simon & Schuster, 1983.
Childs, Marquis W. *Eisenhower, Captive Hero: A Critical Study of the General and the President.* New York: Harcourt, Brace, 1958.
Eisenhower, David. *Eisenhower at War: 1943–1945.* New York: Random House, 1986.
Eisenhower, Dwight D. *Crusade in Europe.* Garden City, N.Y.: Doubleday, 1948.
Eisenhower, Dwight D. *The Papers of Dwight David Eisenhower.* 9 vols. Edited by Alfred D. Chandler Jr. et al. Baltimore: Johns Hopkins University Press, 1970–1978.
Ferrell, Robert H., ed. *The Eisenhower Diaries.* New York: Norton, 1981.
Hatch, Alden. *General Ike: A Biography of Dwight D. Eisenhower.* New York: Henry Holt, 1944.
Lyon, Peter. *Eisenhower: Portrait of a Hero.* Boston: Little, Brown, 1974.
Perret, Geoffrey. *Eisenhower.* Holbrook, Mass.: Adams Media, 1999.

Elkins, Stephen Benton

Lambert, Oscar D. *Stephen Benton Elkins.* Pittsburgh: University of Pittsburgh Press, 1955.

Endicott, William Crowninshield

Choate, Joseph H. *Memoir of William Crowninshield Endicott.* Cambridge, Mass.: J. Wilson and Son, 1904.
Lawrence, William. *William Crowninshield Endicott.* Boston: Merrymount, 1936.

Eustis, William

Barnaby, James. *A Sermon Delivered at Salisbury, Mass., on the Death of His Excellency William Eustis, February 13, 1825.* Newburyport, Mass.: W. and J. Gilman, 1825.

Forrest, Nathan Bedford

Henry, Robert Selph. *"First with the Most" Forrest.* Indianapolis, Ind.: Bobbs-Merrill, 1944.
Wills, Brian Steel. *A Battle from the Start: The Life of Nathan Bedford Forrest.* New York: HarperCollins, 1992.

Gage, Thomas

Alden, John R. *General Gage in America: Being Principally a History of His Role in the American Revolution.* Baton Rouge: Louisiana State University Press, 1948.

Gates, Horatio

Nelson, Paul David. *General Horatio Gates: A Biography.* Baton Rouge: Louisiana State University Press, 1976.
Patterson, Samuel W. *Horatio Gates: Defender of American Liberties.* New York: Columbia University Press, 1941.
See also Burgoyne, John.

Geronimo

Debo, Angie. *Geronimo: The Man, His Time, His Place.* Norman: University of Oklahoma Press, 1989.
See also Crook, George.

Goethals, George W.

Bishop, Joseph B., and Farham Bishop. *Goethals, Genius of the Panama Canal: A Biography.* New York: Harper and Brothers, 1930.

Gorgas, William C.

Dolan, Deward F., Jr. and H. T. Silver. *William Crawford Gorgas: Warrior in White.* New York: Dodd, Mead, 1968.
Gorgas, Marie D., and Burton J. Hendrick. *William Crawford Gorgas: His Life and Work.* Garden City, N.Y.: Doubleday, 1924.

Grant, Ulysses S.

Badeau, Adam. *Military History of Ulysses S. Grant from April 1861 to April 1865.* 3 vols. New York: Appleton, 1868–1881.
———. *Grant in Peace: From Appomattox to Mount McGregor.* Hartford, Conn.: S. S. Scranton, 1887.

Catton, Bruce. *U. S. Grant and the American Military Tradition*. Library of American Biography. Boston: Little, Brown, 1954.
——. *Grant Moves South*. Boston: Little Brown, 1960.
——. *Grant Takes Command*. Boston: Little Brown, 1968.
Fuller, John Frederick Charles. *The Generalship of Ulysses S. Grant*. Civil War Centennial Series. New York: Dodd, Mead, 1929.
Grant, Ulysses S. *Personal Memoirs of U. S. Grant*. 2 vols. New York: Charles L. Webster, 1885–86. Numerous later editions, including E. B. Long, ed. Cleveland: World Publishing, 1952.
Lewis, Lloyd. *Captain Sam Grant*. Boston: Little, Brown, 1950.
McFeely, William S. *Grant: A Biography*. New York: Norton, 1981.
Grant, Ulysses S. *The Papers of Ulysses S. Grant*. 20 vols. to date. Edited by John Y. Simon. Carbondale: Southern Illinois University Press, 1967– .

Greene, Nathanael

Greene, Francis Vinton. *General Greene*. New York: Appleton, 1893.
Thane, Elswyth. *The Fighting Quaker: Nathanael Greene*. New York: Hawthorne Books, 1972.

Halleck, Henry

Ambrose, Stephen E. *Halleck: Lincoln's Chief of Staff*. Baton Rouge: Louisiana State University Press, 1962.
Halleck, Henry W. *Elements of Military Art and Science*. New York: Appleton, 1846.
——. *International Law: Or Rules Regulating the Intercourse of States in Peace and War*. New York: D. Van Nostrand, 1861.

Hamilton, Alexander

Cooke, Jacob E. *Alexander Hamilton*. New York: Scribner, 1982.
Hacker, Louis M. *Alexander Hamilton in the American Tradition*. New York: McGraw-Hill, 1957.
Hamilton, Alexander. Lodge, Henry Cabot, ed. *The Works of Alexander Hamilton*. 9 vols. Edited by Henry Cabot Lodge. New York: Putnam, 1885–86.
McDonald, Forrest. *Alexander Hamilton: A Biography*. New York: Norton, 1979.
Miller, John C. *Alexander Hamilton: Portrait in Paradox*. New York: Harper & Brothers, 1959.

Harmar, Josiah

Peckham, Howard H. "Josiah Harmar and His Indian Expedition." *Ohio State Archeological and Historical Quarterly* 55 (1946): 227–41.
Thornbrough, Gayle, ed. *Outpost on the Wabash, 1787–1791: Letters of Brigadier General Josiah Harmar*. Indianapolis: Indiana Historical Society, 1957.

Harrison, William Henry

Cleaves, Freeman. *Old Tippecanoe: William Henry Harrison*. New York: Scribner, 1939.

Holt, Joseph

Bateman, Roger. "The Contributions of Joseph Holt to the Political Life of the United States." Ph.D. dissertation, Fordham University, 1958.

Hurley, Patrick Jay

Buhite, Russell D. *Patrick J. Hurley and American Foreign Policy*. Ithaca, N.Y.: Cornell University Press, 1973.
La Moore, Parker. *"Pat" Hurley: The Story of an American*. New York: Brewer, Warren and Putnam, 1932.
Lohbeck, Don. *Patrick J. Hurley*. Chicago: Henry Regnery, 1956.

Hussein, Saddam

Karsh, Efraim, and Inari Rautsi. *Saddam Hussein: A Political Biography*. New York: Free Press, 1991.

Jackson, Andrew

James, Marquis. *Andrew Jackson: The Border Captain*. Indianapolis: Bobbs-Merrill, 1933.
Remini, Robert V. *Andrew Jackson*. 3 vols. New York: Harper and Row, 1977–84.

Jackson, Thomas J.

Chambers, Lenoir. *Stonewall Jackson*. 2 vols. New York: Morrow, 1959.
Farwell, Byron. *Stonewall: A Biography of General Jackson*. New York: Norton, 1992.
Henderson, G. F. R. *Stonewall Jackson and the American Civil War*. 2 vols. London: Longmans, Green, 1898.
Vandiver, Frank E. *Mighty Stonewall*. New York: McGraw-Hill, 1957.

Johnson, Harold K.

Sorley, Lewis. *Honorable Warrior: General Harold K. Johnson and the Ethics of Command*. Lawrence: University Press of Kansas, 1998.

Johnston, Joseph E.

Johnston, Joseph E. *Narrative of Military Operations, Directed, during the Late War between the States*. New York: Appleton, 1874.
Symonds, Craig L. *Joseph E. Johnston*. New York: Norton, 1992.

Kearny, Stephen Watts

Clarke, Dwight L. *Stephen Watts Kearny: Soldier of the West*. Norman: University of Oklahoma Press, 1961.

Knox, Henry

Brooks, Noah. *Henry Knox: A Soldier of the Revolution*. New York: Putnam, 1900.
Callahan, North. *Henry Knox: General Washington's General*. New York: Rinehart, 1958.
Denzil, Justin F. *Champion of Liberty, Henry Knox*. New York: Julian Messner, 1969.
Drake, Francis S. *Life and Correspondence of Henry Knox, Major General in the Revolutionary Army*. Boston: S. G. Drake, 1873.

Lafayette, Marquis de

Gottschalk, Louis. *Lafayette in America*. France: L'espirit De Lafayette Society, 1976.

Lee, Henry

Boyd, Thomas A. *Light-Horse Harry Lee: A Biography of Washington's Great Cavalryman*. New York: Doubleday, 1966.
Royster, Charles. *Light-Horse Harry Lee and the Legacy of the American Revolution*. New York: Knopf, 1981.

Lee, Robert E.

Connelly, Thomas L. *The Marble Man: Robert E. Lee and His Image in American Society*. New York: Knopf, 1977.
Cooke, John Easton. *A Life of Gen. Robert E. Lee*. New York: Appleton, 1871.
Freeman, Douglas Southall. *R. E. Lee: A Biography*. 4 vols. New York: Scribner, 1934–1935.
Lee, Robert E. *The Wartime Papers of R. E. Lee*. Edited by Clifford Dowday and Louis H. Manarin. Boston: Little, Brown, 1961.
Nolan, Alan T. *Lee Considered: General Robert E. Lee and Civil War History*. Chapel Hill: University of North Carolina Press, 1991.
Thomas, Emory H. *Robert E. Lee: A Biography*. New York: Norton, 1995.

Lewis, Meriwether

Ambrose, Stephen E. *Undaunted Courage: Meriwether Lewis, Thomas Jefferson, and the Opening of the American West*. New York: Simon & Schuster, 1996.
Bakeless, John. *Lewis and Clark: Partners in Discovery*. New York: Morrow, 1964.

Lincoln, Abraham

Ballard, Colin R. *The Military Genius of Abraham Lincoln*. London: Oxford University Press, 1926. Reprint ed., Cleveland: World, 1952.
Bruce, Robert V. *Lincoln and the Tools of War*. Indianapolis: Bobbs-Merrill, 1956.
Donald, David Herbert. *Lincoln Reconsidered: Essays on the Civil War Era*. New York: Knopf, 1956.
——. *Lincoln*. New York: Simon & Schuster, 1995.
McPherson, James M. *Abraham Lincoln and the Second American Revolution*. New York: Oxford University Press, 1990.
Randall, James G., and Richard N. Current. *Lincoln the President*. 4 vols. New York: Dodd, Mead, 1945–1955.

Lincoln, Benjamin

Cavanagh, John Carroll. "The Military Career of Major General Benjamin Lincoln in the War of American Revolution, 1775–1800." Ph.D. dissertation, Duke University, 1969.

Lincoln, Robert Todd

Goff, John S. *Robert Todd Lincoln: A Man in His Own Right*. Norman: University of Oklahoma Press, 1969.

Longstreet, James

Eckenrode, H. J., and Bryan Conrad. *James Longstreet: Lee's War Horse*. 1936. Reprint ed. Chapel Hill: University of North Carolina Press, 1986.
Longstreet, James. *From Manassas to Appomattox: Memoirs of the Civil War in America*. Philadelphia: J. B. Lippincott, 1896.
Piston, William Garrett. *Lee's Tarnished Lieutenant: James Longstreet and His Place in Southern History*. Athens: University of Georgia Press, 1987.
Wert, Jeffry D. *General James Longstreet, the Confederacy's Most Controversial Soldier: A Biography*. New York: Simon & Schuster, 1993.

MacArthur, Douglas

Hunt, Frazier. *The Untold Story of Douglas MacArthur*. New York: Devin-Adair, 1954.
James, D. Clayton. *The Years of MacArthur*. 3 vols. Boston: Houghton Mifflin, 1970, 1975, 1985.
Lowitt, Richard, comp. *The Truman-MacArthur Controversy*. Berkeley Series in American History. Chicago: Rand McNally, 1967.
MacArthur, Douglas. *Reminiscences*. New York: McGraw-Hill, 1964.
Manchester, William. *American Caesar: Douglas MacArthur, 1880–1964*. Boston: Little, Brown, 1978.
Miller, Francis Trevelyan. *General Douglas MacArthur: Fighter for Freedom*. Philadelphia: John C. Winston, 1942.
Petillo, Carol Morris. *Douglas MacArthur: The Philippine Years*. Bloomington: Indiana University Press, 1981.
Weintraub, Stanley. *MacArthur's War: Korea and the Undoing of an American Hero*. New York: Free Press, 2000.
Whitney, Courtney. *MacArthur: His Rendezvous with History*. New York: Knopf, 1956.

Macomb, Alexander

Macomb, Alexander. *The Practice of Courts Martial*. New York: Samuel Coleman, 1840.
Richards, George H. *Memoir of Alexander Macomb: The Major General Commanding the Army of the United States*. New York: McElrath, Bangs, 1833.

March, Peyton C.

Coffman, Edward M. *The Hilt of the Sword: The Career of Peyton C. March*. Madison: University of Wisconsin Press, 1966.
March, Peyton C. *The Nation at War*. Garden City, N.Y.: Doubleday, Doran, 1932.

Marshall, George C.

Bland, Larry I., ed. *The Papers of George Catlett Marshall*. 1981–1991.
———. *George C. Marshall Interviews and Reminiscences for Forrest C. Pogue*. Lexington, Va.: George C. Marshall Research Foundation, 1991.
Frye, William. *Marshall: Citizen Soldier*. Indianapolis: Bobbs-Merrill, 1947.
Marshall, George C. *Memoirs of My Services in the World War, 1917–1918*. Boston: Houghton Mifflin, 1976.
Moseley, Leonard. *Marshall: Hero for Our Times*. New York: Hearst, 1982.
Payne, [Pierre S.] Robert. *The Marshall Story: A Biography of General George C. Marshall*. New York: Prentice-Hall, 1951.
Pogue, Forrest C. *George C. Marshall*. 3 vols. New York: Viking, 1963–73.

Mauldin, William Henry

Mauldin, Bill. *Up Front*. New York: Henry Holt, 1945.

McClellan, George B.

Eckenrode, Hamilton J., and Byron Conrad. *George B. McClellan: The Man Who Saved the Union*. Chapel Hill: University of North Carolina Press, 1941.
Hassler, Warren W., Jr. *General George B. McClellan: Shield of the Union*. Baton Rouge: Louisiana State University Press, 1957.
McClellan, George B. *The Armies of Europe*. Philadelphia: J. B. Lippincott, 1861.
———. *McClellan's Own Story: The War for the Union, the Soldiers Who Fought It, the Civilians Who Directed It, and His Relations to It and to Them*. New York: Charles L. Webster, 1887.
Sears, Stephen W. *George B. McClellan: The Young Napoleon*. New York: Ticknor and Fields, 1988.

McHenry, James

Brown, Frederick J. *A Sketch of the Life of Dr. James McHenry*. Baltimore: Maryland Historical Society, 1877.
Steiner, Bernard. *The Life and Correspondence of James McHenry*. Cleveland, Ohio: Burrows Brothers, 1907.

Meade, George G.

Cleaves, Freeman. *Meade of Gettysburg*. Norman: University of Oklahoma Press, 1960.
Meade, George G., and George G. Meade Jr. *The Life and Letters of George Gordon Meade, Major General United States Army*. Edited by George G. Meade Jr. 2 vols. New York: Scribner, 1913.

Meigs, Montgomery

Weigley, Russell F. *Quartermaster General of the Union Army: A Biography of M. C. Meigs*. New York: Columbia University Press, 1959.

Miles, Nelson A.

DeMontravel, Peter R. *A Hero to His Fighting Men: Nelson A. Miles, 1939–1925*. Kent, Ohio: Kent State University Press, 1998.

Johnson, Virginia Weisal. *The Unregimented General: A Biography of Nelson A. Miles*. Boston: Houghton Mifflin, 1962.

Miles, Nelson A. *Personal Recollections and Observations of General Nelson A. Miles, Embracing a Brief View of the Civil War; or, From New England to the Golden Gate, and the Story of His Indian Campaigns, with Comments on the Exploration, Development, and Progress of Our Great Western Empire: Copiously Illustrated with Graphic Pictures by Frederic Remington and Other Eminent Artists*. Chicago: Werner, 1896.

———. *Serving the Republic: Memoirs of the Civil and Military Life of Nelson A. Miles*. New York: Harper and Brothers, 1911.

Monroe, James

Ammon, Harry. *James Monroe: The Quest for National Security*. New York: McGraw-Hill, 1971.

Cresson, William P. *James Monroe*. Hamden, Conn.: Archon, 1971.

Gershon, Noel B. *James Monroe: Hero of American Diplomacy*. Englewood Cliffs, N.J.: Prentice-Hall, 1969.

Gilman, Daniel C. *James Monroe*. Boston: Houghton Mifflin; New Rochelle, N.Y.: Arlington House, 1970.

Monroe, James. *The Autobiography of James Monroe*. Edited by Stuart Brown. Syracuse: Syracuse University Press, 1959.

———. *The Writings of James Monroe*. 7 vols. Edited by Stanislaus M. Hamilton. New York: Putnam, 1891–1903. Reprint ed., New York: AMS Press, 1969.

Morgan, George. *The Life of James Monroe*. New York: AMS Press, 1969.

Morgan, Daniel

Callahan, North. *Daniel Morgan, Ranger of the Revolution*. New York: A. S. Barnes, 1876.

Higginbotham, Don. *Daniel Morgan: Revolutionary Rifleman*. Chapel Hill: University of North Carolina Press, 1961.

Murphy, Audie

Graham, Don. *No Name on the Bullet: A Biography of Audie Murphy*. New York: Viking, 1989.

Murphy, Audie. *To Hell and Back: The Epic Combat Journal of World War II's Most Decorated G.I.* New York: MJF, 1949.

Simpson, Harold. *Audie Murphy: American Soldier*. Hillsboro, Tex.: Hill College Press, 1982.

Patton, George S.

Blumenson, Martin. *Patton: The Man Behind the Legend, 1895–1945*. New York: Morrow, 1985.

D'Este, Carlo. *Patton: A Genius for War*. New York: HarperCollins, 1995.

Essame, H. *Patton: A Study in Command*. New York: Scribner, 1974.
Farago, Ladislas. *Patton: Ordeal and Triumph*. New York: Ivan Obolensky,1963.
———. *The Last Days of Patton*. New York: McGraw-Hill, 1981.
Patton, George S. *The Patton Papers*. 2 vols. Edited by Martin Blumenson. Boston: Houghton Mifflin, 1974.
———. *War As I Knew It*. New York: Bantam, 1980.

Pershing, John J.

Goldhurst, Richard. *Pipe Clay and Drill: John J. Pershing, the Classic American Soldier*. New York: Reader's Digest, 1977.
O'Connor, Richard. *Black Jack Pershing*. Garden City, N.Y.: Doubleday, 1961.
Palmer, Frederick. *John J. Pershing, General of the Armies: A Biography*. Harrisburg, Pa.: Military Service, 1948.
Pershing, John J. *My Experiences in the World War*. 2 vols. New York: Frederick A. Stokes, 1931.
Smythe, Donald. *Guerrilla Warrior: The Early Life of John J. Pershing*. New York: Scribner, 1973.
———. *Pershing: General of the Armies*. New York: Scribner, 1986.
Vandiver, Frank E. *Black Jack: The Life and Times of John J. Pershing*. 2 vols. College Station: Texas A. & M. University Press, 1977.

Pickering, Timothy

Clarfield, Gerard H. *Timothy Pickering and American Diplomacy, 1795–1800*. Columbia: University of Missouri Press, 1969.
———. *Timothy Pickering and the American Republic*. Pittsburgh, Pa.: University of Pittsburgh Press, 1980.
Pickering, Octavius, and Charles W. Upham. *The Life of Timothy Pickering*. 14 vols. Boston: Little, Brown, 1867–1873.

Poinsett, Joel Roberts

Putnam, Herbert Everett. *Joel Roberts Poinsett: A Political Biography*. Washington, D.C.: Mimeoform Press, 1935.
Rippy, J. Fred. *Joel R. Poinsett, Versatile American*. Durham, N.C.: Duke University Press, 1935. Reprint ed., New York: Greenwood, 1968.
Stille, Charles J. *The Life and Service of Joel R. Poinsett*. Philadelphia: Historical Society of Pennsylvania, 1888.

Pontiac

Peckham, Howard H. *Pontiac and the Indian Uprising*. Chicago: University of Chicago Press, 1947.

Porter, Peter Buel

Cozzens, Frederick S. *Colonel Peter A. Porter: A Memorial Delivered before the Century in December 1864*. (Includes a sketch of the life of Porter's father, Peter B. Porter.) New York: D. Van Nostrand, 1865.

Powell, Colin L.

Powell, Colin L., with Joseph E. Persico. *My American Journey*. New York: Random House, 1995.

Proctor, Redfield

Partridge, Frank C. *Redfield Proctor: His Public Life and Services*. Montpelier: Vermont Historical Society, 1915.

Pyle, Ernie

Pyle, Ernie. *Here Is Your War: Story of G.I. Joe*. New York: Henry Holt, 1943.
Tobin, James. *Ernie Pyle's War: America's Eyewitness to World War II*. New York: Free Press, 1997.

Ramsey, Alexander

Ryland, William J. *Alexander Ramsey: Frontier Politician*. Philadelphia: Harris and Partridge, 1941.

Rawlins, John Aaron

Wilson, James H. *The Life of John A. Rawlins: Lawyer, Assistant Adjutant-General, Chief of Staff, Major General of Volunteers and Secretary of War*. New York: Neale, 1916.

Reed, Walter

Bean, William B. *Walter Reed*. Philadelphia: University of Pennsylvania Press, 1982.
Truby, Albert E. *Memoir of Walter Reed*. New York: Paul B. Hoeher, 1943.

Ridgway, Matthew B.

Ridgway, Matthew B. *Soldier: The Memoirs of Matthew B. Ridgway*. New York: Harper and Brothers, 1956.
———. *The Korean War*. New York: Doubleday, 1967.

Rogers, Bernard W.

Rogers, Bernard William. *Cedar Falls–Junction City: A Turning Point*. Department of the Army Vietnam Studies. Washington, D.C.: Government Printing Office, 1974.

Rommel, Erwin

Irving, David. *The Trail of the Fox: The Life of Field-Marshall Erwin Rommel*. 1978.
Young, Desmond. *Rommel: The Desert Fox*. New York: Harper and Row, 1965.

Roosevelt, Theodore

Beale, Howard. *Theodore Roosevelt and the Rise of America to World Power*. New York: Collier, 1956.
Harbaugh, William Henry. *Power and Responsibility: The Life and Times of Theodore Roosevelt*. New York: Collier, 1961.

Root, Elihu

Jessup, Philip C. *Elihu Root*. 2 vols. New York: Dodd, Mead, 1938. Reprint ed., Hamden, Conn.: Archon, 1964.
Leopold, Richard W. *Elihu Root and the Conservative Tradition*. Boston: Little, Brown, 1854.

St. Clair, Arthur

St. Clair, Arthur. *A Narrative of the Manner in Which the Campaign against the Indians, in the Year 1791, Was Conducted, Under the Command of Major-General St. Clair*. Philadelphia: Jane Aitken, 1812. Reprint. New York: Arno, 1971.
——. *The St. Clair Papers: The Life and Public Service of Arthur St. Clair. Soldier of the Revolutionary War; President of the Continental Congress and Governor of the NorthWestern Territory, With His Correspondence and Other Papers*. 2 vols. Cincinnati: Robert Clarke, 1882.
Wilson, Frazer Ells. *Arthur St. Clair, Rugged Ruler of the Old Northwest: An Epic of the American Frontier*. Richmond, Va.: Garrett and Massie, 1944.

Santa Anna, Antonio Lopez de

Santa Anna, Antonio. *The Eagle: The Autobiography of Santa Anna*. Edited by Ann Fears Crawford. Austin, Tex.: Pemberton, 1967.

Schofield, John M.

McDonough, James L. *Schofield, Union General in the Civil War and Reconstruction*. Tallahassee: Florida State University Press, 1972.
Schofield, John M. *Forty-Six Years in the Army*. New York: Century, 1897.

Schwarzkopf, H. Norman

Cohen, Roger, and Claudio Gatti. *In the Eye of the Storm: The Life of General H. Norman Schwarzkopf*. London: Cape, 1991.
Schwarzkopf, H. Norman, with Peter Petre. *General H. Norman Schwarzkopf: The Autobiography. It Doesn't Take a Hero*. New York: Linda Grey Bantam, 1992.

Scott, Hugh L.

Harper, James W. "Hugh Lenox Scott: Soldier-Diplomat." Ph.D. dissertation, University of Virginia, 1968.
Scott, Hugh L. *Some Memories of a Soldier*. New York: Century, 1928.

Scott, Winfield

Eisenhower, John S. D. *Agent of Destiny: The Life and Times of General Winfield Scott*. New York: Free Press, 1997.
Elliott, Charles Winslow. *Winfield Scott: The Soldier and the Man*. New York: Macmillan, 1937.
Long, Laura. *Fuss 'n' Feathers: A Life of Winfield Scott*. New York: Longmans, Green, 1944.
Scott, Winfield. *Memoirs of Lieut.-General Scott, LL.D. Written by Himself*. 2 vols. New York: Sheldon, 1864.

Sheridan, Philip H.

Morris, Roy, Jr. *Sheridan: The Life and Wars of General Phil Sheridan*. New York: Crown, 1992.
O'Connor, Richard. *Sheridan, the Inevitable*. Indianapolis: Bobbs-Merrill, 1963.
Rister, Carl Coke. *Border Command: General Phil Sheridan in the West*. Norman: University of Oklahoma Press, 1944.
Sheridan, Philip H. *Personal Memoirs of P. H. Sheridan, General, United States Army*. 2 vols. New York: Charles L. Webster, 1888.

Sherman, William T.

Athearn, Robert G. *William Tecumseh Sherman and the Settlement of the West*. Norman: University of Oklahoma Press, 1956.
Lewis, Lloyd. *Sherman: Fighting Prophet*. New York: Harcourt, Brace, 1932.
Marszalek, John F. *Sherman: A Soldier's Passion for Order*. New York: Free Press, 1993.
Merrill, James M. *William Tecumseh Sherman*. Chicago: Rand McNally, 1971.
Miers, Earl Schenck. *The General Who Marched to Hell: William Tecumseh Sherman and His March to Fame and Infamy*. New York: Knopf, 1951.
Sherman, William T. *Memoirs of General W. T. Sherman: Written by Himself*. 2 vols. New York: Appleton, 1875. Reprint ed., Bloomington: Indiana University Press, 1957.
———. *Sherman at War*. Edited by Joseph H. Ewin. Dayton, Ohio: Morningside, 1992.

Stanton, Edwin McMasters

Flower, Frank A. *Edwin McMasters Stanton: The Autocrat of Rebellion, Emancipation, and Reconstruction*. Akron, Ohio: Saalfield, 1905. Reprint ed., New York: AMS Press, 1973.
Pratt, Fletcher. *Stanton: Lincoln's Secretary of War*. New York: Norton, 1953.
Thomas, Benjamin Platt, and Harold M. Hyman. *Stanton: The Life and Times of Lincoln's Secretary of War*. New York: Knopf, 1962.

Steuben, Friedrich Wilhelm von

See von Steuben, Friederich Wilhelm.

Stimson, Henry Lewis

Current, Richard N. *Secretary Stimson: A Study in Statescraft*. New Brunswick, N.J.: Rutgers University Press, 1954.

Hodgson, Godfrey. *The Colonel: The Life and Wars of Henry Stimson, 1867–1950*. New York: Knopf, 1990.
Morison, Elting E. *Turmoil and Tradition: A Study of the Life and Times of Henry L. Stimson*. Boston: Houghton Mifflin, 1960.
Stimson, Henry L., and McGeorge Bundy. *On Active Service in Peace and War*. New York: Harper, 1917. Reprint ed., New York: Octagon, 1971.

Taft, Alphonso

Leonard, Lewis A. *Life of Alphonso Taft*. New York: Hawke, 1920.

Taft, William Howard

Anderson, Judith Icke. *William Howard Taft: An Intimate History*. New York: Norton, 1981.
Duffy, Herbert S. *William Howard Taft*. New York: Minton, Balch, 1930.
Pringle, Henry F. *The Life and Times of William Howard Taft*. 2 vols. New York: Farrar and Rinehart, 1939. Reprint ed., Hamden, Conn.: Archon, 1964.

Taylor, Maxwell D.

Kinnard, Douglas. *The Certain Trumpet: Maxwell and the American Experience in Vietnam*. Washington, D.C.: Brassey's, 1991.
Taylor, John M. *General Maxwell Taylor: The Sword and the Pen*. Garden City, N.Y.: Doubleday, 1989.
Taylor, Maxwell D. *The Uncertain Trumpet*. New York: Harper and Brothers, 1959.
——. *Responsibility and Response*. New York: Harper and Row, 1967.
——. *Swords and Plowshares: A Memoir*. New York: Norton, 1972.
——. *Precarious Security*. New York: Norton, 1976.

Taylor, Zachary

Bauer, K. Jack. *Zachary Taylor: Soldier, Planter, Statesman of the Old Southwest*. Baton Rouge: Louisiana State University Press, 1985.

Tecumseh

Edmunds, R. David. *Tecumseh and the Quest for Indian Leadership*. Boston: Little Brown, 1984.
Sugden, John. *Tecumseh: A Life*. New York: Henry Holt, 1998.

Truman, Harry S.

Hamby, Alonzo L. *Man of the People: A Life of Harry S. Truman*. New York: Oxford University Press, 1995.
Haynes, Richard F. *The Awesome Power: Harry S. Truman as Commander in Chief*. Baton Rouge: Louisiana State University Press, 1973.

Upton, Emory

Ambrose, Stephen. *Upton and the Army*. Baton Rouge: Louisiana State University Press, 1964.

Vance, Cyrus Roberts

McClellan, David S. *Cyrus Vance*. Totowa, N.J.: Rowman and Allanheld, 1985.

Villa, Francisco "Pancho"

Katz, Friedrich. *The Life and Times of Pancho Villa*. Stanford, Calif.: Stanford University Press, 1998.

von Steuben, Friedrich Wilhelm

Palmer, John M. *General von Steuben*. New Haven, Conn.: Yale University Press, 1937.

Wainwright, Jonathan Mayhew

Schultz, Duane P. *Hero of Bataan: The Story of General Jonathan M. Wainwright*. New York: St. Martin's, 1991.

Washington, George

Flexner, James Thomas. *George Washington*. 4 vols. Boston: Little, Brown, 1965–72.
———. *Washington: The Indispensable Man*. Boston: Little, Brown, 1974.
Freeman, Douglas Southall. *George Washington*. 7 vols. New York: Scribner, 1948–57.
Lodge, Henry Cabot. *George Washington*. American Statesmen Series. 2 vols. Boston: Houghton Mifflin, 1889.
Marshall, John. *The Life of George Washington, Commander in Chief of the American Forces . . . and First President of the United States*. 5 vols. Philadelphia: C. P. Wayne, 1804–1807.
Washington, George. *The Diaries of George Washington, 1748–1799*. 4 vols. Edited by John C. Fitzpatrick. Boston: Houghton Mifflin, 1925.
———. *The Writings of George Washington, 1745–1799*. 39 vols. Edited by John C. Fitzpatrick. Washington, D.C.: Government Printing Office, 1931–44.

Wayne, Anthony

Boyd, Thomas Alexander. *Mad Anthony Wayne*. New York: Scribner, 1929.
Preston, John Hyde. *A Gentleman Rebel: The Exploits of Anthony Wayne*. New York: Farrar & Rinehart, 1930.
Tucker, Glen. *Mad Anthony Wayne and the New Nation: The Story of Washington's Front-Line General*. Harrisburg, Pa.: Stackpole, 1973.

Wedemeyer, Albert C.

Eiler, Keith E., ed. *Wedemeyer on War and Peace*. Stanford, Calif.: Hoover Institution Press, 1987.
Wedemeyer, Albert C. *Wedemeyer Reports!* New York: Henry Holt, 1958.

Weeks, John Wingate

Washburn, Charles G. *The Life of John W. Weeks*. Boston: Houghton Mifflin, 1928.

Westmoreland, William C.

Furguson, Ernest B. *Westmoreland: The Inevitable General*. Boston: Little, Brown, 1968.
Westmoreland, William C. *A Soldier Reports*. Garden City, N.Y.: Doubleday, 1976.

Wilkins, William

Liscombe, R. W. *William Wilkins, 1778–1839*. New York: Cambridge University Press, 1980.

Wilkinson, James

Hay, Thomas Robson, and Morris Robert Werner. *The Admirable Trumpeter: A Biography of General James Wilkinson*. Garden City, N.Y.: Doubleday, Doran, 1941.
Jacobs, James Ripley. *Tarnished Warrior: Major General James Wilkinson*. New York: Macmillan, 1938.
Shreve, Royal Ornan. *The Finished Scoundrel: General James Wilkinson*. Indianapolis: Bobbs-Merrill, 1933.
Wilkinson, James. *Memoirs of My Own Times*. Philadelphia: Abraham Small, 1816.
———. *Wilkinson: Soldier and Pioneer*. New Orleans: Rogers Printing, 1935.

Wood, Leonard

Hagedorn, Hermann. *Leonard Wood: A Biography*. 2 vols. New York: Harper & Brothers, 1931.
Hobbs, William Herbert. *Leonard Wood: Administrator, Soldier, and Citizen*. New York: Putnam, 1920.
Lane, Jack C. *Armed Progressive: General Leonard Wood*. San Rafael, Calif.: Presidio, 1978.
Marcosson, Isaac F. *Leonard Wood: Prophet of Preparedness*. New York: John Lane, 1917.
Wood, Leonard. *Our Military History: Its Facts and Fallacies*. Chicago: Reilly and Britton, 1916.

Woodring, Harry Hines

McFarland, Keith D. *Harry H. Woodring: A Political Biography*. Lawrence: University Press of Kansas, 1975.

Wotherspoon, William Wallace.

Wotherspoon, William Wallace. *The Training of the Efficient Soldier*. Philadelphia: American Academy of Political and Social Science, 1905.

York, Alvin Cullum

Andrews, Peter. *Sergeant York: Reluctant Hero*. New York: Putnam, 1969.
Lee, David D. *Sergeant York: An American Hero*. Lexington: University Press of Kentucky, 1985.
Skeyhill, Tom. *Sergeant York: Last of the Long Hunters*. Chicago: John C. Winston, 1930.
York, Alvin. *Sergeant York: His Own Life Story and War Diary*. Edited by Tom Skeyhill. Garden City, N.Y.: Doran, 1928.

IV. SELECTED TOPICS

A. Serving the Nation

Caswell, John E. *Arctic Frontier: United States Explorations in the Far North*. Norman: University of Oklahoma Press, 1965.
Coakley, Robert W. *The Role of the Federal Military Forces in Domestic Disorders, 1789–1878*. Washington, D.C.: Government Printing Office, 1988.
Coffman, Edward. *The Old Army: A Portrait of the American Army in Peacetime, 1784–1898*. New York: Oxford University Press, 1986.
Cooper, Jerry M. *The Army and Civil Disorder: Federal Military Intervention in Labor Disputes, 1877–1900*. Westport, Conn.: Greenwood, 1980.
DeVoto, Bernard, ed. *Journals of Lewis and Clark*. Boston: Houghton Mifflin, 1953.
Foner, Jack D. *The United States Soldier between Two Wars: Army Life and Reforms, 1865–1898*. New York: Humanities, 1970.
Foster, Gaines M. *The Demands of Humanity: Army Medical Disaster Relief*. Washington, D.C.: Government Printing Office, 1983.
Goetzmann, William H. *Army Exploration in the American West, 1803–1863*. New Haven, Conn.: Yale University Press, 1959.
Jones, Vincent C. Manhattan. *The Army and the Atomic Bomb*. Washington, D.C.: Government Printing Office, 1985.
Kemble, Robert C. *The Image of the Army Officer in America: Background for Current Views*. Westport, Conn.: Greenwood, 1973.
Linn, Brian McAllister, and Bill Linn. *Guardians of Empire: The U.S. Army and the Pacific 1902–1940*. Chapel Hill: University of North Carolina Press, 1997.
Schubert, N. Frank. *Vanguard of Expansion: Army Engineers in the Trans-Mississippi West, 1819–1879*. Washington, D.C.: Government Printing Office, 1981.
Todd, A. L. *Abandoned: The Story of the Greely Arctic Expedition, 1881–1884*. New York: McGraw-Hill, 1961.

B. Minorities and the Army

Arnold, John. *Buffalo Soldiers: The 92nd Infantry Division and Reinforcements in World War II, 1942–1945*. Manhattan, Kans.: Sunflower University Press, 1990.
Barbeau, Arthur E., and Florette Henri. *The Unknown Soldiers: African-American Troops in World War I*. New York: Da Capo, 1996.
Dlackerby, H. C. *Blacks in the Blue and Grey: Afro-American Service in the Civil War*. Tuscaloosa, Ala.: Portals, 1979.
Bowers, William T., William M. Hammon, and George L. MacGarrigle. *Black Soldier/White Army: The 24th Infantry Regiment in Korea*. Washington, D.C.: Government Printing Office, 1996.

Burton, William L. *Melting Pot Soldiers: The Union's Ethnic Regiments*. Ames: Iowa State University Press, 1988.

Cox, Clinton. *The Forgotten Heroes: The Story of the Buffalo Soldiers*. New York: Scholastic, 1996.

Davis, Lenwood G., George Hill, and Benjamin O. Davis Jr. *Blacks in the American Armed Forces, 1776–1983: A Bibliography*. Westport, Conn.: 1984.

Fletcher, Marvin E. *The Black Soldier and Officer in the United States Army, 1891–1917*. Columbia: University of Missouri Press, 1932.

Fowler, Arlen. *The Black Infantry in the West, 1869–1891*. Westport, Conn.: Greenwood, 1971.

Glatthaar, Joseph T. *Forged in Battle: The Civil War Alliance of Black Soldiers and White Officers*. New York: Free Press, 1990.

Higginson, Thomas Wentworth. *Army Life in a Black Regiment and Other Writings*. New York: Penguin Classics, 1962.

Kenner, Charles L. *Buffalo Soldiers and Officers of the Ninth Calvary, 1867–1898: Black and White Together*. Norman: University of Oklahoma Press, 1999.

Langellier, John P. *American Indians in the U.S. Armed Forces, 1866–1945*. Harrisburg, Pa.: Stackpole, 2000.

Lanning, Michael Lee. *The African-American Soldier: From Crispus Attucks to Colin Powell*. New York: Carol, 1999.

Leckie, William H. *The Buffalo Soldiers: A Narrative of the Negro Cavalry in the West*. Norman: University of Oklahoma Press, 1967.

Lee, Ulysses. *The Employment of Negro Troops*. Washington, D.C.: Government Printing Office, 1966.

MacGregor, Morris J., Jr. *The Integration of the Armed Forces, 1940–1965*. Washington, D.C.: Government Printing Office, 1981.

Nalty, Bernard. *Strength for the Fight: A History of Black Americans in the Military*. New York: Free Press, 1986.

Schubert, Frank N. *Black Valor: Buffalo Soldiers and the Medal of Honor, 1870–1898*. Wilmington, Del.: Scholarly Resources, 1997.

Scott, Edward Van Sile. *The Unwept: Black American Soldiers and the Spanish–American War*. Montgomery, Ala.: Black Belt, 1995.

C. Women in the Army

Bellafaire, Judith A. *The Army Nurse Corps: A Commemoration of World War II Service*. Washington, D.C.: U.S. Army Center of Military History, n.d.

Cosner, Shaaron. *War Nurses*. New York: Walker, 1988.

Flikke, Julia O. *Nurses in Action: The Story of the Army Nurse Corps*. Philadelphia: Lippincott, 1943.

Haskell, Ruth G. *Helmets and Lipstick*. New York: Putnam, 1944.

Jackson, Kathi. *They Called Them Angels: American Military Nurses of World War II*. Westport, Conn.: Praeger, 2000.

Monahan, Evelyn M., and Rosemary Neldel-Greenlee. *All This Hell: U.S. Nurses Imprisoned by the Japanese*. Lexington: University Press of Kentucky, 2000.

Norman, Elizabeth M. *We Band of Angels: The Untold Story of American Nurses Trapped on Bataan by the Japanese*. New York: Random House, 1999.

Shills, Elizabeth A., ed. *Highlights in the History of the Army Nurse Corps*. Washington, D.C.: Government Printing Office, 1981.

Treadwell, Mattie. *The Women's Army Corps*. Washington, D.C.: Government Printing Office, 1954.

D. Reserve Components

Hill, Jim Dan. *The Minute Man in Peace and War: A History of the National Guard*. Harrisburg, Pa.: Stackpole, 1964.

Mahon, John K. *The American Militia: Decade of Decision, 1789–1800*. Gainesville: University of Florida Press, 1960.

——. *History of the Militia and National Guard of the United States*. New York: Free Press, 1983.

E. Organization and Administration

Barr, Ronald J. *The Progressive Army: US Army Command and Administration, 1870–1914*. New York: St. Martin's, 1998.

Chambers, John Whiteclay, II. *To Raise an Army: The Draft Comes to Modern America*. New York: Free Press, 1987.

Gabriel, Richard A., and Paul I. Savage. *Crisis in Command: Mismanagement in the Army*. New York: Hill and Wang, 1978.

Hewes, James E., Jr. *From Root to McNamara: Army Organization and Administration, 1900–1963*. Washington, D.C.: Government Printing Office, 1975.

Hittle, James D. *The Military Staff: Its History and Development*. Harrisburg, Pa.: Military Service, 1944.

McNeely, Alexander Howard. *The War Department, 1861: A Study in Mobilization and Administration*. Studies in History, Economics, and Public Law, no. 300. New York: Columbia University Press, 1928.

Millett, John D. *The Organization and Role of the Army Service Forces*. Washington, D.C.: Government Printing Office, 1954.

Palmer, John Mcauley. *America in Arms: The Experience of the United States with Military Organization*. New Haven, Conn.: Yale University Press, 1941.

Powers, Patrick W. *A Guide to National Defense: The Organization and Operations of the U.S. Military Establishment*. New York: Praeger, 1964.

Ries, John C. *The Management of Defense: Organization and Control of the U.S. Armed Forces*. Baltimore: Johns Hopkins Press, 1964.

Romjue, John L. *The Army of Excellence: The Development of the 1980's Army*. Washington, D.C.: Government Printing Office, 1997.

Thian, Raphael P., comp. *Legislative History of the General Staff of the Army of the United States, 1775–1901*. Washington, D.C.: Government Printing Office, 1901.

Wilson, John B. *Armies, Corps, Divisions, and Separate Brigades*. Washington, D.C.: Government Printing Office, 1987.

——. *Maneuver and Firepower: The Evolution of Divisions and Separate Brigades*. Washington, D.C.: Government Printing Office, 1999.

F. Education and Training

Ambrose, Stephen. *Duty, Honor, Country: A History of West Point*. Baltimore: Johns Hopkins University Press, 1966.

Ball, Harry P. *Of Reasonable Command: A History of the U.S. Army War College*. Carlisle Barracks, Pa.: Alumni Association of the U.S. Army War College, 1983.

Brereton, T. R. *Educating the U.S. Army: Arthur L. Wagner and Reform, 1875–1905*. Lincoln: University of Nebraska Press, 2000.

Chapman, Ann W. *The Army's Training Revolution, 1973–1990*. Washington, D.C.: Government Printing Office, 1994.

———. *The Origins and Development of the National Training Center, 1976–1984*. Washington, D.C.: Government Printing Office, 1997.

Ellis, Joseph, and Robert Moore. *School for Soldiers: West Point and the Profession of Arms*. New York: Oxford University Press, 1974.

Fleming, Thomas J. *West Point: The Men and Times of the United States Military Academy*. New York: Morrow, 1969.

Forman, Sidney. *West Point: A History of the United States Military Academy*. New York: Columbia University Press, 1950.

Masland, John W., and Laurence I. Radway. *Soldiers and Scholars: Military Education and National Policy*. Princeton, N.J.: Princeton University Press, 1957.

Moten, Matthew. *The Delafield Commission and the American Military Profession*. College Station: Texas A. & M. University Press, 2000.

Nenninger, Timothy K. *The Leavenworth Schools and the Old Army: Education, Professionalism, and the Officer Corps of the United States Army, 1881–1918*. Westport, Conn.: Greenwood, 1978.

Palmer, Robert R., Bell I. Wiley, and William R. Keast. *The Procurement and Training of Ground Troops*. Washington, D.C.: Government Printing Office, 1948.

Pappas, George S. *Prudens Futuri: The U.S. Army War College, 1901–1967*. Carlisle Barracks, Pa.: Association of the U.S. Army War College, 1967.

G. Doctrine

Galvin, John R. *Air Assault: The Development of Airmobile Warfare*. New York: Hawthorne Books, 1969.

Grotelueschen, Mark E. *Doctrine under Fire: American Artillery Employment in World War I*. Westport, Conn.: Greenwood, 2000.

Jamieson, Perry D. *Crossing the Deadly Ground: United States Army Tactics, 1865–1899*. Tuscaloosa: University of Alabama Press, 1994.

Johnson, David E. *Fast Tanks and Heavy Bombers: Innovation in the U.S. Army, 1917–1945*. Ithaca, N.Y.: Cornell University Press, 1998.

Odom, William O. *After the Trenches: The Transformation of U.S. Army Doctrine, 1918–1939*. College Station: Texas A. & M. University Press, 1999.

Romjue, John L. *American Doctrine for the Post–Cold War*. Washington, D.C.: Government Printing Office, 1997.

H. Logistics

Coakley, Robert W., and Richard M. Leighton. *Global Logistics and Strategy: 1943–1945*. Washington, D.C.: Government Printing Office, 1969.

Colley, David P. *The Road to Victory: The Untold Story of World War II's Red Ball Express*. Washington, D.C.: Brassey's, 2000.

Fuson, Jack C. *Transportation and Logistics: One Man's Story*. Washington, D.C.: Government Printing Office, 1994.

Gough, Terrence J. *U.S. Army Mobilization and Logistics in the Korean War: A Research Approach*. Washington, D.C.: Government Printing Office, 1987.

Heiser, Joseph M. *A Soldier Supporting Soldiers*. Washington, D.C.: Government Printing Office, 1991.

Huston, James A. *The Sinews of War: Army Logistics, 1775–1953*. Washington, D.C.: Government Printing Office, 1966.

Leighton, Richard M., and Robert W. Coakley. *Global Logistics and Strategy: 1940–1943*. Washington, D.C.: Government Printing Office, 1955.

Magruder, Carter B. *Recurring Logistical Problems as I Have Observed Them*. Washington, D.C.: Government Printing Office, 1991.

Ruppenthal, Roland G. *Logistical Support of the Armies, Volume I: May 1941–September 1944*. Washington, D.C.: Government Printing Office, 1953.

———. *Logistical Support of the Armies, Volume II: September 1944–May 1945*. Washington, D.C.: Government Printing Office, 1959.

Shrader, Charles R. *United States Army Logistics, 1775–1992: An Anthology*. 3 vols. Washington, D.C.: Government Printing Office, 1997.

Westover, John G. *Combat Support in Korea*. Washington, D.C.: Government Printing Office, 1987.

I. Branches of the Army

Beck, Alfred M. et al. *The Corps of Engineers: The War against Germany*. Washington, D.C.: Government Printing Office, 1972.

Bergen, John D. *Military Communications: A Test for Technology*. Washington, D.C.: Government Printing Office, 1986.

Brophy, Leo P., and George J. B. Fisher. *The Chemical Warfare Service: Organizing for War*. Washington, D.C.: Government Printing Office, 1959.

Brophy, Leo P., Wyndham D. Miles, and Rexmond C. Cochrane. *The Chemical Warfare Service: From Laboratory to Field*. Washington, D.C.: Government Printing Office, 1959.

Clancy, Tom, with John Gresham. *Special Forces: A Guided Tour of U.S. Army Special Forces*. New York: Berkeley, 2001.

Coll, Blanche D., Jean E. Keith, and Herbert H. Rosenthal. *The Corps of Engineers: Troops and Equipment*. Washington, D.C.: Government Printing Office, 1958.

Condon-Rall, Mary Ellen, and Albert E. Cowdrey. *The Medical Department: Medical Service in the War against Japan*. Washington, D.C.: Government Printing Office, 1998.

Cosmas, Graham A., and Albert E. Cowdrey. *The Medical Department: Medical Service in the European Theater of Operations*. Washington, D.C.: Government Printing Office, 1992.

Cowdrey, Albert E. *The Medic's War*. Washington, D.C.: Government Printing Office, 1987.

Dastrup, Boyd L. *King of Battle: A Branch History of the U.S. Army's Field Artillery*. Fort Monroe, Va.: Office of the Command Historian, 1992.

Dod, Carl C. *The Corps of Engineers: The War against Japan*. Washington, D.C.: Government Printing Office, 1966.

Downey, Fairfax. *Sound of the Guns: The Story of the American Artillery*. New York: David McKay, 1955.

Dzwonchyk, Wayne M. *Aviation*. Washington, D.C.: Government Printing Office, 1986.

Fine, Leonore, and Jesse A. Remington. *The Corps of Engineers: Construction in the United States*. Washington, D.C.: Government Printing Office, 1972.

Finnegan, John Patrick, and Romana Danysh. *Military Intelligence*. Washington, D.C.: Government Printing Office, 1999.

Gillett, Mary C. *The Army Medical Department, 1775–1818*. Washington, D.C.: Government Printing Office, 1981.
——. *The Army Medical Department, 1818–1865*. Washington, D.C.: Government Printing Office, 1987.
——. *The Army Medical Department, 1865–1917*. Washington, D.C.: Government Printing Office, 1995.
Ginn, Richard V. N. *The History of the U.S. Army Medical Service Corps*. Washington, D.C.: Government Printing Office, 1997.
Kleber, Brooks E., and Dale Birdsdale. *The Chemical Warfare Service: Chemicals in Combat*. Washington, D.C.: Government Printing Office, 1965.
Mahon, John K., and Romana Danysh. *Infantry, Part I: Regular Army*. Washington, D.C.: Government Printing Office,1972.
McKenney, Janice E. *Air Defense Artillery*. Washington, D.C.: Government Printing Office, 1985.
——. *Field Artillery*. Washington, D.C.: Government Printing Office, 1985.
Raines, Rebecca Robbins. *Getting the Message Through: A Branch History of the U.S. Army Signal Corps*. Washington, D.C.: Government Printing Office, 1996.
Risch, Erna. *Quartermaster Support of the Army: A History of the Corps, 1775–1939*. Washington, D.C.: Government Printing Office, 1962.
Ross, William F., and Charles F. Romanus. *The Quartermaster Corps: Operations in the War against Germany*. Washington, D.C.: Government Printing Office,1965.
Starr, Stephen Z. *The Union Cavalry in the Civil War*. 3 vols. Baton Rouge: Louisiana State University, 1979–1985.
Stauffer, Alvin P. *The Quartermaster Corps: Operations in the War against Japan*. Washington, D.C.: Government Printing Office,1956.
Stubbs, Mary Lee, and Stanley Russell Connor. *Armor-Cavalry, Part I: Regular Army and Army Reserve*. Washington, D.C.: Government Printing Office, 1969.
Terret, Dulany. *The Signal Corps: The Emergency (to December 1941)*. Washington, D.C.: Government Printing Office,1956.
Thompson, George Raynor, and Dixie R. Harris. *The Signal Corps: The Outcome (Mid 1943 through 1945)*. Washington, D.C.: Government Printing Office, 1966.
Thompson, George Raynor et al. *The Signal Corps: The Test (December 1941 to July 1943)*. Washington, D.C.: Government Printing Office, 1957.
Wardlow, Chester. *The Transportation Corps: Responsibilities, Organization and Operations*. Washington, D.C.: Government Printing Office, 1951.
——. *The Transportation Corps: Movements, Training, and Supply*. Washington, D.C.: Government Printing Office, 1956.
Wiltse, Charles M. *The Medical Department: Medical Service in the Mediterranean and Minor Theaters*. Washington, D.C.: Government Printing Office,1966.
Wright, Robert K. *Military Police*. Washington, D.C.: Government Printing Office, 1992.

J. Equipment, Uniforms, and Weapons

Anderson, Christopher J. *Patton's Third Army*. Mechanicsburg, Pa.: Stackpole, 1997.
——. *The U.S. Army Today: From the End of the Cold War to the Present Day*. Mechanicsburg, Pa.: Stackpole, 1997.
——. *Grunts: U.S. Infantry in Vietnam*. Mechanicsburg, Pa.: Stackpole, 1998.
Conger, Elizabeth Mallett. *American Tanks and Tank Destroyers*. New York: Henry Holt, 1944.

Cox, Curt Hamilton, and John P. Langellier. *Longknives: The U.S. Cavalry and Other Mounted Forces*. Mechanicsburg, Pa.: Stackpole, 1996.

Field, Ron. *The Mexican–American War: 1846–47*. Washington, D.C.: Brassey's, 1997.

——. *The Spanish–American War 1898*. Washington, D.C.: Brassey's, 1998.

Forty, George. *US Army Handbook: 1939–1945*. New York: Barnes and Noble, 1995.

Green, Michael, and Gladys Green. *Weapons of Patton's Armies*. Madison, Wis.: Motorbooks International, 2000.

Hazlett, James C., Edwin Olmstead, and M. Hume Parks. *Field Artillery Weapons of the Civil War*. Newark: University of Delaware Press, 1983.

Hofmann, George F., and Donn A. Starry, eds. *Camp Colt to Desert Storm: The History of U.S. Armored Forces*. Lexington: University Press of Kentucky, 1999.

Howard, Gary, and Roger Pennington. *America's Finest: U.S. Airborne Uniforms, Equipment and Insignia of World War Two*. Mechanicsburg, Pa.: Stackpole, 1994.

Langellier, John P. *Bluecoats: The U.S. Army in the West, 1848–1897*. Mechanicsburg, Pa.: Stackpole, 1995.

——. *The War in Europe: From the Kasserine Pass to Berlin, 1942–1945*. Mechanicsburg, Pa.: Stackpole, 1995.

——. *Fix Bayonets: The U.S. Infantry from the American Civil War to the Surrender of Japan*. Mechanicsburg, Pa.: Stackpole, 1998.

——. *Redlegs: The U.S. Artillery from the Civil War to the Spanish–American War*. Mechanicsburg, Pa.: Stackpole, 1998.

——. *Sound the Charge: The U.S. Cavalry in the American West, 1866–1916*. Mechanicsburg, Pa.: Stackpole, 1998.

Manucy, Albert. *Artillery through the Ages: A Short Illustrated History of Cannon, Emphasizing Types Used in America*. Washington, D.C.: Government Printing Office, 1949.

McAfee, Michael J., and John P. Langellier. *Billy Yank: The Uniform of the Union Army 1861–1865*. Mechanicsburg, Pa.: Stackpole, 1996.

Mountcastle, John W. *Flame On! U.S. Incendiary Weapons, 1918–1945*. Shippensburg, Pa.: White Mane, 1999.

Rentz, Bill. *Geronimo!: U.S. Airborne Uniforms, Insignia and Equipment in World War II*. West Chester, Pa.: Schiffer, 1999.

Ripley, Warren. *Artillery and Ammunition of the Civil War*. New York: D. Van Nostrand Reinhold, 1970.

Stanton, Shelby L. *U.S. Army Uniforms of the Korean War*. Mechanicsburg, Pa.: Stackpole, 1992.

——. *U.S. Army Uniforms of the Vietnam War*. Mechanicsburg, Pa.: Stackpole, 1992.

——. *U.S. Army Uniforms of World War II*. Mechanicsburg, Pa.: Stackpole, 1995.

Wilson, Dale. *Treat 'Em Rough!: The Birth of American Armor, 1917–20*. Novato, Calif.: Presidio, 1989.

Woodhead, Henry, ed. *Echoes of Glory: Arms and Equipment of the Civil War*. Alexandria, Va.: Time-Life Books, 1991.

Younger, Robert. *Civil War Battle Flags of the Union Army and Order of Battle*. New York: Knickerbocker, 1997.

K. Army Art

The Army at War: A Graphic Record by American Artists. Washington, D.C.: Government Printing Office, 1944.

Crane, Aimee, ed. *Art in the Armed Forces*. New York: Hyperion, 1944.

Lanker, Brian, and Nicole Newnharn. *They Drew Fire: The Soldier Artists of World War II.* New York: HarperCollins, 2000.

MacKenzie, DeWitt. *Men without Guns.* Philadelphia: Blakeston, 1945.

Soldier Art. Fighting Forces Series. Washington, D.C.: Infantry Journal Press, 1945.

Sullivan, Gordon R. *Portrait of an Army.* Washington, D.C.: Government Printing Office, 1991.

———. *Soldiers Serving the Nation.* Washington, D.C.: Government Printing Office, 1995.

L. Bibliographies and Information Sources

Blewett, Daniel K. *American Military History: A Guide to Reference and Information Sources.* Englewood, Colo.: Libraries Unlimited, 1995.

Higham, Robin, and Donald Mrozek, eds. *A Guide to the Sources of United States Military History.* Hamden, Conn.: Archon, 1975. Supplement I, 1981. Supplement II, 1984.

Lang, Jack C. *America's Military Past: A Guide to Information Sources.* Detroit: Gale Research, 1980.

Jessup, John E., and Robert W. Coakley, eds. *A Guide to the Study and Use of Military History.* Washington, D.C.: Government Printing Office, 1970.

M. Chronologies, Dictionaries, and Encyclopedias

Atkinson, James W. *The Soldier's Chronology.* New York: Garland, 1993.

Chambers, John Whiteclay. *The Oxford Companion to American Military History.* New York: Oxford University Press, 1999.

Heitman, Francis B. *Historical Register and Dictionary of the United States Army, from its Organization, September 29 1789, to March 2 1903.* Washington, D.C.: Government Printing Office, 1903.

Jessup, John E., and Louis B. Ketz., eds. *Encyclopedia of the American Military: Studies of the History, Traditions, Policies, Institutions, and Roles of the American Armed Forces in War and Peace.* 3 vols. New York: Scribner, 1994.

Lang, Walt. *United States Military Almanac.* New York: Military Press, 1989.

Shrader, Charles R., ed. *Reference Guide to United States Military History.* 5 vols. New York: Facts on File, 1991–1994.

About the Author

Clayton R. Newell retired from the U.S. Army in 1992 with the rank of lieutenant colonel. During his 27 years of active duty, he served in a variety of infantry and field artillery assignments in Vietnam, Germany, and the United States. He is a graduate of Arizona State University, the U.S. Army Command and General Staff College, and the U.S. Army War College and has done graduate study in history at Old Dominion University. He served on the faculty of the Army War College, where he was director of Joint Operations Concepts, and he held the John J. Pershing Chair of Military Planning and Operations. He completed his military career as the chief of historical services at the U.S. Army Center of Military History in Washington, D.C.

Since his retirement, Newell has published a number of books and articles on a wide variety of military subjects. As a military consultant, he has done extensive work researching, writing, and editing after-action reports on the U.S. Army's operations in the Balkans. He is a research fellow of the Institute for Land Warfare and was on the board of directors of the Army Historical Foundation for eight years.

Newell is the author of *The Framework of Operational Warfare* (New York: Routledge, 1991); *Lee vs. McClellan: The First Campaign* (Washington, D.C.: Regnery, 1996), a History Book Club selection; and *The Historical Dictionary of the Persian Gulf War* (Lanham, Md.: Scarecrow Press, 1999). He was the primary editor and contributor to *On Operational Art* (Washington: Government Printing Office, 1994), a collection of essays by prominent military theorists and senior military officers. While at the Center of Military History, he wrote three of the brochures in the World War II Commemoration series: *Burma 1942, Central Pacific,* and *Egypt–Libya.* He has written articles for the *Encyclopedia of the American Military* (New York: Scribner, 1994), *The D-Day Encyclopedia* (New York: Simon & Schuster, 1994), and *Reference Guide to the United States Military* (New York: Facts on File, 1995). His articles and book reviews have also appeared in *Army, Army Historian, Army History, Defense and Diplomacy, Field Artillery Journal, Infantry, Military Review,* and *Parameters.*